John Feinstein is the author of *A Good Walk Spoiled*, which was a *New York Times* bestseller in both hardback and paperback and won the 1995 William Hill Sports Book of the Year Award in Britain. A regular commentator on NPR, Feinstein writes for the *Washington Post Sunday Magazine* and *Golf* magazine, and lives in Bethesda, Maryland.

ALSO BY JOHN FEINSTEIN

A March to Madness
A Civil War
A Good Walk Spoiled
Hard Courts
Forever's Team
A Season Inside
A Season on the Brink
Play Ball
The First Coming
Running Mates (A Mystery)
Winter Games (A Mystery)

THE MAJORS

IN PURSUIT OF GOLF'S HOLY GRAIL

John Feinstein

WARNER BOOKS

A *Warner* Book

First published in Great Britain in 1999
by Little, Brown & Company
This edition published in 2000 by Warner Books

A CIP catalogue record for this book
is available from the British Library.

ISBN: 0 7515 2992 3

Printed and bound in Great Britain
by Clays Ltd, St Ives plc

Warner Books
A Division of
Little, Brown & Company (UK)
Brettenham House
Lancaster Place
London WC2E 7EN

This is for Brigid Bernice Feinstein.
May she be as wonderful as her namesakes.

Contents

I

April Flowers

1

Playing for History

Shortly before 6 o'clock on a sun-splashed April Sunday in Georgia, David Duval walked across the narrow stone bridge named in honor of Gene Sarazen that leads to the 15th green at the Augusta National Golf Club. Everywhere Duval looked, he saw people. Augusta's 15th is one of golf's great theaters. There is water in front of the narrow green and behind it too. Huge loblolly pine trees, one of Augusta's signatures, line the right side of the hole, and there is a grandstand to the left of the green between the putting surface and the 16th tee. When the players cross the Sarazen Bridge, they are only a few feet from the grandstand, walking in the afternoon shadow that it casts. Each player receives a resounding ovation as he passes, the shouts and cheers growing a little louder as the day wears on.

Duval's golf ball was sitting on the front of the green, about 18 feet from the flagstick. He had hit his second shot there, an almost perfect three-iron, and now he would have a putt for an eagle three. His playing partner, Jim Furyk, had hit his second shot over the green into the water, and he walked briskly ahead of Duval to see what he had to deal with in order to try and save par.

Just as Duval crossed from the stone bridge back onto green grass, he heard a murmur come from the stands and instinctively looked up at the scoreboard that sits to the right of the green. The name at the top of the board was Fred Couples, because he had been the leader at the end of the third round. Through twelve holes, Couples had been eight under par for the tournament, the same number Duval had reached when he had birdied the par-five 13th hole a few minutes earlier. Being tied for the lead on Sunday at the Masters is no small thing, but Duval had stayed very calm after pulling even with Couples. After all, Couples still had both of Augusta's back-nine par-fives — 13 and 15 — left to play, and, since both are easily reachable in two, Duval figured Couples still had the advantage.

But now, reacting to the crowd's murmur, Duval glanced up at the board and saw what everyone else had just seen. Next to Couples's name in the slot for the 13th hole, the scorekeeper had slid a large red numeral 6. Duval stared at it for a moment because he wasn't quite sure if it meant what he thought it meant. Maybe, he thought, they'll realize it's a mistake in another second and take it down. But no one was making any such move. Somehow, Couples had made a double-bogey seven at the 13th hole, meaning he had dropped from eight under for the tournament to six under.

Duval wears wraparound sunglasses on the golf course to protect his contact lenses from wind and dust. But the dark glasses do more than that. They allow Duval an extra measure of privacy from prying eyes and cameras. Now, those eyes and cameras could not see how wide his eyes had gotten. He took a deep breath and leaned on his putter, trying to look as casual as possible. But his heart was pounding so hard he was certain everyone around the green could hear it thumping. He was leading the Masters by two shots and staring at a very makable eagle putt. For one brief moment, Duval allowed the kind of thought he tries to avoid at all costs to infect his brain. If I make this putt, I'm going to win the Masters, he thought.

Furyk had played his fourth shot onto the green. It was Duval's turn to putt.

One of the most popular and pointless mind games that golfers like to play is called It's Just Another Tournament. They play this game four times a year at the four events that clearly are not just another tournament: the Masters, the U.S. Open, the British Open, and the PGA. Every golfer knows that if he wants a legacy that goes beyond having made a good living, he must win one of the game's four majors.

Because winning a major is so difficult, because the pressures that are brought to bear late on a Sunday afternoon can be mentally and emotionally crippling, golfers constantly tell themselves and anyone who is willing to listen that it really isn't that big a deal.

"You know, a lot of great golfers have never won a major," Greg Norman, who has won two but lost many others, once insisted. When a listener asked Norman to list all those great players who had never won a major, Norman paused. Then he smiled and said, "Okay, a lot of *good* players have never won a major."

Exactly. Although winning a major championship does not guarantee greatness, not winning one guarantees that you will never be considered great. Deep in his heart, every golfer knows this. He knows there will always be a blank page on his golfing résumé if he doesn't win a major.

Mark O'Meara knew all this. He knew that he would always be asked about not winning a major title until and unless he won one. Publicly, O'Meara repeated the mantra that players in his position repeat if only to keep themselves sane: "If I never win a major, I'll still have had a very good career," he said over and over when the question came up. Then he would point out that he had won the U.S. Amateur title in 1979 and many people considered that a major. "I've never won a *professional* major," he would say.

Euphemisms aside, O'Meara knew that if he hadn't won fourteen times on the PGA Tour and hadn't been one of the game's more consistent players for fifteen years, he would never have had to answer the dreaded "major" question. But he had been asked the question repeatedly, enough times that he had half-jokingly said earlier in the week that he would like to win the Masters if only so he would never have to answer the question again.

O'Meara was far too pleasant a man to snap at anyone for asking the question, but he was sensitive about it. A year earlier, when Jaime Diaz of *Sports Illustrated* had written a piece headlined "King of the Bs," about O'Meara, he had been hurt and insulted. He believed his record was better than that of a 'B' player — even the *best* 'B' player. But deep down he knew the point Diaz was making. You could win at Pebble

Beach forever — O'Meara had won there five times — and it wouldn't be good enough until you won on one of golf's four special weekends.

Now, as Duval lined up his putt at 15, O'Meara and Couples were walking off the 14th tee. Duval led them both by two shots, but their mindsets at that moment were very different. Couples had believed all week that he was going to win the tournament. He had won in 1992, and everything seemed to be aligned for him to win it again in 1998. He had led or been tied for the lead ever since Thursday afternoon, when he had started birdie-birdie-birdie. But now, in the wake of the double bogey that had caused all the murmuring at 15, Couples was trying to regroup emotionally.

O'Meara had no such traumas to deal with. He had trailed Couples almost all day and was two strokes behind him standing on the 13th tee. Fifteen minutes later, he and Couples had walked off the green dead even. He knew Duval was two shots and two holes ahead, but there was plenty of time to catch him. At a moment when all sorts of crazy thoughts could have been raging inside his head, O'Meara felt relaxed. One more time he told himself what he had been saying all day long: "When you've been in position to win on tour, you've done a good job closing the deal. Today should be no different."

Of course it was different, as Duval's pounding heart could attest. He had spent the whole day playing the "it's just another tournament" game, but it wasn't working now. It hadn't been working since the 10th hole, when he had chipped in to get within two shots of the lead and had realized that another of golf's oft-repeated clichés was now very much in play: "The Masters doesn't begin until the back nine on Sunday." It was Sunday, he was on the back nine, and the tournament was very much under way.

Duval has always been a deliberate player. He took even more time than usual looking at his eagle putt, knowing what making it would mean. Finally, he stood over the ball, took the putter back, and watched the ball roll right at the hole. "Halfway there," he said, "I thought I'd made it." So did everyone else. The crowd began to stand in anticipation of the ball dropping. "Three feet out, I was *sure* I'd made it," Duval said.

But nothing is certain on the greens at Augusta until the ball actually disappears into the hole. This time, at the last instant, the ball took a tiny turn left, just enough to leave it an inch from the left edge of the cup. Duval stared in disbelief for a couple of seconds as the crowd oohed in shared dismay. Again, the sunglasses hid his emotions. He walked up and tapped in for the birdie.

Furyk had made a bogey six after his trip to the water and was now at five under. Duval was nine under. He had a three-stroke lead on Couples and O'Meara as he walked to the 16th tee. "That's what I kept telling myself," he said later. "I still had a three-shot lead. I knew Fred and Mark still had 15 to play, so you had to figure they would at least get to seven [under] there. But I was thinking if I made three pars, the absolute worst-case scenario was a playoff."

Which is why he played his six-iron shot conservatively at the par-three 16th to the right side of the green, away from the water. If he had been tied for the lead or a shot behind, he would have aimed at the flag, located, as it always was on Sunday, on the left side of the green where the water could come into play. Leading by three, Duval wasn't about to mess with the water. His shot landed safe and dry on the right side, but instead of funneling toward the hole, as shots often do on that green, it came to a halt, 40 feet to the right of the flag. "That meant, no matter what I did with my first putt, I was going to have an eight-to-ten-foot putt for par," Duval said. It was an eight-footer, and it stopped rolling inches shy of the cup. Bogey. The lead was two.

Duval parred 17 and parred 18, missing a 20-foot putt for birdie at 18 that started out left and stayed left, ending up two feet below the hole. When he walked off the green, Couples and O'Meara were playing the 17th hole. Couples had bounced back from the disaster at 13 to eagle the 15th, meaning that he and Duval were now tied. O'Meara had birdied 15 and just missed his birdie putt at 16. He was one shot back of the two leaders.

Duval carefully went through his scorecard in the scorer's tent, signed his card, and was greeted coming out of the tent by several members of Augusta National. Since a playoff was a very real possibility, they wanted to sequester him someplace where he could have privacy, away from the media, away from the crowds. The spot offered was the cabin named for tournament and club cofounder Bobby Jones that sits to the left of the 10th tee. Duval and his girlfriend, Julie McArthur, along with his caddy, Mitch Knox, and his agent, Charlie Moore, were shepherded to the Jones Cabin. There Jackson Stephens, the chairman of the club, was waiting. He congratulated Duval on his play and offered him a seat in front of the television set.

Couples and O'Meara were on the 18th fairway. Couples was in the fairway bunker on the left side. Once, in 1988, Sandy Lyle had made birdie from that bunker to win the Masters. But that had been a near miracle. Realistically, Couples would have to work to make par. O'Meara was safely in the fairway, but, since he was one shot back, Duval quickly figured that the worst he could do was play off, and since a bogey for Couples wasn't out of the question, he might win the tournament without hitting another shot.

Couples played his shot from the bunker, and as soon as he hit it, Duval knew his chances of winning had improved considerably. Couples didn't even bother to watch the ball come down, turning from it in disgust almost as soon as it left his club. His assessment was right. The ball flew into the front right bunker up by the green. Couples would have to get up and down to tie.

The camera shifted to O'Meara, perfectly positioned in the fairway in almost the same position Duval had occupied 20 minutes earlier. As O'Meara stood over his ball, CBS put a font on the screen that said, "O'Meara, −8." Duval gagged. "Isn't he minus seven?" he asked.

"He birdied seventeen," Jack Stephens said.

Duval hadn't known that. He had assumed that both players had parred 17. Since he had narrowly missed a birdie from the spot where O'Meara now stood, Duval knew that O'Meara could birdie from there and the tournament would be over. O'Meara's second shot flew onto the green and stopped in almost the exact same place from which Duval had putted 20 minutes earlier. Duval breathed a small sigh of relief. At least O'Meara hadn't knocked the flag down. The putt would be 20 feet with a wicked right-to-left break. Certainly makable for a great putter like O'Meara, but not easy by any means.

O'Meara and Couples walked to the green, the applause raining down on them. This wasn't the kind of victory walk Tiger Woods had experienced a year earlier with a 12-shot lead, but the applause was warm and generous for two talented and popular players. Couples, now hoping for a playoff, played a fine bunker shot to about six feet. A three-way playoff seemed possible, even likely.

Perhaps the only person not thinking in those terms was O'Meara. "As I was lining the putt up, it occurred to me that if I wanted to win the Masters, I was going to have to make a putt someplace," he said. "I thought to myself, why not right now? Why go back down the 10th? Why not end this here?"

Unbeknownst to O'Meara, many in the crowd were already scrambling down the 10th fairway, trying to get into position for the playoff they were sure would begin there in a few minutes. It was just after 7 P.M. and the sun was slowly beginning to retreat into the Georgia pines, the warm day beginning to cool as dusk slowly moved in.

O'Meara and his caddy, Jerry Higginbotham, looked the putt over carefully. Both agreed it would probably break about "one or one and a half cups left," O'Meara said later. In other words, the break was about the width of the cup — 4¼ inches — he was aiming for and then about half that much again. But as he went to get over the putt, something in O'Meara's gut told him the putt would break just a little more than that. His experience on the greens at Augusta, built up over fourteen years of playing the golf course, told him that there is always a little more break in a putt than you think you see. And he knew, just *knew* that the final Sunday hole location at Augusta would be in a tricky spot.

Jack Stephens knew too. He had played the golf course a lot more than O'Meara and had putted to that hole location often. As O'Meara got up over the putt, he looked at Duval and said, "Don't worry about a thing, David. *Nobody* makes this putt."

Duval knew he had missed it. So had Furyk, who had been on almost the same line, just a couple of feet farther away. He took a deep breath.

So did O'Meara, who had long ago put aside any notion that this was just another tournament. He knew now that this moment, right here, right now, was what he had played golf for all his life. All the money, all the other victories, the huge house he had built for his family in Florida, were distant memories. This was a putt for history, the putt of his life.

"As soon as it left the club, I knew I had hit a good putt," he said. "I could see it tracking toward the hole, but I could also see it was starting to die to the left."

If he had believed his eyes rather than his gut, the putt would have followed the same path that Duval's and Furyk's had. But because he had played it just a little more to the right, the putt began to break an instant later than the others had. Behind the hole, many of the spectators began standing as the ball began to dive. O'Meara stood frozen, not wanting to think it might be in, not wanting to deal with the disappointment of thinking for a moment that he had won the Masters and then having to walk to the 10th tee for a playoff.

Just before the ball got to the cup, it began to veer left. "Another inch and it's wide," O'Meara said.

But that inch wasn't there. The ball caught the left side of the cup and disappeared. O'Meara's arms were in the air, a wave of disbelief and relief pouring over him. He never smiled. His game face was so set that the smile didn't come until later. Higginbotham was pounding him on the back and Couples was congratulating him. O'Meara was more stunned than thrilled. He had never once led the tournament in four days. Until now. On his final putt, on the final hole. The only time when it mattered.

In the Jones Cabin, there was a brief silence when the putt disappeared. Jack Stephens, having finally seen someone make that putt, stood up and shook hands with Duval. "Well, David, great playing," he said. "We'll look forward to seeing you again next year."

Duval stood there, his eyes blank. He felt as if someone had kicked him very hard in the stomach. He had finished second on tour seven different times. Each time it had been disappointing. But not like this. Two months later, retelling the story, he leaned forward and took a deep breath. "I swear to God," he said, "just thinking about it again makes my stomach hurt all over."

Duval now knew the difference between all other golf tournaments and the four majors. The pain. "Never, ever, have I felt like that at the end of a golf tournament," he said. "It was as if every bit of adrenaline and energy I had ever had just went right out of me. Right then I understood what the majors are all about. Really and truly understood for the first time."

Several hours later, Mark O'Meara also understood. He had gone through all the rituals of victory after making his putt: the green jacket ceremony in the Butler Cabin; the public ceremony on the putting green; talking to the print media, then the TVs. He had sat at the victory dinner in the clubhouse that night, accepting congratulations all around, proudly wearing the green jacket. As dessert was being served, O'Meara sat back in his chair and a wave of exhaustion came over him.

Suddenly, something occurred to him. He had no idea how much money he had made for winning the tournament. "First time in my life," he said. "I won the golf tournament and six hours later, I didn't have a clue how much the winner's check was for."

The check was for $576,000. But if it had been for $576 or $5.76, O'Meara wouldn't have cared. Most of the time, professional golfers play for money. It is how they are measured at the end of each year. But four times a year, the money becomes completely irrelevant. They are playing for history.

2

Before the Masters
Was the Masters

Although it may seem that the four major championships have been the four major championships forever, that isn't even close to being the case. In fact, there is considerable disagreement on exactly when the notion of golf's current Grand Slam came into being. As recently as 1953, when Ben Hogan became the first and only man to win the Masters, the U.S. Open, and the British Open in the same year, he didn't even play in the PGA. What's more, he never returned to Great Britain to defend the title he had won at Carnoustie or anytime thereafter.

Imagine a golfer in today's world somehow pulling off the miracle of winning the first three majors in a year and then passing up the PGA. It just wouldn't happen. Of course, Hogan's decision was based at least in part on the difficulty of rushing back from Great Britain and then going through seven days of match play at a time when he still hadn't completely recovered from the 1949 automobile accident that almost killed him. But, even so, if a player today had to crawl around the course for a chance at sweeping the four majors he would do just that.

The first major championship was, of course, the Open Championship staged in 1860 at Prestwick, Scotland. The first Open wasn't really an open, since it was open only to professionals. Willie Park won the 36-hole event, shooting a 174 to beat Old Tom Morris by two shots.

A year later, the Open did become open, allowing amateurs to compete, and the results were similar: Old Tom Morris was the winner, Park the runner-up. In fact, the two men dominated the event, Morris winning it four times, Park three, during the first eight years the championship was conducted. Their string was broken only in 1865, when Andrew Straith beat Park by two shots to win the title. Park and Morris then won the next two Opens before Young Tom Morris — son of Old Tom — won the next four tournaments.

A year later, in 1872, the tournament was moved away from tiny Prestwick for the first time, to the Old Course at St. Andrews. For the next twenty years it was rotated among three courses — Prestwick, St. Andrews, and Musselburgh. In 1892, Muirfield was added to the rotation. That was also the first year that the championship was extended to 72 holes, Harold H. Hilton winning with a score of 305. Two years later, the Open was played outside Scotland for the first time, at Royal St. George's, in the south of England.

A year later, shortly before the Open was played for the thirty-fifth time (there hadn't been a tournament in 1870 because Young Tom Morris had retired the championship belt by winning it three straight times and no one had yet come up with something else to play for), the U.S. Golf Association decided to hold a national championship of its own. It was held at Newport Country Club, 36 holes played on the same 9-hole course in one day. The winner was Horace Rawlins, who shot 173. In 1898, for the fourth U.S. Open, the USGA matched its British counterpart by extending the event to 72 holes. But it was only in 1900, when the great Harry Vardon ventured across the Atlantic to win the championship, that the Open played in the U.S. began to approach the status of the Open played in Great Britain.

To this day golf people argue about which Open carries more prestige. In Europe, there is little doubt that most golfers and golf fans consider winning the British Open the number one achievement in golf, with the Masters second and the U.S. Open third. In the United States, the number one spot is a split decision between the Masters and the U.S. Open, with the British Open third. Only the PGA finishes the same in every poll in every corner of the globe—fourth—a fact that rankles those who run it.

The PGA of America held its first championship in 1916, a match play event won by James M. Barnes. World War I caused a two-year gap before Barnes successfully defended his title in 1919. In the 1920s, the PGA gained cachet because of the men who won it: Walter Hagen in 1921, Gene Sarazen the next two years, and then Hagen the next four. In 1923, Sarazen and Hagen staged one of the great matches of all time, Sarazen winning the 36-hole final on the second hole of sudden death.

Seventy-one years later, when Augusta National chairman Jack Stephens introduced Sarazen on opening day of the 1994 Masters as one of the honorary starters, he noted that Sarazen had won the second Masters in 1935, that he had won the British Open in 1932, and that he had won the U.S. Open in both 1922 and 1932. "Hey Jack," the ninety-two-year-old Sarazen said, "you forgot the PGA. I won that twice, you know."

Such seems to be the fate of the PGA.

In fact, in 1930 when Bob Jones won his historic Grand Slam, the four events that made up the Slam were the U.S. and British Opens and the U.S. and British Amateurs. In those days it wasn't automatic that a top golfer turned professional, because it wasn't a terribly lucrative profession. Almost all pros held club jobs in addition to playing in tournaments and, to a cultured man like Jones, who held a law degree, the notion of playing golf to make a living was absurd. As late as the 1950s very good players passed up the chance to turn pro because it was such an uncertain way to make a living. Only the very top players made big money. It wasn't until Arnold Palmer came along and brought both corporate America and TV to the game that the tour started to become the place to be for almost anyone who showed an ounce of ability.

A little more than a year after winning his Slam, Jones and his friend Clifford Roberts purchased a piece of property in Augusta, Georgia, called Fruitlands Nursery. On July 15, 1931, the lead story in the *Augusta Chronicle* carried the headline "Bobby Jones to Build His Ideal Golf Course on Berckman's Place." (The Berckman family had owned the nursery.) The subheadline read: "National Club Will Be Headed by Great Golfer." The somewhat hyperbolic news story began this way: "Bobby Jones, King of the links for probably all time, whose superiority in golf has been displayed on the finest golf courses in the entire world, has come to Augusta to build his ideal golf course."

Jones's prestige and Roberts's business acumen got the golf course built and the club started although it was in the midst of the depression.

Most of the charter members — fifty-nine men who paid $350 each to join — were from New York, men who did business with Roberts. The club opened in January 1933, and Jones and Roberts began planning an invitational golf tournament right from the start. The first Masters was played in 1934, with Horton Smith beating Craig Wood by a shot to win. It was known then as the Augusta National Invitational because Jones thought the term "Masters," which Roberts preferred, pretentious. By 1938 Jones gave up that battle, since most people — players included — were using the Roberts terminology, and the tournament has been known as the Masters for the last sixty years.

Since then a number of books have been written about the history of the club and the golf tournament, the best and most recent being Curt Sampson's *The Masters: Golf, Money, and Power in Augusta, Georgia*, which was published in 1998. Sampson explains in detail the difficult beginnings the club had, the trouble it often had in paying bills, and, perhaps most amazing, the lack of interest in the tournament locally until well after World War II. Not only was it easy to buy a ticket to the Masters in the early days, Roberts and company did everything but plead with people to take them.

That did not mean the tournament did not have an impact on the golf world. From the moment Gene Sarazen hit his "shot heard round the world," the four-wood second shot he holed for a double eagle at the 15th hole during the final round in 1935, the Masters and Augusta National became an important part of the golf year. The Sarazen Bridge is named in Sarazen's honor as a tribute to that famous shot. What many people don't remember is that the double eagle didn't win the tournament for Sarazen but put him into a tie with Craig Wood, who was already in the clubhouse. The next day Sarazen won a 36-hole playoff by five shots. (Wood did finally win the tournament in 1941.)

Although some insist that the Masters was considered one of golf's major events from 1934 on, others insist that it wasn't until after World War II that it acquired that sort of prestige. Regardless, there is little doubting the fact that all the majors — and golf in general — became far more significant after Arnold Palmer and Jack Nicklaus arrived on the scene.

Saying that in no way diminishes the greatness or importance of men like Jones and Sarazen and Hagen and Hogan and Byron Nelson and

Sam Snead. Golf was certainly popular during their time and there are those who will get up and walk out of the room — including Dan Jenkins, perhaps the best recent chronicler of golf — if you imply that anyone has yet lived who could strike a ball as purely as Ben Hogan.

But Palmer and Nicklaus took golf to new levels of popularity. Part of it was simply timing. Palmer, coming to golf in the 1950s, just when television was becoming a force in American life, was as significant to golf as the fall of the Berlin Wall was to Germany. Whether winning or losing, and Palmer tended to do both spectacularly, Palmer was irresistible. He had the smile, the outgoing personality, the famous belt hitch, and the ability that few athletes have to make the public feel both his joy and his pain.

Palmer won his first Masters — and his first professional major — in 1958. During the next four years he dominated the game and, in doing so, took all the majors and his sport to new heights. He won a second Masters in 1960, then followed that up by shooting 65 in the last round of the U.S. Open to come from seven shots behind to win. It has been said and written by many that the '60 Open was the greatest golf tournament ever played, in part because of what Palmer did on the final afternoon, beginning the round by driving the green at the par-four first hole and going on from there to win, but also because of who was on the leader board at Cherry Hills Country Club that day.

The runner-up to Palmer in that tournament was a fat twenty-year-old amateur named Jack Nicklaus. He played the last 36 holes that day with forty-eight-year-old Ben Hogan, seriously in the hunt at a major for the last time. When the day was done (Hogan finished four shots back) Hogan's comment was "I just played with a kid who should have won the tournament."

The '60 Open was one of those rare moments in a sport where three different generations cross paths: the aging Hogan, who could still hit the ball as well as anyone but couldn't buy a putt; the thirty-year-old Palmer, who was at the peak of his powers; and the rising Nicklaus, who hit the ball prodigious distances but hadn't quite figured out how to win yet.

A month later, with two legs of the now-established Grand Slam under his belt, Palmer made the trip to St. Andrews to play in the British Open. The world's oldest championship had been largely ignored by

American players even after Hogan's victory in 1953 because the travel was so difficult and the Open purse so small. Although transatlantic airplane flights were common by the mid-1950s, they still took nine to ten hours and were very expensive. Palmer loved to fly, had plenty of money, and wanted to play at St. Andrews. He finished second there to Kel Nagle — losing by a shot — but he returned the next two years, winning at Royal Birkdale in 1961 and at Troon in 1962. Most of the top American players followed Palmer's example and the British Open was reborn.

Palmer won his third Masters in April 1962 and would have won his second U.S. Open that June except that the fat kid who had so impressed Hogan, now a twenty-two-year-old pro, beat him in a playoff. That tournament was a turning point for both men. It was a launching pad for Nicklaus and the beginning of the end for Palmer as a dominant player. His win at the British Open a month later was his sixth major as a pro. He was only thirty-two. But he would win only one more major — the '64 Masters — and a number of his near misses over the next few years would be inflicted on him by Nicklaus.

During that period, Nicklaus was considered golf's black hat, the anti-Palmer. Palmer was handsome and trim, comfortable with the galleries, friends with the media, a fast player who kept everyone in suspense wondering if he would succeed or fail. Nicklaus was overweight, self-conscious about his appearance and the fact that when he succeeded it often meant Palmer failed. He was opinionated but awkward with the media, painfully slow as he methodically thought his way around the golf course, and was so good that he often took the suspense out of golf tournaments.

He won his first Masters in 1963, then after finishing second to Palmer the next year came back to win by *nine* (over Palmer) in 1965. When Tiger Woods made history in 1997, winning the tournament by 12 shots in a performance that left people gasping and wondering if he had made Augusta National obsolete, he broke the record set by Nicklaus thirty-two years earlier (and later tied by Raymond Floyd) by exactly one shot. In 1965 there were no metal woods, no perimeter-weighted irons, and no lob wedges. Nicklaus shot 271. Two years later he broke Hogan's U.S. Open record of 276, shooting 275 at Baltusrol Golf Club, including a final-round 65 to win by four — over Palmer.

Nicklaus may not have been popular during this period, but he was good for golf. And even better for the majors. There was no doubting his greatness, and he gave golf something it needed: a rivalry. Later, when Palmer started to fade, Lee Trevino and Tom Watson came along to give Nicklaus rivals. In the minds of many, Palmer and Nicklaus will always be inseparable the same way that Mantle and Mays, Evert and Navratilova, and Ali and Frazier are inseparable in baseball, tennis, and boxing. In truth, Palmer and Nicklaus may go beyond that. Even though they have always been keen rivals, both in golf and in business, their friendship has grown over the years to the point where they're more like Burns and Allen or Huntley and Brinkley. Theirs is an act that will live on in people's minds long after the act splits up.

Nicklaus made the majors more important than they had ever been, not only by playing so well in them but by making it clear that other golf tournaments paled in significance next to them. He built his entire year around peaking on four weekends and made no bones about it. In every profession, people copy the person who is the best, and as Nicklaus continued to win majors and talk about them, other players began trying to do the same thing.

Twenty-five years ago, then PGA Tour Commissioner Deane Beman and his predecessor Joe Dey created the Players Championship, hoping that it might someday become a fifth major or perhaps usurp the PGA's spot as the fourth major. Today, the Players is played on a very good golf course, it has the year's best field because of the way it is selected, a huge purse that is larger than any of the four majors, hours and hours of TV coverage, and the respect of all golfers everywhere because of the way it is run. And when Greg Norman, who won the event in 1994, was forced to withdraw in 1998 because of a shoulder injury, this is what his agent said: "Greg is very disappointed. He was hoping to use this event as a really good warm-up for the Masters."

One could almost hear current commissioner Tim Finchem groan out loud when he read that comment. A warm-up for the Masters. Ouch. But that is the truth of the matter. It isn't that the Players or the other events on tour don't matter; they do. They just don't matter as much.

"The week of a major just has a different feel to it than the other weeks," said Tom Watson, who should know, having won eight of them. "There's more tension during the practice rounds. You pay more attention to the golf course and the greens than to whatever bets you may have going. You start focusing on Monday morning rather than Thursday morning. It's almost like taking a final exam. The other tests matter, you want to study hard for them, but this is the final. This decides your grade."

Nicklaus won fifty-five midterms (nonmajors) on the PGA Tour and, along with Palmer, holds the record for most consecutive years (seventeen) with at least one win on tour. But the number that people associate most often with Nicklaus is eighteen, the number of professional major titles that he won. Toss in his two U.S. Amateur titles and the number becomes twenty. One person who counts Nicklaus's two Amateurs as majors is Tiger Woods, who is the only man to win the Amateur three times. Ask Woods how many more majors he needs to catch Nicklaus and, without hesitation, he will say, "sixteen." In other words, Woods believes he has four majors — three Amateurs and the '97 Masters — already put away.

Another person who subscribes to that theory is Palmer, who literally bristles if someone mentions his seven major titles. "Eight," he will say quickly, "and the Amateur may have been the toughest of them all."

That certainly may have been true in 1954, when Palmer won the Amateur, and it may very well have been true in 1959 and 1961, when Nicklaus won his. But it is less true today because few top amateurs retain their amateur status once they finish college. Most turn pro. Only on rare occasions — forty-four-year-old Tom McKnight, the 1998 runner-up being an example — does a true amateur, an adult who works for a living and plays golf, reach the final of the Amateur. The USGA recognized this fact eighteen years ago when it created the Mid-Amateur championship, a national event for amateurs twenty-five and older. "It was created to give the working amateur something to play for where he wouldn't come up against a bunch of pros in training," said USGA executive director David B. Fay. "Let's face it, most of the kids [like Woods] who have a chance to win the Amateur will be pros in the near future."

That isn't to say winning the Amateur is easy. It is a grueling competition that begins with 312 players playing 36 holes at stroke play, the low 64 qualifying for match play. The winner must then win six matches, including a 36-hole final. To do what Woods did — winning eighteen straight matches over three years — is extraordinary. But the simple fact in today's world is that most people think of the majors as the Masters, the U.S. and British Opens, and the PGA. And Nicklaus's eighteen victories in those four events — seven more than anyone else — is considered the watershed number in the sport. It is to golf what Roger Maris's sixty-one home runs used to be to baseball. The difference is this: Maris was surpassed in 1998, not once but twice. Most golf people believe Nicklaus's record will never be broken.

3

Return to Augusta

Of course it wasn't that long ago that a lot of people were convinced that it was only a matter of time until Tiger Woods broke Nicklaus's record and every other record that had ever been set in the game of golf.

This was in the spring of 1997, in the wake of Woods's stunning professional debut in a major championship. Woods had played in the Masters twice as an amateur, finishing forty-first in 1995 and missing the cut in 1996. By the time he arrived in Augusta in 1997, he had already won three times in seven months as a pro, been chosen as *Sports Illustrated*'s Sportsman of the Year, been labeled the Messiah by his father, had become a multimillionaire, had been on the cover of almost every magazine on the planet, had awed even his fellow pros with his length off the tee, and, perhaps most amazing, was the favorite to win the Masters at twenty-one.

Nicklaus had started a lot of the hype a year earlier when he had claimed, after playing a practice round with Woods, that the young prodigy would win more Masters "than Arnold and I did *combined*." That number was ten — six for Nicklaus, four for Palmer. Reporters sitting in the interview room when Nicklaus made the statement almost laughed out loud. No one other than Nicklaus had won more than eleven professional majors. Nicklaus had just said flat out that Woods would win eleven Masters.

As brilliant as he was, there was no way Woods should have been able to deal with all the hype and pressure being heaped on him. He did — and made it look easy. After shooting 40 on the front nine on Thursday, he played the last 63 holes of the golf tournament in a stunning 22 under par. He led by three on Friday night, by nine on Saturday night, and by 12 on Sunday night. "He's a boy among men," Watson said on Saturday as Woods ran away from the field, "and he's showing the men how to play."

Woods's victory wasn't just an amazing performance by a young superstar, it was a major social and political event in American history for the simple reason that he was black. Woods's father, Earl, was part African-American, part Native American, and part caucasian. His mother, Kultida, was from Thailand. Woods liked to call himself a "cablinasian." Regardless of what percentage of him was African-American, what percentage Thai, what percentage white, what percentage Native American, the bottom line was that he was a man of color, which meant that he was a man who would not have been eligible for membership in the PGA before 1963 because of the PGA of America's "caucasians only" clause. It also meant that he came from a group of people who quite clearly had once not been welcome at Augusta National — except in subservient roles.

For many years Augusta National had been a symbol of the old south, a place that clung to segregation much the same way George Wallace had, only without the state troopers. During the first forty years the Masters was played, the only black men seen inside the ropes were those carrying golf bags. There were other blacks at Augusta: groundskeepers, waiters, busboys. But no members and no one playing in the Masters.

Clifford Roberts, who had become the sole master of the Masters after Bob Jones's death in 1971, insisted that the tournament wanted black players and would welcome them when they qualified. But during the 1960s, when both Charlie Sifford and Pete Brown won events on the PGA Tour, neither was invited to play in the Masters even though both were clearly qualified. It was only after the qualifying rules were changed to make any winner on tour an automatic invitee that Lee Elder got into the field by winning the Firestone Classic in 1974.

Roberts's defenders — and he has many of them — will point out that it was Roberts and the membership that brought about the change in the rules. That is certainly true. It is also true that it was not until 1991 that Augusta National invited an African-American, Ron Townsend, an executive with Gannett, to join the club. The reason Townsend was invited to join was an incident known in golf history simply as "Shoal Creek."

In 1990, the PGA Championship was scheduled to be played at Shoal Creek, a relatively new club outside Birmingham, Alabama. The tournament had been held there in 1984. The course had received good reviews from the players, so the PGA of America decided to return there six years later. In an interview with a local newspaper before the 1990 tournament, Hall Thompson, who was the founder and president of Shoal Creek as well as an Augusta National member, was asked what would happen if an African-American applied for membership in his club. "That just wouldn't happen in Birmingham," Thompson replied.

That comment set off a hailstorm of controversy that almost resulted in the tournament being moved to another site. In the end, Shoal Creek agreed to invite Louis Willie, a local African-American businessman, to join the club immediately as an honorary member while awaiting formal approval as a full member, and the PGA of America, the PGA Tour, and the U.S. Golf Association all agreed that in the future they would not hold events at clubs that discriminated on the basis of race. Religious and sexual exclusion were still deemed acceptable. The following spring, Ron Townsend was invited to join Augusta National. Four years later, a second African-American, Charlotte banker Bill Simms, joined the club, although he resigned two years later.

On the morning of Woods's historic victory in April 1997, eighty-three-year-old Charles Yates, one of Augusta's original members and its unofficial historian, insisted that Cliff Roberts was misunderstood. "I guarantee you that Cliff's up there [Roberts committed suicide in 1977] right now with a big smile on his face," Yates said. "He knows this is good for golf, that it will bring the game to more people, and there was nothing he cared about more than that."

That is not the image most people had of Roberts, who was known as a tyrannical, my-way-or-the-highway leader. The men who have succeeded Roberts as club chairman — Bill Lane, Hord Hardin, Jack Stephens, and, last spring, Hootie Johnson — all have been considered more reasonable and approachable than Roberts. And yet, just as Roberts forced CBS to remove Jack Whitaker from its telecasts thirty-three years ago because he referred to the crowd around the 18th green as "a mob," Stephens did the same thing to Gary McCord in 1994 for making references to "body bags" behind the 17th green and for saying the greens were so fast they appeared to have been "bikini-waxed."

Augusta is an authoritarian place regardless of who is in charge. The club's approach has always been the same: The Masters is *our* tournament. If you do not like the way we put it on, you are welcome not to participate. And, if you do participate, you will be asked to behave in a certain way. If you cannot do that, you will be asked (told) to leave.

The attitude of the men who run the club and the tournament is perhaps best explained by the lines of red-lettered type that appear on the flip side of every pairings sheet issued during the Masters. The back side of the pairings has a map of the club and a mockup of the scorecard. At the top of the page, impossible to miss, is the following:

MESSAGE FROM: ROBERT TYRE JONES (1902–1971) President in Perpetuity, Augusta National Golf Club . . .

In golf, customs of etiquette and decorum are just as important as rules governing play. It is appropriate for spectators to applaud successful strokes in proportion to difficulty, but excessive demonstrations by a player or his partisans are not proper because of the possible effect upon other competitors.

Most distressing to those who love the game of golf is the applauding or cheering of misplays or misfortunes of a player. Such occurrences have been rare at the Masters, but we must eliminate them entirely if our patrons are to continue their reputation as the most knowledgeable and considerate in the world. (written in April 1967)

Of course the rules of etiquette and decorum didn't apply just to the patrons. Several years ago, on an unusually hot Augusta afternoon, Bev Janzen, the wife of two-time U.S. Open champion Lee Janzen, was walking the golf course in order to watch her husband play. After several holes, her feet were so hot inside her shoes she thought she might pass out. So she took them off. She hadn't walked fifty yards when there was a gentle tap on her shoulder. She turned to find a Pinkerton guard standing behind her. "Ma'am, I'll have to ask you to put your shoes on," the Pinkerton said. "No bare feet."

Bev Janzen started to point out how hot it was, how far she had walked, the fact that she was a player's wife. Then she looked at the face of the Pinkerton and realized she was wasting her time. Without a word, she put her shoes back on.

Almost everyone has a story like that one. One longtime Augusta rule that is almost universally ignored is the one asking that the players play only one ball during practice rounds. Players will routinely play two and three balls on a hole, especially those who show up early, arriving on the weekend before the tournament in order to play the course in virtual solitude before the course is overrun by fans — patrons in the Augusta vernacular — for the three practice days before the tournament begins on Thursday.

On the Sunday before the 1998 tournament, a sparkling spring day, a number of players were on the golf course. Corey Pavin walked up to the first tee, glanced at the sign that reads, "Practice rounds — use one ball only," and hit four balls off the first tee. A few minutes later, David Ogrin arrived and hit just two tee shots. Like Pavin, he set off down the first hole alone with his caddy. Several minutes later, three-time Masters champion Nick Faldo walked onto the first tee accompanied by Fanny Sunneson, his longtime caddy, and Brenna Cepelak, his girlfriend. Just as Faldo was about to tee his ball up, club chairman Jack Stephens drove up, resplendent in the green jacket worn only by members and Masters champions. Seeing him, Faldo stiffened into a mock salute. Stephens came through the ropes, shook hands with Faldo, and gave Cepelak a kiss. After a few minutes of banter, Stephens got back in his cart and watched Faldo tee off.

Faldo hit one ball.

One person who wasn't in Augusta on that April Sunday afternoon in 1998 was the defending champion. A lot had happened to Tiger Woods since that historic day a year earlier when he had blown everyone away and become the first minority player to win the Masters or any other major championship.

The Masters had been Woods's fourth victory in seven months on tour. His win had sent the entire golf world and most of the country into Tiger-mania. Everything he did was news. When he turned down President Clinton's invitation to take part in a ceremony commemorating the fiftieth anniversary of Jackie Robinson's breaking of the baseball color line, it was news. When he refused to sign a golf ball for a charity auction for fellow player Billy Andrade, it was news. When he won his first tournament following the Masters, the Byron Nelson Classic, it was news. When he won again at the Western Open in early July — his sixth victory in ten months on tour — it was, of course, big news. And it was very, very big news when he didn't win the U.S. Open, finishing tied for nineteenth.

But the biggest news Woods made was not of his own doing. In fact, at the moment that the trouble was beginning, Woods was playing the back nine at Augusta, finishing off his Masters victory. It began when a CNN television crew asked 1979 Masters champion Fuzzy Zoeller, who had just finished his final round, the same question everyone else was asking: What do you think about Tiger?

Few golfers in history have ever been more media-friendly than Fuzzy Zoeller. He is a gregarious, funny man who loves to tell jokes, crack one-liners, and entertain anyone and everyone he comes in contact with. Maybe he thought his answer to the question was funny or entertaining. But with a national TV camera rolling, Zoeller picked the wrong time and the wrong place to try to be funny.

"Little boy's playing great out there," Zoeller began. "Just tell him next year not to serve fried chicken at the [champions] dinner." Zoeller stopped, turned away from the camera, and then turned back and said over his shoulder, "Or collard greens or whatever the hell it is they serve."

Zoeller has apologized on several occasions for his comments. He has explained over and over again that he meant nothing by it and that he was just kidding around. Many of his friends have pointed to his exemplary record over a period of many years in race relations and said it is unfair to wipe all that out because of a thirty-second slipup. What no one has ever been able to explain is what Zoeller was thinking at the moment that he made the comments.

Calling Woods a little boy might have been acceptable because Woods was only twenty-one. Watson had called him a "boy among men," the day before, and clearly hadn't meant anything derogatory by it. It was a reference to Tiger's age. The fried chicken comment was borderline — extremely borderline — but Zoeller might have survived it with a quick apology. But the last line, the one he turned back to the camera to make, was the killer, especially the part about "whatever the hell it is *they* serve."

When Zoeller's comments were aired a week after the Masters as part of a CNN golf show, all hell broke loose. Very quickly, Zoeller's longtime sponsor, Kmart, canceled its deal with him, reportedly worth about $1 million a year. Zoeller apologized once, then twice, while withdrawing from the Greater Greensboro Open because the tournament had been threatened with pickets if he played. He publicly pleaded with Woods to call him so he could apologize personally and explain what had happened.

Neither Woods nor his agents at the International Management Group were in any rush to lessen Zoeller's pain. IMG is one of the most powerful sports entities on the planet. It practically runs professional tennis — which may partially explain the sport's recent pratfall in popularity — and it controls large chunks of the golf world: top players, major tournaments around the world, the world golf rankings, numerous television deals, and, perhaps most important, it has managed Arnold Palmer since Palmer's early days on tour. It was Palmer's friendship with IMG founder Mark McCormack that led to the formation of the company that is now an all-powerful multimillion-dollar corporation.

But IMG didn't manage Zoeller. In essence, that made him a nonperson in their eyes. The man who managed Woods was Hughes Norton, an IMG employee for twenty-five years, a man who when asked what he hoped his legacy would be once answered, "I want to be remembered for making rich people richer."

If you listened to the Norton version of world history, Greg Norman would be renting carts and selling golf shirts out of a pro shop if not for him. Curtis Strange probably would never have won anything more important than the Virginia state championships. And Tiger Woods wouldn't have a single endorsement. To Norton, the best way to sum up the Kingdom of Tiger was to paraphrase Louis XIV: "Le Tigre C'Est Moi." Norton not only didn't care if Zoeller was suffering, he undoubtedly had a good laugh over it. In Norton-world you were with us or against us. Zoeller, a nonclient, went in the against column.

Of course the boss could have stepped in and told Norton and all the other IMG hangers-on that enough was enough, Zoeller knows he made a mistake, he's said he was sorry, now let's accept the apology and get it over with. But Woods was in no rush to do that, not because of any small-minded IMG-like motives but because he was genuinely hurt and angry by what Zoeller had said.

Woods had come to believe during his first year on tour that most people didn't understand him. "No one has ever been through what I'm going through," he often said, accurately and with a large dose of well-deserved arrogance. Woods trusted a small group of people: his parents, a couple of friends from his days at Stanford, a small group of loyal media types, and, at least in terms of business, Norton and company. He honestly believed that most of the media was waiting to jump on him when he made mistakes, that large chunks of the public wanted to see him fail, and that a lot of the players were jealous of him.

He knew players whispered behind his back about all the attention and the contracts and the entourage. He knew some of them had half-jokingly changed the initials of the PGA Tour to TGA — Tiger Golf Association. But he also thought — correctly — that most of them respected his game and his competitiveness and understood that his presence was good for their game.

That's why Zoeller's words hurt. Woods believed that even if Zoeller thought he was joking there had to be some anger behind the words. He wasn't smiling when he spoke, and the last phrase, "whatever it is *they* serve," had almost been said behind clenched teeth. If IMG or his dad had been pushing him to respond quickly, Woods probably would have. But they weren't, and he was hurt enough and angry enough that he felt no need to rush to Zoeller's rescue.

It was pressure from other players — specifically IMG clients Brad Faxon and Steve Elkington — that finally elicited a public response from Woods, who issued a statement three days after Zoeller's apology and withdrawal from Greensboro saying he accepted Zoeller's apology.

Several weeks later, the two men had an arranged olive branch lunch at Colonial Country Club that probably should have been on *Court TV* or *Geraldo Live*. Each agreed to try and put any hard feelings behind him.

Publicly, both did exactly that. Privately was another story. Woods said it best for both of them one night in San Diego ten months later: "I forgive him," he said. "But I can't forget."

Now, it was April again, the dogwoods were in bloom in Augusta, and the golf world was making its way to the golf course that Cliff Roberts and Bob Jones, with a large assist from architect Alister MacKenzie, had created. Neither Woods nor Zoeller would be among the early arrivals. Each knew that returning to this particular place would mean being asked questions about the incident all over again.

Augusta National and the Masters had come a long, long way since their beginnings. Palmer and Nicklaus had made the tournament into a major sports event, rather than just a major golf event, with their victories — Palmer four, Nicklaus five from 1963 through 1975 before tacking on a miraculous sixth in 1986 long after he had graduated from fat phenom to slender icon — and the prestige and importance of the Masters had grown steadily.

The club had gotten quite rich because of the Masters but not nearly as rich as it could have. The price of a ticket for the four days of the tournament had been fixed at $100 for years, and the club sold only 25,000 of them. Ticket scalpers did boom business — selling the passes for up to $8,000 apiece in 1997 — but if you were one of the fortunate few who were on the ticket list, you paid $100. Needless to say, if the Lords of Augusta raised the price for the week to $500 or even $1,000, there would be very few dropouts. And if there were, the waiting list for tickets was so long that it had been cut off twenty years earlier.

Parking was free. Food on the grounds cost about half — or less — of what concessions at most sports events cost. The huge souvenir tent located just inside the main gate was jam-packed from morning till evening with people lining up for hours just to get inside. The lines were sometimes so long it would not have been inappropriate to put up signs like the ones at Disney World that say, "45 minutes from this point." Masters memorabilia — hats, shirts, sweaters, sweatshirts, raingear, socks, mugs, glasses, prints, keychains, scorecards, golf balls — wasn't cheap but it wasn't outrageous. And, like everything else, if the prices had been doubled, every item would still sell out during the week. What's more, tournament week is the only week of the year when Masters memorabilia is on sale. Unlike Wimbledon, which had taken its logo global to cash in on its prestige, the members at Augusta make their killing — about $7 million gross — in a week and figure that is enough.

And then there was television. Right from the beginning, Clifford Roberts had insisted that the club retain almost complete control of the Masters telecasts. CBS had been the first network to televise the tournament, and forty-two years later it was still the only network that had televised it. CBS and Augusta always had a one-year contract, which kept the network on a very short leash. One mistake too many and the Lords could be on the phone to ABC or NBC in an instant.

If the membership had been willing to let CBS or any other network run their telecasts the way other golf telecasts were run, they probably could have gotten four or five times more than the reported $4 million CBS paid. NBC had paid the U.S. Golf Association $13 million a year in 1995 to wrest the rights for the U.S. Open from ABC. In return, NBC and cable's ESPN gave the Open wall-to-wall coverage from Thursday to Sunday — about thirty-five hours of live coverage. The more hours they were on the air, the more opportunity the network had to sell commercial time, which it did — usually about thirteen minutes of commercials per hour.

CBS and cable partner USA Network are allowed ten hours of live Masters coverage. Each hour contains exactly four minutes of commercials — two minutes for Travelers Insurance and two minutes for Cadillac — period. Although the front nine had been wired with TV cables for years, coverage from there was still limited. More often than not, by the time TV went on the air the leaders were already on the sixth or seventh hole. Most golf fans can close their eyes and describe Augusta's back nine in minute detail. But, unless they have been inside the hallowed gates, they have rarely seen the front nine, especially the first six holes.

Jack Stephens, who stepped down as club chairman in May 1998, was a firm believer that the front nine should remain off-limits to television. His belief was that limiting the TV coverage made watching the

Masters more special. He also believed there should be some benefits to being on the grounds — like seeing the parts of the golf course people couldn't see on TV. That was part of the Masters tradition of servicing the patrons. His successor, Hootie Johnson, says he agrees with that philosophy. Stephens thought seeing the back nine on Sunday was plenty for most people, that they didn't need to see the leaders walking to the range or chatting with their caddies on the putting green. That's what people often see with the extended coverage now provided by the other three majors.

Once, when someone asked Stephens if he liked to watch the Super Bowl, he smiled beatifically and said, "The fourth quarter."

And so, while much is made about the millions the Masters brings into the Augusta National coffers, the truth is the club could easily make four or five times more than it makes. But the members would rather retain complete control over their tournament, over the telecast, and — perhaps most important — their privacy than rake in more money. Everyone who belongs to the club knows that talking about the club to outsiders is strictly forbidden. Only the chairman is allowed to speak for the club and, at least in Stephens's tenure, the chairman took advantage of that privilege exactly once a year — Masters Wednesday at 11 A.M. In Stephens's case one of the reasons for his reticence was that he was not comfortable in the spotlight. A billionaire businessman with a quick, sharp sense of humor, Stephens always appeared at ease during his annual meeting with the media. But according to those who know him, Masters Wednesday was his least favorite day of the year. "He's in a cold sweat until the press conference is over," according to one friend.

In fact, in recent years Stephens had turned a lot of the chairman's public duties over to others. He shared the podium during his press conference with Will Nicholson, a former president of the U.S. Golf Association who is Augusta's chairman of competitions. That means Nicholson runs the actual golf tournament, playing a major role in setting up tee locations and hole locations, putting together Thursday's pairings, dealing with problems as they come up during the week, and overseeing changes in the course from year to year.

Often, Stephens would defer to him to answer specific questions about the condition of the golf course, new hole locations, the speed of the greens (Augusta National *never* reveals exactly how fast the greens are), or any changes in the tournament itself. Nicholson, who is sixty-nine, is as outgoing and comfortable in the spotlight as Stephens was shy about it. In addition to sitting in on the press conference, Nicholson has MC'd the Sunday awards ceremony since 1995. Stephens, who is seventy-three, has had some health problems in recent years (including a stroke last August shortly after he had stepped down as chairman) and probably decided to give up running the awards ceremony after struggling to get through it in 1994. In addition to a slight quaver in his voice, Stephens had a lot of trouble pronouncing the name of the new champion, José María Olazabal. He tried mightily, but pronounced it "Oh-la-Za-bul," rather than the correct "Oh-la-tha-bul." Olazabal gave him a thumbs-up for coming a lot closer than many people do, but nonetheless Stephens had to be embarrassed.

A year later, shortly before the final round was scheduled to begin, Stephens called Nicholson into his office and asked him if he would mind taking charge of the awards ceremony. Nicholson was surprised, but not shocked. A year earlier, Stephens had turned the TV awards ceremony over to club vice-chairman Joe Ford. Traditionally, the club chairman has always sat in during the TV awards ceremony, always asking the champion the first question. This has led to some hysterically awkward moments, the most memorable probably being the moment in 1980 when Hord Hardin began by saying to Seve Ballesteros, "Now Seve, just how tall are you?"

Nicholson has run the ceremony on the putting green the last four years almost without a hitch. His only troublesome moment came that first year, when he went through the lengthy ritual of introducing each foreign golf association that had sent a representative or representatives to the tournament. Nicholson went to the bottom of the list he had in front of him, thanked them all, and asked for a round of applause. Then he turned the page and saw that he still had about fifteen countries to go. Without missing a beat he looked up and said, "Do I get a mulligan?"

At Augusta the members get as many mulligans as they want.

Almost every golfer who has ever played in the Masters has vivid memories of his first trip to Augusta National. Without fail, they can describe pulling up to the entrance to Gate Two and driving ever so slowly down

Magnolia Lane. There probably isn't a more romanticized strip of road anywhere in the world than the 250 yards that leads from the gate to Founders Circle, where one turns right to reach the parking lot reserved during tournament week for the players.

The giant trees — magnolias of course — that shade the road give it a unique intimacy. During tournament week, no one can walk in Gate Two and only players and members can drive in. If spectators try to walk up Magnolia Lane from the clubhouse end of the road, one of the ever polite Pinkertons turns them away. This is hallowed ground.

"The first time we ever drove in, it took us about half an hour to get down Magnolia Lane because I was hanging out the window gaping and my wife was hanging out the other side taking pictures," said Scott McCarron, who first qualified for the tournament in 1996. "It was as if you were pulling into Valhalla or something."

Many are surprised by how small golf's Valhalla turns out to be. The white clubhouse that sits at the end of Magnolia Lane is three stories and connects via a short walkway with the one-story building that houses the men's grill and the locker room. Down a sloping hill from the locker room is the pro shop and the bag room. Everything else at Augusta spreads out from these main buildings. There are ninety-four cabins, many of them to the left of the clubhouse — if one is looking at it from Magnolia Lane — and winding around the putting green toward the 10th hole. The cabins are actually cottages, most of them two stories with a two-bedroom suite on each floor, that the three hundred members can rent when they come to the club to play or, when available, during the Masters. From there, they can order room service or eat in the clubhouse. Contrary to what many think, the National — as it is called by locals — is not as sexist as some other all men's clubs. Women can play the golf course and eat in the clubhouse. The only place they are not allowed is the grillroom, which has signs posted on the doors that say "gentlemen only." That prohibition is lifted during Masters week, when reporters — male and female — are allowed inside.

To the left of the putting green is the par-three course, which many believe is the most beautiful spot on the grounds. It was built in the late 1950s, largely at the behest of Clifford Roberts, and meanders its way through the trees and around two lakes. Near the first tee of the par-three course is a stone drinking fountain that has three plaques commemorating each winner of the annual par-three tournament, which dates back to 1961. No one has ever won the par-three tournament and the Masters in the same year, which has given rise to the legend of the par-three jinx. The closest anyone has come to breaking the jinx was in 1990, when Raymond Floyd won the par-three and then led the Masters until he bogeyed the 17th hole late Sunday and lost a playoff to Nick Faldo. Some players swear they will put a ball in the lake at number nine rather than win the par-three.

The three most important cabins on the grounds are all located near the putting green. Just off the clubhouse is the Clifford Roberts Cabin — not to be confused with ten other cabins located below the pro shop that are named in his honor. This is the cabin where Roberts lived when he was at Augusta and the place where he ate his last meal on the fateful night of July 4, 1977, when he walked down to the par-three course and put a bullet through his head.

A few yards from where Roberts shot himself is the Eisenhower Cabin, built specifically for President Dwight D. Eisenhower, a close friend of Roberts's who made forty trips to Augusta during his presidency and too many to count after he left office. Almost everywhere you turn at Augusta there is something named for Ike: the lake behind the cabin (which is where Roberts's body was found); the large tree on the left side of the 17th fairway, so named because so many of the president's tee shots landed in it that he pleaded with Roberts to cut it down; and the three-story cabin itself, which still bears the presidential seal. The cabin was built with a basement for the specific purpose of giving the Secret Service a place to set up headquarters and is the largest cabin on the grounds.

In between the Roberts Cabin and Ike's Cabin is Butler Cabin, best known to the public as the place where CBS stages its awards ceremony and the spot where the leaders are customarily taken to be interviewed. CBS uses the basement of Butler, the top two floors remaining in the hands of the members. Everyone who goes into the CBS studio circles to the back of the cabin, which looks out at the par-three course. The studio itself is a 14-by-22-foot room with two cameras, three hard-backed chairs on a raised platform, and a fireplace that makes the set look cozy and regal at once. Just off-camera behind the set is a small kitchen, and there are two small rooms off the main ones that are used by production people and technicians.

Bill Macatee has worked in the cabin for twelve years now, first as the host of the Thursday-Friday USA telecast, and in recent years as host for both USA and for CBS on the weekends. Over the years, Macatee has developed a routine of taking a walk out the door of the cabin to sit on the edge of the par-three course for a few minutes before the telecast begins. It gives him a chance to relax and puts him in the mood to wax poetic — which may be in the CBS contract — about the beauty of the place.

As is often the case with personnel at Augusta, the same Pinkerton guard has been on the door that leads to the cabin for as long as Macatee can remember. Each day when Macatee walks out of the cabin, the guard will greet him warmly and tell him to enjoy his walk. Macatee will return the greeting, take his walk, and return about twenty minutes later. And, without fail, the guard will say to him, "Mr. Macatee, do you have your pass?"

One can only hope that the day never comes when Macatee leaves the pass inside and the Masters telecast opens with a shot of empty chairs inside Butler Cabin.

If you want to understand the history and lore of Augusta, the place to begin is inside the clubhouse. Just inside the door on the parking lot side is the front desk where members check in when they arrive to spend a few nights. Copies of the *New York Times* and the *Wall Street Journal* can be picked up there each morning on the way to breakfast.

Although there is a small dining area on the first floor, most members prefer to make their way up the winding steps to the room known as the library. The walls on the steps are filled with pictures of the club's charter members. At the top of the steps sits an old-fashioned ballot box presented to the club by the Royal and Ancient Golf Club, which administers both the British Open and, along with the USGA, all the rules of golf. The box says very simply: "Candidates for membership in the R@A, Admit./Reject."

A few steps to the right at the top of the steps is the library. It is here that the Champions Dinner is held each Masters Tuesday. The Victory Dinner is also held in this room on Sunday night. The room is filled with bookcases containing books on golf that date back to the nineteenth century and also has cabinets devoted to Bob Jones, Clifford Roberts, and Dwight D. Eisenhower (known of course as Ike's Cabinet). Roberts's cabinet contains, among other things, a pair of Roberts's glasses, a copy of the book he wrote in 1976 called "The Story of Augusta National Golf Club," and a ball he used to make a hole in one on November 14, 1971.

In the corner of the library is a plaque listing the winners of the club's annual jamboree. One of the 1998 winners, according to the plaque, was Ron Townsend, Augusta's first African-American member. The library leads to the porch, the most pleasant place to eat at Augusta and about as nice as any spot anywhere. The porch, which has ten tables and comfortable wicker chairs, overlooks the veranda, the putting green, and, through the branches of the famed giant oak tree where members, players, and media pause to meet and greet, the first tee.

At the back end of the second floor is a large oak door that leads to the champions locker room. If you are a Masters champion this is the one place you can go during Masters week to escape the prying eyes of the media and the public. In 1997, after shooting 81 to miss the cut, Nick Faldo fled to the champions locker room because, as he said later, "I was in complete shock and couldn't think of a thing to say." A nonchampion wouldn't have had that luxury. The locker room downstairs is open to the media — much to the disgust of the men who work in there. When John Daly held an impromptu press conference in front of his locker two days before the 1998 tournament, one of the veteran locker-room attendants, Roland Gray, known to one and all as Mule, stalked away from the scene muttering, "Damn press doesn't belong in here. All they do is block traffic."

Actually the press rarely blocks traffic in the locker area. Most players conduct their interviews under the tree, traditionally stopping en route to the locker room once they are inside the roped-off area of the veranda. Most reporters who venture into the locker room do so in search of a specific player or to leave a note on his locker. They do not linger. They know exactly how Mule feels about their presence.

They cannot, however, wander in and out of the champions locker room. Like everything else at Augusta, the champions room is not that large. In fact, each champion has to share locker space with another champion. Each man has a half-locker with his name on it. As often as possible, current players are paired with past champions who are either deceased or do not attend the Masters. That gives them more room. Two-time champion Tom Watson shares space with the late Claude Harmon. Craig Stadler is paired with Craig Wood; Sandy Lyle with Cary Middlecoff; Fred Couples with Ralph Guldahl; Raymond Floyd with Ben Hogan; Ben Crenshaw with another Texan, Jimmy Demaret. Occasionally current players locker together. Nick Faldo and Gary Player are together. Perhaps in 1999, Tiger Woods and his best friend, Mark O'Meara, will be paired. In '98, Woods, then the most recent champion, shared with Jack Burke the locker closest to the door that leads to the porch. On the Sunday before the tournament began, Woods's green jacket had already been hung in his locker. The rest of the jackets would be laid out by Tuesday, in time for the Champions Dinner. Only the current Masters champion is allowed to remove a green jacket from the club grounds.

Two steps from where Woods would locker is the door leading to the porch. From the porch, one can look past the flagpole on Founders Circle all the way up Magnolia Lane. When a golfer gets a chance to stand or sit on that porch, knowing what must be achieved to gain entrance, the feeling of accomplishment must be overwhelming.

There is a back door to the champions locker room that leads to a small hallway that connects to the library. There are several telephones in the hallway and a flight of steps — green carpeted of course — that lead to the Crow's Nest, the spot where amateurs have traditionally stayed while playing in the Masters. Once, the Crow's Nest had bunk beds and a ladder that could be pushed up to the wall so that someone in the top bunks could climb to the windowsill early in the morning and peer outside to check the weather.

Now, the bunk beds are gone, replaced by five single beds that are spread out in four small rooms, all of which lead to a large common area. The large window is still there but the ladder has gone the way of the bunk beds. If someone staying in the Nest wants to know the weather, he can sit down at one of the card tables in the common room and click on the TV. Each closet has a white bathrobe in it with the Masters crest.

There are historic pictures on every wall: one shows the nursery before the golf course was built, another is a picture of the clubhouse, and another is of Billy Joe Patton, one of a handful of amateurs who seriously contended in the Masters. There is also a framed postcard, dated January 13, 1933, which was sent from "The Robert T. Jones Golf Course." Another picture shows Jones, wearing plus fours, playing St. Andrews in 1936.

One can't help but wonder how many amateurs have slipped down the fifteen steps late at night to walk into the hallway and then sneak through the back door to the champions locker room, thinking, someday, I'll be in here.

Arnold Palmer made it; so did Jack Nicklaus and Tiger Woods. And in 1999, twenty years after he stayed in the Crow's Nest, Mark O'Meara would join them.

4

In Search of Green

With very few exceptions, players look forward to Masters week more than any other.

Unlike at the other majors, which change locations each year, everything is familiar — unless of course you are an awed rookie. Most players stay in the same house each year, drive the same route to the golf course, eat in the same restaurants, see the same friends. Traditions grow up for each of them that are a part of the week, whether it is a Wednesday night pre-Masters cookout or having a relative or friend caddy during the laid-back par-three tournament. To this day, Jim Furyk, who almost won in 1998, insists that his best Masters moment came in 1997 when his mom caddied for him during the par-three and he handed her his putter on the ninth hole and urged her to take a crack at a 10-foot birdie putt. Shaking like a leaf, she rolled the putt in, engendering one of the loudest roars ever heard at Augusta.

Players will usually start arriving in Augusta as early as the Thursday before the tournament starts. Upon registering, each is given a player number — #1 is reserved for the defending champion and the rest are handed out in order of arrival — a player badge, and the keys to a white Cadillac that is his for the week. Each is also given a player gift, usually china with the Augusta National crest on it. The first player to arrive in

1998 was Darren Clarke, the burly Northern Irishman who had finished tied for second in the British Open in 1997 and was playing in his first Masters. Lee Janzen wasn't far behind Clarke, and after that they began arriving in a steady trickle: Gabriel Hjerstedt, another Masters rookie, was followed by Scott McCarron and Furyk, who had gotten into the habit of showing up for the weekend before the tournament because he loved the quiet before the grounds were stormed on Monday.

Fred Couples didn't get to Augusta until Sunday night. But no one was more excited to be back than he was. Couples had played in the Masters thirteen times. He had won it in 1992 — his first and only major title — had finished in the top ten seven times, and had never missed the cut. He loved the golf course, the atmosphere, the week.

This year was even more special than past years. For the first time in his life, Fred Couples was in love. Madly, hopelessly in love. This might sound strange for a man who had been married once, engaged another time, and had had countless other opportunities with countless other women. But this was different.

His first marriage, to Deborah Morgan, had grown out of a teenage infatuation that had started when he was a sophomore at the University of Houston. She was two years ahead of him in school — although, as he learned later, quite a bit more than two years older than he — a tennis player with an athlete's body and a huge appetite for fun and life. They were married a year after Couples dropped out of school to turn pro and, as his career took off, the marriage began crashing. It was really over long before he won the Masters, but didn't become the trashy stuff played out in the tabloids until after he had won at Augusta and become the world's best-known player.

After Deborah came Tawnya Dodds, also a little older than Couples, someone he enjoyed and respected and probably loved. But in love — no. He tried to convince himself that he was in love with her, even got engaged to her, but eventually both realized it wasn't meant to be. By early 1996, the relationship was over.

And then came Thais Bren. In a sense, the timing when they met could not have been worse. It was early 1997 and Couples was, to use his words, "a mess." His dad had been diagnosed with cancer, the same disease that had killed his mother three years earlier. The back problems that had plagued him since 1994 were troubling him again. And then, during the week of the Los Angeles Open, he met this beautiful young woman who had two beautiful young children. She was sweet and funny, and all Couples could think about was spending time with her. But there was a problem: she had cancer. Couples can still remember her saying to him early on, "Listen to me, you're a young man, you have your whole life ahead of you, you don't need all this." Couples had looked her in the eye and said, "I'm a big boy. I know what I want."

They went from there.

In a funny way, although the opposite often seems to be the case if you listen to him talk, Fred Couples has always known what he wanted. He was the youngest of Tom and Violet Couples's three children, ten years younger than Tom Jr. and two years younger than Cindy. They lived in a small house in West Seattle, small enough that Fred remembers sharing a room with his brother and sister until they moved into a bigger house when Fred was in the third grade. "I was devastated," Couples said. "I didn't want to go to school because I missed all my friends so much."

Tom Couples worked for the Seattle Parks and Recreation Department all his adult life, starting on the grounds crew as a teenager, eventually being put in charge of all the facilities at West Seattle High School. When Fred was young, he and his dad would go out most nights and find a semipro baseball game to watch, often when the sun went down and the temperatures cooled, sitting in the car near the field watching the game and talking ball.

It was baseball that bonded the Couples family. And it was baseball that led Fred Couples to golf. Tom Couples had been an excellent semipro baseball player in his day, a powerful left-handed-hitting first baseman who was still talked about with awe in Seattle when Fred was growing up. Tom Jr. was also a superb player, a pitcher who was good enough to win a scholarship to Seattle University. He played there for four years and then signed with the New York Yankees, playing for a year in their farm system before a sore arm and the realization that he probably wasn't good enough to ever be a big leaguer brought him home.

Tom Jr. was young Fred's hero as a kid. He can remember being his batboy from the time he was in second grade right through the Seattle U. years. It was there that Fred met Steve Dallas, who was Tom's catcher and pal. Often, Steve would come over to the house so that Tom could pitch to him, and little Fred would stand at the plate and hold a bat up so that his brother had a target to work with.

As it turned out, Steve Dallas's real passion was golf. His father was a club pro, and one day he took Fred to the golf course to caddy for him. Fred loved it and kept going back. As payment, Dallas gave Fred a cut-down set of clubs, 3-, 5-, 7-, and 9-iron. Fred grabbed them with a base-ball grip, began slapping the ball around, and quickly got hooked on the game. Dallas saw his potential, taught him a proper grip and a stance, and turned him loose at Jefferson Park, a municipal course in West Seattle. Soon, Fred was playing for 10-cent skins on the par-three course with teenagers and adults and, soon after that, playing with anyone he could find on the adult course.

"I was okay," Fred remembered. "I could slap the ball around, but I was really little then. I won a lot of skins on the par-three course but not so many when we moved to the big course."

By the time Fred was thirteen, he was dividing his time between golf, baseball, and soccer. That summer, he went out for a baseball team for fourteen- and fifteen-year-olds because his father was one of the coaches and he wanted to play for him. He made the team, but before the season began each player had to produce a birth certificate. "The funny thing," Couples said, "is that they did it to keep any older kids from sneaking in." This time they caught a younger kid. Couples wasn't fourteen, so he couldn't play with the fourteen-year-olds. He went back to try out for the twelve- to thirteen-year-old team but tryouts were over. The team had been picked. "So I just said, 'Fine, I'll play golf.'"

And so he did. By the end of that summer he was shooting consistently in the 70s and starting to make a mark in local junior tournaments. By fifteen, he was good enough to qualify for the U.S. Public Links Championships. Golf became his passion. He got a job picking up balls at a local driving range every night. He would arrive at 9 o'clock — an hour before closing — and walk along the fences hitting balls into the middle of the range. When the range closed, he would pick the balls up and go home. He spent afternoons at the golf course, playing constantly. "My mom loved it," he said. "I'd come home from school and ride my bike to the course. She always knew exactly where I was."

By his junior year, a lot of colleges were recruiting him, especially on the west coast. He chose the University of Houston, in part because it offered the best scholarship — tuition and books — but also because, unlike some schools, he didn't have to go and try out for the coach. He arrived at Houston a shy, naive freshman with a lot of game. Two of his suitemates that year were Blaine McCallister, now a longtime pro, and Jim Nantz, who would grow up to be the number one voice of golf on CBS. "Jim was the serious guy in the group," Couples remembered. "We all thought he'd be president someday."

It was during Couples's freshman year that he first began to think seriously about playing golf for a living. He had met Lee Trevino once at a clinic in Seattle and had been awed by him, but he had never seen a pro tournament in person. In April 1978, Couples and his pals went out to the Houston Open one day. Couples loved it: the atmosphere, the sounds, the beauty of the place. "I remember watching Orville Moody putt," he said. "He was putting cross-handed and he just slapped at the ball. We cracked up watching the guy."

Later that day Couples noticed that the guy he and his friends had been laughing at had shot 64. It wasn't until later that Couples found out that Moody was a U.S. Open champion. "Blew me away," he said. "I followed golf as a kid. Tom Weiskopf was my favorite, and of course I remember Palmer and Nicklaus. But Orville Moody? No way did I know who he was."

A year later, after playing very well as a sophomore at Houston, Couples took another step toward the pros when he qualified for the 1979 U.S. Open at Inverness in Toledo, Ohio. He was nineteen years old and he took his mom with him to the championship. "I remember being terrified to go into the locker room," he said. "All those stars. I was too shy to even say hello. I just spent time with my mom and kept playing practice rounds all day long."

The practice paid off. Couples made the cut — but not without a moment of terror. Playing the 18th hole on Friday, he hit his ball into a bunker. For reasons that he can't explain to this day, he kicked at some pebbles as he was walking into the bunker. When he walked into the scorer's tent, a USGA official said to him, "Don't sign your card. There may have been a rules violation in that bunker."

Couples knew he was right on the cut line. Terror seized him. How would he feel if he had to go home and tell everyone that he had missed the U.S. Open cut because he had foolishly kicked a few pebbles in a bunker? P. J. Boatwright, the USGA's late rules guru, came into the tent and guided Couples to an empty bunker on the now-empty front nine. "Show me what you did, son," Boatwright ordered. Couples complied.

Boatwright smiled. "You're okay, son. That's no problem."

Because Couples hadn't been trying to improve his lie and hadn't been set in a stance, he lived to play the weekend. The next day, he was paired with Lee Trevino. "I was so nervous I couldn't even see my ball on the first tee," he said. "Trevino was great. To this day, whenever we play, he says, 'Yeah, you're just like you were the first time I played with you.'"

Not quite. Couples shot 80 that day. But the next day, paired with the only other amateur left in the field, John Cook, he shot 71. That was good enough to tie for forty-eighth place and make him low amateur — by a shot — over Cook, who was the reigning U.S. Amateur champion. Couples went back to Houston filled with confidence and had an excellent junior year. By this time he had all but abandoned any pretense of trying to graduate — "I did what I had to in order to stay eligible and that was it" — but was still planning to come back for his senior year. He left for the summer planning to play in the U.S. Amateur as his last event of the summer and then return to enroll for the fall semester.

He never made it back.

The Amateur was played that summer at Pinehurst's famed No. 2 course (the site of the 1999 U.S. Open) and Couples arrived with a ticket back to Houston in his pocket. He was medalist for the 36 holes of stroke play and won his first three matches to reach the quarterfinals, where he played Jim Holtgrieve. In those days, the Masters still invited all four U.S. Amateur semifinalists to the following year's championship, the one proviso being that you still had to be an amateur to accept the invitation. Couples knew a spot in the Masters was at stake when he played Holtgrieve. He lost on the first hole of sudden death.

Distraught, Couples decided not to go to Houston. Instead, he somehow traded his ticket to Houston for a ticket to California and flew there to see Deborah, who lived near Anaheim. He didn't tell his parents where he was going because they never really approved of the relationship since Deborah was older than Fred and acted a lot older than Fred. He stayed in Long Beach with friends of the family, casually telling them that he had told his parents he was staying with them for a few days. Back at Houston, Nantz and his buddies suspected he was with Deborah but weren't quite sure since he hadn't called them either.

A couple of days after arriving, Couples went to play golf at a public course called El Dorado. The pro was named Larry Benson, and when Couples mentioned he had just come from playing in the U.S. Amateur, Benson asked him if he wanted to play with him. He was getting ready to play in the Queen Mary Open in a few days and could use some competition. "I played really well," Couples said. "Afterward I asked Larry if there was any way I could get into the Queen Mary Open. He told me that amateur qualifying had been the previous week and the only way I could get in was if I turned pro. I didn't think I wanted to do that, but the next day I came back and played really well again. So I just said, 'You know what? I'm turning pro. I want to play.' I went in the next day to sign up, and they said to me that if I did this, I couldn't go back to college. I said, 'Who cares, big deal.'"

On the opening day of the tournament, Couples bumped into an old friend from Houston named Tom LaMore. "I see you turned pro," LaMore said. "Have you signed up for Q-School?"

"Signed up for what-school?" Couples answered.

He had no idea what the PGA Tour Qualifying School was. He hadn't thought that far ahead. All he had thought about was playing in the Queen Mary Open. Back then, it cost $500 to enter the qualifying tournament (today it costs $4,000). For Couples, it might as well have been $4,000 because he didn't have anything approaching $500. Once again, LaMore saved him, convincing his uncle to loan Couples the money. He wired it to the PGA Tour the next day — hours before the deadline for entering.

In the meantime, Couples played in the Queen Mary with Deborah as his caddy. On the second day, he accidentally bent his putter and, after finishing the next hole, he tried to straighten it on a nearby tree and ended up breaking it. When Deborah saw that he had broken his putter, she thought he had thrown a tantrum over a missed putt. She threw down the bag and stormed off saying, "I'm not caddying for you if you can't behave like an adult." Couples was amused by this since he had seen her break tennis racquets in anger. But he chased her down, convinced her he hadn't thrown a fit, and she returned to the bag.

Couples played well in the tournament, finishing tied for eighth with another young pro named Mark O'Meara. They each made $1,800. That night, flush with his success, Couples finally called home. "I knew I hadn't behaved very well and they were probably worried," he said. "But I was so excited about the way I had played, I figured everything would be okay."

He figured wrong. His dad answered the phone. Couples can only remember his father yelling at him — really yelling — once during boyhood. He and some friends had been playing hockey in the backyard at the end of a rainy spell and somehow got the idea that heaping mud on the neighbor's house would be a cool thing to do. The neighbor showed up at the door that night and Tom Couples let Fred have it. Most of the time the disciplinarian was his mom. "She did the yelling," he said. "With dad, he would give you a look and you knew."

Tom Couples didn't yell this time either. Fred explained that he had been in California with Deborah, he was sorry he hadn't called but a lot was going on, he had turned pro and played in this tournament and won $1,800 for finishing eighth and . . .

He never finished the sentence. Tom Couples hung up on him. A few minutes later Fred called back. His mom answered this time. She asked for details. What would he do next? Where would he go? Had he spoken to anyone at Houston? "She calmed the waters," Fred remembered. "But my dad was very, very angry. And disappointed. I hadn't exactly handled things well that week."

The twist to the story was that none of it would have happened if not for Jim Holtgrieve. If Couples had beaten him in the Amateur quarter-finals, he never would have given up his spot in the 1981 Masters to turn pro. But once he lost to Holtgrieve and wasn't in the Masters — years later he blocked the memory so completely that he thought he had *beaten* Holtgrieve and then lost to Hal Sutton — going back to school, especially with Deborah no longer there, wasn't enough incentive to keep him from making the move.

Couples stayed in California to practice until Q-School, which was only a few weeks away. In those days, Q-School was held twice a year (now it is held only once) and there were two stages each time, not three. Couples stayed with O'Meara during the first stage, which they both survived, and then moved on to the finals. There were twenty-two spots available. Couples bogeyed the last hole and finished twenty-second.

"To this day I have no idea what I would have done or what would have happened next in my life if I hadn't made it," he said. "Knowing me, I probably would have been done."

Instead, he was off to play the PGA Tour at the age of twenty-one. A friend of his uncle's agreed to sponsor him, which meant he had enough money to buy a car and pay his bills for the first few months of travel. Which was a good thing, since he wasn't making any money. This was 1981 and the old "rabbit" system was still in place. That meant only the top sixty money winners were fully exempt on tour each year. If you were a Q-School graduate, you played in Monday qualifying events each week to get into tournaments. Because everyone drove from stop to stop, the Q-Schoolers were constantly hopping from place to place, hoping to get into tournaments. Thus, the term rabbit.

Couples hopped all over the west coast, qualifying for exactly one tournament. He shot 76–76 in San Diego and missed the cut. After he had failed to qualify for the Bing Crosby Pro-Am, he was officially zero for the west coast. He remembers sitting in the locker room after another failed Monday, talking with Mike Donald, who was also a young tour rabbit at the time. "You know, I have absolutely no idea what I'm doing out here," he said to Donald. "All I do every week is drive to get someplace on Sunday, play a practice round, go out on Monday and play lousy, and then spend the rest of the week looking for a place to play so I can go do the same thing again the next Monday. I'm lost."

Donald, who became close to Couples during the next few years, liked to recount that story after Couples became a star, because the notion of Fred Couples clueless and hopeless on the golf course seemed like a fantasy by then.

Things finally got better for Couples when the tour shifted to Florida. He got into Arnold Palmer's tournament at Bay Hill, made the cut, and cashed his first check for $660. He made another cut at Doral and another $2,200. Then, at New Orleans, he broke through, finishing tied for fifth. He made $12,500, paid off his car and his sponsor, and kept getting better from that point forward. He ended the year on a high note, finishing second in the Pensacola Open. That locked up his spot in the top sixty and nudged him ahead of fellow rookie O'Meara on the money list (fifty-third to fifty-fifth). But O'Meara won rookie of the year and the Rolex watch that went with it because the voting took place before Pensacola. To this day Couples often tells O'Meara he owes him a watch.

Once he was established on tour, Couples didn't look back. He won for the first time in his third year, winning a five-man playoff at the Kemper Open. He knocked a five-iron to a foot at the second playoff hole, and when he tapped in the birdie putt — "I almost lipped it out I was so nervous," he said — here came Deborah, blond hair flying, racing across the green and leaping into his arms. The picture of her wrapped around Fred made most newspapers and golf magazines around the country.

"You know, if things had turned out differently, we would probably have the picture around someplace and we'd take it out every so often and laugh," Couples said, thinking back to that giddy day. "Now when I think about it and what happened, it's funny, but it's also a little bit sad."

The victory at Kemper made Couples a budding star. He was twenty-three, with boyish features, an easy smile, and a very striking blonde wife. He also had the kind of sweet swing most players would kill for. When he won the Players Championship the following year and finished seventh on the money list, it seemed to be only a matter of time until he became one of the game's dominant players.

But it wasn't as easy as Couples made it look. He won only once more during the next five years and, although he was a consistent money winner, didn't crack the top ten on the money list at all during that time. A lot of people wrote Couples off as a major talent with minor ambition, someone who was content to make a lot of money but didn't want the responsibilities that came with stardom.

It's certainly true that being a star has never been Couples's raison d'être. But that wasn't why he didn't become one as quickly as some thought he would. It wasn't until 1986, when he began working with Paul Marchand, that he had someone who worked with him on his swing on a regular basis. He and Marchand made changes in his swing and his approach to the game that, as is often the case, made things worse before they got better.

What's more, his marriage was slowly falling apart. He and Deborah had married after he turned pro, but Deborah was never really happy with the life of a tour wife. She continued working, running the tennis pro shop at Indian Wells, even after Fred began to make a lot of money. Then she got interested in polo and was often off playing polo. Almost inevitably, they grew apart. Couples thinks the deterioration of his marriage may have had something to do with the improvement of his golf game.

"I just made a point of focusing more on my game, of working at it a little harder, of caring about it a little more," he said. "The golf course became the place where I was happiest. It gave me good feelings about myself that I wasn't getting away from the course."

The turning point probably came in 1989 when he played on the Ryder Cup team for the first time. Raymond Floyd, who was the captain, saw loads of unrealized potential. Couples lost a critical singles match on the 18th hole and sat by the side of the green crying uncontrollably. From that weekend on, Floyd became a mentor and close friend.

"It was really simple stuff," Couples said, looking back. "I remember we had a talk once about playing par-fives. He asked me how many eagles I made at par-fives most weeks. I said, one, maybe every so often two. He said if that was the case, why was I always trying to fly my second shots right at the flag. More often than not, I was taking away any margin for error that way and if I missed the shot at all, I was going to make par or bogey. But if I played for the fat of the green, I had all the power I needed to get the ball comfortably on and from there I would almost certainly make no worse than birdie and occasionally make an eagle."

More mature, more focused, more driven, Couples exploded in 1991, winning twice, finishing third four times, and ending up third on the money list. Two of the thirds were in majors — the U.S. and British Opens — and when 1992 began there was no doubt who was the best player in the world never to have won a major.

Couples didn't hold the title for long. He played the best golf of his life to win the Masters. That was his third win of the year and it was still April. Davis Love III was also having a career year, winning three times in less than two months, and the two of them both went over $1 million in earnings earlier in a year than anyone had done before. They were going to be the game's next great rivalry.

But there was turmoil in Couples's life. He and Deborah had been living separate lives for a while at this stage, but she suddenly turned up at the Masters, tapping on the window at his house while he and Marchand were sitting in the living room the night before the tournament began. She stayed the week, but reconciliation was not a possibility. She also showed up at the British Open, causing a famous scene in a bar one night when she began dancing on tables. Clearly distracted, Couples (who wasn't in the bar) missed the cut and left without Deborah. The divorce that followed was very ugly, very public, and very expensive. Even now, Couples has trouble talking about it.

"It just didn't have to end the way it did," he said, shaking his head. "The funny thing about it is, she probably would have ended up with more money if we had just sat down and said, 'Okay, you take this, I'll take this.' But she didn't want it that way, so a lot of money was wasted on lawyers. It was a joke."

Couples didn't play nearly as well during the rest of 1992 but still ended up as the leading money winner and player of the year. The next year he dropped to tenth on the money list while the tabloids had a field day with the divorce. By then he was dating Tawnya Dodds and feeling much more comfortable about the direction of his life.

But everything changed on the morning of March 6, 1994. Couples was on the range at Doral warming up for the final round of the Doral-Ryder Open. He was just starting to swing a little bit harder with his eight-iron when he took a swing and felt a bomb go off in his back. The scream of pain could be heard up and down the range. If Marchand hadn't been standing right there, Couples might have fallen flat on his face. Marchand caught him, and Couples gamely tried to straighten up and lean on his eight-iron for a moment. No way. He was helped into the fitness trailer, where he was able to lie down while a doctor was sent for. At one point, Jon Brendle, one of the PGA Tour's rules officials, came in to see how Couples was doing. It was getting close to his tee time and Brendle needed to know for certain if Couples was withdrawing.

"Wait a second, Jon, let me give this a try," Couples said. He got off the table he was lying on, took one step, and fell down in a heap.

Since that day, Couples's life has never been the same. He has deteriorating disks in his back and they won't get better. He has been on and off the tour because of his back problems. Long airplane rides always give him trouble. There is no doubting the importance of Marchand and his longtime caddy, Joe LaCava, but no one is more important to Couples professionally these days than Tom Boers, the back specialist from Columbus, Georgia. Couples went to see him after Doral on the recommendation of Jim McKay, Phil Mickelson's caddy, and has worked with him ever since.

"It's better now than it's been in a long, long time," he said early in 1998. "But it's never going to be completely better. I've learned to live with it. I can't practice for long periods of time, and I can't play as many weeks as I might like to. But I can still play and I can still compete. I'm still pretty good and at times I can be very good."

Things didn't get better after the Doral incident. Couples's mom had been fighting cancer for the better part of a year, and she began to get very sick shortly after Doral. On May 8, 1994 — Mother's Day — she died.

Couples became the tour's enigma. There were moments when he looked ready to dominate again. He won the Buick Open in August 1994 but could play only fifteen times the next year. He won the Players Championship in 1996 and had a great chance to win the British Open before fading on the back nine on Sunday. And then came 1997. The year was a complete nightmare. First, his dad was diagnosed with cancer. Then, shortly after he met Thais she had to undergo cancer surgery. The rest of the year was a blur to Couples. One minute he was in Switzerland with Thais at the clinic where she was being treated, the next he was in Seattle with his dad, who was yelling at him to get back out on tour. Couples's mind wasn't on golf very much and he finished fifty-fifth on the money list. He stopped playing in the fall so he could go home and be with his dad. Given his dad's attitude, this wasn't as obvious a decision as it appeared to be.

"It doesn't matter what he's saying to you, you need to go spend the time with him," Davis Love told him one day in September. "Even if you just sit there and talk about the Mariners or Seahawks, you should be there."

Couples knew Love was right. He went back to Seattle and spent hours and hours with his dad. Sometimes they talked, sometimes they didn't. But Couples knew he had done the right thing by being there. Tom Couples died on Thanksgiving Day.

Couples began 1998 hoping he could start all over again. Thais's cancer was in remission. He was spending more and more time with her and her kids in Los Angeles and loving every minute of it. In February he shocked himself by winning the Bob Hope Desert Classic, beating Bruce Lietzke in a playoff. A month later, Marchand flew to Florida to spend the week with him at Bay Hill. They spent long hours on the range, working on a swing that would enable Couples to hit the ball left-to-right more often. Couples has always been a pronounced fader, so adept at hitting the ball right-to-left that other players on tour will talk about trying to hit a "Freddy slice." But Couples was convinced that if he wanted to win at Augusta again, he had to be able to draw the ball. A draw was very helpful at number two, number five, and number nine, and an absolute necessity at number thirteen. Couples came out of the Bay Hill sessions feeling better about his swing and his game than he had in a long time. He played well at Bay Hill and at the Players.

His back felt good. His game felt good. And he absolutely couldn't wait to show Augusta to Thais. "She can't wait," he said during the Players, "because she's sick of hearing me talking about it."

5

Warming to the Task

By Monday morning, everyone has arrived at Augusta. In 1998, the last two players to check in were, appropriately enough, Arnold Palmer and Jack Nicklaus. They were entitled.

The Masters is the only event in sports where more people show up to watch practice than actual play. That's because more people are allowed to show up for the practice rounds than for the tournament itself. Until 1995, the gates of Augusta were opened on Monday, Tuesday, and Wednesday and anyone who showed up could buy a ticket and walk in. But as the fascination with the Masters grew, the crowds for the practice rounds became thicker and thicker. Tour operators who couldn't get tickets for the Masters began selling tickets to people for the practice rounds because they knew they could get everybody in.

Things were so bad in 1994 it became almost impossible to walk around the golf course. The Lords of Augusta never reveal attendance figures, but the guesses on the crowds for the first half of the week that year ranged as high as 85,000 a day. Something had to be done.

A lottery was started for practice round tickets. Beginning in 1995 anyone wanting to purchase practice round tickets had to send in an application for tickets. If they made the cut, the tickets arrived by mail. If they didn't, their check came back in the mail. Again, the Lords won't reveal the cutoff number, but estimates put the practice round crowds nowadays at somewhere between 40,000 and 50,000. That is considerably more than the 25,000 who get tickets for Thursday to Sunday.

Often it seems that those who come to the practice rounds don't really come to watch golf. After all, the golf being played isn't real, unless you count a $10 nassau involving millionaires as real golf. So, while they may walk down to Amen Corner or stand around the 18th green to watch the stars walk up the hill, most fans spend their time on the practice days doing two things: buying souvenirs and taking pictures of one another. Here we are in front of the clubhouse. And here we are watching Arnold Palmer tee off. Here we are watching all the people who are watching Arnold Palmer tee off.

It is understandable. If you can't actually see the Masters, the next best thing is being able to say you were *at* the Masters. And bring home pictures and souvenirs as proof.

No one in the world was more excited to be at Augusta than Kenny Bakst. But Bakst was a long way from being an awed spectator. He came carrying golf clubs, not a camera. In fact, Bakst had probably spent more time on the grounds at Augusta National in the months leading up to the Masters than any club member or anyone else in the field. And he had loved every minute of it.

"I actually feel a little bit melancholy today," he said on Monday afternoon. "I've waited for this for months and now I realize in a few days it's going to be over."

It was an amateur's trip to Fantasy Island that had started the previous August in Dallas, when Bakst won the USGA's Mid-Amateur championship, played at the Dallas Athletic Club, by hitting a seven-iron four feet from the hole to birdie the 18th hole of the final to win one up. Winning a national championship was a thrill for Bakst, but the best part of it all was the final perk given to the Mid-Amateur champion: a spot in the Masters.

Since its beginnings, the Masters has always held spots open in the field for amateurs, a tribute to Bob Jones, generally considered the game's greatest amateur player. Once upon a time the entire U.S. Walker Cup team was invited, and, until 1989, all four U.S. Amateur semifinalists were included in the field. But with the game becoming more and more dominated by professionals and the best amateurs consistently turning pro younger and younger, the Masters has cut back on amateur participation. Now, there are only five guaranteed slots for amateurs: the U.S. Amateur champion and runner-up, the British Amateur champion, the U.S. Public Links Champion, and the Mid-Amateur champion.

The Mid-Am is the event most likely to produce a true amateur — as opposed to, as USGA executive director David Fay puts it, "pros in training" — because a player has to be twenty-five to enter. Most players who are twenty-five and still amateurs aren't likely to turn pro in the future.

Bakst fit that profile. A golf junkie, he is the third of five children, the son of not one but two single-digit handicappers. He began playing with his older brother Peter long before he was old enough to get on the golf course at the Long Island club his parents belonged to, so he spent a lot of time on public courses and on the driving range. By the time he was twelve, he was hooked on the game, so much so that he would spend hours in his room at night practicing his swing. "I literally wore a groove into the carpet with my club," he said.

He and Peter, who was two years older than he was, were close to being scratch players before they graduated from high school and both chose Stanford. Peter found other things to do there, but Kenny stuck with golf. "My goal was to be a pro," he said. "I thought I was good enough and that's what I worked at my first two years in school."

He didn't work very much at school though, which concerned his parents. His father, a heart surgeon, had always thought that Kenny would be the one who followed in his footsteps. He had an aptitude for math and science but no real passion for medicine. Still, when his parents urged him to quit golf as a junior to improve his grades, he agreed. "In the back of my mind I think it had occurred to me that this might not be my profession," he said. "Even if the answer wasn't medicine, I figured I'd better be in position to go to grad school if I wanted."

His grades went up and he returned to the golf team as a senior. By now he had filled out and grown and had become a very good ball striker. A number of his teammates believed he had the game to make it on tour. Bakst wasn't so sure. Often, he would play a round where he would hit seventeen greens and shoot 72 while someone else would hit eleven greens and shoot 68.

"I just didn't have the short game to go with my long game," he said. "My friends told me I'd learn it on tour but I didn't think that was necessarily true. I had played a lot of golf for a lot of years. Why would I think that just because I was playing it for a living with all that added pressure that I would suddenly get it."

There was more. Bakst played well in college, but he didn't tear up the Pacific-10 or the national tournaments. Often, he would come home from tournaments disappointed in himself, frustrated because he hadn't made any putts or contended in the final round. Golf, he knew, was often about failure, even for the very best players. "You can go weeks, months, even years not playing well," he said. "I didn't think I had the temperament to deal with a job where I would feel as if I was failing for long stretches of time."

And so, he gave up the dream and went to law school at Southern California. He practiced for three years in Los Angeles, moved back to New York, went into the real estate development business, and made a lot of money. He met Suzanne Pearl through mutual friends in 1987, and they were married a year later. Jonathan was born in 1992, William in 1995.

"I have never regretted my decision," he said, sitting comfortably in the clubhouse that had become a home away from home for several months. "If I was graduating from college now, I might have thought differently. There's *so* much more money out here now. There are more endorsements. There's the Nike Tour as a fallback if you aren't on the big tour. It's a totally different landscape.

"But even with all that, I'm not sure. I look at the way you live on tour, even if you do well, the transient nature of it, how tough it is on families, and I don't know if I would be happy regardless of the money involved."

Bakst was never swayed from his decision. He played a lot of high-level amateur golf, winning club championships, and competed successfully in tournaments in the New York area. He qualified five times for the U.S. Amateur and five times for the Mid-Amateur. But prior to 1997 he had never made an impact in any of them.

Then it all came together during one perfect week in Dallas. The hardest part — other than waiting out a rain delay that caused the final to be pushed back twenty-four hours — was trying not to think about playing in the Masters. After he had beaten Tim Jackson in the semi-finals, Jackson, who had won the Mid-Am in 1991 and played in the Masters, read his mind as they shook hands. "Just go out tomorrow and play a great round of golf," he said. "Don't think about the Masters at all."

Bakst knew that would be impossible. He called home that night to tell his family not to come to Dallas for the final. "Things were going so well I didn't want to change anything," he said. When Peter got on the phone, he told his brother he agreed with the decision. "If you lose, I don't want to be around," he said. "And if you win, we're all going to the Masters anyway."

So much for not thinking about the Masters.

But Bakst managed to keep his emotions under control and his mind in the present in the final, coming from two down with six holes to play to win. Once he rolled in his final birdie putt and knew he was in the Masters, he decided he was going to enjoy the experience since there was no way of knowing if he would ever get back. "I wanted to come here and play as well as possible," he said. "But I also wanted to savor the entire thing, enjoy it for all it was worth."

Augusta National allows anyone who has qualified for the Masters complete access to the club and the golf course once it reopens in October. (The club closes from late May until mid-October each year so the course will not be torn up in the searing heat of Georgia summers and because few members would venture there in summer anyway.) Bakst took full advantage of his punched Masters ticket. He made four trips to Augusta, flying down from New York for long weekends, often playing the course by himself each day until the sun was almost down. On his first trip down, Bennie Hatcher, a veteran Augusta National caddy, was assigned to carry his bag. Bakst soon learned that Hatcher had caddied for — among others — Arnold Palmer and Lanny Wadkins in the days prior to 1983 when the club required players to use the local caddies during the tournament.

Bakst and Hatcher became a team. Bakst played fourteen rounds at Augusta prior to tournament week, becoming so familiar to most club employees that they greeted him with a casual "Hi, Kenny" whenever he walked into the clubhouse. After his first formal practice round on

Monday of tournament week, Bakst spent so long talking to reporters about what it was like to play in front of thousands of people alongside two-time Masters champion Ben Crenshaw that he arrived at the clubhouse thirty minutes after the kitchen had stopped serving lunch. Bakst was about to venture onto the grounds to find a concession stand when one of the waiters tapped him on the shoulder. "Tell me what you want, Kenny," he said quietly, "and I'll get it for you."

Bakst had flown into Augusta on Friday because he wanted to spend a couple more days on the golf course before it was overrun with people and because he wanted to sleep in the Crow's Nest before his family arrived and have the full amateur experience at Augusta. Everyone else — Suzanne and the two boys, his parents, three of his four siblings, and a host of friends — came in Sunday, which was Bakst's fortieth birthday. The family had rented a house for the week and the birthday party was held there on Sunday night.

Bakst would begin his forties in grand style: on Monday he would play with Crenshaw and Scott McCarron. On Tuesday he had a game with a couple of old-timers named Palmer and Nicklaus. "I think I'm more nervous about Tuesday than I am about Thursday," he said, only half-joking. Crenshaw was a friend with whom he was involved in a golf course project. That was how their practice round had come about. Palmer and Nicklaus were a different story. With the help of the USGA, Bakst had written to each of them, wondering if there was any chance he might play a practice round with him during Masters week. He got gracious letters back from both men saying they would love to play with him — on Tuesday.

Whoops. Bakst was overbooked. "How in the world do you tell Arnold Palmer or Jack Nicklaus you can't do it on Tuesday because you've got a game?" he said.

The answer was easy: you play with both of them. Bakst called Palmer's longtime assistant Doc Giffin and explained his dilemma since he had received Nicklaus's letter first and had already said yes to Nicklaus. Giffin told him not to worry about a thing. Then he went about making the necessary arrangements.

As much as Bakst had played the golf course, as familiar as he had become with the club, he wasn't prepared for what greeted him on Monday morning. All the visualization he had done through all the months of preparing had been inside the ropes: seeing shots he would need to play, putts he would have to make, the handshake and hellos with Palmer and Nicklaus.

"I never, for whatever reason, put a picture of all the people in my mind," he said.

They were there on Monday. Everywhere. Bakst walked onto the driving range, looked around, and saw a packed grandstand behind him and people packed four and five deep against the ropes on either side. "First time in my life I had to take deep breaths on the driving range to get control of myself," he said. "It was unreal."

The day was unreal too, a classic April day in Augusta, the flowers and dogwood in full bloom, the golf course spectacular. Bakst was in a daze most of the way around, trying to listen to the advice Crenshaw was giving him about the golf course but drinking everything in at the same time.

And then came Tuesday. The introductions to Palmer and Nicklaus. Warming up again with thousands watching. This time, the walk to the first tee was a little calmer. He and Fred Funk, who was the fourth member of the group, waited for Nicklaus and Palmer to arrive. They came separately, the crowds parting as if Moses had raised his staff for each of them to walk onto the tee. As the round went on, Bakst noticed that they almost never arrived at a tee or a green together. First one, followed by the ovation. Then the other. "They know how to do this," he said to Funk at one point.

Once the cheers and screams for the two icons had quieted, arrangements were made. They would play a $10 nassau, young guys (Funk and Bakst) against old. It was time to play. "Okay, Kenny," Palmer said, "why don't you lead us off."

Bakst almost looked behind him to see which Kenny Palmer was addressing. He wanted to say something like "You talkin' to me?" Clearly, Palmer was talking to him. Legs quaking, aware of thousands of eyes on him, he somehow got his ball teed up. He looked at the yawning bunker at the top of the hill on the right side of the first fairway and tried to imagine the course empty, the way he had seen it so many times. He swung, connected, and — miraculously — the ball soared down the fairway.

Nothing to this game.

For the next several hours, Bakst felt as if he were floating around the golf course. He even played well enough that he and Funk won the match from Nicklaus and Palmer. When the round was over, Nicklaus made a point of telling him how impressed he was with his game. Then he had to go. Something about a ceremony honoring him for playing in forty straight Masters.

Bakst walked up the hill from behind the 18th green to the oak tree and found several writers from the New York area — familiar faces now — waiting for him. Suzanne and Jonathan and the family were there too. "I'll just be a few minutes," he said to Suzanne. He tilted his head in the direction of the writers. "I gotta talk to the guys for a few minutes and then we'll go."

With that, like a seasoned veteran, he walked over to the writers to tell them how he and his partner had outplayed Nicklaus and Palmer at Augusta National in front of thousands of people. Later, Nicklaus would comment that he had rushed off without paying his debt.

"He paid," Bakst said. "He paid in spades."

Practice rounds at the majors aren't like practice rounds at other golf tournaments. Amateurs like Bakst aren't the only ones who make special arrangements prior to tournament week with the game's stars. In 1996, when he won Palmer's tournament at Bay Hill to qualify for his first Masters, Paul Goydos accepted the trophy from Palmer, thanked him, and then said, "Will you play a practice round with me at Augusta?"

"Only if you lose the beard," Palmer said, a reference to the scruffy goatee Goydos had been sporting for several weeks.

Goydos lost the beard.

In 1995, knowing that Palmer was planning to make his last appearance in the British Open at St. Andrews, Tom Watson made pretournament arrangements to play a practice round with Palmer and Nicklaus. "I figured it might be my last chance to do something like that," said Watson, who has won the British five times himself. He even went so far as to arrange for — and insist on — a picture of the group as it crossed the eleventh-century bridge over the Swilcan Burn at 18.

At other times players try to set up practice rounds for different reasons. John Daly and Fuzzy Zoeller always play practice rounds together at the majors, Zoeller having been Daly's big-brother figure and best friend on tour for years. At the U.S. Open in 1997, Daly approached Tiger Woods about playing a practice round. Initially, Woods said yes. Later he learned that Daly was planning to bring Zoeller along, hoping that 18 holes together might do more good than the famous Forced Lunch a few weeks earlier at Colonial had done. When Woods realized what Daly was planning, he canceled the date, then set out that morning at 6:30 to play a practice round alone. He was less than pleased when Tom Meeks of the USGA rode out to tell him the golf course wasn't open yet.

The Woods-Zoeller soap opera was still a major topic of conversation as the practice rounds got under way. Zoeller had arrived in town giving anyone and everyone who asked a firm no comment whether the question was about the menu for the Champions Dinner Tuesday night, his feelings about Tiger, the weather, the golf course, or anything else.

It was sad to see Zoeller in such a sour mood, because that isn't who he is or has been during his years on tour. Zoeller had gone from apologetic in the wake of his comments a year earlier, to resigned, to angry. When *Golf World* columnist Tim Rosaforte had written a column in March implying that Zoeller still owed Woods an apology, Zoeller had gone ballistic. That's it, he told friends, I'm not talking to any of them anymore.

Woods was as heartily sick of the topic as Zoeller was and kept insisting it was all old news, water under the bridge, all in the past — pick your cliché. Clearly though, there was simmering resentment between the two men. Even so, the general sentiment was that once the Champions Dinner was over and done with, everyone would be able to bring closure to the issue.

Monday at Augusta is like the first day of school for the players. Everyone is excited to be back, the new kids look around in awe, and greetings and old war stories are exchanged by almost everyone. By Tuesday, everyone begins to settle in and get serious about preparing for the golf tournament.

Which means two things: pace of play on the golf course comes to a near halt, and tempers begin to fray. By lunchtime on Tuesday, players were coming off the golf course screaming about how long it was taking to get around. "How much chipping and putting can you do?" asked Jim

Furyk, who walked in after nine because he got tired of waiting at every hole.

Furyk had started out on number one with Tom Watson and Scott Hoch. It had taken them an hour to play three holes. When they got to the par-three fourth and found two groups on the tee and another on the green, that was it for Watson. "I'm walking in," he told Furyk. "This is ridiculous."

Furyk and Hoch tried cutting over to the seventh hole to see if things might open up there a little. They didn't. They played three more holes and quit too.

Tiger Woods, Mark O'Meara, and John Cook played a little later that day and found the going a bit smoother. One way or the other, the threesome was going to play 18 holes because they had arrived Monday afternoon and needed to see the entire golf course, since it closed early on Wednesday and there was talk of rain being on the way.

"No matter how well you know the course, you need to get a feel for it because it changes every year," O'Meara said. "It isn't like at the other majors where you may not know the course at all, but you still need to check things out."

O'Meara, Woods, and Cook had all flown into Augusta on Monday on the private plane that Woods leased. O'Meara and Cook had been close friends for twenty years, dating back to the days when they had competed as amateurs and then to their early years on tour when they had been neighbors in California. Each had been a U.S. Amateur champion — Cook in 1978, O'Meara a year later, when he had beaten the defending champion in the final. Each had made a lot of money on tour and had a lot of success. O'Meara had won fourteen tournaments, Cook nine. They had both played on Ryder Cup teams. Each had flirted with winning the British Open: O'Meara in 1991, when he had started the last round in second place only to watch Ian Baker-Finch blow the field away by shooting 29 on the front nine; Cook the following year, when he had missed a two-foot birdie putt on the 17th hole that would have given him a two-shot lead with one hole to play.

O'Meara had turned forty-one in January, Cook would be forty-one in October. Cook had three children, O'Meara two. Each had gone through a puzzling slump several years earlier. Cook, after winning three times in 1992 and finishing second in two majors (the British Open and the PGA), went winless for three years, dropping from third on the money list in '92 to ninety-seventh in '95. He was so discouraged he talked of retirement. O'Meara never quite got to that point, but he also slipped. After winning five tournaments between 1989 and 1992, he went two years without a win, sliding from eleventh on the money list in '92 to eighty-sixth two years later.

Then, both had revived and started winning again. Their slumps had come at a time in life when many golfers struggle. Each began to resent time on the road away from their families. Their kids had reached the age where they were doing new and different things all the time and often the dads missed out. Because golfers peak later in life than athletes in other sports, they often face family issues that their peers in other sports never face. The conundrum was best described once by Tom Kite: "When you're at home, you feel as if you're missing something not being on tour. When you're on tour you *know* you're missing something not being at home."

O'Meara made things easier for himself by building a huge home for his family outside Orlando, in Isleworth, the exclusive Arnold Palmer/IMG-backed golfing community. Although he admitted he was distracted during the building of the house, being in Florida made travel much easier most of the year (not to mention the tax benefits — there is no Florida income tax). Cook had seen how much O'Meara enjoyed Isleworth and had decided late in 1997 to build his own house there.

He had flown to Orlando the week before Augusta to meet with his builder and to play some practice rounds with O'Meara and Woods, who had moved to Isleworth in 1996 after turning pro, mostly for tax purposes. The older men were keenly aware of the pressure Woods would be facing the next week. They were also aware of their own relatively poor records at the Masters: O'Meara had one top-ten finish (a tie for fourth in 1992) in fourteen appearances; Cook had never finished in the top twenty in twelve trips to Augusta.

On Sunday night, the three players all had dinner at O'Meara's house. O'Meara had played well throughout the week. Earlier that day the three men had played 27 holes and O'Meara had outplayed Woods thoroughly in their ongoing battle to be the unofficial King of Isleworth. "I clipped him pretty good," O'Meara said the next day, relaxing in the locker room at Augusta. Generally, the two played $5 nassaus. O'Meara had won $100. "He kept double- and triple-pressing on the par-fives," O'Meara said. "I told him that wasn't fair when he was hitting six-iron to the greens and I was hitting three-wood. He said, 'You got a putter, don't you?'"

O'Meara had a very good putter, as he had proven to Woods that day and during his seventeen years on tour. The friendship that had grown between O'Meara and Woods since they had become neighbors was a classic odd-couple case. Their backgrounds as players could not have been more different. Woods had been trained for golf from the cradle forward, appearing on the *Mike Douglas Show* to show off his skills at the age of four. By the time he was fourteen he was already a blip on the golf horizon with IMG hot on his family's trail.

O'Meara didn't play golf at all until he was thirteen. His dad worked as a traveling representative for a number of furniture companies and the family was constantly being uprooted. By the time he became a teenager, O'Meara had lived in nine different homes in seven states — North Carolina, New York, Michigan, Ohio, Texas, Illinois, and California. The family finally settled down in Mission Viejo, California, in a house that overlooked the Mission Viejo Country Club.

O'Meara can remember playing nine holes of golf once before then. That changed quickly over the next few years. "When you move around a lot, you have trouble making friends," he remembered. "At times I felt like I had spent my whole life being the new kid in school. When we got to Mission Viejo, golf became my best friend. I started playing a lot, started to get better, and got completely hooked."

The club became his home away from home. O'Meara hung around the pro shop, cleaning clubs and carts, picking up range balls, anything just so he'd be allowed to practice and play the course. One of the assistant pros at Mission Viejo, an older man named Bob Harriett, eventually took O'Meara under his wing and helped teach him the game. "At first he thought I was a nuisance," O'Meara remembered. "But after a while, when he saw I was really interested, he worked with me."

O'Meara improved quickly. He played on a state championship team in high school and was recruited by, among others, UCLA. He seriously considered going there but decided on Long Beach State because it was an hour closer to home and he could commute. "To be honest with you, I wasn't ready to leave home," he said. "This way, I didn't have to."

Like most successful pros, O'Meara gives a lot of credit for his success to his wife. The touring pro's wife has to play mother and father at home when her husband is away, has to deal with the ups and downs that are an inevitable part of the game, has to try to bring normality to a life that is anything but normal. O'Meara goes a step further: he credits his wife with helping get his career started.

He was a junior at Long Beach State playing in a charity event at Mission Viejo that was run by the singers Jimmy Seals and Dash Crofts. O'Meara was paired with Lennie Clements, who had grown up down the road in San Diego and would also go on to play on tour. O'Meara vividly remembers walking onto the 13th tee and seeing a very attractive girl standing there. She was working for the tournament as a spotter and, since play was backed up, O'Meara decided to introduce himself.

Her name was Alicia Lauria. O'Meara asked her if she went to school in the area and she said she did. Four-year school, O'Meara wondered. Or maybe one of the many junior colleges nearby. Not exactly. Like Mark, Alicia was a junior — at Dane Hills High School.

Whoops.

O'Meara was twenty-one, Alicia was seventeen. "At that age, a four-year age difference is a big deal," he said, laughing now at how uncomfortable he felt that day. "Now, it seems like nothing. But it wasn't nothing back then."

Age difference or no age difference, O'Meara was smitten. He began to see Alicia, first just as friends. "A lot of our dates were at the driving range," he said. "She liked golf, but she hadn't learned how to play yet."

The key, for O'Meara, was that Alicia really liked the game. He had been dating someone else who disliked the game and that had hurt both the relationship and, O'Meara believed, his game. Now, spending time with someone who liked golf and didn't resent his commitment to it, he was far more relaxed. Eighteen months after meeting Alicia, O'Meara won the U.S. Amateur title. At that point he was certain about two things in his life: he wanted to take a shot at playing professionally and he wanted Alicia there with him.

He kept his amateur status for another year, in part because he wanted to go back to school to get his degree in marketing and because he wanted to play in the Masters. Like most players, he has distinct memories of that first trip to Augusta. "One thing I remember is standing in my boxer shorts up in the Crow's Nest and being able to look out the window and watch the guys tee off," he said. "I thought that was kind of neat."

The first day he played with Fuzzy Zoeller, who was the defending champion, and parred the first hole. He walked to the second tee thinking, well, no matter what happens I can always say I parred the first hole I played at the Masters. He was still congratulating himself when he hooked his drive at number two into the trees and a few minutes later made a rock-solid 10-foot putt for a rock-solid double bogey. Welcome to the real world. He ended up shooting 80–77 and missed the cut by a wide margin. Even so, he left with no regrets.

It took him five years to get back. He turned pro in the summer of 1980, making the transition official by signing a contract with the Hogan Company. O'Meara had played with Hogan clubs in college and, during the rainy final of the U.S. Amateur, had pulled out a Hogan umbrella. The company noticed and offered him $5,000 to sign with them when he turned pro. O'Meara was thrilled, especially when his contact person, Chip Bridges, suggested he should fly to Forth Worth and sign the deal in Ben Hogan's office.

O'Meara was so excited he did three things he almost never did: went out and got a haircut, put on a sports coat, and wore a tie. He was a lot more nervous meeting Ben Hogan than he had been playing John Cook in the Amateur final. "He couldn't have been nicer that day," O'Meara said. "I was there for an hour. He told me all about how he had struggled for all those years. He said he finally got to the point where he decided he had to get off the tour and completely revamp his game or just quit altogether. That was when he went to the desert and spent hours and hours day after day trying to find his swing. He was never a natural."

That day marked the beginning of a friendship between Hogan and O'Meara. "Sometimes he treated me like his grandson," O'Meara said. "Other times he treated me like a stranger."

One year, O'Meara arrived in town to play in the Colonial Invitational and went straight to Hogan's office because his swing teacher, Hank Haney, was with him and Haney was dying to meet Hogan. When they got to the office O'Meara and Haney were told that Mr. Hogan (as everyone called him) had just left to go to Shady Oaks Country Club for lunch — a routine he followed every day. Rather than just show up there unannounced with Haney, O'Meara called over to the club to make sure Hogan didn't mind if he brought Haney with him. When Hogan came to the phone, O'Meara gingerly asked if it would be okay to bring his good friend and teacher to meet him.

There was a pause at the other end of the line.

"Mr. Hogan, are you there?" O'Meara asked.

"Yes I am," Hogan said.

"Well then, would it be okay if I brought Hank over?"

"No, it wouldn't."

Another pause. O'Meara waited, wondering if Hogan would suggest another time or tell him why it wasn't okay. All he got was silence.

"Mr. Hogan?" he said again.

"Mark, are you coming to the [Hogan company] dinner tonight?"

"Yes sir, I'll be there."

"Good, see you then."

The line went dead.

Haney never did get to meet Hogan.

On another occasion, O'Meara flew into town after winning a tournament in Japan. He and Hogan went to a far end of the range at Shady Oaks, and, Hogan, ever-present cigarette dangling from his mouth, watched O'Meara hit a few balls. O'Meara felt good, confident coming off a victory, and he figured he was impressing the old man. O'Meara kept hitting shots; Hogan said nothing. Finally, O'Meara walked back to where Hogan stood.

"Well, Mr. Hogan," he said, "what do you think?"

Hogan took the cigarette out of his mouth. "Awful," he said.

O'Meara almost gagged.

Having signed with Hogan, O'Meara set his mind on the future. First came Q-School. He played well at both stages and got his playing card for 1981. He and Alicia had planned to get married on Valentine's Day but that would have come smack in the middle of the PGA Tour's west coast swing. So they pushed the wedding up to December 20. Their honeymoon was two days in Coronado, highlighted by a trip to the San Diego zoo. Then, with $3,000 borrowed from Mark's dad, they flew to Australia. Mark played in two events there, another in New Zealand, and came home with $7,000 in winnings. He repaid his father, he and

Alicia bought a Volkswagen Rabbit, and they set off to find their fortune on the PGA Tour.

"We had no house, no apartment, nothing," O'Meara said. "Everything we owned was in that Rabbit. I can't ever remember having a better time."

He was a tour rabbit driving a Rabbit. O'Meara played eleven straight weeks, skipped a week, then played twelve more weeks. Like his fellow rookie Fred Couples, he was fighting to make what was then the magic top sixty. Unlike Couples, who couldn't break an egg on the west coast, O'Meara got off to a good start. He made the cut at the Bob Hope and cashed a check for $1,600. Then he finished eighth at Phoenix and made $8,000, which might as well have been a million as far as Mark and Alicia were concerned.

Eventually, he finished fifty-fifth on the money list. The next year should have been easy. The tour decided to go to the all exempt format for 1983, meaning that the top 125 money winners would be fully exempt. It seemed like a piece of cake — except O'Meara lost his game someplace. Maybe it was buried in the trunk of the Rabbit, but he couldn't find it. By the time he got to the Hall of Fame Classic at Pinehurst in October, his game was in shambles and he was in serious danger of missing the 125 and landing back in Q-School.

On the first day of the tournament, he shot a 76. Miserable, he slogged to the range, although the exercise seemed pointless. He hit shots left, hit them right, hit them fat, hit them thin. At one point he turned around and saw a young man dressed in clothes that made him believe he was some kind of pro, standing and watching him, arms folded as if he was analyzing what he was doing.

"You know, feel free to make a suggestion," O'Meara said. "Any suggestion at all."

Instead of doing that, the young man walked over to O'Meara and introduced himself. His name was Ken Crow and he was one of the teaching assistants at Pinehurst. He had a friend who he thought might be able to help.

"Bring him out," O'Meara said. "Bring all your friends. Bring anyone you can find."

A few minutes later Crow returned with his friend. His name was Hank Haney.

"What's the problem?" Haney asked.

"It's pretty simple," O'Meara said. "I can't hit the ball."

Haney asked him to hit a few shots. He watched silently. O'Meara kept waiting for him to say something. Anything. Finally, he did. "You got a few minutes?" he asked. "Let me buy you a Coke so we can talk."

They went into the clubhouse and sat down. For the next hour, Haney explained his theory of the golf swing and how it differed from what O'Meara was doing. At another time, another place, O'Meara might have written it off as technical mumbo-jumbo. But not at this time or this place. What Haney was saying made sense. They agreed to work together and see what happened. O'Meara made the cut that week and made just enough money to hang on to his card — he was 119th on the money list. He then spent most of the next eighteen months making the trek to Pinehurst whenever he had free time. "There were times we hit balls when there was snow on the range," he said. Gradually, O'Meara's swing changed, becoming less flat, and less likely to cause him to lose the ball left — his biggest problem.

The work paid off. He improved to seventy-sixth on the money list in 1983, then exploded the following year, winning his first tournament (Milwaukee) and finishing second on the money list. That was the year he and Alicia bought their first house. "It cost $80,000 and I didn't think we could afford it," he said. "Then the next week I won at Milwaukee and made $54,000."

For the next nine years he was as steady as anyone on tour. He won money and he won tournaments. He made his first Ryder Cup team in 1985, just missed it in '87, then made it again in '89 and '91. Then came the mid-thirties slump. His daughter, Michelle, was born in 1987, son Shaun arrived two and a half years later. By 1993, O'Meara found himself looking at hotel room windows as if they had bars on them. He felt trapped. Intellectually, he knew what was going on. But it didn't help emotionally. It didn't make leaving the kids any easier. By late 1994, he wasn't sure he wanted to play or could play anymore.

The nadir came at the Canadian Open. O'Meara can still describe the moment in vivid detail. "I was on the 15th tee at Glen Abbey Country Club. It's a par-three. Seven-iron shot that day. I took the club out of the bag, teed my ball up, and got over it. All of a sudden, it occurred to me that I had absolutely no idea how I was going to get the ball onto the green. I mean none. I wasn't thinking of getting close to the pin, right of it, left of it, fading the ball, drawing the ball. I had none of those thoughts. I was absolutely, completely frozen. It was as if I had never played the game."

O'Meara went home and talked it over with Alicia. He could quit if he wanted to. He would be thirty-eight in January. He had won eight times on tour and had made plenty of money. Or, he could buckle down and understand that life isn't perfect, that the payback for making the money he made was being on the road. "I needed to dig in and work at what I was doing or get out," he said.

He dug in. He won twice in 1995 — including at the Canadian, a remarkable 180-degree turnaround in twelve months — and jumped from eighty-sixth on the money list to tenth. A year later, he won twice again and was fifth on the money list. Then Woods showed up at Isleworth and O'Meara became his big brother figure. But Woods did as much for O'Meara as O'Meara did for him. A month after turning forty, O'Meara won back-to-back events: the AT&T Pebble Beach Pro-Am (for the fifth time, holding off a fast-closing Woods at the finish) and the Buick Invitational in San Diego. He was probably playing as well as he had in his life.

That was the good news. The bad news was that all of that winning, especially when coupled with his friendship with the passionate, driven Woods, made people wonder all over again why O'Meara had never been able to deliver in the majors. For a player of his caliber, his record in the most important tournaments was quite ordinary — he had a total of seven top-ten finishes in fifty-six starts in majors. In '95, '96, and '97, with his game flourishing again, he had one top-ten finish in a major — a tie for sixth at the '95 PGA. His best chance to win had come in 1988 at the U.S. Open, when he finished one stroke out of the Curtis Strange–Nick Faldo playoff.

All that winning in nonmajors and not contending in majors was what had caused Jaime Diaz to label him the King of the Bs. O'Meara continued to insist it didn't bother him that much. But deep down, he knew better.

"If anything, I had hurt myself over the years by trying too hard," he said. "I would think, you're a good player, you should play well, you need to play well, in these tournaments. Then I wouldn't and the frustration would build. It wasn't as if I didn't have chances, I did, but not as many as I thought I should have had.

"Everything is different at a major. The whole week feels different, from the atmosphere in the locker room to all the extra media to not playing in a pro-am. I always knew, bottom line, I'd had a good career. But I also knew I hadn't put a period — an exclamation point — on it."

Just as O'Meara had been impressed with the way Woods had played the week before the Masters in '97 — especially when he shot a 59 one day at Isleworth — Woods and Cook were impressed with what O'Meara was doing pre-Masters in '98. Joe Louis, the owner of Isleworth and a close friend of O'Meara's, was so impressed with what he saw when he played with O'Meara that week that he abandoned his practice of placing several bets on several players and decided to put all his money — a substantial amount — on O'Meara.

The odds he got were 33 to 1.

"I don't think very many people were thinking about me when the week started," O'Meara said. "People were thinking about Tiger and Ernie [Els] and Justin [Leonard] and David [Duval]. The young guns. Which was understandable. I don't think anyone even asked me about not winning a major early in the week. It was almost as if it wasn't an issue anymore."

It certainly wasn't an issue to the men running the tournament. They invited fourteen players to come to the interview room prior to the start of the tournament. O'Meara wasn't one of them.

Which was fine with him. Flying into Augusta on Monday, O'Meara was almost as concerned with what he knew would face Woods as he was with his own plans and hopes for the week. He gave Woods a pep talk, reminding him that he didn't have to win the Masters every single year of his life to be a success. "I told him he should enjoy the week for himself and not worry about anyone else," O'Meara said later. "He shouldn't worry about the fans or his folks or IMG or [swing teacher] Butch [Harmon] or anyone else in the world. He should play for himself and enjoy what he had achieved. If he won again, great. If he didn't, there would be a lot of other years."

O'Meara also lectured Woods a little bit as he does on occasion. He had been reading quotes from Woods all winter and spring about how tired he was because of all the pressures and responsibilities heaped on him. "Stop saying you're tired," he said. "You're twenty-two years old. You shouldn't be tired. You can give yourself a break whenever you want. Don't always talk about how tough you have it. You want to find out a little bit about what's tough, get yourself a VW Rabbit and drive it from event to event for a while. Then come talk to me."

O'Meara smiled retelling the story. "You know what?" he said. "That might be a great thing for Tig to do. Give him a little perspective."

If those words had come from almost anyone but O'Meara, Woods probably would have sloughed them off. In fact, a year earlier even if they had come from O'Meara, they probably would have been ignored.

But this was a very different Tiger Woods than the cocky, arrogant kid who had blown the golf world away a year earlier at Augusta. He was still cocky and arrogant, but he was a lot more mature, a lot more willing to listen to good advice, and a lot more aware of his own flaws — as a golfer and a person.

He had won six times during his first ten months on the PGA Tour, including his mind-blowing 12-shot victory at the previous year's Masters, but hadn't won in the ten months leading up to the Masters. He had played well enough to lead the tour in stroke average and had been in contention often. But he hadn't won. He had finished nineteenth, twenty-fourth, and twenty-ninth in the three majors that followed the Masters in '97, after some people had predicted he would walk off with the Grand Slam.

For a while, he had made golf look easy. Since then golf had looked just a little bit harder.

But Woods wasn't different because of his golf. He was different because he was learning every day, whether it was from friends like O'Meara or from nonfriends like players and members of the media who had been critical of him. Whether he admitted it or not — and he didn't — some of the criticism stung and some of it rang true. He was smart enough to know he shouldn't have blown off President Clinton and Rachel Robinson, and he should have signed the golf ball for charity that fellow player Billy Andrade had asked him to sign.

Beyond that, most important perhaps, Woods now seemed to understand that no matter how often his managers at IMG told him he was never wrong, there had been times he had been wrong. That caused him to look at the IMG people differently and at himself more critically. He understood that he wasn't perfect — on or off the golf course. If Mark O'Meara told him it would be a good idea to stop talking about how tired he was all the time, then maybe he would stop talking about how tired he was all the time.

That didn't mean he didn't occasionally get snappish with questioners and it didn't make him any more comfortable with the frenzied crowds he found himself surrounded by at times. There had been occasional death threats. He wasn't going to hide out because of them but he was aware of them. In today's climate, he would have been a fool not to be.

Woods returned to Augusta with mixed emotions. Naturally, the place evoked great memories. It would always be the place where he had won his first major as a pro, a place where he had made a huge breakthrough, for himself as a golfer and for minorities everywhere. But he wasn't comfortable with all the hoopla that had surrounded the victory. It was, he understood, a big deal. It was different than Justin Leonard or David Duval winning at Augusta for their first major title. He understood that clearly.

Just as clearly he understood that what Augusta had once stood for would never go away completely. His hero as a kid had been Charlie Sifford, who, in spite of the fact that he had won on the PGA Tour in the 1960s, had never been invited to play in the Masters. Sifford felt deep resentment for the men who ran the club then and still felt it in 1997 when Woods won. No matter how gracious the club members were to him in the wake of his victory, Woods couldn't help but harbor some of Sifford's old resentment. It would have been disloyal not to.

And so, while he understood that this was an important week for him and while he desperately wanted to defend his title if only because this would be the perfect place to start winning again, he didn't want to make the event or the club any bigger than he had to. He thought it was cool to see his green jacket hanging in the locker and his name on the champions locker right next to Jackie Burke's. But he wasn't going to tear up when someone asked him if he felt nostalgic coming back to this place.

"I don't have time for that right now," he said.

He did manage a smile when someone asked him if God came to him and told him he could win just one major this year and he had to choose it, which one would he choose. "The way I am," he said, "I would probably argue with him and say why can't I have all four?"

Twenty-five years earlier, Jack Nicklaus would no doubt have had the same argument with God. In 1972, he had made a run at winning all four majors in the same year, winning the Masters and the U.S. Open before coming up one stroke short at the British Open, finishing second to Lee Trevino. Nicklaus was never as outwardly confident about his game as Woods, but he believed in himself every bit as much. He believed in himself so much that in 1998, at the age of fifty-eight, arthritic hip and all, he still honestly thought that winning the Masters again was not entirely out of the question.

That was why, when Jack Stephens presented Nicklaus with a plaque on Tuesday afternoon honoring him for playing in forty Masters — and winning six — he noted that there was a little bit of blank space at the bottom of the plaque, "just in case."

The ceremony was held next to the chipping green, which is a few yards from where Magnolia Lane bumps into Founders Circle. It was another gorgeous Georgia day, the afternoon sun slowly moving west. Nicklaus had expected to give a set speech, thanking everyone, talking about how honored he was to be honored. After that would come his annual pre-Masters press conference, which would end only because Nicklaus would need to leave for the Champions Dinner. Once Nicklaus started talking, it was difficult to get him to stop.

But a funny thing happened to Nicklaus as he gave his little set speech. When he started to talk about his wife, Barbara, the words suddenly stopped coming so easily. A large lump came into his throat when he tried to explain what she had meant to him, how proud he was of their five children and the life they had built together. "That doesn't usually happen to me," he said later. "But when I thought about Barbara and this place and all the years of coming here together . . ."

For once, Nicklaus didn't need to say another word.

Perhaps never in the history of the tournament had the Champions Dinner been so anticipated. Would Fuzzy eat a cheeseburger? Or crow?

Of course no one except the champions themselves and club chairman Jack Stephens was going to know the answer to that or any of the other riveting questions of the evening firsthand because they were the only ones invited. This was about as exclusive a dinner as you could find: no wives or relatives or buddies. No club members except the chairman. Byron Nelson had been the unofficial master of ceremonies for years and Sam Snead had traditionally gotten up as the evening wound down to tell some of his jokes — none of which could be told in mixed company. Snead was absent this year, though, because he had been taken to an Augusta hospital shortly after he and his son had arrived from Florida earlier in the day. The hospital reported that he might have suffered a stroke.

The man who had come up with the idea for the dinner, Ben Hogan, had stopped coming a number of years prior to his death even before he had health problems. But most of the champions came back for the camaraderie and the stories. A couple admitted they came back because of the $5,000 honorarium the club paid each of them.

The dinner is held upstairs in the clubhouse in the library. A green jacket is required for admission. Even though the previous year's champion technically sets the "menu," as a matter of tradition, the guests can order anything they want off Augusta's regular dinner menu. Most of the time protocol dictates that you eat what the champion eats, but not always. In 1989, when Scotsman Sandy Lyle requested haggis, there were a lot of steaks ordered off the regular menu.

If there was one man in the room other than Woods who was guaranteed to eat a cheeseburger, french fries, and a milkshake, it was Zoeller. He was hoping against hope that the dinner would finally bring closure to the nightmare that had started for him fifty-one weeks earlier. So was Woods. He did everything he could to be the gracious host, thanking everyone for being there and for eating the cheeseburgers — which most of them did. When the dinner was over, he and Zoeller walked out and told reporters individually that a good time had been had by all, the food had been delicious, and the past was the past and thank goodness now that the dinner was over maybe everyone else would take that approach too.

Of course they would. For forty-eight hours.

6

Counting Down . . .

By Wednesday morning, the atmosphere has changed from first day of school to last day before finals.

The pairings for Thursday morning have been issued. Now everyone knows when they will play and who they will be playing with. The golf course is quickening and the greens are getting harder and faster with each passing day. The veterans shake their heads at the rookies and say, "But this is nothing. Wait till tomorrow." Everyone knows that sleep will not come easily.

"Once they hand out those pairings late Tuesday, it's as if you've gone from 'Gee, isn't it great to be here' to 'Wow, there's important work to do,'" said Jeff Sluman, who was playing in his eleventh Masters. "Getting the pairings at Augusta is a little bit like getting your tax return. It isn't something to joke about."

The pairings are put together at lunchtime on Tuesday by three men: Will Nicholson, Phil Harison, and Fleming Norvell. They make their way to the top floor of the press building, which was built in 1991 after the old Quonset Hut that had been used for the media became so outdated that reporters were just about sitting on each other's laps.

There, in the pairings room, they sit around a table with the entire field in front of them. On one wall is a board with slots for each player's name. At the Masters, pairings are done only for Thursday. Unlike the other majors and normal full-field events, the Masters re-pairs based on scores after the first round because it has a relatively small field. Some of the pairings work is easy because it is automatic. The three honorary starters, Gene Sarazen, Sam Snead, and Byron Nelson, tee off at 8 A.M. Each will hit a drive and then retreat to the clubhouse, although most people are pretty convinced that Snead, who is eighty-five, could easily handle playing the entire golf course. Out of deference to Sarazen, who is ninety-six, and Nelson, who is eighty-six and hobbled by hip problems, Snead settles for one swing.

The next few pairings involve the older past champions who still take advantage of the lifetime exemption the Masters grants to all champions. Doug Ford, the 1957 champion, who turned seventy-five in 1998, is always in the first pairing at 8:15. Ford has played in more Masters (forty-six) than anyone else, and many thought he would retire after breaking Sam Snead's record of forty-four in 1997. Ford has not made the cut since 1971 and his continued presence in the field has been the subject of great debate in recent years because he clearly cannot hit the ball far enough to have a chance to compete on the golf course anymore. Five times he has withdrawn after one round. In 1997, not wanting to withdraw while in the process of breaking Snead's record, he played the second round — and shot 94.

And yet, for all the grumbling about Ford, the fact is, he has a right to play and, perhaps more important, he isn't taking a spot away from anyone else. And so there he was on the board again, this time paired with sixty-six-year-old Gay Brewer, the 1967 champion. Next came two more "seniors," Billy Casper, the 1970 champion, and Charles Coody, who won a year later. The second-oldest man in the field was Arnold Palmer, but he wasn't placed in the early pairings for the simple reason that, even at sixty-eight, regardless of what he might shoot, Palmer was still one of the big draws at Augusta — or anyplace else he played. Palmer was placed in the 10:12 slot along with Jay Haas — another Wake Forest alumnus. Three-time champion Gary Player and Tommy Aaron, the other sixty-somethings in the field, also received later times in deference to the fact that both were still considered good enough to have a chance at making the cut.

Once the senior slots are filled, the amateurs are taken care of: the

U.S. Amateur champion always plays with the defending champion. That meant Tiger Woods would play with twenty-year-old Matt Kuchar, a Georgia Tech sophomore with a big smile and a lot of game. Tim Clark, the Public Links champion, was paired with Player for the simple reason that both are from South Africa. British Amateur Champion Craig Watson drew Sandy Lyle for the same reason — both are Scottish. Kenny Bakst would play with Ben Crenshaw because the committee knew they were friends. "We do what we can to make the amateurs comfortable," Nicholson said. Joel Kribel, runner-up in the Amateur, drew 1987 champion Larry Mize no doubt because Mize is one of the most easygoing players on tour and a good partner for someone who is bound to be nervous.

The so-called big names go next, spread out across the day so as to keep the crowds from getting too thick in any one part of the golf course and to help television. Unlike other golf tournaments, including the other majors, the television people are not consulted before the pairings are done. But they are given consideration. Nicholson, Harison, and Norvell know when Japanese and European TV are on the air and try to have their players on the golf course at those times, if possible. Woods and Kuchar were assigned a 1:30 time, meaning they would just be reaching the back nine when the USA cablecast came on the air. Fred Couples and Greg Norman were set to go an hour earlier. Justin Leonard and Nick Price were scheduled for 1:12; Tom Lehman and Colin Montgomerie (a British Open champion with the number one British player) would go off at 1:48; Ernie Els and David Duval were given a 2:15 slot. Other than the preset Player-Clark and Lyle-Watson pairings, there was only one pairing that didn't include at least one American: Nick Faldo and David Frost.

Once the glamour pairings are done, the rest of the field is filled in around the names already on the board. The process rarely takes more than a couple of hours. All three men have been through the routine before and rarely do they have to agonize over their decisions. The names — eighty-eight of them in 1998 — are placed into the slots, copies are made, and the word goes out. Ford and Brewer would lead the field onto the golf course at 8:15. Mark Brooks and Scott Simpson — each a past champion of a major tournament, each with a reputation as a slow player — would be the last men out at 2:42.

The pairings arrived in the locker room shortly after two o'clock on Tuesday and everyone began studying them. David Duval sat in front of his locker studying the sheet. Across from him, Colin Montgomerie was doing the same thing.

Duval shook his head. "Two-fifteen," he said. "I was hoping to go early. I like playing with Ernie [Els] but I wish it was earlier."

Everyone wants an early tee time at Augusta. Not the 8:15 old men's slots, but pre-noon. Generally speaking, players prefer to play in the morning because the greens aren't as spiked up and there is usually less wind. At Augusta, a morning tee time is even more valued because, unlike other tournaments where those who play early Thursday play late Friday and vice versa, everyone is re-paired at Augusta after Thursday and the leaders go out late the last three days.

"It means if you're in contention you're going to play late all four days," Duval said, still looking at the sheet. "I'd like to get up and get at it at least once. Especially the first day."

He looked up from the sheet at Montgomerie, who had just finished hiring a caddie for the week, Joe Collins, one of the Augusta regulars. Montgomerie's tour caddy, Alister McLain, had been forced to fly home because of a disc problem in his back. Montgomerie is a man whose day can be ruined by a slow-changing traffic light, and now, on the eve of the Masters, he was without a man he had worked with successfully for six years. He figured to be in a less-than-lighthearted mood.

"You okay, Monty?" Duval asked quietly.

"A bit concerned actually, David," Montgomerie said.

Duval nodded. "I understand."

"Yes," Montgomerie said, his face still quite sober, "I'm concerned with the future of David Duval, wondering like the rest of the golf world if this is going to be the week that he finally breaks through, puts all the disappointments behind him, and finally wins his first major."

For a split second Duval didn't get it. Then he saw Montgomerie starting to crack up and he started to laugh along with him.

"Hey, I really appreciate the concern," he said. "I'll try not to let you down."

The exchange would have shocked most people. After all, Montgomerie was the sour, dour Scotsman Americans loved to hate. Duval was the passionless kid behind the sunglasses, the anti-Tiger whose version of a fistpump was to adjust his glasses. At the U.S. Open in June, one local San Francisco columnist would begin a piece on him by writing, "David Duval has the personality of a divot."

Neither man was anything like his image. Montgomerie could certainly be cranky and he was mercurial to say the least. But he was also quite clever and funny, one of the brightest men on any golf tour, someone who could — as he had just proven to Duval — make fun of himself. No one was asked about his lack of a major title more than Montgomerie. He had lost a playoff at the U.S. Open in 1994, a playoff at the PGA in 1995, and had lost to Els by a shot at the Open in 1997, missing a six-foot putt on the penultimate hole that proved to be the difference. What's more, his British Open record — no finish higher than eighth, four missed cuts in the last eight years — was generally considered a national disgrace that ranked just behind Cornwallis's surrender at Yorktown.

Montgomerie felt the pressure to break through and win a major. Unlike some players, he didn't deny it. He was quite honest about the fact that he knew a player with his record — he had been the leading money winner in Europe for five straight years — should have a major title on his résumé. But as long as it wasn't there, he was going to have to deal with questions about it. And if he had to do that, he figured he might as well joke about it whenever he could.

Duval was a perfect audience for him. At twenty-six, he was eight years younger than Montgomerie and hadn't had anything approaching the close calls in majors that Montgomerie had. In fact, in eleven majors as a pro (he had twice qualified for the U.S. Open as an amateur) Duval had never been in the top ten. His best finish had been a tie for fourteenth at the 1996 British Open. His best major might have been his first — the 1990 U.S. Open at Medinah, which he qualified for as an eighteen-year-old college freshman. There, he shot three straight even-par rounds and when he birdied three of the first six holes on Sunday he was on the leader board. "I saw my name go up there, I went into shock and proceeded to shoot 43 on the back nine," he remembered, laughing now at the all-too-predictable outcome of that day.

And yet, in spite of his lack of experience as a contender, he arrived at Augusta as one of the favorites, a notion he found baffling given his record and relative lack of experience. He was still only twenty-six and was only in his fourth year on tour. Even so, he was right there with Montgomerie on the infamous best-player-never-to-have-won-a-major list, and knew that the question was going to follow him around the world until he removed himself from it by winning one. What had put him on the list was a streak of torrid golf that had started the previous October when he closed the 1997 season by winning the last three tournaments he played in — Williamsburg, Disney, and the Tour Championship. In four weeks (he had skipped Las Vegas) he went from being asked when he was going to break through and win a golf tournament to when he was going to win a major. He had then tacked on a fourth victory at Tucson in February to raise those issues all over again.

Duval viewed a lot of the frenzy around him with a sense of detached bemusement. He wanted very much to win golf tournaments and to win majors and to take his place among the world's best players because he honestly thought he was good enough to do those things. But he was way, way past viewing setbacks in golf as a reason to wallow in self-pity. He might get angry for a little while if he played poorly; he might second-guess himself after a mistake. But none of that was likely to last very long. Duval had too many other things to spend his emotional energy on to invest too much of it in golf.

"I decided long ago that none of us are dealt more than we can handle," he said, relaxing one night in a quiet restaurant. "I've been dealt some things in my life, but I don't go around acting as if I'm the only one who has burdens. Everyone has burdens."

Perhaps so. But not everyone has watched his twelve-year-old brother die after he has given him his bone marrow at the age of nine to try and save his life. Not everyone has watched that death tear apart his parents' marriage during his teenage years.

David was the second of Bob and Diane Duval's three children, three years younger than Brent, five years older than Mary. He says now that he has only a few memories of Brent, admitting that part of the reason for that is that while the memories can make him smile, they can also make him cry.

He remembers how close Brent and his little sister were. He was her protector, her hero. David and Mary got along, but not like Brent and Mary. The boys were very different, but still close. Unlike David, who began going to the golf club with his father — a golf pro — at a young age, Brent was more into fishing and the outdoors. In David's memory, it was Brent who taught him to fish and took him fishing. He bonded with his dad through golf, with his brother through fishing.

"I remember we spent a lot of time together fishing," he said. "We never kept anything we caught, just threw it back. That's the way I fish now. I like the sport of it, the challenge, but I have no desire to keep the fish once they're caught."

Duval remembers his brother as energetic, "always the first one up the steps to class, always a leader." He also remembers watching that change. "At first he dropped back to the middle of the class, then he was the last one up the steps. Then he started lagging behind. You knew something had to be wrong."

Something was: aplastic anemia, a serious blood disease. The doctors said Brent Duval needed a bone marrow transplant. They did blood tests on Bob and Diane and David. Somehow, David knew he was going to be the match. "It never occurred to me that it would be anybody but me," he said. "He was my brother. It was meant to be me."

He was playing basketball on a friend's driveway when his dad drove up and confirmed what he had already known: he was the match. They packed the car and headed north from Jacksonville to Cleveland before sundown. The situation was that urgent. Once they got to Cleveland, David had to be tested once more to be certain that his marrow would be a match for Brent. Once that was confirmed, the surgery would be performed forty-eight hours later.

"But because I was only nine, they couldn't give me anesthesia twice in such a short period of time," he remembered. "So when they opened me up to do the matching test, they did it without any drugs." He winced at the memory. "It was like lying down on a table and having someone stick a needle in your back and open you up. The pain was unbelievable." He smiled. "I think most of the scars are gone."

The physical ones anyway. The surgery was performed in January 1981. For a while, Brent improved. His body seemed to be accepting the new bone marrow. David went back and forth to Florida on several occasions, visiting whenever he could get away from school. His parents were in Cleveland almost full-time. At one point, Brent was able to leave the hospital briefly. But he soon became sick again. This time it was pneumonia. His body didn't have the strength — or enough white blood cells — to fight it. On May 17 — Duval still remembers the date — he died.

There is no way to measure the grief of a family that loses a son or a brother. The Duvals were no different. Bob and Diane's marriage began to founder. They separated shortly after Brent's death, then reconciled a year later. David was conscious of the fact that his parents were fighting a lot and that both were dealing with a lot of anger and pain. What had been a happy home before Brent's illness became an extremely unhappy one. David went searching for an escape from the sadness in his life and found it on the golf course.

"I got in the habit of spending hours and hours at the golf club by myself," he said. "Sometimes I would just go out by myself and play. Or I would practice. And practice. I could stand in a bunker all afternoon dripping with sweat in the middle of the summer and hit shot after shot. I loved it. I found that I preferred playing alone, practicing alone."

Years later, when his father told him that he believed golf became his escape from Brent's death, David initially rejected the notion. But as he grew older, he began to believe his father was right. Even now, he enjoys solitude. On the range, he prefers to find a spot off by himself and hit balls. A lot of players see the range — especially in the late afternoon — as a place for socializing and telling jokes. Duval rarely participates. "I like being by myself," he said. "It's something I was comfortable with when I was young and something I'm still comfortable with now."

Not surprisingly, the hours and hours of practice began to pay dividends for Duval as a teenager. He became one of the top junior players in the country and was recruited by most of the big-name golf schools. If Florida State had recruited him from day one, he might have ended up there. Both his parents went to school there, and Duval had grown up as a fanatic Florida State football fan. But the golf program wasn't terribly well organized in 1989, and by the time anyone contacted Duval he had all but decided to go to Georgia Tech. "If they had called earlier it might have been different," he said. "But by the time they got around to it I felt pretty comfortable with the idea of playing for Puggy."

Puggy was Tech golf coach Puggy Blackmon, a tough, tell-it-like-it-is sort who was perfect for the very cocky young Duval. Of course Duval had plenty to be cocky about. He was a first-team All-American as a freshman and went on to become one of three players in NCAA history to be a first-team Division 1 All American four years in a row. (Phil Mickelson and Gary Hallberg were the other two.) As a junior, he was given a sponsor's exemption into the Bell South Classic in Atlanta and actually led the event for three days before fading on Sunday. The following spring he was the college player of the year.

College wasn't always a great time in Duval's life, despite his success on the golf course. His parents' on-again, off-again marriage finally split for good, and Duval could see whenever he visited her that his mother was struggling emotionally. He felt helpless. His dad was doing better, working toward the day he turned fifty and could take a shot at the Senior Tour. Still, the divorce and all that was involved brought back memories of Brent and all that had happened after his death.

But none of the troubles at home affected his golf. Again, the game became his escape. He worked endlessly and kept improving. He had filled out — perhaps too much — to a stocky 6 feet, 200 pounds, and could hit the ball great distances off the tee.

Needless to say, all the big-name agents were pounding on his door by the end of his senior year. Duval listened to them all and finally settled on IMG because he felt being with the biggest and most experienced company would be to his advantage. But he insisted on a clause in the contract naming Hughes Norton as his agent. "He was in charge of the golf division, so I figured he was their best guy," he said. "I wanted to be with the best guy."

He was with Norton for two years. Then came IMG's great Tiger chase, which was led by Norton. "He dropped me like a bad habit," Duval said, able to laugh about it now. At the time, Duval was on the PGA Tour and doing just fine, but he wasn't the Next Great Player in the Annals of Golf. Duval agreed to say with IMG after Charlie Moore was assigned to his account. He was — and is — comfortable with Moore, so all is well with IMG and Duval. And Norton? "No hard feelings," Duval said. "Hughes takes care of Hughes. I understand that. It's one of the things that makes him good at what he does."

Both Duval and IMG had high hopes when Duval finished his fourth year at Tech. He left school a little less than a year shy of a degree, having never really gotten terribly interested in all the technical classes he had to take there. "I knew when I chose Tech that I wasn't going to have much interest in engineering or math classes," he said. "If I had gone to a school with more of a liberal arts curriculum, it might have been different. But to be honest, when I chose a college I was thinking that golf was going to be my career and I made my decision based on what I thought was best for my golf. That might not sound so great, but how is it different than someone choosing a school because they think it's the best way for them to get to medical school?"

The difference may be that the margin of error in golf is slimmer. Almost anyone with a 3.5 GPA and good board scores will get into some med school. In golf, you can have a 4.0 average in college — as in player of the year, four-time All-American — and you are guaranteed nothing. Duval found that out quickly. He played the second half of 1993 on the Nike Tour, hoping to win enough money, even with a late start, to make the top ten on the money list, which would have earned him a spot on the '94 PGA Tour without going through the torture of Qualifying School.

He almost pulled it off. His second week on tour, he won, and he played steadily throughout the fall. He won the season-ending Nike Tour Championship, but because a last-minute decision had dropped the prize money from $250,000 to $200,000, he came up $2,000 shy of tenth place, finishing eleventh. If the initial prize money offering hadn't changed, Duval would have won $45,000 instead of $36,000 and his ticket to the tour would have been punched right there.

He didn't mind. "I had played very well and given the fact that I played only nine tournaments, finishing eleventh on the money list was a big boost for my confidence," he said. "Plus, being eleventh got me straight to the Q-School finals, which should have made my life a lot easier."

Should have. Duval arrived at PGA West the first week of December apprehensive, knowing that Q-School was a one-shot, six-round deal with the top forty players and ties from a field of 180 players making it to the tour. He played nervously for three days and went into the fourth round in jeopardy of missing the round-four cut when the field was cut to ninety players and ties. For eight holes on that fourth day, he continued to play poorly. Finally, with almost no hope to make the cut, he stopped playing tentatively and birdied five of the last ten holes.

That put him at one-under-par 287 for the four days. All day the word on the course had been that one under was the number. When Duval birdied the difficult 18th hole on the Dunes Course at LaQuinta Country Club, he breathed a deep sigh of relief. He had played horribly for 62 holes and gotten his act together just in time.

Or so he thought. Since there is no computerized scoring at Q-School and since Duval was playing at the second course being used for the event, he walked off 18 not knowing what the cut was. He got into his car and made the five-minute drive over to the Jack Nicklaus Resort Course, which was the headquarters for the tournament. Before going inside for lunch, he checked the scoreboard. At that moment, one under was in, but scanning the board, Duval noticed that there were a lot of low numbers early in the day.

Feeling a little bit less sure than he had walking off 18, he went inside to eat lunch. When he returned thirty minutes later, he felt even less sure. "The arrow was moving too fast," he said.

The arrow is just that — a little red arrow that scorekeepers place next to the last name that is inside the cut line. Naturally, as the day wears on and more scores come in, the arrow moves up. Duval didn't like the trend. For the next hour, he and his caddy, Jeff Webber, stood in front of the board and watched the arrow move. Dusk closed in and the last scores were being posted. About ten minutes before the last group checked in, Duval watched the arrow move from the last name listed at 287 to the last name listed at 286.

For once, the players had miscalculated the number. It had been two under, not one under.

Jim Furyk had already left for the day when the arrow moved. When he heard what had happened to Duval and the others at one under, he swallowed hard. On his 18th hole he had banged a 25-foot birdie putt 10 feet past the hole. "I was two under, so I figured I had a shot to play with," he said. Almost casually, he knocked the 10-foot par putt in, wanting to make it because there were still two days to play, but not desperate since he figured he had a shot to play with. As it turned out, that 10-footer kept him alive.

Two days later, Furyk, after shooting 69–71 the last two days, got his playing card — right on the number. By then, Duval was back home in Jacksonville pondering his future.

Actually, there wasn't much for Duval to ponder. He would have to go back to the Nike Tour. This did not exactly send him into paroxysms of joy. He hadn't minded the idea of playing for a few months on the Nike, but he always assumed that when his first full year as a pro came around, he would spend it on the big tour. Now that option didn't exist.

"I sulked about it for a while," he said. "I was used to getting my way in golf, to being successful. This was the first real setback I'd ever had."

Midway through 1994 he still hadn't come out of his funk. He wasn't playing nearly as well as he had the previous fall and was looking a return trip to Q-School squarely in the eye. That was when he decided to take a week off, fly to Atlanta, and spend some time with his old college coach.

Blackmon is not a cry-on-the-shoulder kind of guy. He told Duval that what had happened was almost inevitable. "Golf humbles everyone sooner or later," he said. "Now is your turn. The important thing is how you deal with it. It isn't as if you stopped being a good player — you didn't. You just have to go back out and play and stop worrying about where you are or what you're playing for."

Duval knew his old coach was right. He returned to the Nike Tour with renewed vigor and, although he didn't win a tournament, he became the most consistent player out there, finishing second once, third three times, and in the top ten ten times. By the end of the year it all added up to eighth place on the money list and — finally — his ticket to the PGA Tour.

When he looks back on that year, Duval now believes it hastened his path to stardom rather than delaying it. Failing to make the tour on his first try was a humbling experience, one that was healthy for him. Playing on the Nike Tour taught him to appreciate the trappings of the big tour when he got there, and it also taught him to play aggressively, because the only way to make serious money in a $200,000 tournament is to finish in the top five.

It didn't take Duval very long to make the adjustment to playing on the PGA Tour. At the season-opening event in Hawaii, he made the cut on the number, then shot 64 on Saturday and jumped into a tie for ninth by Sunday. A week later in Tucson, he did even better, finishing sixth. As a Nike Tour graduate, Duval wasn't automatically in every event, but a top-ten finish is supposed to guarantee you a spot the next week, regardless of where you stand in golf's pecking order.

A lot of players like to begin their year in Phoenix. In fact, so many fully exempt players entered there that Duval, top ten or no top ten, couldn't get in. Duval got mad, then figured out a way to get even: he finished second the next week at Pebble Beach, then finished second again two weeks later at the Bob Hope Desert Classic. He left the west coast third on the money list without any need to worry about being left out of events in the future.

In almost any other year, Duval would have been a lock for rookie of the year. He set a rookie earnings record with more than $882,000 in prize money and finished eleventh on the money list. But both Woody Austin and Justin Leonard had great years too, each winning just under $750,000. And Austin did something Duval and Leonard didn't do: he won a tournament, the Buick Open. On that basis, he won rookie of the year. "I had no problem with that," Duval said. "We're out here every week to win a golf tournament. Woody did it. Justin and I didn't."

Not winning first became an issue for Duval late in 1995 and came up more and more often in 1996. He finished second twice again and third twice. He was around the lead on Sunday a lot, a sign of consistency, but couldn't seem to close the deal. Just as veteran players with multiple tour wins get asked the dreaded "how come you haven't won a major" question, Duval found himself facing the almost as dreaded "you've been in contention but haven't won a tournament" question. Duval understood why it came up and tried to deal with it patiently when it did.

But dealing with the media was not — and is not — his favorite sport. Because he is shy by nature, he doesn't have much interest in talking about himself under any circumstances, and he certainly isn't comfortable — understandably — when reporters ask him what are for most people routine questions about his family background. A simple question like "Do you have brothers and sisters?" can be an ordeal for Duval.

Duval is one of the brighter people on tour, a voracious reader who quotes Mark Twain as easily as most golfers quote Jim Nantz. But he starts to squirm when people start labeling him as some kind of intellectual just because his taste in reading goes beyond *USA Today*. Ask him why he often seems uncomfortable in press conferences and he will laugh and say, "Do you know how many times I've been asked about the sunglasses and the beard?"

The answer is: just about every week.

Duval started wearing sunglasses on the golf course in college. He wears contact lenses, and one year at the ACC Tournament, the weather was windy and the air full of pollen. Duval was getting dust in his eyes and they were tearing up on him because of the pollen. Sunglasses solved both problems. He went on to win the tournament. Since then, he has worn sunglasses, most recently wraparound Oakleys, for the simple reason that he is under contract for six figures annually to the company. "But if I wasn't under contract I'd still wear the glasses," he said. "They're a part of my equipment."

The beard has come and gone since he arrived on tour. He first grew it one week just for a change of pace. He played well. The beard stayed. Then he started getting all kinds of questions about it. "It almost became controversial," he said, shaking his head at the notion. Even tour commissioner Tim Finchem sidled up to him one day at a tournament and said, "When are you going to shave?"

Certainly not anytime soon after that. Duval doesn't view himself as a rebel, but he is loath to do anything because it is expected of him. He didn't grow a beard or start wearing sunglasses so that people would talk about him, but he isn't going to stop doing either just because people do talk about them.

Some people like the look. Titleist, another of his sponsors, has told him to keep it because they like the idea of having at least one player who looks different on the golf course. Others think Duval looks too cold and intimidating and, with his tendency not to emote anyway, isn't likely to be a fan favorite anytime soon. Duval has always figured he would let his golf answer those critics.

And he has done just that. He moved up to tenth on the money list in 1996 in spite of not winning again, but found the going in 1997 frustrating. He had decided late in 1996 that he needed to change his physique. Returning from a run in Atlanta one morning, he stepped on a scale and found himself staring at the number 226. Too much. Way too much. He changed his diet, eliminating fast food and things he loved like Mexican pizza. He put himself on a regular running regimen — fifteen to eighteen miles a week — "nothing crazy, but steady stuff." He had never been a big red meat eater, but he cut it out entirely. He also began training with weights on a regular basis to try and replace some of the fat with more muscle.

The new discipline and training worked. He dropped forty pounds in a little more than six months. He felt stronger on the golf course, less likely to tire in the heat or on Sundays. But he also had to get used to his new body, and for a good part of '97 he wasn't the player he had been the previous two years.

It wasn't that he played poorly. There were two more second place finishes, but he wasn't nearly as consistent as he had been in the past. And he was not chosen for the Ryder Cup team, which had been one of his primary goals. Some people criticized Tom Kite for choosing Fred Couples and Lee Janzen over Duval as the captain's picks, but Duval isn't one of them. "The only reason I wasn't on that team was me," he said. "I didn't play well enough to make it. Tom went for experience, which was certainly understandable, and it wasn't as if I had lit up the world during the summer."

But he did light up the world during the fall. The turning point may have come at the Buick Classic in Calloway Gardens, Georgia. Having watched the American Ryder Cup team lose without him the previous week, he arrived there angry with himself for not playing well enough to be on the team. He had never played well in the Buick, but this time he ended up ninth even though he didn't make a putt all week. By the time he got to the Michelob Challenge the following week at Williamsburg, he was convinced it was finally his time to win. He felt so good about his game that he even made an uncharacteristic crack to two TV reporters that they better keep a close eye on him during the week because he was ready to break through.

Not that it was easy. Duval trailed Duffy Waldorf by three shots going into the last round. Then he led Waldorf and Grant Waite by two on the back nine before fading just enough to create a three-way playoff. But on the first hole of the playoff he hit a five-iron 12 feet from the hole and nailed the birdie putt. Finally, he thought, things went my way at the end instead of the other guy's way.

Gone were the questions about closing the deal. A week later he won again, this time beating Dan Forsman in a playoff at Disney. Then he finished off his season by winning the Tour Championship. In three weeks he had won $1,269,000 and jumped to second on the money list for the year, finishing with $1,885,308. Only Woods made more. When he won again early in the year at Tucson, there were some golf people saying he was the best player in the world. Duval bridled at that notion.

"I've played well," he said. "But you can't put me in the same sentence with Tiger or Ernie Els or, for that matter, Davis Love or Greg Norman. Justin [Leonard] has won a major. I haven't."

Deep down, though, he believed that might change soon. Especially if he had the support of people like Colin Montgomerie.

7

Jinxes and Crystal,
and Then Came the Rain

In 1997, the weather in Augusta had been so hot in February and March that the famous azaleas and all the various flowers that make the golf course at the National so stunning had bloomed too early. By the arrival of the Masters field and the CBS cameras, whose job it was to send out breathtaking pictures of the golf course to an eager nation, many of the azaleas were dying. And so, even though Rae's Creek is dyed every year so that it looks bluer than blue on TV screens, nothing could be done to bring the azaleas back. "You can't spray 365 acres of flowers," said one Masters expert.

That would not be a problem in 1998. The azaleas had bloomed at exactly the right time and the golf course had never looked better. Rae's Creek was still dyed blue, but the flowers didn't need any help at all. The weather at the beginning of the week was perfect — until Wednesday afternoon.

Less than an hour before the golf course closed at 3 P.M. so final preparations for Thursday's first round could begin, the skies opened. The annual par-three tournament was under way, and most of the fans were packed around the picturesque little mini-course over behind Ike's Cabin when the storms rolled in. They came quickly and with a great deal of noise — thunder and lightning — sending everyone scurrying for cover.

Scott McCarron was about to walk from the range to the first tee of the par-three course when the horn blew. He took a look at the blackening sky, shook his head, and said, "We're done for the day. I guarantee it."

To some players, canceling the par-three is a disappointment. They enjoy the loose atmosphere, the camaraderie with the crowds, the chance to show off a little when a mistake doesn't really matter. Kenny Bakst had put his five-and-a-half-year-old son Jonathan into a miniaturized version of the white Augusta National caddy's jump suit and teed off early. Olin Browne, playing in his first Masters, had his not-quite-ten-year-old son Olin Jr. out there with him. Other players brought friends or other relatives to caddy. Few carried the forty-pound bag that players normally use on the golf course. They either grabbed a little Sunday bag or just carried three or four clubs with them. If Jonathan Bakst was a candidate to be the smallest caddy ever to work the par-three, there was little doubting who had been the biggest: 7-foot-1-inch San Antonio Spurs center Tom VanDorn, who had looped for Corey Pavin two years earlier. The most amazing thing about VanDorn's appearance was that the caddy master actually had a jump suit that fit him.

As it turned out, Scott McCarron's prediction was accurate. The siren that sounded at 2:34 P.M. turned out to be the bell tolling for the par-three contest. Only six players actually finished nine holes and, as a result, Sandy Lyle was declared the winner with a score of 24. That is a very high winning score. The winning score when the "full field" — usually about half the Masters field — finishes is normally around 21 or 22. The record for the course, a rather stunning seven-under-par 20, is coheld by two past Masters champions, Art Wall and Gay Brewer. Wall, who won the Masters in 1959, shot his 20 six years later, and Brewer, the 1967 champion, shot his 20 six years after winning his green jacket. In all, nine Masters champions have won the par-three event — but only one of them, Ben Crenshaw, won a Masters after winning the par-three. Crenshaw won the Masters in 1984, won the par-three in 1987, and then came back to win a second Masters eight years later.

One of the legends of Augusta holds that winning the par-three is a jinx, since no one has ever won both the little tournament and the big one in the same year. Most players laugh the jinx off. Some do not. All go onto the golf course firing at the flags because a hole in one gets you

Augusta crystal — glasses, bowls, vases — without dealing with the jinx. There was only one hole in one before the rains came, by David Duval at the second hole. The ace was worth more than just crystal to Duval since he, John Daly, Fuzzy Zoeller, and Tommy Tolles had each put up $1,000 for an ace. Even though none of them got to finish the round, Duval's ace counted and the other three had to pay up.

One person who took the par-three jinx seriously was McCarron. "If I ever come to the ninth hole with a chance to win the par-three, the ball is going in the water," he said. "I'm here to win the real thing, not just some nice crystal." (The par-three winner takes home Augusta crystal, as does anyone who makes an eagle during the real tournament or in the par-three.)

That McCarron would be discussing the notion of winning the Masters at this stage of his life is part of one of the more remarkable comeback stories in the recent annals of golf history. As the 1998 tournament began, McCarron was thirty-two and in his fourth year on the PGA Tour. Five years prior to that, he had quit the game for good after graduating from UCLA because he had no future in the sport. He had been kicked off the UCLA golf team, lost his scholarship, and then came back to play — putting left-handed — as a walk-on. "The only reason I went back," he said, "was because guys on the team get to play at Bel Air Country Club. I knew I wasn't going to be a pro. I'd had the yips since high school. The dream was dead."

The dream had started very early. McCarron comes from a long line of jocks. His grandfather, Al McCarron, was a minor league baseball player for the San Francisco Seals who took up golf in his fifties and became a single-digit handicapper. In his seventies, Al McCarron shot his age so often that a golf ball company that offered a free golf ball to anyone who sent in a certified scorecard showing that a person had shot his age wrote him a note asking him to send in the scorecards a dozen at a time so they could simply ship him a dozen balls at a time.

Al's son Barry inherited his jock genes. He was one of the best baseball players ever to come out of San Mateo High School, and he signed with the St. Louis Cardinals after graduation. He played Triple-A ball for four years, first in the St. Louis organization and then with Chicago Cubs farm teams. But he never made it to the big leagues, perhaps because of his penchant for partying (at least according to what his son has heard) or perhaps because he wasn't quite as driven as he should have been (also according to what his son has heard) and retired from baseball at the age of twenty-two.

He was a food salesman for several years and then got into the golf business in large part because he had taken up the game after quitting baseball and quickly fell in love with it. He steadily built an embroidery business, selling golf shirts at a time when that business was beginning to boom.

Scott was the proverbial chip off the old block, a natural athlete who was good at everything he did. The first toy he remembers owning was a cut-down golf club and he swung it everywhere until he was able to go to the golf course with his dad and start using the real thing. By the time he was five, he had won his first golf tournament — a father-son event. Barry McCarron was a scratch player by then and he saw in Scott the ability to get to the highest level that he had never quite reached.

"I think he believed that his father had never pushed him hard enough when he was a kid," Scott said, looking back. "Everyone talks about how much ability my dad had, but I guess he also had a very good time when he wasn't playing. Maybe he felt he squandered some of his talent because of that and he wanted to make sure he didn't let me make the mistakes he had made."

What developed — not surprisingly — was the classic dad-pushes-son relationship. Scott can still remember his father making him cry on the golf course during a tournament because he was so critical of him. Gloria McCarron became the mediator between her husband and her son when things got tense, which they often did.

Nonetheless, Scott blossomed as a player. By the time he got to high school, he had given up both baseball and tennis to focus on golf even though he was very good at both. He continued to win junior tournaments consistently and, as a senior, was recruited by all the west coast powers: Stanford, Arizona, UCLA. In the end, he chose UCLA over Stanford mostly because he thought being five hundred miles south of his parents' home in the Bay Area would be healthy for him.

It was just before Scott left for college that Barry McCarron sat down to talk to him about his future. He had come to understand that he had, at times, made life difficult for his son and he wanted him to think of golf as something to do for himself rather than for his father. "I guess he knew that from that point on it was going to be up to me," Scott said. "I didn't understand it then, but I was playing golf for *him*, not for me. He was smart enough to figure out that wasn't healthy for either one of us. The problem was, I didn't know it yet."

And wouldn't really know it for years to come. Scott McCarron isn't sure what it was that made his father sit him down for that talk. But it might have been the yips. There is no more dreaded disease in golf than the yips. It is one of those words golfers don't even like to say because if you don't say it maybe it will go away. Almost all golfers get the yips at some point in their lives, usually later rather than sooner, but not always. The yips are nerves so bad on the green that it becomes impossible to hold a putter steadily enough to put a smooth stroke on the ball. You jump, your putter jumps, the ball jumps — and very rarely does it jump into the hole.

Barry McCarron had been fighting the yips for years. Like all those afflicted, he tried everything to combat them. He putted side-saddle, cross-handed, with a long putter. He would have putted standing on his head if that would have helped. And then, late in his senior year of high school, Scott came down with the yips too. There is no scientific evidence to prove that the yips are genetic, but maybe all those years of watching his dad struggle, or perhaps all the pressure he had faced trying to be a star, finally crashed on him.

Off he went to seek fame and fortune at UCLA — and the yips went right along with him. "It was awful," he said. "Here I am, on scholarship, ready to go down there and be a star and I can't make a putt to save my life. The fact that I played as well as I did that first year is a tribute to how well I hit the ball tee to green. Because I couldn't putt at all."

Naturally, McCarron began looking for answers. His coach, Eddie Merrins, was convinced that his problems were technical, that if he could find a way to keep his head still, or move his eyes over the ball more, or not get ahead of it, he would putt better. McCarron knew better. And so, midway through his sophomore year, at a tournament in Arizona, he decided to putt side-saddle. It worked. He putted better than he had since high school and finished in the top ten in the tournament.

That was the good news. The bad news was, when Merrins, who had not gone with the team to the tournament, found out what McCarron had done, he threw him off the team.

"To be fair, it was more a last straw thing," McCarron said. "He didn't bounce me just for that. He was an old school guy. He didn't want us joining fraternities, so I pledged a fraternity. He didn't like long hair, I grew my hair long. Maybe I was reacting to all those years with my dad. But when I putted side-saddle, he thought I had done it as a rebellious thing. I hadn't. I had done it as a desperate thing. But he tossed me."

He also pulled his scholarship. The timing could not have been worse. A year earlier, his father's business had been wiped out by a flood that destroyed a warehouse full of shirts. Because the warehouse was on a flood plain, there was no flood insurance. Barry McCarron had to file for bankruptcy.

Somehow he came up with the money to send Scott back to UCLA as a junior. By now, Scott had given up any hopes of playing golf professionally. Even if he had still been on the team, the fact was he couldn't putt. You can't make a living playing golf if you can't putt. So he changed his focus. He tried out for the tennis team — UCLA has one of the best tennis teams in the country and he just missed making the team — and actually put a little time into schoolwork. He thought he might want to go to law school and he knew he would have to get his grades up to do that.

But the golf bug was still there. When he came back to school the following year, he asked Merrins if he could try out for the team as a walk-on. He had spent the summer putting left-handed and actually felt comfortable with it. Merrins said he could compete in the team's four-round tryout tournament if he wanted but he would be given no special favors as an ex-team member. The tournament was 54 holes — you played four rounds and your best three counted. After his first three rounds, McCarron was 10 shots ahead of the field. He didn't even bother playing a fourth round, going to a football game instead. He made the team easily.

Golf was different for him this time. He played well at times but, even though he putted better, he still wasn't good enough to think about a professional career. At the end of his senior year his dad asked him if he wanted to help him start a new golf apparel business. That sounded like a challenge to him, so he agreed.

The next few years were difficult. McCarron had met Jennifer Megquier at UCLA and they had dated off and on, then much more on than off. After graduation, she had moved to New York to work for a magazine. When Scott visited her, he realized he didn't like the idea of her living three thousand miles away from him. "I wasn't necessarily ready for marriage," he said. "But I certainly wasn't ready to have her there while I was in California."

He asked her to move back to the west coast. She did. Eventually Scott got around to being ready for marriage. By then, the business he and his dad had started was struggling. They actually had two companies, but neither was making much money. Scott had twice been able to convince banks to give them substantial loans, largely by taking the bankers on the golf course and impressing them with his game. But he wasn't happy.

And a funny thing had happened to his golf game. He had figured out a way to make putts. He had gone to a Senior PGA Tour event, the Raley's Gold Rush, in the spring of 1991 and noticed that a lot of the players were using long putters. It wasn't as if he had never seen a long putter before, but as he watched it seemed to him that the long putter and the split-handed grip that the players used kept them steady. He knew a lot of senior players had suffered with the yips and this seemed to be the most frequent answer they came up with to deal with them.

He went home and built a long putter in his garage. Almost from the start, he felt comfortable with it. He knew it looked funny, especially in the hands of someone who was just turning twenty-six, but he didn't care. He was making putts again. He entered the Mid-Amateur championship that summer, qualified, and made it all the way to the quarterfinals. It was his best golf result in years. He was hitting the ball longer and longer and gaining confidence.

He was also miserable at work. And so, at the end of the year, he made a decision. First he sat down with Jennifer, then with his father. He wanted to give golf one more real shot. He honestly believed he had the talent to play the game, especially with the new putter. Jennifer thought he should do whatever he thought would make him happy. His father was decidedly unhappy.

"Ironic, I guess, that me wanting to play golf would be upsetting to him after all those years as a kid," he said. "I understood. The business was struggling and I'm sure he felt like I was deserting him. But it wasn't working for me. I wanted to give it a shot."

A friend agreed to loan him $8,000 to get him started. Off he went to play mini-tour events anyplace he could find them. His goal was to get his game in shape to qualify first for a foreign tour, make some money, and then try for the PGA Tour's Q-School in the fall of 1992. He just missed in final qualifying for the Asian Tour, which was probably a good thing, since he would have been miserable spending three months over there without Jennifer, who certainly couldn't afford to quit her job at that point in their lives.

Then he and Jennifer went to Canada for the 36-hole qualifying event for the Canadian Tour. "Jennifer came to caddy," he said. "She had a pull cart, so she didn't have to carry the bag. She didn't know anything about golf, so it was just something we thought would be fun. A bonding thing."

Not quite. McCarron parred the first hole, then double-bogeyed the second hole, and made a 10 on the third hole, losing two golf balls in the process. At one point, when he tried to play a shot out of a hazard, Jennifer suggested it might be easier if he just dropped a ball on dry land. She might have been right, but Scott certainly wasn't soliciting suggestions at that point. "I guess you can't tell your wife the three 'ups' of caddying," he said, able to laugh about it now — 'show up, keep up, and shut up.' I had played three holes and basically I'm already dead," he said. "I was, to put it mildly, aggravated."

He managed to make a par-five on the fourth hole and, as they walked to the fifth tee, one of his playing partners, who was keeping his card, asked him what he had made on the hole. "Five," McCarron answered.

"Honey," Jennifer said, "I think you made a four."

"No," McCarron said. "It was a five."

"I really think it was four."

"Oh you do, do you? So you think after playing golf for twenty-five years that I can't keep score? You think you know more about the game than I do because you've been out here for four holes? Is that what you think? Well you know what? You don't. You don't know anything. You're fired!"

McCarron was now eight over par for four holes *and* he had just fired his wife. Jennifer left the pull cart sitting there and walked away in tears. For some reason, she didn't leave altogether, instead seeking solace from the families of McCarron's playing partners, who no doubt were telling her that they knew a number of very nice single young men.

It took McCarron six holes to figure out that not qualifying for the Canadian Tour probably wasn't worth making his wife miserable. He finally walked over, apologized profusely, and was forgiven. The McCarrons agreed on one thing when the day was finally over. Jennifer's career as a caddy was finished.

McCarron entered the PGA Tour's Q-School that fall and promptly shot about a million, failing to come even close to making it past the first stage. He was frustrated and baffled. He knew he was a better player than he had shown, and yet he couldn't figure out how to get himself to calm down enough to play up to his potential. A friend suggested he see a sports psychologist. McCarron knew a lot of successful players had worked with psychologists, so he decided it was worth a try. The man he went to see was Glenn Albaugh, who not only had a background in psychology but had been a golf coach at the University of the Pacific for years.

Albaugh taught McCarron the basics: developing a preshot routine, focusing more on his target rather than his swing, visualizing good shots, learning to put bad shots behind him and move on to the next shot. "For some guys, maybe that stuff wouldn't be a big deal," McCarron said. "But for me, it was exactly what I needed. I had no focus on the golf course except for desperately wanting to do well. This changed all that. I began playing better almost right away."

He started to make money on the mini-tours, and this time when he went to Canada to qualify for the tour — with a new caddy — he not only made it, he won the qualifying event. He played solidly in Canada, finishing twenty-second on the money list, and came back home in the fall convinced he was at least ready to make it to the finals of the Q-School, which would put him onto the Nike Tour for 1994.

He was almost right. He cruised through the first stage. Then came the critical second stage. All those who got through and reached the finals were assured of no worse than a spot on the Nike Tour. McCarron couldn't handle the pressure. "Missed by two shots," he said. "I was crushed."

He had now given two years of his life to trying to make it to the tour. He was twenty-eight. He had no job, almost no money and, at least for the next year, very little future in golf. He took a long ride on his mountain bike and sat on a rock all by himself staring into space for a long, long time. He knew he wasn't ready to quit. If Jennifer could deal with it, he had to give it one more year. She could. And he did.

This time he decided to play the Hooters Tour. The Hooters is a large step below the Nike Tour. It is sponsored by the restaurant chain known for scantily clad waitresses and barely edible food. The Hooters events are played in tiny towns, most of them in the south, with a weekly purse of $100,000 and a $500 entry fee. Players can play as long as their money holds out.

Coming up with the entry fee each week was a challenge for McCarron. He stayed in private housing most weeks to save on hotel money, and when another player would fly home for a week, McCarron would often volunteer to drive his car to the next stop to make a few extra bucks. Jennifer had to keep working, so he was lonely and miserable a lot of the time.

But his golf was good. He contended consistently and, after ten weeks, was leading the tour's point standings. Since the winner of the points race receives a $100,000 bonus at the end of the year, McCarron was in position to come into a giant windfall — as long as he kept playing every week. That's what players do on the Hooters. They play every week because they can't afford not to.

Jennifer had come out to visit him for one week earlier in the year. As fate would have it, she had returned home pregnant. The McCarrons were thrilled. But Jennifer had a miscarriage. Scott told her he would be on the next plane home. No, she said. There's nothing you can do now. Stay out there and play. Win the bonus. There will be other chances for us to start our family. Scott knew she was right. For a week, he tried. But he couldn't focus on golf. He felt as if he was deserting Jennifer. They needed to share their grief. He quit the Hooters Tour and flew home.

"It's a decision I never regretted for a minute," he said. "Even if it had ruined my golf career, it would have been the right thing to do."

As it turned out, it didn't ruin anything. McCarron returned to playing on the Golden State Tour in California because he could get home in a couple of hours from any of the events. In August he won the highest-paying event on the tour, the Long Beach Open, and a first prize check of $25,000. A week later, he won another tournament and another $8,000. That was $33,000 in two weeks, more than Jennifer's salary — which they had been living on — for the entire year.

"We were rich," he said. "I mean, richer than rich. We figured if we lived to be a hundred we could never spend that money."

Maybe having a few extra dollars relaxed him. Or maybe winning and playing well gave him the confidence boost he needed. Either way, McCarron was now convinced his time at Q-School had come. But every step seemed more difficult than the next. At the opening stage, McCarron was in a comfortable position after 36 holes, but somehow misread his tee time for the third round and showed up just in time not to be disqualified, but late enough to start the round with a two-shot penalty. Flustered, he dropped back that day and spent the entire last round on the bubble. He finally made a late birdie to get in by one shot.

The second stage, the one that had thrown him a year earlier, was even tougher. With five holes to play on the last day, McCarron thought he was in serious trouble. Not only was he right on the cut line, but he was nervous, spraying shots all over the golf course. "I couldn't hit a green," he said. In fact, he missed the last five greens. And, in every case, he got the ball up and down: five straight one putts. He made the cut right on the number. Any miss at any of those holes and he would have been gone.

Now, at least, he was assured a place on the Nike Tour. But he wanted more than that. At the Q-School finals in Greenlefe, Florida, he was in trouble right from the start. Three straight rounds of 73 left him needing a superb fourth round just to survive the 72-hole cut from 180 to 90 players. He figured he needed to shoot 67 to give himself a chance. For 17 holes he played almost perfect golf, and he arrived at 18 needing a par to shoot 67. Again, nerves got the best of him. He fanned a drive way right, hitting it directly into the hazard he had to avoid to have a chance to make par. Disgusted, he headed up 18, apologizing to his brother-in-law, who was caddying for him, for being such a choking dog. But when they got to the drop area adjacent to the hazard, they found something funny: McCarron's golf ball. The ball had caught a branch and pitched forward, missing the hazard and landing in a patch of rough where he actually had a swing at the ball. From there, he got it to the green, rolled his 50-foot birdie putt to within six feet, and then made the testy par putt, his knees knocking all the way.

Once more, he had survived, right on the number. Given a life he thought he didn't have, he played excellent golf the last two days and made the tour with a shot to spare. When he made his par putt on the 108th and final hole of the week, Bill Britton, a man who had survived the rigors of Q-School on four different occasions, shook his hand warmly and said, "Welcome to the PGA Tour."

McCarron was still not quite sure where he was or where he was going. He was reeling from exhaustion, physically and emotionally. He went back to his room to take a shower, so he could go back and watch the late scores come in and make sure he was, indeed, going to the PGA Tour. Standing in the shower thinking about the disappointments and the close calls, the lucky break on 18 two days earlier, and Britton's words, it all crashed on him. "I just broke down completely," he said. "Stood there under the water crying like a baby."

He was crying again eleven months later, but this time for a different reason. Courtney McCarron arrived on Halloween, a healthy, happy baby. By then her dad had finished his first year on the tour and pulled off another miracle, finishing third at Las Vegas in the second-to-last event of the year to vault himself from 212th to 128th on the money list. Since there were four non-PGA Tour members in the top 125 that year, McCarron was officially 124th. What's more, if he hadn't kept his card, McCarron would not have been able to go to Q-School because Courtney was due during the second stage of Q-School, and McCarron wasn't going to miss that for anything. Fortunately, he got to see his baby born and continue his golf career.

He had survived a year on tour, and he and Jennifer were parents. But life still wasn't easy. Earnings of $147,371 sounded like a lot, but after travel expenses and taxes, McCarron was hardly rich. Especially when the people who had bought out one of the companies he and his father had started had the original loan called and came looking for the money. "I needed about $200,000 in cash," he said. "To put it simply, I didn't have it."

The week before he flew to New Orleans in late March 1996 to play in the tournament there, McCarron decided he had no choice but to file for bankruptcy. He would do it during the Masters, when he was back home, since he had not qualified for Augusta. On the day before the tournament began, McCarron took Courtney for a walk in her stroller to a mall near the hotel. He was morose, wondering what this latest turn would mean for his future and for his family.

"I was standing there gazing in the window of this novelty store and I saw this poster of an island green," he said. "Underneath the picture it said, 'In the middle of every challenge, lies an opportunity.' I looked at Courtney and said, 'Sure, why not? Why not make this an opportunity?'"

In the movies, the hero goes out and wins the golf tournament, pays off his debts, and lives happily ever after.

In real life, McCarron went out, won the New Orleans golf tournament, paid off his debts, and has, for the most part, lived happily ever after. He beat Tom Watson coming down the stretch that week and suddenly life changed radically. He had a first place check of $270,000, a two-year winner's exemption that gave him a secure spot on tour through 1998, a spate of new endorsement offers, and a cherished spot in the Masters. Instead of flying home to file for bankruptcy, McCarron paid his debts and flew to Augusta. He amazed everyone — including himself — by staying in contention almost the entire week before finishing tied for tenth, which earned him an automatic trip back for 1997. In a period of three weeks, he went from a struggling journeyman pro to one of the tour's bright young stars.

All of a sudden people noticed how far he hit the ball, how quick his smile was, how sharp his sense of humor could be. "I went from frog to prince almost overnight," he said.

The young prince proved his win was no fluke a year later when he won his second tournament, in Atlanta, and finished 1997 twenty-fifth on the money list with winnings of more than $852,000. A second daughter, Cassidy, arrived at the end of the year and the McCarrons moved into a spacious new house in Rancho Murieta. McCarron was being asked to go to meetings involving potential members of the Presidents Cup team and, when people talked about players not named Woods who could win the Masters, his name came up.

"If I'm going to win a major, I think my best shot is at Augusta," he said. "Every year I know the golf course a little better, know the greens a little better, feel a little more comfortable with the surroundings. I think I'm ready to seriously challenge now."

When he and Jennifer had first driven down Magnolia Lane in 1996, they had been hanging out the windows taking pictures, giddy just to be there. This time, McCarron flew in on Saturday (although he couldn't play that day because the airline lost his golf clubs) and arrived at the golf course early Sunday with a very serious look on his face.

"I honestly believe," he said, "that I'm ready to win this thing."

He was not alone.

In fact, when the players headed for their homes late Wednesday afternoon, the list of those convinced they could win — or would win — was a long one. Woods, no matter how uncomfortable he might feel with the trappings of the club, loved the golf course. Duval, who had been the world's hottest player for six months, thought his time had come. Justin Leonard had just won the Players Championship two weeks earlier and was beginning to think he had the game — and the putter — to compete at Augusta. Tom Watson was having the best year of his career at the age of forty-eight.

And then there was Couples. He had been like a little kid in the weeks leading up to the tournament, telling Thais time and again how much she was going to love Augusta. She had finally turned to him one night and said, "Let's just wait until we get there. Then I can tell you that you were right."

Couples had a feeling about this Masters. He had asked Paul Marchand, his longtime teacher, to fly in from Houston during the week of the Bay Hill Classic in Orlando to work on his swing with Augusta in mind. Marchand had moved him back from the ball a little bit, allowing him to draw the ball more easily when he wanted to, something he knew he would have to do at Augusta on number two, five, nine, 13, and 14.

Although Couples was a natural left-to-right player and Augusta was supposed to be set up for the right-to-left player, he had always had the length to play the golf course well. Now he wanted to play it better.

"Everything we did at Bay Hill was with Augusta in mind," he said. "As we were hitting shots, I kept picturing different tees at Augusta and where the ball needed to go. I came out of there feeling great."

He had run into his old pal Jim Nantz in Houston on the Sunday before the tournament, and Nantz, who has an encyclopedic memory, started reminding him of the parallels between 1998 and 1992; the tournament would be played on the same dates; it would end on Easter Sunday; he had been playing well; there was a new woman in his life. Couples listened to everything Nantz said with one ear, thinking for the most part that his friend was just trying to give him a pep talk. He flew into Augusta on Sunday night and drove to the golf course Monday morning to register. It was when he was handed his player badge that Couples began wondering for the first time if perhaps Nantz was on to something: "It was number seventy," he said. "That was my number in ninety-two. The only reason I remember is that Jim came up to me on the morning of the last round that year and said to me, 'Shoot your badge number and you'll win.' And that was what I shot."

Mark O'Meara had badge number 73. It had absolutely no significance to him. He had never played that well at the Masters, and a lot of people wondered if his relatively low ball flight would keep him from ever playing that well at Augusta. "People always said my best shot to win a major would be at the British because of my ball flight," he said. "I understood what they were saying. But I still thought I had a chance if I could ever get the right attitude going."

Easier said than done. O'Meara wasn't even being asked the "majors" question that week. He had become a nonfactor. He wasn't invited to the press room before the tournament, and when reporters did stop to talk to him it was usually to ask him if he thought Woods was in the right frame of mind to defend his title. All of which was fine with O'Meara. He went through his preparations the same way he had always done in the past.

Then, on Tuesday, he did something different. When he went to the sign-up board for the par-three tournament and saw that all the slots were filled in until 4:40, he paused. O'Meara was fully aware of how important the par-three is to Augusta's members, and he had always enjoyed it in the past. He had never once skipped it. Mark O'Meara, the golfing good guy, always showed up to give everyone a laugh or two during the par-three.

Not this time. He put the pen down. "Four-forty was late," he said. "I didn't want to be at the golf course that late. I wanted to get here Thursday morning charged up and ready to go. I wanted this year to be different."

The first difference came Wednesday afternoon. While most of O'Meara's fellow pros waited in the rain, first to see if play would begin again, then for traffic to clear after play was called off, O'Meara was back at his house resting. He had played his last practice round in the morning, hit some balls, and been long gone when the rains came.

8

The Squire and Friends

It can be argued that golf's best day each year is opening day at Augusta. At all majors, the atmosphere on Thursday morning is charged. Everyone has been waiting and talking and speculating for three full days about what might happen, and now, at last, something is actually going to happen.

The locker room is a little quieter than most weeks on tour, players making — as Jeff Sluman once pointed out — a lot more trips to the bathroom than they do on a normal Thursday.

But the Masters begins in a way no other golf tournament begins. The other three majors all send their first players off close to dawn because, with fields of 156 players, the only way to get the entire field in before dark is to get everyone started shortly after the sun comes up. The first player off the tee at the other three majors is, often as not, someone whose main claim to fame in golf may very well turn out to be that he was once the first player to put a ball in the air at a major championship.

At the Masters, the first player to strike a ball is the man everyone in golf calls the Squire: Gene Sarazen. The second is Lord Byron: Byron Nelson. The third is the Slammer: Sam Snead. Among them they won six Masters (three Snead, two Nelson, one Sarazen), nineteen majors (seven Sarazen, seven Snead, five Nelson), and 171 tournament titles in all. None of the three is ever given a badge number. In the slot where their player numbers would normally be placed on the first tee, each is assigned a different number every year. In 1998 Sarazen had 96, Nelson 86, and Snead 85. No one had to ask what those numbers meant. "I swear I get older every year and they don't," Sarazen joked once. Even at ninety-six, he still went to the range on Thursday morning for a few swings to get loose. "I'm just not sure I can do it this year," he said. He had said that before.

At Augusta, the field rarely consists of more than ninety players. In 1998, there were eighty-eight starters. That means everyone can play in twosomes on Thursday and there is no need to tee anybody off before 8 o'clock in the morning. It is a more comfortable way to begin for everyone: players, fans, officials, even those who have to get the golf course ready. They are still out very early, but not as early as at the U.S. Open (for example), where most people responsible for running the golf tournament are at the course before 5 A.M. on Thursday and Friday.

The gates open on Thursday morning at Augusta at 7:30. That gives everyone time to get to the first tee for the opening ceremony, scheduled for 8 o'clock. Every year, without fail, the parking lots begin to fill well before 7:30 even though people know they will be waiting in line for the gate to open. They don't mind. They just want to be certain they aren't late.

In 1998, no one was going to be late. Because the rain had saturated the course, club officials had decided to delay the start by at least an hour to give the grounds crew extra time to work on the greens. Each year players marvel at how much faster the greens are at Augusta on Thursday than they are on Wednesday. "It's as if they have some magic elixir they pour on them on Wednesday night," Brad Faxon, one of the tour's best putters, said. "That's one thing you have to understand when you play your practice rounds. The greens you putt on Monday, Tuesday, and Wednesday are going to be entirely different than what you putt on Thursday."

Other golf tournaments talk about the speed of their greens constantly. Green speed is measured by something called a stimp-meter (invented by a man named Stimp), which is really a simple device from which a ball is rolled onto the green. The number of feet that it rolls once it is rolled off the stimp onto the green is the green's speed. In other words, if the ball rolls 10 feet, the greens are — in golf vernacular — stimping at 10. Anything over 10 is considered faster than average, 12 is getting near the danger point, and anything from 13 on up is considered lightning. At the U.S. Open, which prides itself on fast greens, the stimp rarely gets above 12 and, more often than not, maxes out in the 11 to 12 range.

How fast are the greens at Augusta? No one knows for sure because the members won't tell. "We don't want people focusing on that," Will Nicholson said. "We want them focusing on the quality of the golf course and the golf tournament."

Which is all fine. But naturally when people are denied information, they want it more. And they will speculate. "Well, let's see, the USGA keeps it at about twelve at the Open," Brad Faxon said one day. "I'd say Augusta is about sixteen."

Sixteen! "Okay, maybe fifteen," Faxon said, being slightly less hyperbolic. "Put it this way. They're faster than anything else you'll putt on in your entire life."

Everyone has a story about the greens at Augusta. The most famous may involve two-time Masters champion Seve Ballesteros, who barely tapped a birdie putt on the 16th one day in 1986 and watched it roll 20 feet past the cup. He almost took a full swing at the next putt and was 10 feet short. Then he missed the bogey putt for a four-putt five. Later, in the press room Ballesteros was asked what happened at the 16th. He shrugged and said in his Spanish accent, "I mees, I mees, I mees, I make." Then he stormed back to the champions locker room and began screaming at Tom Watson (as if he had any control) that the 16th green should be blown up.

Everyone has a story like that. In 1996, Jeff Sluman had an eight-foot birdie putt at the second hole. He tapped the putt gingerly down the slope, thought he had made it, and watched the putt rim out. Then it started rolling. By the time it stopped, he had a 50-footer coming back for par.

"It gets to the point sometimes of being ridiculous," Greg Norman once said. "That's why putting the ball in the fairway is so important. Because if you aren't in position to aim for a certain quadrant of the green, you have almost no chance to two-putt."

It is also why some people say the Masters is nothing more than a putting contest. Which is a vast oversimplification. But the greens and the hole locations are a constant source of discussion during Masters week. The hole locations are chosen each night by a committee that includes club members, rules officials from various golfing bodies, and David Graham, a man who won both the U.S. Open and the PGA. Nicholson goes along on the hole-locating excursions whenever he has time in order to be — his description — "the conservative member of the group." In other words, if he thinks a hole location may produce 50-foot second putts, he is likely to object to it. "We want them tough, but fair," he says.

Fair, of course, being a relative word.

The rain was going to make greens stimping at Faxon's hyperbolic 16 — or even 12 or 13 — just about out of the question no matter how long the start was delayed. Soft greens at Augusta can be a disaster because then the players can fly the ball right at the pins without fear of ending up in an impossible spot over the green. But mother nature always seems to find a way to protect this particular golf course. Which is why Thursday dawned cold and windy. Combine raw weather with wet fairways that would provide little roll and the golf course would play long and, with slower greens, tough but fair. Just the way Nicholson and his band of merry men would want it.

It was almost 9:30 by the time the course was deemed ready for play. Sarazen was the first of the three legends to arrive, driven up to the first tee at 9:22 dressed in his trademark knickers and white floppy hat. He wore a green sweater to protect himself from the wind and carried a cane that he didn't appear to need onto the tee. Jack Stephens, in his green jacket and his own white floppy hat, waited to greet him.

When the opening ceremony is held at 8 in the morning, the first tee is crowded. But now, starting ninety minutes late, there wasn't an inch of free space within 200 yards of the tee. Just about everyone on the grounds who wasn't on the range warming up to play was jostling for a view as Nelson and Snead arrived to join Sarazen. "We might have drawn a crowd if we had waited till noon," Stephens said wryly.

Stephens is the only person who uses a microphone on the first tee at Augusta. Phil Harison, who has been the starter for the tournament since 1947, has never used one. Harison's introductions are the soul of simplicity. He stands up, clears his throat, and says, "Fore please, now driving . . ."

"My job is to make the players as comfortable as I can," Harison said. "Walking on the first tee here is a very nervous moment for most of them. I talk with them if they want to talk, leave them alone if they want to be left alone. But I try to keep the introductions short and sweet. The people here know who they are and what they've done. They just want to get on the tee and get the first shot down the fairway. They don't need me holding them up by reciting their life history."

Harison is a local insurance man, an unusual Augusta member in that he was invited to join the club when he was only twenty-one. He and his brother Gummy shared the starter's duties for forty years until Gummy's death. Now, Harison handles the job by himself except when he needs a brief break. Then another member, Fleming Norvell, fills in for him.

As always, Harison sat nearby waiting his turn while Stephens did the honors for the three legends. There had been serious doubt forty-eight hours earlier about whether Snead would make it to the ceremony. When his son Jack checked him into the hospital on Tuesday, it had been feared he had suffered a stroke. Twenty-four hours later, the hospital said he had just been a victim of fatigue and he was sent home to rest up for the big morning.

The opening ceremony is so simple and brief that if you blink — or don't show up early enough to get a decent view — you are apt to miss it. Stephens always began the same way every year.

"Good morning," he would say.

And, like a good first-grade class, the entire crowd would answer back: "Good morning."

You almost expect the Pledge of Allegiance to come next.

Stephens would then give a brief history of the three great men on the tee, putting a little extra emphasis on their Masters victories.

"We're fortunate to have Sam here," Stephens said. "He was threatening to knock out some hospital windows if necessary to get here. I understand he can also kick the ceiling too."

At that moment, on cue, Snead kicked his right leg into the air over his head, smiling as if to say, "Didn't think I could do it, did you?"

Like everyone else, Stephens stared at Snead in disbelief for a moment, then plowed on. "Well then, it's time to begin the 1998 Masters. Gene, would you lead us off?"

Sarazen nodded and walked to where his grandson, Gene Ilnicki, had teed the ball up for him. He went through a brief preshot routine, glanced down the fairway, which by now was packed with people on both sides, took the club back in a graceful arc, and sent the ball up in the air a good 150 yards down the fairway. Right down the middle. At ninety-six. "Didn't know if I could do it," he said softly, a smile curling his lips for a moment. The appreciative murmur quickly turned to full-blown applause.

Nelson was next, the ball teed up for him by his wife, Peggy. His swing was quicker, crankier, as a result of hip surgery a couple of years earlier that has made pivoting difficult. He couldn't quite get through the ball and it dove right on him, but it still had plenty of carry, making it about halfway up the hill to the yawning bunker on the right side of the fairway. More warm applause followed Nelson off the tee.

Snead didn't need anybody to tee the ball up for him. He sauntered onto the tee, took a practice swing, looked down the fairway once, took the club back, and cracked the ball almost to the top of the hill, a good 230 yards down the fairway. Where Sarazen and Nelson drew murmurs, Snead got a gasp. He loved it. He watched the ball land, picked up his tee, and walked off triumphant, as if to say, "Fatigue my . . ."

Stephens had a huge grin on his face when Snead was finished. The entire ceremony had taken less than five minutes. "Thank you very much, everybody," he said. "The show is now on the road."

Twelve minutes later, Phil Harison introduced the first pairing of the tournament, Doug Ford and Gay Brewer. It was 9:44, meaning the tournament was 90 minutes behind schedule and the temperature still hadn't reached 60 degrees. It would be a long, tough day for everyone — especially the older players. That was clear when Ford's opening tee shot didn't travel quite as far as Snead's shot had gone. Still, he managed to par the first two holes and, as the weather warmed, thoughts of a respectable score no doubt danced through his mind.

The rest of the field followed Ford and Brewer onto the golf course and, as the day wore on, the story lines that are a part of every Masters began to unfold.

As Ford and Brewer made their way up the hill on number one, six names were on every leader board around the golf course: Tiger Woods, Ernie Els, Justin Leonard, Davis Love III, Matt Kuchar, and Craig Watson. They were — in order — the 1997 Masters, U.S. Open, British Open, PGA, U.S. Amateur, and British Amateur champions. Every year at the Masters, the winners of those six events begin Thursday on the leader board. Since each leader board has slots for ten names, the six champions will remain on the board at least until they have started play and dropped behind five other players.

The Thursday crowd is very different from the practice day crowds. It is older, to say the least. "It's a mature crowd," Justin Leonard said with a grin. The Masters is the toughest ticket in sports. The last time there was a public sale was in 1972. The waiting list for those trying to get tickets was cut off in 1978. Each ticket is red-bordered with a picture of the clubhouse in the middle and the $100 price for the week at the bottom. It also has a number that allows the club to track it if it is lost or turns up in the wrong hands. If someone misbehaves on the grounds, his ticket is removed, the number traced back to the owner, and that person is removed from next year's ticket list. No one misbehaves at Augusta.

The most unlikely opening day story belonged to none other than Brewer, who looked anything but sixty-six as he worked his way around the golf course. On a day when one player would break 70, Brewer shot a remarkable round of even-par 72, highlighted by a par at the 12th that came after he put his tee shot in the water and then holed a wedge from the drop area.

"What an incredible round," Fred Couples said later. "That's the story of the day." Couples had shot 69 to lead the tournament, which was also one of the stories of the day. He began with three straight birdies, going right to the top of the leader board, and hung on in the wind the rest of the round. "Every time I started to get down [caddy] Joe [La-Cava] told me I had to hang in there if I wanted to beat Gay," he said, joking but not joking.

One by one, players came stumbling off the 18th green, exhausted and bleary-eyed from battling the wind and the golf course all day. Any talk that the golf course had been made obsolete by Woods's record-breaking performance had disappeared. Wind is a golf course's ultimate protection and it had protected Augusta on opening day. Only Couples broke 70. Three players — Scott Hoch, Paul Stankowski, and José María Olazabal — were at 70. Five others shot 71. When the long day finally ended at dusk, there were still ten players on the golf course. The ninety-minute delay at the start had made it impossible to get everyone in before dark since the last tee time had been pushed back from 2:42 to 4:12.

It was shortly after 8 o'clock when officials began telling players that they were free to stop playing. David Duval and Ernie Els were on the 16th tee when they were told they had the option to play the hole or come back at 7:30 the next morning to finish the round. Duval looked at the swirling winds, felt the chill that had been increasing by the minute, and looked at Els. "I don't know about you, Ernie," he said. "But I'd rather take my chances in the morning."

Els nodded. "I'm with you."

It had already been a long day for both players. Neither had been thrilled with their tee time — 2:15 — and the delay had pushed them back to 3:45. On tour, players like to use their early day most weeks to spend some extra time on the range in the afternoon, then catch up on their rest. They understand that if they are in contention on Saturday there will be no chance to work on their game after the round because they will be expected to come to the press room and, in all likelihood, it will be close to dark before they are finished there. "Even if you get done before dark you're probably too tired to go do anything anyway," Duval said.

After waiting for what had seemed like forever, Duval had crushed his drive off the first tee so far past the fairway bunker that he only had a nine-iron left to the green. "A lot of pent-up energy right there," he said. From there, he butchered the hole, leaving his second shot 30 feet short of the pin and three-putting for an extremely annoying bogey. Standing on the second tee, Duval had to have a talk with himself. "I just reminded myself that everyone was making bogeys and I had used one up early," he said. "I had to bear down and not waste any more shots."

He did that, birdieing the second and then going into a grinding routine for most of the front nine. The basic approach most players take to

Augusta is this: get through the first seven holes without any disasters, then attack. The only true birdie hole among the first seven is the par-five second. Par on any other hole is a good score, any birdie is a bonus. The two front-nine par-threes — numbers four and six — are two of the most difficult par-threes anywhere in major championship golf.

The second par-five on the course, number eight, is the longest of the par-fives, the one reached in two least often. But it is still a hole where a player has a chance to make birdie. Nine through 12 are all fraught with danger but also can be birdie holes, especially if one drives the ball well at nine, 10, and 11. Twelve is rarely more than a seven-iron shot but the tales of disaster are part of Augusta legend. Then comes the three-hole stretch where a player has to make a move: the short par-fives at 13 and 15, which sandwich 14, a tricky par-four where most players are content with par. If you play 13–14–15 in 4–4–4 you will be in good shape. To really make a move you have to throw in a three at one of the three. The par-three 16th is the last hole where water comes into play. The 17th is one of the holes the Lords of Augusta have toughened for 1999 because the once-infamous Eisenhower tree had essentially been taken out of play. Most of today's players hit the ball long enough to make the tree not a factor, and get through the hole with a driver and a short iron. And finally comes 18, a hole where two perfect shots will give you a great birdie chance and anything less will mean trouble. A very good finishing hole.

Every golf fan in America knows the back nine at Augusta, having seen it on TV year after year. What surprises people when they first see the golf course in person is the steepness of the hills. "I remember the first time I walked down 10 and 11 I couldn't believe how sharp the inclines were," Justin Leonard said. "And 18 is completely different than it looks on television. You can't imagine how steep that hill is going up to the green."

By contrast, most people know little about the front nine because they see it on TV only in bits and pieces. The Lords have allowed CBS a little more latitude each year and viewers do get to see some of the front nine, but not much. The first hole is one of the more difficult opening holes in golf, and no one — other than those with tickets or invitations to play — ever sees it.

Duval was very happy to get to the turn at even par and thrilled to birdie the 11th. He didn't birdie 13 or 15, but that wasn't as disappointing as it normally would be since very few people were even attempting to reach either green in two. Fifteen was the talk of the tournament. Woods had all but destroyed the hole a year earlier, actually hitting nine-iron second shots there. This time, he laid up with his second shot. So did everyone else in the field with the exception of Phil Mickelson and Scott McCarron. Mickelson missed the green but still made birdie. McCarron, who had just double-bogeyed the 14th to go three over par for the day, absolutely hammered a three-wood over the water. Then he made his 60-footer for eagle. That was the only three of the day on the hole. Before darkness fell there had been an 11 (Ignacio Garrido) and two tens (Costantino Rocca and Bill Glasson).

The eagle was a round saver for McCarron, who managed to get in at one-over-par 73, a score he was thrilled with under the circumstances. Duval was one under par standing on the 16th tee and figured since he had to get up early the next morning anyway, he might as well see if the conditions would be calmer than they were at that moment. "I didn't want to get up early to finish but I had no choice," he said. "I still figured I was in good position being where I was and the lead being sixty-nine."

He was in good position. So was Woods, who had also shot 71 playing with his successor as U.S. Amateur champion, Matt Kuchar. If the day had a hero — other than Gay Brewer — it was Kuchar, who strolled around Augusta with a huge grin on his face all day, a stark contrast to Woods's intense game face. Kuchar also played superbly. He was two under par through fourteen holes, then seemed to be in deep trouble when he double-bogeyed 15 and hit his tee shot in the water at 16. But he knocked his third shot at 16 to within a foot to salvage a bogey, then birdied 17 to get in at even-par 72 — not bad for a college sophomore who had a bunch of tests coming up in a week at Georgia Tech.

As the day wound down and the scores went up, a buzz began to make its way around the press room. Because the round could not be finished before dark, that would mean a delayed start on Friday. In order to finish the second round Friday, the committee had taken the unusual step of pairing the players in threesomes to save time. On the board, listed one after the other, were three players who had shot 71: Woods, Zoeller, Montgomerie. A little figuring told you all you needed to know:

as long as Duval didn't birdie one of the last three holes to shoot 70, the third-to-last group off the tee Friday would be those three men.

Woods and Zoeller hadn't been paired together anyplace in the year since the infamous Zoeller comments. Now they would be together, at Augusta of all places, with the entire world watching. And, as a bonus, the third member of the group would be Montgomerie, who a year earlier had been in second place after 36 holes and had talked that evening about how much he thought his previous experience in major championships would aid him the next day when he was paired with Woods. The scores the next day had been Woods 65, Montgomerie 74. The next day Montgomerie shot 81 and finished tied for thirtieth. So much for experience.

It didn't take long for the press to come up with a name for the potential Friday threesome: the Sunshine Boys. There would not be a lot of yucking it up going on in that group.

The only person who might have been less happy on Thursday evening than the Sunshine Boys was Mark O'Meara. His day had started reasonably enough with a one-under-par 35 on the front nine, but the back nine had been a disaster. It began with a bogey on 10, when he had tentatively left a six-foot uphill par putt short, and had ended two hours later when he tapped in for a 39 that gave him an opening two-over-par 74. Given the other scores, it wasn't awful. O'Meara was furious.

"Seventy-four was the absolute highest score I could have shot that day," he said. "I'm not saying it should have been 68 or 69, but it shouldn't have been any more than 70 or 71."

Worse than the number was the route to the number. O'Meara is one of the best, most confident putters on the tour. Standing over the putt on number 10, it had occurred to him that he had no idea how he wanted to hit the putt, where he wanted to hit it, or how he planned to get it into the hole. "I was all wishy-washy," he said. "First I worried I'd yank it left, then I worried I'd yip it right. I ended up gimping it up there short. I was furious with myself. You can't putt anyplace like that, much less at Augusta. You start leaving uphill putts short you are in trouble."

O'Meara spent a little time in the locker room after he had finished, then decided to go to the putting green. His longtime teacher and friend

Hank Haney went with him. O'Meara threw a couple of balls down and began hitting putts, his jaw locked in anger. "You know it wasn't a bad round," Haney said. "You actually played pretty well."

O'Meara is not a man who gets angry very often. Now, he was angry. "Hank, I stink," he said. "You can't win this tournament if you're standing over a six-foot putt *hoping* to make it."

Haney understood O'Meara's frustration. He tried soothing him one more time. "Look at the scores," he said. "Look how tough the golf course played for everyone today." O'Meara wasn't buying. "That's bull," he said. "You know it and I know it. That round should have been a 71 at most. It's the same old story."

Later, O'Meara would admit that he was feeling a little bit of panic. In one sense he was in a great position because no one was all that interested in his 74. He had become yesterday's news. Once upon a time he had been one of the first people mentioned in BPNTHWAM (best player never to have won a major) discussions. Now he was an afterthought, coming long after Duval and Montgomerie and Phil Mickelson. The general thinking was that, at forty-one, his time had come and gone. He was still a good player, but these days he received more notoriety for being Woods's sidekick/mentor than for his fourteen career victories.

None of that was on O'Meara's mind at that moment on the putting green. He wasn't ready to sit back and be the aging mentor to the young superstar. As many times as he had repeated the mantra about not needing to win a major to feel complete, he was well aware of what people said about that hole in his résumé. Like anyone else, he cared about what others thought. The King of the Bs label was like an itch that needed salve. There was only one way to apply it.

He knew he could take some of his frustration out on Haney. They had worked together for more than sixteen years now and Haney would understand. He did. "Okay, Mark," Haney said, dropping the pep talk. "Let's try something." Gently, he took O'Meara's head in his hands and tilted it forward. Normally teachers don't like to make adjustments to a player's technique in the middle of a major. But Haney figured there was nothing to lose now. "I think you need to get your eyes over the ball a little more. It looks to me like you're aiming right. Try lightening your grip a little bit too."

O'Meara put his head down in the position where Haney wanted it. He loosened his grip on the putter and rolled a few putts. Bingo, they started rolling smoothly right at the hole. Still, O'Meara didn't get too excited. "I had rolled the ball well on the practice green that morning," he said. His stroke did feel better, though, smoother. He began to give himself a talking to, reminding himself to free up and let the ball roll. Maybe he had been aiming right. Maybe a death grip on the putter wasn't the answer. Try easier, he told himself. He spent another thirty minutes on the putting green with Haney and then went home to relax. He was five shots out of the lead. On Thursday, that meant nothing — if you played well on Friday.

9

Freddie and the Sunshine Boys

Once the Masters is under way most players try to get into a routine that is almost identical every night. Few of them venture into Augusta's restaurants, in part because the town isn't exactly San Francisco (there is a note on the inside of the menus at the local Red Lobster informing customers that they are dining in the place selected by *Augusta* magazine as having "the best seafood" in Augusta) and because any player who is the least bit recognizable will have a tough time getting through a meal without getting writer's cramp from signing autographs. The other option of course is to offend people by saying no.

So most stay in. Everyone brings friends and family to Augusta. Since just about every player in the field rents a house (standard price for the week is $5,000 to $8,000 unless you choose to go really upscale) there is usually plenty of room for everyone. Some players go so far as to rent two houses, one for those in their entourage who want to stay up late, the other for the golfer, who needs a decent night's sleep. Olin Browne, playing in his first Masters, had done that. "We have the frat house and the house of sanity," he said. "I'd love to hang out in the frat house more, but I can't."

In many ways Browne was a typical Augusta rookie in that he wanted to savor every bit of the experience that he could. At thirty-eight he had no idea if he would ever be back. He had agreed to write a diary for the *Augusta Chronicle* all week and his son, Olin Jr., was his caddy in the par-three tournament. Most of the people that he had ever been on a first-name basis with had called him at some point for tickets. He had accommodated as many people as he could.

Tickets are a major issue for the players. Each player is allowed to buy eight tickets for the four days of tournament play at the standard price of $100 for the week. There are no comps and, supposedly, no one can get extras. "I just have a feeling that if Jack [Nicklaus] needs extras he gets them," David Duval said. "And you know what? He should."

Players can buy extra tickets for the practice days, and some will actually bring in two waves of friends — one group for the practice days and one group for the tournament days. That way they can at least get a few more people inside the hallowed gates. Brad Faxon had done that. He had several friends coming for the practice days, then others arriving Wednesday night for the tournament.

Faxon always looks forward to Augusta because he loves everything about the place. But he had never looked forward to it more than this year. He was hoping that the tournament would mark both an ending and a beginning for him after an eight-month period that had been a living hell.

Faxon was thirty-six, a fifteen-year tour veteran who had known solid, consistent success since his days as a college star at Furman. Three times he had qualified for the U.S. Open as an amateur and he had made the cut and been low amateur at Oakmont in 1983. Later that year, he made it through Q-School on his first try and had never gone back. He had won five times on tour and been a member of the last two U.S. Ryder Cup teams. He and his wife, Bonnie, had three adorable daughters ages nine, seven, and two. What's more, Faxon was one of the best-liked and most respected players in the game. He had been a member of the Tour Policy Board and was one of those people who was always being quoted on golf issues by the media because he was thoughtful and honest, no matter what the topic. He even dabbled in journalism himself, writing an occasional guest column for *Golf World* magazine.

Faxon was someone who never backed away from an issue. When a number of American players skipped the British Open in 1996, complaining about the costs and the difficulty of the golf courses, Faxon ripped them. "Anyone who is exempt and doesn't come over here to play shouldn't be allowed to be on the Ryder Cup or Presidents Cup team," Faxon said. He went on to directly criticize Scott Hoch, who not only was exempt and hadn't gone over to play but had criticized the event in general and the Old Course at St. Andrews specifically. The comments cost him $500, because the PGA Tour doesn't like members publicly criticizing other members (regardless of what the constitution says about free speech), and earned him the enmity of Hoch.

A quick perusal of Faxon's bio in the tour's media guide told you a lot about him. Under "special interests," Faxon wrote: "all sports, except hunting and fishing." Since about 90 percent of his fellow pros would list hunting and/or fishing as their special interests, Faxon was clearly sending a message.

If not liking hunting and fishing made Faxon a nonconformist in his chosen world, it certainly didn't make him an outcast. Faxon was that rare person who could be different, be proud of being different, and still engender respect.

The first half of 1997 had been one of the best periods of his life. He was playing the best golf of his career, riding a lengthy hot streak that had started at the 1995 PGA when he had shot a 63 on the last day to move up to fifth place for the championship. That was nice, but what was important was that the fifth place finish put him on the Ryder Cup team for the first time. "In some ways that round was more satisfying than the days when I've won tournaments," he said. "I went out there knowing I had to shoot a great round to have any chance to make the team and I did it. It was a wonderful feeling."

He finished second four times in 1996, which was aggravating, but he had such a consistent year — he didn't miss a single cut — that he made more than $1 million and finished eighth on the money list. Then, the following April, the week before the Masters he won at New Orleans, ending what had been an almost five-year victory drought. He was so hot at that point that some people picked him as one of the favorites to win the Masters. Naturally he missed the cut — the first time he had ever failed to play the weekend at Augusta. He came right back to finish second the next two weeks and was over the million-dollar mark in earnings before the year was half over.

That's when his life came crashing down around him. He had just returned from the British Open, where a 67 on the last day had vaulted him to a twentieth place finish, and was playing at the Greater Hartford Open, a week he enjoyed because it was close to his home in Barrington, Rhode Island. It was a chance to play in front of friends and family, and Faxon looked forward to it. This time, though, it was different. He came home from Hartford on Sunday night. That was when Bonnie told him she wanted a divorce.

As with any marriage that goes bad, there had been warning signs and tension before the actual split. Most of the problems with the Faxons could be traced to the lifestyle a professional golfer must live. Two weeks a year — Hartford and the CVS Classic in Sutton, Massachusetts — the tour came to Faxon or at least close by. The rest of the time, Faxon had to go to the tour. Travel is a fact of life for all professional athletes, but it is often more difficult for golfers because they tend to peak later and can keep making a good living while their children are growing up. Faxon turned thirty-six the week after Bonnie delivered the news that she wanted out of the marriage. Most athletes are contemplating retirement or already retired at thirty-six. Faxon was playing the best golf of his life and believed the best was yet to come.

"I remember saying to Bonnie once that I understood that it was tough for her with the kids when I was on the road," Faxon said, his voice filled with sadness one afternoon the following winter. "But if I gave up golf, came home, and found some kind of job that kept me off the road, then I really wouldn't be me anymore, would I? It isn't that you don't love your family or want to be with them, but when you do this for a living it becomes a part of who you are and what you are. I think if I had given it up, we would have both been terribly unhappy in the long run."

The separation devastated Faxon. His parents had divorced when he was nine and he remembered how awful that had been. His younger sister had been about the same age as his middle daughter, Emily, was at the time, and the split had been very difficult for her. "It affected me a great deal, but I was two years older than my sister," he said. "I think it was much worse for her."

Faxon knew that the divorce would inevitably bring sadness into the life of his children and he hated that. He also knew that he would have to deal with the divorce publicly because he was a public figure. Again, he was more concerned about how Melanie and Emily, who were old enough to understand what was happening, would deal with that since they were bound to hear about it at school.

He had been looking forward to playing on the Ryder Cup team again, but he knew that even that would now be an ordeal because he would have to answer questions about his private life. Colin Montgomerie unintentionally made matters worse when, in analyzing the American team, he said, "Brad Faxon's going through a divorce. You can't possibly expect him to play well."

Months later, Faxon could laugh — sort of — about the comment. "That was just Colin being honest," he said. "What he said was true. I just wish he hadn't said it."

The rest of the year was difficult. Faxon spent a lot more time with lawyers than with his golf clubs. Eventually an agreement was hammered out under which Bonnie Faxon agreed to continue living in Bristol County so that the children would be near their father. They would stay with her when Brad was away making his living and with Brad when he was home. In return, Bonnie received 50 percent of Brad's assets — a little more than $2 million when all was said and done. Some of Faxon's friends had urged him to fight Bonnie harder on the financial terms but he had decided against that for two reasons: his priority was keeping the kids close to him and he didn't want the divorce to get ugly because he knew what that would do to the kids.

The final papers had been signed on February 23, the week before the tour moved from the west coast to Florida. Not surprisingly, Faxon had played miserably on the west coast and he hoped that signing the papers — even though the divorce wouldn't be final for another ninety days — would bring some measure of closure to what had been an awful six months. Realistically, though, he knew absolute closure was out of the question.

"This is going to go on for the rest of my life," he said. "Bonnie is still the mother of my children. We still have to deal with one another. Fortunately, we can talk to one another civilly. That isn't a problem. But everything is going to be different from now on, for me, for the girls. It has to be."

He and Bonnie were civil, but that didn't mean things were easy or simple. One morning Faxon called home before he went out to play and Bonnie wouldn't let him talk to the girls. They had been up too late the night before, she said. She went on to say that it was Brad's fault they had been up too late because the week before when he had them he had let them stay up later than normal. She was right. They had been off from school, so he had let them stay up a little later. An argument about the difference between school nights and non-school nights had followed, and Faxon had gone out to play with golf about the farthest thing from his mind.

"That will get better with time, I know that," he said. "We'll all make adjustments. I'll get used to being mother and father when I'm home and to worrying about some of the things Bonnie used to take care of. That's all fine. But any notion that this is somehow something that you put behind you is just silly. You don't."

Masters week had always been something Faxon looked forward to. This year was no different, although the cast of characters would be different. A couple of high school friends who had become newfound bachelor buddies were coming down, as were some old friends. Every year Faxon tried to bring people to the Masters who had never been before. This year he was bringing Steve Ruggerio and Paul Schwab down for the first time. Ruggerio was, by his own description, the biggest Jack Nicklaus fan in history. Schwab was, according to Schwab, the biggest Arnold Palmer fan in history. Ruggerio was so fanatic that during big tournaments he would often call the press room every fifteen minutes if the event wasn't on television to get updates on Nicklaus. Schwab's nickname at his golf club was "King," in honor of Palmer.

Faxon had scheduled what he thought would be his friends' dream practice round for Wednesday. He and his best friend on tour, fellow Rhode Islander Billy Andrade, were going to play a practice round with Palmer and Nicklaus. The day turned out even better than Faxon could have imagined. Schwab left the house at 6:30 because he wanted to be sure to be in the parking lot when Palmer arrived, which wouldn't be until 9:30. When Palmer got there he had his personal assistant, Doc Giffin, and his longtime friend and dentist, Howdy Giles, with him. Schwab — naturally — recognized Giffin and Giles and introduced himself to them. Both were impressed that he knew exactly who they were. He explained he was down for the week with Brad Faxon. Friendships were quickly formed.

Later, Faxon let Ruggerio drive his courtesy car — the tournament gives each player a Cadillac to use during the week — down Magnolia Lane. As if that wasn't enough, he got Nicklaus to give him one of his golf balls with the famous "Jack" imprint on them. When Faxon handed the ball to Ruggerio, his friend said, "Do you realize I'm going to have to go out and spend $3,000 to get this thing mounted?"

To top the day off, when the round was over, Giles and Giffin not only introduced their new friend Schwab to the King but Giles took a picture of Schwab with his hero. "It was the greatest day of their lives," Faxon said, laughing. "I can't remember the last time I had so much fun."

Faxon was having so much fun he almost forgot about his troubles at home for a few hours. He was starting to feel more confident about his game, having played better in Florida than he had on the west coast. Like a lot of players, he came to Augusta with two goals in mind. The first, naturally, was to win the tournament. But if that didn't happen, the next best thing was to finish in the top twenty-four because that would ensure a return trip the next year without having to sweat out making the top thirty on the money list or winning a tournament or making the top sixteen at the U.S. Open or the top eight at the PGA. Those were the other routes back to Augusta for those who hadn't won the tournament.

Fred Couples had talked after the first round about the luxury of having won the tournament because it meant a player had a lifetime exemption. "We all want to be able to come back here year after year," he said. "Because I won here, I don't ever have to worry about that again. I really think that helps me because I can come here and go for broke. To me, there's no difference between second and fiftieth because I'm coming back here forever no matter what. But to guys who haven't won, making the top twenty-four is bound to be in the back of their mind."

This was Faxon's seventh straight Masters. He felt very comfortable with the golf course, knowing he was a good enough putter to handle the greens and that the wide open fairways made his occasionally wild driver less of a problem than at the U.S. Open, where any wayward drive almost guaranteed a bogey. "I always feel prepared when I get here because the week or two before the tournament I sit around and visualize the golf course," he said. "I know it that well now that I can do that. I picture shots and putts and pin positions, and by the time I get here I feel I'm really ready to play. Every year, I feel like my chances to win here get better. Winning is the ideal. But until I win I want to make sure I get back here every year. I can't imagine not being here. It would kill me."

Faxon had gotten off to a reasonable start on Thursday, shooting 73. Friday nerves at Augusta are different than Thursday nerves. On Thursday everyone has a nervous stomach because it is the first day of a major. On Friday, everyone — even the leaders — has the cut on their mind when they step onto the first tee. It is not out of the question for one (or more) of Thursday's leaders to be slamming their trunk and heading for home on Friday. Augusta is a golf course with little margin for error, and wild scoring swings — in both directions — are a part of the tournament's lore.

In 1985, Curtis Strange shot 80 on Thursday and then came back with a pair of 65s to take the lead. He was still leading the tournament on Sunday afternoon when he put balls in the water on both 13 and 15, opening the door for Bernhard Langer. The flip side of that story was Mike Donald. Playing in his first Masters in 1990, Donald shot an amazing 64 on Thursday. Twenty-four hours later on the same golf course he shot 80.

This year was no different. Once again the golf course was windy and cold right from the start. By the time the ten players who hadn't finished on Thursday got through the last few holes and the golf course crew got finished with its work, the second round didn't begin until the same time the first round had started: 9:30. To avoid another losing battle with darkness, tournament officials decided to send everyone off in threesomes, the first time in fifteen years that radical step had been taken.

Because of the threesomes and because the windy conditions forced everyone to take longer than normal selecting clubs, play slowed to a near halt by the middle of the day. The pace was so slow that players found themselves waiting on the second tee since almost everyone waits in the fairway there to play their second shot to the reachable green. "You get backed up on the second tee and you know it's going to be a very long day," said Fred Couples, whose group didn't make it to the 18th green until 7:30 after teeing off at 2:20. "It was definitely a day that tested your patience."

One person who felt none of that was Kenny Bakst. He had shot an aggravating 82 on Thursday, aggravating because he had hit the ball well enough to score much better but hadn't been able to make any putts. He even incurred a penalty shot on the 17th green when the wind moved his ball after he had addressed it.

Bakst was paired on Friday with 1973 champion Tommy Aaron and Italy's Costantino Rocca, who had enjoyed the dubious honor of being paired with Woods on the final day a year earlier, meaning he would someday be the answer to the trivia question Who was playing with Tiger Woods on the day he broke the Masters scoring record?

All day long, Bakst worked to shoot the best score he possibly could. His dream of making the cut had essentially gone out the window on Thursday, and any possibility of a Strange-like turnaround disappeared when he shot 39 on the front nine. But Bakst never stopped smiling. He understood where he was and what he was doing and how much this week would mean to him long after it was over.

He and Aaron and Rocca were the third group of the day to reach the 18th tee. The first four players had been sent out in twosomes since 88 divided by three equals 29 and ⅓ and you can't divide a golfer up three ways — even at Augusta. But the two twosomes had become a twosome and a onesome when Doug Ford, who had talked about withdrawing after shooting 86 on opening day, made good on his threat after 27 holes, saying he had sprained an ankle. It had taken him 46 shots to complete nine holes and rather than limp home — literally and figuratively — with another score in the 90s, he headed for the clubhouse. It was the sixth time he had withdrawn without finishing two rounds. Would he be back in 1999 for his forty-seventh Masters? Absolutely, he said.

Bakst had three-putted the 17th green by knocking his first putt off the green, but he was grinning broadly as he walked onto the 18th tee. "I guess I had to do that once to see what it felt like," he said. He hit his last Masters tee shot, then spotted his son Jonathan walking outside the ropes. "JB, come here," he said, calling him by his nickname. He reached under the rope, picked Jonathan up, and walked down the fairway carrying him in his arms. No doubt some rule of the Masters was broken, but no one cared. Here was a father who would someday remind his son about the afternoon he carried him down the 18th fairway at Augusta National during the second round of the Masters.

Bakst finished his week by holing a 15-foot par putt. He threw his arms in the air in triumph as the 18th hole gallery gave him a rousing ovation. It was the longest putt he had made in two days. His 82–78 would leave him ten shots outside the cut. It hardly mattered. No one walked off the 18th green all week with a bigger smile on his face than Kenny Bakst.

At the same moment that Bakst was walking onto the 18th green drinking in everything he could see and hear, three men walked to the first tee with their faces blank, looking for all the world as if they had been condemned to five hours in purgatory.

No doubt that was exactly the way Tiger Woods, Fuzzy Zoeller, and Colin Montgomerie felt. Scott Hoch, who often said what others were thinking but wouldn't dare say, had set the tone on the putting green. "What's it going to be," he asked, "pistols at ten paces?"

Everyone shook hands on the first tee and off they went, followed by a huge gallery and most of the media horde. To make matters worse, the pace of play was so slow that they had to wait on almost every hole. During those waits, each player chatted with his caddy or stared into space. The usual chitchat between golfers killing time was nowhere to be found.

Zoeller did break out of his funk once. On the seventh hole, after he and Woods had both hit excellent approach shots and heard no applause as they were walking up the fairway, Zoeller walked onto the green, looked at how close the two shots were, and muttered, "Are these people handcuffed?" Woods cracked up. Augusta's galleries are notorious for being tough to please. This was a perfect example.

That was the lightest moment of the day. All three players struggled. Woods managed a 72, which left him four shots off the lead; Zoeller shot 74 and Montgomerie 75. None of them was in a mood to talk much when the round was over. Zoeller stopped to talk behind the 18th green very briefly. "It was no big deal, so don't make a big deal out of it," he said. "He [Woods] is a person like everybody else. It was a gentlemen's round."

But his true feelings about the entire affair seeped through a moment later when he cut off questions and started walking toward the clubhouse. "Excuse me, boys," he said as he began walking. "Oops. I'm sorry. I guess it's not politically correct to say 'boys.' I apologize."

Woods also insisted the whole thing was no big deal, that it was all a media creation, and that he and Zoeller got along just fine.

Of course they did. In much the same way that the losing presidential candidate pledges his complete support to the winner on election night.

As always, some of Thursday's heroes became Friday's victims. Gay Brewer's sixty-six-year-old body simply couldn't handle the windswept course a second straight day. His tee shots kept getting shorter and shorter, his shots to the greens longer and longer. By the time he was done, he had shot 86 and looked every minute of his age. Olin Browne's journal, which had been so full of pep and vigor on Friday morning, came to a skidding halt on Saturday morning after he began his round with a quadruple-bogey eight at the first hole and went on to shoot 80, missing the cut by two shots. In sixty-two years, no one had ever made an eight at the first hole during the Masters. At 10:20 in the morning, Scott Simpson became the first man in tournament history to do it. Three and a half hours later, Browne became the second.

Three-time champion Nick Faldo didn't do much better than Browne, shooting 79 after an opening 72. He would have made the cut if he hadn't missed an 18-inch putt on the final hole. The only good news for Faldo was that he didn't have to hang around until Sunday to present the green jacket as the defending champion the way he had to in 1997 after missing the cut. Paul Stankowski, who had been in second place after an opening 70, shot exactly 10 shots higher on Friday and made the cut right on the number.

As always, a number of big names missed the cut. Tom Watson, who had once made twenty-one straight Masters cuts before missing by one shot in 1996, missed by one for the second time in three years, shooting 73–78, dooming himself with a double-bogey seven at the 15th hole. A host of past champions missed the cut: Raymond Floyd, Sandy Lyle, Larry Mize, Ben Crenshaw, Seve Ballesteros, and the seniors Arnold Palmer, Tommy Aaron, Billy Casper, Charles Coody, and Brewer. The last four weren't surprising. What was surprising was Tom Lehman, one of the most consistent Masters performers of the '90s, shooting 80–76, and Nick Price shooting 76–75.

Greg Norman, the man most tormented by the Masters, quietly shot 78–76, patiently answered questions under the tree, saying he hadn't played all that badly, and then headed off to have shoulder surgery. He would be gone from the game for eight months.

Two of the grand old men of the game did make it to the weekend: three-time champion Gary Player shot 77–72, and at sixty-two became the oldest player in Masters history to make the cut; and Jack Nicklaus made the cut for the thirty-sixth time in forty years with a solid 73–72 for 145. Two amateurs also survived: Joel Kribel at 149 and the effervescent Kuchar, who rebounded from a 40 on the front nine on Friday to shoot 36 on the back nine. That gave him 72–76 for 148 and a spot in the weekend lineup.

Jim Furyk also made the cut. In fact, he made it easily, shooting 33 on the back nine for a 70 that, along with his opening 76, put him a comfortable four shots inside the number. It also left him seven shots behind the two leaders, Fred Couples and David Duval. When he walked off the 18th green Friday afternoon, Furyk wasn't thinking about the leaders. He was just thankful that he had gotten his act together before the tournament had become a complete disaster. "On the ninth tee all I was thinking about was trying to make the cut," he said. "Now I can go out tomorrow and see if I can make a move."

Three hours earlier, Furyk had been sitting on his golf bag on the ninth tee fuming. He was six over par for the tournament. What's more, he had been warned twice for slow play, meaning he was one warning away from a one-shot penalty. Given the pace of play and given the fact that his group was now sitting and waiting for the group in front to clear the fairway, Furyk wasn't at all happy with being singled out.

"We did get behind," he said. "And I know the rules at Augusta are different than on tour but I never dreamed I would get two bad times, especially when we had caught up by number eight. At least I thought we had caught up."

According to rules official Mike Shea, who had been monitoring the group of Furyk, Billy Mayfair, and Darren Clarke, they had not yet caught up. And so, when Furyk took more than fifty seconds to play his third shot to the eighth green because he was uncertain what club to play in the swirling winds, he had gotten his second warning.

A month shy of turning twenty-eight, Furyk had emerged as one of the tour's most consistent players. In 1997 he had set a tour record by making $1,619,000 without winning a tournament. It was not a record that thrilled him. He was pleased with thirteen top-ten finishes and with finishes of T-5 (tied for fifth), fourth, and T-6 in the U.S. Open, the British Open, and the PGA. He was thrilled to make the Ryder Cup team. But what he really wanted to do was win again. He had won twice on tour, in Las Vegas in 1995 and in Hawaii in 1996. Making a lot of money and being consistent were very nice. But winning was nicer.

That Furyk had become as good a player as he was would have shocked anyone who had taken a look at his swing. It was a swing teacher's nightmare, full of loops and swirls. It looked almost like something a trick shot artist might try. But it worked. He had worked with only one teacher in his life — his dad — and Mike Furyk had never once attempted to change his son's swing. It was the way he swung the club naturally, and he was able to repeat it over and over and make consistent contact. That was what mattered in a golf swing, not aesthetics.

Mike Furyk had learned the game in college, often sneaking out to play because his father, who had worked in a western Pennsylvania steel mill all his life, disdainfully described golf as a doctor's game. Mike Furyk became very good very quickly, but he didn't want his dad to know he played. One day, he met up with a group and impressed them with his play. At the end of the round they asked him his name. When he told them, they looked at him and said, "Are you Mike Furyk's boy?"

They were friends of his dad's from the steel mill. Mike begged them not to tell his dad they had played golf with him. "Leave it to us," they said. They explained to Mike Furyk Sr. that not only was golf a game for those who didn't practice medicine, but that his son had a knack for it. If it was okay with his buddies from the mill, it was okay with Mike Furyk. From that day on, Mike Jr. could play all the golf he wanted.

Jim's father was good enough to become a club pro but gave it up to become a sales rep for a golf company when Jim was a little boy. That kept him on the road at times, but when he was off the road he had more time to spend with his only child. Jim began going to the golf course with his father when he was very young. His main interest was in his father's golf cart, which he loved to put into reverse whenever his dad got out to hit a shot. "Dad liked to play fast," Jim remembered. "He would hit, jump back in the cart, and hit the gas. He backed into trees, water fountains, you name it. He never got mad though. He just said if he was dumb enough not to check on me, then whatever he got, he deserved."

Even if cart sabotage was what seemed to interest Jim most, Mike Furyk wanted to be sure his son didn't become a golf course junkie. He ordered him off the golf course until he was twelve. "If you still want to play then, you can," he said. "In the meantime, play other sports."

Jim did play other sports but he couldn't wait for his twelfth birthday to return to golf. During that summer, he and a friend played every day for two months at a local public course. Jim started the summer shooting in the 120s and ended it breaking 90 consistently. A year later, he was breaking 80. And the following summer he began to dominate junior tournaments in the Lancaster area. He had signed up to play football that fall but decided to focus on golf after his success that summer. Through high school, he was one of the top junior players in the east. Arizona was his college of choice, and after a solid college career he took his funny-looking swing and went off to find fame and fortune as a golfer.

He got through the first two stages of Q-School in 1992, but like a lot of players he wasn't prepared for his first trip to the finals. He played poorly, missing the 72-hole cut, which left him as a partially exempt player on the Nike Tour in 1993. The first six months of the next year were difficult. Since he wasn't fully exempt, he got into only five of the first ten tournaments. He managed to play well enough in those five events that he moved up high enough on the reshuffle (which occurs for the partially exempt players after ten events) that he was playing every week.

But Murphy's Law seemed to be dogging him. In Connecticut, he got off to a great start in the first round and was two under par at the turn. But he pulled the wrong ball out of his bag — a Titleist ball that was legal, but didn't have a legal stamp on it — and when he noticed he had to call four strokes in penalties on himself. This is one of the more obscure rules on tour but one that crops up every so often. In fact, it got Greg Norman disqualified at Hartford in 1996 when he was leading the tournament. Titleist had changed the official name of the ball Furyk was playing. Furyk still had some of the balls with the old name in his bag. Even though the balls were exactly the same as the ones with the new name on them, the balls with the old name technically no longer existed and thus were illegal.

Furyk actually made two birdies after the four-stroke penalty to get back to even par by the time he reached the 18th tee. Since no one knew he had been penalized, the scoreboard near the 18th showed him leading the tournament at four under par. "I stood there looking at that board and wanted to cry," he said.

A few weeks later, in Missouri, Furyk managed to get through a first round with no penalties and no bogies, shooting 66 to lead the tournament. He was staying that week with a friend near the golf course and they went out that afternoon to shoot a few baskets on his backyard court. "Nothing serious, we weren't that dumb," Furyk said. "Just shooting around."

That was enough. Furyk went up for a layup and somehow came down wrong and rolled his right ankle. All the ice in the world couldn't get the swelling down by the next morning, and Furyk hobbled around the course with an untied sneaker on the foot. He was in agony. At one point he hit a shot down a hill near a hazard and had to literally crawl down the hill to hit the shot. He missed the cut by a shot. "Which was probably a lucky break," he said. "If I had played the weekend, I would have finished dead last and made three hundred bucks and been in absolute pain every step I took."

By mid-July Furyk was buried deep on the money list and fairly convinced he was heading for a lost year. It seemed as if every time his game started to come together something crazy knocked him backward. The Nike Tour had moved into its too-hot-to-live stage, and Gulfport, Mississippi, was the tournament site for the week. "It really never got much hotter than four hundred degrees," Furyk remembered.

He made it through three days in the oven in fourth place, easily his best performance of the year. He began the last day hoping to play well enough to move up to second since Bob Friend was leading the field by five shots and Furyk by six. With three holes to play, he was still four back of Friend and had moved into a tie for second. Then he finished birdie, birdie, birdie, watched Friend make a bogey coming in, and suddenly he was in a playoff. He made his fourth straight birdie on the first playoff hole, and in the blink of an eye he had gone from nowhere to having won a tournament.

That meant a $27,000 payday after he had made less than $10,000 the first half of the year. It also gave him fully exempt status on the Nike

Tour through the following year and a giant confidence boost. "It was amazing the way it happened," he said. "Winning never really occurred to me until I made the three birdies at the very end."

As soon as the awards ceremony was over, Furyk raced into the clubhouse to get out of the heat and call his parents. His dad answered the phone. "How'd you do?" he asked when he heard his son's voice.

Furyk opened his mouth, intending to say, "Dad, I won!" but nothing came out. He was completely choked up. "I'm not someone who shows a lot of emotion on the course," he said. "But sometimes when I'm done and I think about what's happened, I'll get very emotional. At that moment, thinking about all the time Dad and I had spent together on the golf course and what this meant to me and, I knew, to him, I just kind of lost it."

After a few seconds of stumbling around, Furyk finally got the words out, leaving his father stunned and speechless on the other end of the phone. Furyk has since won on the PGA Tour and may someday win a major title, but it is probably fair to say that no victory will ever bring more gratification than the one in Gulfport, Mississippi.

The victory catapulted Furyk into the top twenty-five on the Nike Tour money list and gave him an outside shot to make the top ten for the year, which would have given him an automatic spot on the PGA Tour in 1994. He didn't play poorly coming down the stretch, but he ended up twenty-sixth for the year. What was aggravating was going into the Tour Championship in twenty-fourth place and coming out in twenty-sixth in spite of finishing tenth. David Duval won the tournament and Danny Briggs finished second. Both had been behind Furyk on the money list. When they leap-frogged him, he dropped out of the top twenty-five, which meant he had to go back to the second stage of Q-School instead of straight into the finals.

Undaunted, Furyk got through the second stage to reach the finals, which were held that year at PGA West in Palm Springs. This time his approach to the finals was different. He already had full-fledged status on the Nike Tour for 1994, so it was all or nothing — make the top forty and move up, or go back to the Nike. "I already had my fallback position in place," he said. "There was nothing to protect."

That was the year when everyone in the field miscalculated the 72-hole cut, thinking it would be one under par when it turned out to be

Mark O'Meara. From the King of the
B's to the top of the golf world—all in
fifteen weeks. (© *Golf Magazine*/Fred Vuich)

Fred Couples. One of his best years on the course; his best ever off the course. (© *Golf Magazine*/Fred Vuich)

Jim Furyk. Mr. Consistency.
A couple of putts away twice in 1998.

(© *Golf Magazine*/Sam Greenwood)

David Duval. Dealing with uncommon burdens with uncommon grace.

(© *Golf Magazine*/Sam Greenwood)

Lee Janzen. The Terminator—
especially when a U.S. Open is at
stake. (©*Golf Magazine*/Fred Vuich)

Payne Stewart. He lost the Open but
won newfound respect in defeat.
(© *Golf Magazine*/Fred Vuich)

Phil Mickelson. The man who has
everything—except a major.

(© *Golf Magazine*/Sam Greenwood)

Justin Leonard. He never did learn
to speak Spanish, but his putter did
plenty of talking anyway. (© *Golf Magazine/*
Fred Vuich)

two under. Furyk almost casually made a 10-foot par putt on the 72nd hole to finish at two under and didn't even realize how close he had come to missing the cut until he checked the pairings for the next day and noticed that the one-unders weren't playing. He shot 69 the next day to move into serious contention to make the top forty and then came back with 71 on the last day.

"Everyone thought the number was going to be six [under]," he said. "I was right at six playing my last two holes, both with water in play. I was really careful, kept the water out of play, and just missed a thirty-five-footer for birdie at the last hole. I mean it wrapped all the way around the cup and stayed out. I tapped in and thought, okay, you did well. Then I had this awful thought: What if we all miscalculated *again?* What if the number goes to seven? What if that one inch is the difference between being on the tour and not on the tour?"

Everyone who has ever been to Q-School has had moments like that. Fortunately for Furyk, the notion that six would be the number proved correct. He stood in front of the scoreboard throughout the afternoon and watched the scores come in. When he realized that six was safely in — he finished in a nine-way tie for thirty-seventh place — he was so drained and so exhausted that the thought of celebrating never crossed his mind. "I was planning to drive back to Tucson that night," he said. "But I was so tired I went back to my hotel, checked back in, and went to sleep."

Furyk took his parents with him to Hawaii the following January for his first tournament as a full-fledged PGA Tour member. His dad caddied for him, although the two of them almost didn't make it to the first tee. "I went out to the range to warm up the first day and it was very cold and windy," Furyk said, smiling at the memory. "I mean it was really gusting, and there was nothing but dirt on the range, almost no grass. I took out my wedge to get loose, and I was probably a little nervous given the circumstances. I took a nice easy swing and chunked the shot completely. Dirt went flying everywhere and absolutely covered the guy next to me."

Sheepishly, Furyk looked at the guy and said, "Sorry about that."

The guy turned around. It was Lanny Wadkins, the newly named Ryder Cup captain. This side of Raymond Floyd, Wadkins probably has as mean a stare as anyone on tour when he is in the wrong mood. When Furyk saw who it was he had just buried in dirt, he almost burst out laughing from nerves and embarrassment. Fortunately, Wadkins just shrugged it off and returned to his work.

"So I lined up another wedge, took another easy swing, and chunked it *again*."

The dirt flew and Wadkins had so much black on him he could have passed for Gary Player. Furyk didn't know whether to laugh or cry. "Gee, I'm sorry," he said. "Maybe I'll aim a little more in the other direction."

Wadkins just nodded. "That," he said, "would be a nice idea."

"He was probably thinking, who let this rookie out here?" Furyk said. "But he controlled himself."

Lucky for Furyk it was the first day of the first tournament of the year and Wadkins hadn't made his first bogey yet.

Still fighting his nerves — and no doubt wondering when Wadkins was going to pounce on him from behind a tree — Furyk missed the cut in Hawaii. That brought the tour to Tucson, the place where he had gone to college for four and a half years (he went back to graduate after turning pro), meaning Furyk was playing two golf courses he knew in front of a friendly crowd. After one day he was tied for the lead. After two days he was tied for the lead. After three days he was tied for the lead. Finally, on Sunday he faded, but not badly, shooting a 70 to finish tied for seventh.

Because he had been near the lead for most of the weekend, he was all over television — local kid makes good with funky swing — and when he got to Phoenix a week later it seemed as if everyone knew who he was. "I was on the range one day and I turned around and there were about fifty people behind me watching and there was no one else near me hitting balls," he said. "I guess a lot of them came out to see the swing after seeing me on TV the week before. I sat down on my bag and thought, boy, this is a little different."

The Swing and solid play made Furyk, if not a household name, someone who people knew during that first year on tour. The Swing and his willingness to poke fun at himself helped get him a Callaway deal and several commercials with Johnny Miller, Callaway's number one spokesman.

The year couldn't have turned out much better. In May, he was signing autographs behind the 18th green at the Memorial Tournament when he noticed a very pretty blonde watching him. "At least I hoped she was watching me," he said.

She was. Tabitha Skartved was a teacher in Columbus and she was impressed with the way the rookie pro handled himself with kids. He was patient and seemed to enjoy himself as opposed to other players who acted as if signing autographs was a burden. Furyk, who is shy by nature, decided to take a chance on introducing himself. They chatted for a while, he asked her out, and a relationship was born. Four years later, it was still going strong.

Furyk went from seventy-eighth on the money list his first year to thirty-third the next year, capping his season with an October victory in Las Vegas. Then he beat Brad Faxon in a playoff the following January in Hawaii and went on from there to finish twenty-sixth on the money list. That had set up 1997, when he emerged as perhaps the most consistent player on the tour even though he didn't win again. Furyk was convinced he would win again soon, although he had come to Augusta for the third time still not sure if he had the game to be truly competitive on the golf course. Proving just how consistent he was, he had finished T-29 in his first Masters and T-29 in his second. He was hoping to break out of that mold in his third.

For 27 holes it looked as if he would do just that — but in the wrong direction. He had ruined his Thursday round with mistakes on back-to-back holes that had led to double bogeys at the 11th and 12th. When he finally holed out on 18, he had shot 76 — even par on 16 holes but four over par on 11 and 12 — and he was tired and frustrated. As he handed his putter to caddy Steve DuPlantis, he shook his head and said, "I waited all year to play this round and all I get is this."

He wasn't feeling any better sitting on the ninth tee Friday, already two over par for the day and teetering on the brink of a penalty shot for delays. But the holdup on nine turned out to be a blessing. Furyk was able to calm himself down and he almost holed his second shot at the ninth. He birdied there, then made three more birdies without a bogey coming in. He was seven shots behind Fred Couples and David Duval, the coleaders at five-under-par 139. With 36 holes to play, he was back in the ballgame.

Most of the forty-six players who had made the cut still believed they had a chance. The course record at Augusta of 63, held by Nick Price, had been shot on a Saturday in 1986. Under the right conditions, the golf course often yielded scores of 64 and 65. Gary Player had closed with a 64 to win in 1978, and Jack Nicklaus's sixth and most famous victory in 1986 had come after a 65 on Sunday.

The leader board was full of intriguing names when Friday's final threesome — Couples, José María Olazabal, and Paul Stankowski — reached the clubhouse just before dusk. Scott Hoch, who had missed the most famous two-foot putt in Masters history in 1989 to open the door for Nick Faldo, was two shots back of Couples and Duval. "Do I feel this tournament owes me one?" Hoch asked in response to a question. "No. Do I think about that putt sometimes? Yes. Especially when I'm here."

Two shots back of Hoch was a fivesome who all had stories to tell: Woods, the man with all eyes on him, who was clearly fighting his game but hanging near the leaders; 1994 champion Olazabal, who had come back from back problems that had almost ended his career to again be a factor in the game; 1993 PGA champion Paul Azinger, who had beaten cancer but was still struggling to get back to anywhere near the level he had been before his illness ("When was the last time I contended?" he said. "Heck, I don't think I could have contended for my club championship the last couple of years); Phil Mickelson, who, with twelve PGA Tour victories at the age of twenty-seven, was the consensus choice as the current BPNTHWAM; and last, but certainly not least, was Jay Haas, who probably would be the consensus choice among his fellow pros as the NPNTHWAM (Nicest Player Never To Have Won A Major).

One shot further back was another player who hadn't won a (professional) major. Mark O'Meara had shot 70 on Friday. He had made some putts. He was still virtually unnoticed when he left the grounds Friday afternoon, but the smile was back. His wife, Alicia, and their two children had flown into town that day. O'Meara had a feeling it might be a fun weekend.

10

Moving Day at Augusta

The weather changed again on Saturday morning. The swirling winds of Thursday and Friday had become comfortable breezes. The chill in the morning air was gone. By the time the day's first twosome, Corey Pavin and Paul Stankowski, walked onto the first tee at 10:30 A.M., there was no need to wear a sweater. The golf course, which had played to a stroke average of 73.345 the first two days, would be much more playable for the third round. The chance to "go low" would be there. Moving Day — tour terminology for Saturday — could be just that: a day when almost anyone in the field could move into contention.

Saturday wasn't just a big day for the players, it was also a big day for CBS. During the first two days of the tournament, all of their personnel had worked the telecasts that appeared on the USA Cable Network. In one sense, being on USA was no different from being on CBS in that a glitch or a failure to produce pictures and words that met the demands of the Lords of Augusta would be disastrous. Even so, everyone at the network knew the weekend was the real deal; Thursday and Friday were the warmup act.

And that meant nerves were a little bit frayed.

CBS had televised every Masters since 1956. In its lengthy P.R. handout the network proudly referred to the Masters/CBS relationship as "the longest sports marriage in network history." There was no question that the people who wore the green jackets also wore the pants in this relationship.

From 1958 through 1996 the CBS telecasts had been ruled by the iron hand of Frank Chirkinian, the man who proudly answered to the nickname "Ayatollah." Chirkinian had been in charge of golf at CBS for so long there were those who thought that he had directed it on CBS radio before cameras had come along. After being the constant on every Masters telecast for thirty-eight years, Chirkinian had retired at the end of 1996 at age seventy and been replaced by his longtime associate producer, Lance Barrow.

Barrow was forty-four, a stocky Texan who absolutely loved golf and golfers. For years he had been dragged kicking and screaming to do two weeks of tennis a year when the network televised the U.S. Open. He didn't mind doing football (after all, he was from Texas) but if he had his druthers, Lance Barrow would produce golf fifty-two weeks a year. His best friend was Davis Love III and he was close to many of the players he had worked with during eighteen years covering the tour. He was a proud member of Royal Troon, a 14-handicapper who would gladly eat, drink, talk, play, and watch golf every day of every week of every month of every year.

In a sense, no one was better prepared to produce a Masters telecast than Barrow. He had watched Chirkinian up close for years and understood the aesthetics the telecast needed, the importance of letting the pictures do most of the talking. No one, including the Ayatollah, who was on hand spending a lot of time on the veranda, doubted Barrow's ability to make the telecast work.

He had made a seamless transition from the number two chair to the number one chair in 1997, but in a sense, that had been a slam dunk. There was one story to follow on the weekend: Tiger Woods. The network got a record 14.1 rating on Sunday — 44 million viewers — and about all Barrow had to do was keep Woods on camera to have a successful telecast.

This year would be a different test. Woods was still part of the story, but the story had about a dozen moving parts to it on Saturday morning. And perhaps more to come. All the CBS people knew that the pressure of Masters weekend was as real for them as it was for the players. A one-year contract will do that to you, especially when that one-year contract is for an event your network has televised for forty-three straight years and is, arguably, the most important sports property you own. It may explain why CBS Sports president Sean McManus said nothing on Saturday when the man in charge of the upstairs seating in the clubhouse practically accused him and two friends of loitering during lunch. McManus and friends had barely taken a sip of their coffee when the man appeared demanding the table for another party. McManus would have been perfectly justified if he had told the man to buzz off. Instead, he nodded and said they would finish up as quickly as they could.

All of McManus and Barrow's announcers had memorized the Do's and Do Not's of a Masters telecast. It was a lengthy list that included:

- Do Not refer to the gallery or to fans. Do refer to patrons.
- Do Not refer to the front nine or the back nine. Do refer to the first nine and the second nine.
- Do Not under any circumstances hint, imply, or infer that these great players are competing for prize money. Do bring up as often as possible how important the principles of amateurism are to the Masters as exemplified by Bob Jones.
- Do Not *ever* refer to Bob Jones as Jones or Cliff Roberts as Roberts. Do call them by their full names or Mr. Jones and Mr. Roberts.
- Do Not bring up the blue dye in Rae's Creek or the notion that anything artificial has ever been done to the aesthetics of Augusta National.
- Do Not refer to any of the buildings named for President Eisenhower or Bob Jones or anyone else as cottages. Do call them cabins.

And the penalty for violating these rules? Everyone at CBS knew the answer to that too: a McCord/Whitaker scholarship. Jack Whitaker had been banned from CBS telecasts of the Masters after his 1966 reference to the "patrons" around the 18th green as "a mob." Gary McCord had joined Whitaker in purgatory following the 1994 tournament when he had jokingly said that the greens were so slick they looked "bikini-waxed" and had later referred to the fact that the area behind the 17th green was so difficult to escape from that there were body bags lined up back there.

No one was more terrified on this particular Saturday about a McCord/Whitaker scholarship than Sean McDonough. Working the 16th tower, McDonough had slipped a couple of times on Thursday and Friday and had referred to the "gallery" around the green. Once, he had even let the dreaded word "fans" slip into a sentence. McDonough was one of the best young broadcasters going, the son of the great Will McDonough, the longtime *Boston Globe* reporter who had been one of the few newspapermen to successfully make the transition to TV. He was a rising star. He didn't feel like one after two days at Augusta.

"You just wait till this afternoon," he said, smiling. "There are going to be patrons all around that sixteenth green. They'll be behind the green, in front of the green, heck there may be some patrons swimming in the water near the green."

He wasn't kidding. At one point during the telecast later in the day, McDonough used the word patrons six times in three sentences. It was believed to be a new Masters record for, um, patronizing the Lords of Augusta.

There would be no McCord/Whitaker scholarship for Sean McDonough.

Jay Haas was loosening up on the range shortly after noon on Saturday when he saw Butch Harmon, Tiger Woods's swing guru, approaching with a broad grin on his face. Butch Harmon is one of four sons of Claude Harmon, the 1948 Masters champion who also happened to be a great teacher of the game. All four sons grew up to be teachers, though Butch, having helped revive Greg Norman's game in the early '90s before finding big-time fame and fortune with Woods, is the best-known of the brothers. His younger brother Billy, now a teacher in Palm Springs, had once caddied for Haas and was back on the bag this week for old times' sake.

Butch Harmon has a wicked sense of humor, a knack for one-liners, and the ability to take as good as he gives. It is a quality that serves him well in what has become a hugely competitive profession. Now he was fighting a laugh as he walked up to Haas and his little brother.

"Tiger just told me he figures he'll do more talking today on the first hole than he did in eighteen holes yesterday," Harmon said.

Haas cracked up. The line was funny — and true. Woods, having slogged through five hours-plus in the Sunshine Boys pairing on Friday, would be paired with Haas on Saturday. There is no one on tour most players would rather be paired with than Haas.

Haas was forty-four. He has been on tour since 1977 and has won nine times. He has also finished in the top five seven different times in major championships, including a third place at Augusta in 1995. In 1977, as a tour rookie, he finished fifth in the U.S. Open. Twenty years later, he finished fifth in the Open again. "Haven't improved a lick in twenty years," he joked.

Haas has golf and the Masters in his blood. Bob Goalby, the 1968 Masters champion, is his uncle and has been his golfing mentor since he was a boy growing up in St. Louis. Haas first came to Augusta with his uncle when he was a teenager. He was awed by the place then and he is awed by it now. This was the sixteenth Masters Haas had played in. But he hadn't qualified in 1997, which had been an in-your-face reminder to him that unless you win the golf tournament, playing in the Masters is not a forever thing.

"I can remember saying to Curtis [Strange] after we both played well in 1995 but didn't win that we needed to win one of these things soon so we could be guaranteed coming back here for the rest of our lives," Haas said. "I was joking when I said it, but there was a large kernel of truth in it. I know I'm a lot closer to the end now when it comes to playing here than the beginning."

Haas and Strange had been best friends since their days at Wake Forest, when they had been the foundation of some of the best college golf teams in history. On the surface, they were an odd couple, the laid-back, take-life-as-it-comes Haas and the manically intense Strange. "My uncle Bob, who is pretty intense himself on the golf course, once said that he never met anyone who hated a bogey more than Curtis," Haas said with a laugh. "I think that sums him up pretty well."

What people miss is that Haas has a serious distaste for bogeys too. It just doesn't show on his face and in his manner the way it does with Strange. The two men are more alike than people think. Both are devoted family men, Strange to his two sons, Haas to his five children. Both love to watch and talk about sports other than golf, especially basketball, since both went to college in the hoops-crazed ACC. Haas is a year older than Strange, but they turned pro together because Strange passed up his senior year.

His career has been a model of consistency. He has never been in the top ten on the money list in a single season, but he went into 1998 as the sixteenth leading money winner of all time. His first win was in 1978, his most recent one was in 1993, but late in 1998 he almost won again, finishing second at the Texas Open. While Strange became a superstar — leading money winner three times, first player to earn a million dollars in a year, back-to-back U.S. Open titles — Haas purred along quietly making a very good living for his family, playing on Ryder Cup teams, serving on the Tour's Policy Board.

The irony is that Strange has always bridled at his notoriety. He never wanted to be a celebrity, he just wanted to be a great golfer. Haas would have had no problem at all being a celebrity. He has the kind of outgoing personality that makes answering questions from the media or dealing with the public easy for him. Strange has always been bothered when people come up to him for autographs in restaurants and don't know who Haas is. Haas couldn't care less.

But Strange does have one thing Haas would love to have: two major titles on his résumé. As a golfer, Haas understands the importance of the majors. He also knows what winning the Masters meant to his uncle. "It's been thirty years and it's still a memory he cherishes every single day," Haas said. "I know he gets tired of being asked about the DeVicenzo thing on occasion, but what matters to him is that he is a Masters champion."

The DeVicenzo thing is, of course, one of the most embarrassing and still-discussed moments in Masters history. Goalby had actually finished tied with Roberto DeVicenzo after 72 holes, but Tommy Aaron, who was paired with DeVicenzo, had incorrectly given him a four rather than a three on the 17th hole, and DeVicenzo somehow overlooked the error and signed his card with the four on it. Once he did, the four on 17 became his official score even though millions of people had watched him make three. When DeVicenzo, who is an Argentinian, was told what he had done, he uttered one of golf's most memorable lines: "What a stupid I am."

No one will ever know who would have won the 18-hole playoff, but Goalby has had to live with DeVicenzo's mistake as much as DeVicenzo. It is almost as if there is an invisible asterisk next to his name. Every year at Masters time, the incident comes up and golf people debate what should have been done. Some point out that since the Masters pretty much makes up the rules as it goes along, tournament officials should just have said, "The heck with it, we all know he made three, give him a three." Others decry the rule itself, but it has never been changed and is still on the books exactly as it was in 1968. As recently as two years ago, John Huggan, the highly respected columnist for *Golf World* magazine, suggested that Goalby himself should have insisted on a playoff, that he was somehow responsible for what had happened.

All this talk has left Goalby understandably with something of a chip on his shoulder. But to Haas, he is just Uncle Bob, someone he still loves to play with whenever he can. In fact, once Haas knew he was going to be in the '98 Masters he had made plans to come down on Sunday prior to the tournament so he could play a practice round with his uncle Bob. All past Masters champions are invited to the tournament whether they choose to play or not. That means they can participate in practice rounds if they so desire. Haas and Goalby played on a stunning Sunday afternoon, one that Haas had enjoyed (particularly when his sixty-nine-year-old uncle began screaming at himself on the seventh hole for not playing better) every minute of, but it had also been a reminder to him how precious these days at Augusta had become.

"I was out of the tournament in ninety-seven and I really missed it," he said. "It made me realize that I couldn't take coming back here every year for granted. Getting back this year [which he did by finishing fifth at the U.S. Open after having to go through the qualifier just to get in] meant a lot to me. Now if I could just win the thing and get myself to that upstairs locker room for the rest of my life . . ."

For eleven holes on Saturday it looked as if Haas might have a chance to get himself to the upstairs locker room. He and Woods were the third-to-last pairing of the day, with Hoch and Mickelson and Couples and Duval behind them. Even though the conditions were near perfect, no one in the earlier groups was going low. In fact, the only player who had made any kind of move at all was the cherub-faced amateur, Matt Kuchar, who had flirted with missing the cut before finishing strong on Friday to shoot 76 for a total of 148. He blazed out in 32 and got himself onto the bottom of the scoreboard at even par for the tournament.

Kuchar was heading down the 10th fairway when Haas and Woods walked off the first tee. The mood was light because Haas is rarely uptight on the golf course and Woods was delighted to be playing with someone he felt comfortable with. But it didn't stay light for long. Woods three-putted the first green, ending an amazing streak of 113 holes, dating back to the 1996 tournament, during which he had not three-putted one of Augusta's greens.

That set the tone for the early part of his day. He was bunkered at the second and made a par-five — which as far as he was concerned might as well have been a bogey — then he hit his tee shot in the left bunker and made bogey at the fourth; hit it over the sixth and made double bogey when his chip rolled about a foot farther than he wanted it to and ended up going all the way down the hill and off the green; and then bogeyed the seventh hole after missing the green left with a wedge.

At that moment he was five over par for the day, four over par for the golf tournament, and nine shots behind Haas, who was merrily rolling along having made birdies at the second, third, sixth, and seventh. Those seven holes were proof of why golf is such an amazing game. Here was Tiger Woods, King of the World, anointed as God of Augusta forevermore, playing with good old Jay Haas, King perhaps of Greenville, South Carolina, and Haas was killing him. As they walked to the eighth tee, Haas's score for the day was 23. Woods's was 32. If Woods had been getting a stroke a hole from Haas, he still would have been two down.

The double bogey at six had ended another Woods streak. For the first time since he had shot 40 on the front nine during the first round in 1997, his name came off the leader board.

Haas was fully aware of everything that was happening. He knew his name had jumped to the top of the leader board and that he and Fred Couples were leading the championship at that moment. He also knew that his now grim-faced playing partner was ready to take his entire golf bag and throw it (perhaps with Fluff still carrying it) into any water hazard he could find.

After Haas hit his tee shot on the par-five eighth, Woods got up and, with the wind dead in his face, took the hardest golf swing Haas had ever seen anyone take. "The ball got up to about eye level," Haas said, "and it just stayed there like it was on a string. There was absolutely no way to reach the fairway bunker into that wind. He was about two steps past it."

As they walked off the tee, Woods looked at Haas and said, "I had a little bit of the red-ass there."

Haas laughed. "No kidding," he answered.

Haas had hit a good drive, but he was a good 50 yards back of Woods. He hit a full three-wood and was still about 90 yards short of the green. Woods also took out a three-wood, an almost impossible shot given the narrow landing area short of the green. He hit the ball pin high.

"You take a full swing at that?" Haas asked as they walked up the fairway.

"Nah, I choked down on it," Woods said. The two monumental shots seemed to have calmed him down. They had awed Haas. "Those two shots," he said, "cannot be hit by a mere mortal."

Haas was beating the kid by nine shots and still found his ability mind-boggling. Woods birdied the eighth to creep back to three over and then birdied the ninth. "What struck me about Tiger that day was as angry as he was walking to the eighth tee, he didn't blow up and he didn't give up," Haas said. "The mark of a champion isn't how you play when everything is going right, it's how you play when you're struggling. He showed me something that day."

As they walked down the 11th fairway, though, Haas was the man everyone was watching. Other than the superstars, Haas is one of the best-liked men in the game, not only by other players but by fans who have followed him through the years. As he made his way down the hill toward the 11th green, Haas could glance at the scoreboard to the left of the creek at 11 and see that a lot had changed since the beginning of the day.

He and Couples were leading at five under par. Duval, who was struggling with his putter, had dropped back to three under. He was tied at that number with Paul Azinger, who had just birdied the 12th hole, and they were one shot behind Phil Mickelson, who had quietly sneaked up into third place at four under. Another person going quietly along was Mark O'Meara, who hadn't made a bogey all day and had just knocked in a 15-footer of his own at the 12th a few minutes earlier to tie Duval and Azinger at three under.

Haas has played in too many golf tournaments in too many years to get caught up in a Saturday afternoon leader board. But this was Augusta and he had put himself right into the middle of the battle with his front-nine 32. He had also just nailed a six-iron shot to eight feet right of the hole at the 11th and he knew that if he knocked that putt in, he would be leading the tournament all by himself with the two back-nine par-fives still to play.

Haas walked onto the 11th green to a warm ovation. The area from the 11th green to the 13th fairway is one of the most popular spectator spots on the golf course. If you are in the right place, you can watch three groups at once because you can see the 11th green, the entire 12th hole, and the 13th tee. No one can get very close to the players in this corner because the ropes are set up so that no one can get anywhere near Hogan's Bridge, the 12th green, or the 13th tee. But if you are able to find space behind the 12th tee, all three holes are in view. Many people arrive at the 12th tee early in the morning to secure a spot and then wait for the golfers to begin showing up. It is invariably as crowded as any area of the property.

Haas looked his putt over closely and then gave it a confident rap, feeling as if he could make anything on this day. But this time the ball curled below the hole at the last possible second. An opportunity lost. Disappointed but far from disgusted, Haas tapped in.

He then walked back up the gently sloping hill that takes the players backward from the 11th green to the 12th tee. It is a long-standing Masters tradition that each player receives a round of applause as he walks onto the 12th tee. Woods had received warm applause as he preceded Haas onto the tee. Haas expected to get the same thing. But he had forgotten where he was on the leader board and how much people respected him. And so, as he walked onto the tee, he was surprised, maybe even a little bit stunned, when he realized that the entire crowd was on its feet, giving him a rousing ovation.

Standing ovations don't happen that often at Augusta if only because many of Sean McDonough's patrons find getting out of their chairs no small task. This, though, was a real, live, everyone-up standing ovation.

"Maybe my concentration slipped just a tiny bit," Haas said later. "It did surprise me. But I still thought I was all right when I was over the ball."

Hitting first, Woods had flown a gorgeous eight-iron to within five feet of the flag. The 12th was about as benign that day as it can be. There was almost no wind and the flag was middle-right on the green, meaning players had plenty of bailout room if they needed it. Haas selected a seven-iron, plenty of club on a day like this, took the club back and somehow hit the ball about as fat as a pro will ever hit it. His left hand came flying off the club, and the ball was clearly in trouble as soon as it was airborne. As the crowd gasped in disbelief, the ball plopped into the water as several thousand people groaned.

"Just a bad shot at a bad time," Haas said later. "I don't know if my concentration slipped or if I just put a bad swing on the ball, which can happen. It just happened to me at the worst possible time."

How easy was 12 playing that day? This easy: only one player out of forty-six found the water — Haas. It cost him a double-bogey five but beyond that it cost him all the momentum and good feeling he had built up until the moment he missed his birdie putt at the 11th. Until then, he had played a near perfect round of golf. From that point on, everything was a struggle. He didn't birdie either par-five coming home, and he threw in one more bogey at the 17th before he finally got to the clubhouse. He had shot 32 on the nine at Augusta where players rarely expect to go low and 39 on the nine where shooting 30 is not unheard of. Woods, who shot 33 on the back nine, made up eight of the nine shots he had given up to Haas on the first seven holes. When the day was over, Haas had shot 71, Woods 72.

Both were still in contention. But neither man left the golf course feeling very happy.

It was a strange day at Augusta. With the golf course seemingly sitting there waiting for someone to take it apart in the calm conditions, nobody did. The lowest score anyone produced was 67. There were four of them — Davis Love III, Darren Clarke, Per-Ulrik Johansson, and Jim Furyk. The first three had all started the third round 10 shots behind Couples and Duval and moved to the fringes of contention at even-par

216 for 54 holes, six shots behind the leader. Furyk, who had played his last 27 holes in eight under par, moved to two under for the tournament and was only four shots back. Much to his surprise, he was very much in the golf tournament.

At day's end, Couples again had the lead by himself at six-under-par 210. He had turned a struggling round completely around on the 13th hole when he had hit one of the most perfect shots of his life, a three-iron that stopped 18 inches from the hole. It was one of those shots when a player knows as soon as the ball is off the club that he has hit it perfectly. The CBS boom mike in the fairway clearly picked up Couples's concise reaction to the shot: "Oh Baby!" Couples often worried about the presence of the mikes on the golf course because he often has, as he puts it, "an immature mouth," when the ball doesn't perform as it is supposed to. This time there was no problem.

Couples tapped in for an eagle that got him two under par for the day and seven under for the tournament. He came to the 18th hole still at seven under and leading the field by three shots. A three-shot lead going into the last day at Augusta doesn't make you a lock by any means, but it is not a bad position to be in.

Couples never had a chance to ponder what the three-shot lead would have meant. He overcut his drive at the 18th, missing the fairway on the right side, forcing him to punch out of the trees. He chipped to about 10 feet but missed the par putt. It was a disappointing way to end the day, but he had still shot 71 and he had a two-shot lead over Azinger, Mickelson, who had been six under through 16 holes before bogeying 17 and 18, and O'Meara, who had very calmly produced a four-birdies, no-bogeys 68. He led Furyk and Duval, who had finished with a disheartening 74, by three. Haas, José María Olazabal, and Scott Hoch were four back and still in the hunt if they could produce a superb final round. Five back was a fascinating trio: two-time U.S. Open champion Ernie Els, Woods, and a limping fifty-eight-year-old named Jack Nicklaus.

This was the same Jack Nicklaus of whom Woods had said on Tuesday, when asked about playing in forty straight Masters, "I just can't imagine being that old." He hadn't meant any disrespect, but to a twenty-two-year-old, fifty-eight probably sounded like 158. Now Nicklaus, who had played in his first Masters eighteen years before Woods was *born*, had the exact same 54-hole score as Woods.

Nicklaus's name had gone onto the bottom of the leader board at exactly 4:33 P.M., to huge roars everywhere on the golf course, when he birdied the 15th hole. He had stayed at one under par for the tournament when he absolutely rammed a 40-foot putt into the back of the hole for a par at the 18th. "If it doesn't go in, it might still be rolling," he said, grinning.

Everyone knew Nicklaus couldn't win the tournament, right? "Of course I can't win," he said. "But if I could go out there tomorrow and maybe put up a sixty-five . . ."

That was what he had done in 1986. But that was twelve years and a lot of hip and knee and back pains ago. Still, it was Jack Nicklaus. "The guy's unbelievable," Couples said. "When I'm fifty-eight I'll be playing five-buck nassau at the club with my buddies."

Not this weekend, though. On this weekend, Couples would be going back to his rented house for one last dinner with all his friends, and then he would tee it up at 3:10 the next afternoon in the final pairing of the Masters with Mark O'Meara — the same Mark O'Meara he had tied for eighth place in his first pro tournament almost eighteen years earlier, the same Mark O'Meara he had roomed with at Q-School that same fall.

"Three-ten, can you believe that?" Couples asked, staring at the pairings sheet. "It's bad enough you have to sit around being nervous all morning, but three-ten? Are they kidding?"

They weren't kidding. CBS knew perfectly well that with a 3:10 final pairing there was no way they would be off the air at their scheduled time of 7 o'clock. But they didn't want to be off at 7. They wanted the last putt to go into the hole shortly after 7 and the awards ceremony in Butler Cabin to last until about 7:20 or 7:25. That way they would pick up people tuning in for *60 Minutes* and bolster the tail of their Masters ratings, and they would give a big lift to *60 Minutes* with people staying where they were once the green jacket had been presented.

"If all goes well, the last ball goes in the hole at 7:03," said CBS's Rob Correa. "Maybe 7:04 or 7:05."

Regardless of the exact minute, Sunday promised to be a very long day for everyone.

11

The Tournament Begins
on the Back Nine on Sunday . . .

On Saturday night at the Masters, no one goes to bed early.

For those who will be watching on Sunday, it is the last night to party, since almost everyone will head up the road — or in the case of many of the corporate honchos to Daniels Field to fly out in their private jets — on Sunday evening.

For those who will be playing, going to bed anytime before midnight is pointless. "You know it isn't going to be easy sleeping to begin with," Mark O'Meara said. "And the last thing you want is to get up really early and then sit around killing time all morning."

So everyone finds different ways to stay up late.

It was closing in on 8 o'clock by the time Couples finished all of his various postround interviews and left the golf course. He and Thais and his good friend John McLure stopped at an Italian restaurant en route back to the house, and Thais and John went in to pick up take-out to bring back to the house. Couples stretched out in the back seat and closed his eyes. Initially, he decided to lie down to make sure no well-meaning passersby noticed him and stopped to chat, wish him luck, or ask for autographs, but when he put his head back on the seat he realized how tired he was.

"I had played late all three days, and all three days I had to go in and do an hour of media after I was done," he said. "I know that's part of the deal, especially at a major, but it does begin to wear on you."

There may be no feat in golf more difficult than going wire-to-wire with the lead, especially in a major. In the previous sixty-one Masters four winners had led from start to finish: Craig Wood in 1941, Arnold Palmer in 1960, Jack Nicklaus in 1972, and Raymond Floyd in 1976. As dominant as Woods had been in 1997, he had not taken the lead for good until late in the second round. The great players rarely took the lead on Thursday — or wanted to take the lead on Thursday. On his way to winning eighteen major championships, Jack Nicklaus led after all four rounds three times. "I never wanted to go wire-to-wire," he has said. "The best way to play a major is to play good golf on Thursday and Friday and build for the weekend. With luck you peak on Saturday and Sunday."

Of course in golf you can't plan your peak. It isn't like swimming or track where you taper your workouts with an eye toward producing your best performance on one given day. In golf you work and hope your game is where you want it to be when it matters most. This year, more than any year in the past, Couples had tried to bring his game to a peak for the Masters. He had spent four straight days with his teacher, Paul Marchand, working on the practice tee at Bay Hill, the first time he could ever remember practicing that way for four straight days.

The work had paid off for three days. Now, as he waited for Thais and McLure to return to the car, he wondered if he had the emotional energy to get through a Sunday at Augusta. "Physically I knew I'd be fine on Sunday afternoon," he said. "I had really built to the point where I expected to win the golf tournament. I knew that mentally that was the right way to approach it and I felt good about it. But I also knew from experience what a long tough day the last one is at Augusta."

All the players know that. What makes the last day at Augusta different from the last day at other majors is knowing that someone can "go deep," another player term for going low. The golf courses at the other three majors are rarely set up to allow for low scores, especially on Sunday. Yes, Johnny Miller had produced a 63 at Oakmont to win the U.S. Open in 1973; Greg Norman had come up with a 64 to win the British

Open at Royal St. George's in 1993; and Steve Elkington had fired a 64 on the last day at the PGA in 1995, on badly beaten-up greens at Riviera Country Club in Los Angeles. But those rounds were aberrations, near miracles. And the USGA liked to point out that rain the night before had softened the greens at Oakmont to the point where they really weren't "U.S. Open" greens.

If you lead a U.S. Open, a British Open, or a PGA on Saturday night and can produce a round near par, you will have an excellent chance of winning. At Augusta, if the weather conditions are good, you have to start out on Sunday assuming that someone is going to shoot in the mid-60s and you are going to have to produce a number of birdies yourself if you hope to hang on and win.

Couples knew that as well as anybody. He was a bit unhappy with himself because he felt he had let an opportunity slip away in the third round. "I played okay," he said later. "But in that weather, under those conditions, 71 was not a great score. If I had made a couple more putts and shot 68 or 69, I could have really put some distance between myself and everyone else. I was a little bit upset that I didn't do it."

Nonetheless, he led by two and felt the same confidence he had felt all week. Once he had been handed his player badge and it was the same number — 70 — as he had been given in 1992, he had started to buy into all the Jim Nantz notions about omens and karma. Starting the tournament with three straight birdies had confirmed all that and he had gone from there.

He sat around that night watching a baseball game and then *Sportscenter*, trying to make it as close to a normal Saturday night as possible. But he knew better. Everyone knew better. Jim Furyk watched his dad fire up the grill, ate his dinner quietly, and then stayed up watching *Forrest Gump* on video after everyone else had gone to bed. David Duval sat up in bed reading because he knew he wasn't going to fall asleep. Mark O'Meara was doing the same thing as Couples — spending a quiet night with his family, trying to keep things as normal as possible — when his phone rang. It was Hank Haney. He was in Atlanta at an airport hotel. He was supposed to fly out in the morning to run a clinic in the afternoon, but he couldn't do it. "I'm driving back in the morning," he said. "I have to be there."

O'Meara had been hearing from his friends about omens too. His car dealer in Orlando, Kevin White, had told him just before he left for Augusta that he had dreamed O'Meara won the Masters. Joe Louis, the owner of Isleworth, always liked to make a couple of bets on players during the major championships. Often, O'Meara would call him after he got on site to tell him who he thought was playing well. He was supposed to call Louis on Tuesday, but he hadn't because he didn't really have a feel for who was hot and he didn't want Louis making a bet based on bad advice. The next day, Louis had called him to wish him luck. O'Meara had told him he was sorry he hadn't called the day before. "Don't worry about it," Louis said. "I bet all my money on you."

O'Meara was stunned. "What are my odds?" he asked.

"Thirty-three to one," Louis had answered.

Two shots back with 18 holes to play, his odds were now a lot better than that.

The last day at any major has a special feeling because everyone knows that something dramatic is going to happen by nightfall. At the Masters, the feeling is a little bit different because of the golf course.

"You know where the pins are going to be," Jeff Sluman said as he lingered by the first tee waiting for the leaders to tee off. "You know it's going to be very hard but there are going to be birdies out there to make. And you know someone is going to make a run from back in the pack."

Except of course in 1997, when the pack was so far behind Tiger Woods it wasn't even in Georgia.

All the majors stage a tournament within a tournament on Sunday. While the leaders sit around the clubhouse killing time before they go out and decide who will be the champion, the second tier of players go out to try and ensure themselves a spot in the field for next year. At the Masters — prior to 1999 when the number dropped to sixteen — the top twenty-four finishers were automatically invited back for the following year. That number was very much on Brad Faxon's mind when he teed off at 1:10. Faxon was in a three-way tie for twenty-third place beginning the day — eight shots behind Couples. Realistically, he knew he wasn't going to win. But he figured he still had a chance to finish in the top ten and, worst-case scenario, he wanted to make certain he held on to his spot in the top twenty-four.

The day was a struggle. Faxon didn't play badly; in fact he drove the ball very well. But, as had been the case all week, his putter failed him. Faxon has built his career around a putter that often acts as a magic wand. No one succeeds on tour if they can't putt. With Faxon that was always the case times two.

"It was aggravating," he said. "Because I might have hit the ball as well as I've ever hit it at Augusta. But nothing went in."

The 18th hole was Faxon's week — his year — in microcosm. He was even par for the day and suspected he was right on the cusp of the top twenty-four. A birdie would probably lock him in, a par would leave him dangling, a bogey would almost certainly knock him out. There was no way to be sure because there are no electronic scoreboards at any of the majors. Week to week on the PGA Tour the electronic boards tell players exactly where they stand. Any time they walk by a scoreboard it will show the names and the position in the field of the players on that hole. At the Masters, unless you are in the top ten and on a leader board, you have no idea where you stand in relation to the field.

Faxon's gut told him he was right on the bubble. He hit two good shots at 18 to a spot 12 feet below the hole. At least now he had taken bogey out of the equation. His playing partner, Stewart Cink, was also on the bubble. Both players were two over par for the week. Cink had a 20-footer for birdie. Calmly, he rolled his putt in. Now, Faxon had to make his putt to tie Cink. He thought he had made it, but at the last possible second the ball veered below the hole. It had been that way for four days.

"Think about this," Faxon said later. "I had one hundred and twenty-five putts for the week. The winner had one hundred and six and I finished eleven shots behind him."

Putting statistics can be deceiving because they don't count putts from the fringe and don't take into account how close a player hits the ball to the hole throughout the week. But Faxon has been near the top of the list in putting statistics almost his entire career. Everyone on tour would rank him among the top five putters out there. For him 125 putts in any week is almost unheard of.

He walked off 18 with a bad feeling in the pit of his stomach. "Something told me that Stewart making and me missing was going to cost me," he said. When he got into the locker room, a check of the computer revealed that Cink had indeed put himself into the top twenty-four by birdieing 18. If Faxon had made his putt, he would have been tied with Cink at one over par, good for a tie for twenty-third. Instead, he finished one shot further back and was tied for twenty-six. Cink making hadn't hurt him, but missing his own putt had.

"There are still plenty of ways to get in next year," Faxon said softly. "But it would have been nice to get it out of the way right now. I had the chance and didn't get it done."

Another player who had the chance and did get it done was the U.S. Amateur champion, Matt Kuchar. His 68 on Saturday had brought him back to even par for the tournament, and on Sunday he shot a solid, even-par 72 to finish at 288. That left him in a tie for twenty-first place, guaranteeing his return to Augusta in 1999. Not once, it seemed, did he stop smiling.

One person who wasn't smiling at the end of the day was Justin Leonard, who was paired with Kuchar on Sunday. He was happy for Kuchar and admired his ability to stay calm coming down the stretch with the top twenty-four in sight. But Kuchar's caddy almost drove him crazy.

The caddy was Peter Kuchar, Matt's dad. On Thursday, when Peter Kuchar had played cheerleader all the way around the golf course for his son, most people thought it was a nice story. By Sunday the word around the locker room was that the old man never let up and that he was a shameless self-promoter. Since Matt was an amateur, he couldn't pursue any endorsements. According to one clothing company representative, Peter Kuchar had approached him and asked if the company was interested in having *him* wear their clothes. After all, he said, there was nothing illegal about him endorsing a product.

No, there wasn't. But as the rep pointed out, there really wasn't much point in putting someone in their clothing when he would be wearing the Augusta caddy's jump suit over that clothing.

Leonard is a very methodical player. Away from the golf course he likes a good joke as much as anyone. But the last round at the Masters was not a place to be whooping it up as far as he was concerned. He tried to ignore Peter Kuchar's constant cheerleading as best he could. But on the 15th hole, after Matt had hit a fine shot to the green, Peter walked up near the ropes and led cheers for his son.

Leonard, who was about to play his own second shot, waited. Then he got over his ball. The noise continued. He looked up and saw Peter Kuchar still leading cheers. "That was when I just about lost it," he said later. "I mean enough is enough. It's the back nine at Augusta on Sunday. Give me a chance."

Leonard was happy with the way he played, shooting 69 to produce his first top-ten finish (T-8) at Augusta. But he knew that this wasn't going to be the last time he encountered Team Kuchar. At the U.S. Open, the U.S. Amateur champion is paired the first two rounds with the defending U.S. Open champion and the reigning British Open champion. The reigning British Open champion was Justin Leonard. "Something has to change between now and San Francisco," he said. "I don't want to go through that again."

Generally speaking, anyone who is within five shots of the lead going into the last day of a major is thought to have a chance to win. On this day at this Masters, a lot of people were stretching the five-shot rule to six shots because of the identity of three of the players who were six shots behind Couples.

One was Davis Love, who everyone knew could go as deep as anyone in the field on a given day. Love had loads of confidence going into the last day because he had shot 67 on Saturday, because he had won the most recent major prior to the Masters (the '97 PGA), and because two years earlier he had shot 66 on the last day to come within a shot of winning. CBS's Lance Barrow walked through the clubhouse at lunchtime Sunday telling anyone who would listen that Love was the man to watch.

The other two players worth watching who were tied with Love were Leonard, who had won three tournaments in the last year in which he started the last round five shots back of the leader (including the British Open), and Scott McCarron, who had been very steady — 73–71–72 — all week but had yet to have a break-out round. The other three players at 216 weren't considered contenders simply because they lacked experience at Augusta and in major championships: Kuchar, Darren Clarke, and Per-Ulrik Johansson. Clarke had started the last round of the British Open in second place in '97 but had never been in serious contention the last day, after hitting his tee shot out of bounds on the second hole.

From 215 on down to Couples at 210, everyone was a contender. There were five players who had won majors in the past: Couples, Paul Azinger at 212, José María Olazabal at 214, Ernie Els at 215, and Nicklaus, the Olden Bear trying to turn Golden one last time at 215. One stat on Nicklaus put the field in perspective: if you didn't include Gary Player, who was playing in the first twosome of the day, the other forty-four players in the field had won a combined total of twenty-two professional major titles — only four more than Nicklaus alone. Player had won nine, making him one of the great players ever, but still nowhere close to Nicklaus. Among the under-fifty set playing that Sunday only John Daly (two), Els (two), Bernhard Langer (two), and Fuzzy Zoeller (two) had more than one major on his résumé. Els was the only one in that group with a chance to win.

The BPNTHWAM set had several players in contention: Colin Montgomerie at 215, David Duval and Jim Furyk at 213, and Phil Mickelson and Mark O'Meara at 212. Even though he had shot 69 on Saturday, few people expected Montgomerie to be a serious factor. His wife was home in England on the verge of giving birth to their third child. The baby had been due in May but the doctors were now convinced it would be arriving within a week. Montgomerie had already canceled plans to play at the next tour stop at Hilton Head so he could fly directly home from the Masters.

Duval and Furyk were paired together, which pleased both of them. Both lived in Ponte Vedra, Florida, near PGA Tour headquarters, and they occasionally got together for dinner when they were both at home. They were different in more ways than they were similar. Duval was a southerner who was trying very hard to break his habit of chewing tobacco. He loved to fish, thought hunting wasn't a sport — "What's the challenge of shooting something that can't even see you," he said — and probably read more books than anyone on tour, although he had tired of being portrayed as some kind of intellectual. "Jeez, just because I know who Ayn Rand is people want to make me into a scholar," he said, shaking his head.

Furyk knew who Ayn Rand was too, but his reading interests ran more toward *USA Today* and *Sports Illustrated*. He was a northerner who loved all sports but wasn't likely to be found chewing tobacco or hunting or fishing very often — if ever. He was an only child from a close-knit family; Duval was the second of three children from a family that had scattered when he was a teenager, after his brother's death.

Different as they were, they enjoyed each other's company. They had reached the tour a year apart (Furyk in 1994, Duval in 1995) and both were young rising stars, though Duval's recent victory string had earned him a good deal of unwanted notoriety. They teed off at 2:50, each understanding that this was a day that might represent a great opportunity for a breakthrough.

The 3 o'clock pairing was entirely different. Paul Azinger had lived with the BPNTHWAM label until his emotional victory in the PGA in 1993. Two months later he had been diagnosed with cancer. He had become a symbol of courage during the next year, not only coming back from the cancer but becoming an eloquent spokesman for anyone who had ever fought the disease. He had started a golf tournament to raise money for cancer research and spent a lot of time with children who had cancer. "I just try to tell them that I kicked cancer's butt and they can too," he often said.

But the cancer had interrupted his career right at its peak. In 1993 he had been one of the two or three best players in the world, winning the PGA and two other tour events, anchoring the U.S. Ryder Cup team, and finishing in the top three in tournaments an amazing ten times. In three and a half years back since his illness, he had a total of five top-ten finishes and his best finish in thirteen majors had been a tie for seventeenth at the '95 Masters. He had never really liked the golf course very much — he had finished at least third in the other three majors, never higher than fourteenth at the Masters — and he willingly admitted on Saturday that he was surprised to find himself in the second-to-last group on Sunday.

By contrast, Phil Mickelson wasn't surprised to be in that group. With the exception of Woods, Mickelson had dealt with more expectations than anyone in the sport. He had first won on tour as a college junior, winning the Tucson Open, and, two months shy of twenty-eight, already had twelve PGA Tour victories. But because he had won so much, because his game was so spectacular at times — especially around the greens — Mickelson had been dealing with the BPNTH-WAM label almost since the day he turned pro.

To his credit, he never ducked it, never pretended it didn't matter. "I should be contending at the majors," he said. "I believe I'm a good enough player to win them and until I do I'm not going to feel satisfied with myself. But I think I will win one soon."

Mickelson made no bones about the fact that seeing Woods win the Masters at twenty-two, Els win his second U.S. Open at twenty-seven, and Leonard win the British Open at twenty-five the previous year had increased the pressure he felt to win his own major. He had put himself into position with his 68 on Saturday and insisted that the bogeys at 17 and 18 hadn't affected his confidence. Still, it probably wasn't a great omen when he pushed his drive off number one into the trees on the left side.

Everyone, it seemed, started out tight. Not surprising under the circumstances. Woods, hoping to get off to a quick start to get the attention of the leaders, opened with a bogey for the second straight day. So did Duval, the third time in four days he had bogeyed number one.

The feeling among the leaders as they started out was best described by Couples in his own unique way: "I'm actually semi-calm," he said, walking out of the locker room. "But I'm also semi-nervous."

Mark O'Meara felt semi-calm when he walked to the driving range with Hank Haney to warm up. But within seconds, he was semi-nervous. Haney was a wreck. He kept talking about what O'Meara needed to do, what this round could mean, what was at stake, how important a good start was. O'Meara finally stopped him. "Hank, I know," he said. "I know everything. It'll be all right. I've been in position to win before. I know how to win golf tournaments."

If O'Meara needed an omen, he might have found one if he had glanced up at the player board next to the first tee. As each group comes onto the tee, one of Phil Harison's nephews slides the names of the players onto a standing board next to the tee. Next to the name of the player, he posts his player number. When Couples and O'Meara walked onto the tee, their numbers had been reversed. Couples had been given

O'Meara's 73 and O'Meara had been given Couples's lucky 70. Naturally, neither player noticed. Both were staring down the fairway trying to semi-calm themselves.

Only one person was making a move on the front nine and there wasn't a soul within a hundred miles of the place who didn't know exactly who it was. Augusta crowd roars are different than in other places. They are, as Zoeller had pointed out on Friday, harder to come by. They don't really get loud until Sunday, as if the crowd is saving its energy for the day that really matters. And they are distinctive. The roar for Duval is different from the roar for Couples, the roar for Woods different from the roar for Love.

And then there is the Jack roar. It is like no other because it has been building for forty years. It began as little more than a whimper back in the '60s when he was the black hat to Palmer's white hat. It grew through the '70s as he lost weight and gained titles and stature. And it reached a peak in 1986 when he won at Augusta for the sixth time at the age of forty-six, six years after he had last won a golf tournament. The only other player who could produce a roar that would match a Jack roar was Palmer and he hadn't played the weekend at Augusta since 1983 and hadn't been in the top ten since 1967.

Of course Nicklaus hadn't top-tenned in any major since a sixth place finish at Augusta in 1990. His best finish since then had been a twenty-third at the 1991 PGA. He had gotten into the habit of playing well for 36 holes, then fading on Saturday. That was no doubt a product of age. Which was why everyone had been impressed and surprised when he produced a solid 70 on Saturday. Realistically, he couldn't be expected to play as well on Sunday.

He didn't. Instead, he played better. First, there was a birdie at the second. That was fine, but no big deal since most players birdie the second. But then there was a birdie at the third. That produced the first real Jack roar of the day, echoing off the trees and all the way back to the putting green where the leaders were getting ready to tee off. To a man, they looked up from what they were doing and, to a man, they all looked at their caddy or at each other, smiled, and said, "Jack."

A bogey at the fourth quieted things for a few minutes and, after a par at the fifth, Nicklaus was at two under for the tournament. By now, Couples and O'Meara had teed off and Nicklaus was still four shots behind Couples. Not for long. He rolled in a long birdie putt at the sixth and here came the roar again. Duval and Furyk were standing on the third green when they heard it and both broke into broad grins. "How about that guy?" Duval said to Furyk as they walked to the fourth tee.

"It was one of those things," Furyk said later, "where you're locked into what you're doing but the roars were so loud you couldn't help but notice."

Nicklaus was now three under and Couples had joined the first-hole bogey parade, dropping to five under. Suddenly, it was Sunday at Augusta and Jack Nicklaus was two shots out of the lead with 12 holes to play. Was he Joe Hardy? Was the devil lurking in the trees somewhere preparing to collect his soul after he holed out on 18? It was too crazy to be true. People came running — yes, running at Augusta — from everywhere to try to get a glimpse of this. All of a sudden, Couples and O'Meara, the last group on the last day of a major championship, found themselves playing almost by themselves.

"We looked up when we got to the third tee," Couples said, "and it was like, where did everybody go?"

They were all over at the seventh, trying to see Nicklaus. And here he came, almost running down the fairway. Els, his playing partner, who was spotting him thirty years, was walking a good 20 yards behind him, a huge grin on his face because, like everyone else, he couldn't believe what he was seeing. "I was completely awed," he said later. "I almost forgot about playing I got so caught up in rooting for him."

Nicklaus floated his second shot to the elevated seventh green, about 15 feet left of the hole. By now they were roaring while he walked, cheering every step he took. Nicklaus couldn't help himself. He was supposed to be concentrating, but he had this big grin on his face, giving the papal wave as often as he could. He stalked his birdie putt like the Bear of old and then drained it. Els was laughing in disbelief. Nicklaus was four under par, two shots behind Couples — who had birdied the second — and O'Meara — who had birdied two and three — and tied with Mickelson and Azinger for third place.

Couples and O'Meara had reached the fourth tee by now and both had silly grins on their faces. "You know what, Joey," Couples said to his caddy, Joe LaCava. "Good for him. If he can pull this thing off, wow, what a thing that would be."

But he couldn't. Mr. Applegate came calling early. A par at the par-five eighth slowed him down a little. But at the ninth, he hit his wedge eight feet from the hole, giving himself another birdie chance. The putt broke hard right, though, stopping on the edge of the hole. The first loud Jack groan of the day went up, and Nicklaus stood looking at the putt in disbelief for several seconds. As he walked through the ropes to the 10th tee, his step had slowed a bit, the waves came a little bit slower. By now, Couples and O'Meara had both birdied the fourth to get to seven under. Three shots on the back nine at Augusta certainly wasn't out of the question, but it seemed apparent now that the leaders weren't going to come sliding backward. Nicklaus felt as if he could have been out in 31; instead it was 33. He hadn't even noticed the pain in his arthritic hip until just now. After he parred the 10th hole, he walked slowly off the green, limping slightly. He had looked about twenty-eight years old going down the seventh and eighth, perhaps thirty-eight coming up the ninth, forty-eight walking off the ninth, and now fifty-eight. A good fifty-eight, but fifty-eight.

He played a solid back nine — one bogey and birdies at the two par-fives, but the miracle wasn't going to happen. When he rolled his birdie attempt to within two inches at the 18th, Els was standing there trying to root the ball into the hole. Els insisted that he mark his ball so that he could tap in after Els holed out and stand on the green and drink in the cheers. He did just that and, as he hugged his son Steve, who was also his caddy, Els stood on the green a few feet away and joined in the applause. "I had chills," he said later.

So did everyone else. Nicklaus had shot 68, which would be good enough to tie for sixth place. It may not have been a miracle, but it was nothing short of remarkable.

When it became apparent that Nicklaus wasn't going to pull off the greatest upset in sports since the United States hockey team had beaten the Soviet Union in the 1980 Olympics, the championship was left to be decided among the mortals.

O'Meara had started with the hot putter, making a 10-footer for birdie at two, a 30-footer for birdie at three, and a 50-foot bomb for birdie at four. "All I wanted to do was get that one close," he said later. "When it was about halfway there, I thought, Oh my God, it's going in."

It was at that moment that O'Meara first thought he might be on to something special. That thought had occurred to Couples too, because he knew how good O'Meara could be when his putter got hot. But he was still completely confident. He had matched O'Meara's birdie at the fourth, and even though the whole world was focused on Nicklaus at that moment, they stood on the fifth tee tied for first, two shots clear of the field.

No one really expects to go low on the front nine at Augusta on Sunday. If it happens, it is almost a lucky break. The only true birdie hole is the second. The eighth is the longest of the par-fives, reachable in two only for the longest hitters in the field and, even for them, it is a lot easier to miss the green than hit it. The fourth and sixth are two of the tougher par-threes in major championship golf, and none of the par-fours are easy. That's why Augusta's oldest cliché is the one about the golf tournament not beginning until the back nine on Sunday.

"You get to that stretch from thirteen to fifteen and you have to make something happen," Couples said. "Because if you play them even par, you can start out with a one-shot lead and finish with a two-shot deficit."

That was why Nicklaus's early run was so amazing. It was also why neither Couples nor O'Meara gave much thought to the two-shot lead they had on the field. A lot of people were lurking: Mickelson, whose game plan had been to get through the first six holes without a big mistake and then attack, had done that. He was five under playing the seventh hole. So was Azinger, who had just birdied the sixth.

Duval and Furyk had both started slowly. Duval bounced back from his opening bogey to birdie the second, then made four straight pars. On the seventh tee, he was four shots back at three under par. Furyk, who had been playing catchup all week, was five back at two under. Now though, the Mickelson theory about beginning to attack kicked in. Duval birdied seven. Then Duval birdied eight and Furyk eight and nine. Just like that, Duval was five under, Furyk four. Then they both birdied the 10th, Duval chipping in, and their numbers were six and five.

Couples was aware of what they were doing. He was aware of everything. As casual as he may look walking the golf course, he knows exactly what is going on at every moment. He checks the scoreboards constantly. He never plays the mind game some players employ of not checking the board. He wants to know what the other players are doing. "In a way, it's fun," he said. "If you're going bad, hell, it doesn't matter anyway. And if you're going good, you want to know what everyone's doing. Especially at Augusta, where you can make any score on any hole."

Couples thought he had made a big move at the seventh. He and O'Meara both hit wedge shots close to the hole, but O'Meara's putter finally cooled for a moment when he missed from six feet. Couples rammed home his four-footer to take the lead back at eight under, then birdied the eighth while O'Meara settled for par. At that moment, he was two up on O'Meara and *four* up on everyone else. He was settled into the round now, a solid three under par for the day.

At the ninth, he hit a perfect drive all the way to the bottom of the hill. O'Meara, perhaps feeling the pressure of Couples's back-to-back birdies, pulled his tee shot into the trees. When O'Meara got to his ball, his only play was to punch out in front of the green. As he stood in the trees, trying to figure the best route out, Couples stood in the fairway, waiting. As hard as he was trying not to get ahead of himself, he couldn't help it. "I had 107 yards to the hole, a wedge," he said. "Mark has no chance to get his ball on the green. He's looking at bogey. I have a chance for birdie. If that happens, I'm leading by four going to the back nine. Four!

"You know, you tell yourself a million times to go one shot at a time but dammit we are all human. I'm standing there thinking to myself, wow, this thing could be over right here."

Later, Couples would kick himself for letting that thought creep into his head. Because a moment later, after O'Meara had played his shot from the trees, he got just a little bit loose with his wedge shot. There is no room for looseness on the ninth green at Augusta. The front part of the green slopes back to front, and the hill in front of the green is a lot steeper than it looks on TV. In 1996, Greg Norman had spun a wedge from the front of the green all the way down the hill on Sunday. That had led to a bogey that sent Norman to the back nine with his six-shot lead over Nick Faldo down to two. He never recovered.

Now Couples made a mistake similar to Norman's. He didn't get the ball high enough up on the green. He didn't miss by much, maybe a foot or two, but he missed by enough. The ball spun off the green. O'Meara then hit his pitch shot to four feet. His ball landed perhaps a foot farther up the green than Couples's ball. That turned out to be a monumental difference. Annoyed and wanting to be sure he got the ball safely to the pin this time, Couples knocked his third shot 12 feet past the hole. Then he missed the par putt. O'Meara made his.

Wham! In less than ten minutes, Couples had gone from fantasizing about a four-shot lead to the reality of seeing his lead cut to one. "If I'd had a gun walking to the tenth tee," he said, "I'd have shot myself. I mean if you're a hundred and seven yards from the hole with your drive, you can't make a bogey. You just *can't*. It was ridiculous. Now, I had to dig in all over again."

He did, though, producing a solid par at the 10th. Surprisingly, it was O'Meara who played a poor shot at the 10th, laying the sod over a nine-inch and missing the green left. "Worst shot I played all day, no doubt about it," he said. It was the first bogey he had made since the ninth hole on Friday.

Now, though, he was in third place because Duval was on fire. He had made another birdie at the 11th to get to seven under. O'Meara was aggravated by the bogey, but knew it was too early to panic.

By now, the list of potential winners was thinning. Mickelson, having played the first six holes the way he wanted to, had made a bogey on the seventh. He was still hanging in the hunt at four under when he pulled an eight-iron into the water at the 12th. His hopes drowned with the golf ball. Azinger never went away completely all day — in fact he almost chipped in at the 17th to get to within one shot of the lead — but he never got the break that he needed to make a big move.

By the time Couples and O'Meara got to the 13th tee, it looked like a four-man golf tournament. Couples and Duval were tied for the lead at eight under because Duval had birdied 13. O'Meara was two shots back, as was Jim Furyk, but Furyk had only one par-five left to play.

Couples had spent hours and hours on the range with Marchand working on drawing the ball off the tee, the opposite of his natural fade. Three days in a row, he had hit perfect draws with his three-wood on 13, the last one leading to the eagle on Saturday. He set up to hit the exact same shot, but this time he didn't pull it off. Instead, what he got was an ugly pull hook that went screaming over Rae's Creek into the trees and the azaleas on the left. O'Meara took a deep breath. He knew that his chances to win the golf tournament might very well depend on where Couples's ball was and what kind of second shot he had.

Amazingly, Couples had a couple of options. One was to punch it through a hole in the trees at a 45-degree angle and get it safely to the fairway for a reasonable third shot to the green. The other option was to play the ball straight up the path leading through the woods and try to get it hole high to the left of the green. That would be by far the more dangerous of the two shots, but Couples gave it some serious thought. "If it's Thursday, I play it up the path," he said. "It would not have been that hard a shot and I might have ended up still having a chance to make birdie.

"But it wasn't Thursday, it was Sunday. Extra nerves are involved. I didn't want to go down in history as the biggest mental midget ever to lose the Masters. The safe play was the right play."

And so Couples punched the ball between the trees, one hand coming off the club as he did. The ball made it safely to the fairway and it looked as if Couples had dodged the proverbial bullet. He was now 161 yards from the hole and it appeared certain he would walk off the hole with no worse than a par. He could still make birdie. After all, he had gotten up and down from the fairway on Saturday, hitting a three-iron from 205 yards. Now, he was in between six- and seven-iron.

Which was the problem. Couples's golfing instincts told him the right play was a hard seven-iron. He didn't think the creek would come into play unless he completely mishit the ball and he might be able to get it close. LaCava, having just witnessed a near disaster, didn't want to take any risks. "Let's hit six, make sure we get it past the pin, and get out of here," he argued.

The argument made sense. One of the reasons Couples and LaCava have worked so well together for eight years is that LaCava is not a yes-caddy. Couples respects him and his opinions even on those occasions when he disagrees and doesn't listen to what he's being told. Standing in the fairway at 13 he was a little bit shellshocked from the tee shot and the escape. Instead of relying on his gut, he decided to rely on LaCava's counsel to play it safe. "It was good, sensible advice," Couples said. "But it wasn't what I needed to do right there. The blame is with me for not going with my gut."

Couples pulled the six and got over the ball. Another mistake. "I needed time to get my mind back together," he said. "I was going in a thousand directions mentally. I needed to walk up to the green, walk back, calm myself down, make a solid decision, and play the shot. I did none of the above."

What he did was take a half-hearted swing with the six-iron, trying to cut the ball softly into the pin. He got a soft cut — too soft a cut. The ball drifted right and short and splashed into the creek. Couples stared at it as if to say, "This can't be happening."

He had to walk up, drop in front of the creek, and chip on. Two putts later he had made seven and as he walked off the green, the mindset of the Masters had changed. Couples, who had believed for 66 holes that it was his destiny to win this Masters, was no longer so sure. He now trailed by two shots with five to play. O'Meara, who had wondered if Couples was catchable, had now caught him, albeit by Couples slipping rather than by him charging. And, up ahead, Duval, seeing the double bogey go on the board as he walked onto the 15th green, suddenly knew it was his Masters to win or lose. Furyk, even after his bogey on the 15th, stood on the 16th tee thinking if he made three straight birdies he could still have a chance because he at least had the advantage of playing with the man he had to catch.

Truly great players do not roll over and die after a disaster. Couples came back and almost birdied the 14th, just missing a 10-foot putt, and then hit an absolutely brilliant five-iron second shot at the 15th to within three feet. When he made the putt for eagle he had played the critical 13–14–15 stretch in even par by going 7–4–3. Even par through that stretch usually isn't good enough, but Couples was again tied for the lead because Duval had followed his birdie at 15 with a bogey at 16.

In Couples's mind at that moment, the tournament was between him and Duval. "No disrespect to Mark," he said. "But when I walked off thirteen, I was chasing Duval. He became the target. I really almost stopped thinking about Mark, which was probably foolish."

O'Meara had birdied 15, meaning he trailed Couples and Duval by one. He walked onto the 16th tee feeling he was in almost perfect position. The par-fives, where Couples's and Duval's length gave them an advantage, were now behind them and he was just one shot back. He was putting well and, for some reason, he felt calmer than he had thought he might be under the circumstances. "All your life you say, "I'd just like to get into position to win a major and see what happens," he said. "Well, here I was. I was in position to win a major."

O'Meara hit a gorgeous tee shot at 16, a five-iron that stopped just behind the hole. Couples, still pumped up, hit his tee shot just over the green. But he chipped close and saved his par. O'Meara's birdie putt just missed. In the meantime, Furyk was two-thirds of the way to his goal, having birdied 16 and 17 to join O'Meara at seven under. Duval had hit his second shot at 17 to 10 feet and knew he had made the putt. Only it hadn't gone in. "I will never know how those putts at 15 and 17 didn't go in," he said. "I thought I had made them both."

As O'Meara and Couples walked up the slight incline from the 16th green to the 17th tee, O'Meara turned to his caddy, Jerry Higginbotham, and said, "You know what, I can make birdie on these last two holes and win this thing."

Higginbotham wasn't about to argue. He loved hearing his man talk with that kind of confidence. "It was amazing how good I felt coming off of sixteen," O'Meara said. "I hit a great shot in there and a great putt even though it didn't go in."

He and Couples both hit excellent drives at 17 and each hit a nine-iron to about 10 feet. Couples was just outside O'Meara and putted first. He wasn't even close, pushing it two feet past the hole. "Worst putt I hit all week," he said. "I never even put a stroke on it."

O'Meara's stroke was perfect. The ball went dead center. It was at that moment that Duval was being taken to the Jones Cabin, having missed his birdie putt at 18. Furyk had come much closer to making his putt, a curling 25-footer that stopped two inches below the cup. If it had gone in, four players would have been tied for the lead. Drained by the effort he had made trying to catch the leaders and coming up two inches shy, Furyk tapped in.

Three men were tied for the lead at eight under. Duval was finished, O'Meara and Couples were on the 18th tee. O'Meara, pumped up and confident, hit a perfect tee shot to the right of the fairway bunker. Couples, not feeling nearly as good and with Saturday's overcut drive into the woods still on his mind, aimed for the bunker, hoping his natural cut would move the ball safely to the right. This time, though, the ball didn't cut. It went dead straight into the bunker.

In the CBS tower, Nantz, still searching for omens, pointed out that Couples had hit his tee shot into that same bunker in 1992 and gone on to win. Then, though, he had a two-shot lead. Now he had an eight-iron in his hands and 135 yards to the hole. He took too much sand, and the ball popped up right and headed straight for the front bunker, right of the green. Couples didn't even look. "I was mad at myself," he said. "It was a bad shot."

O'Meara and Higginbotham weren't certain if the right shot was a six- or a seven-iron. Understanding that he was pumped up by the magnitude of the moment, O'Meara said he liked seven-iron, preferring to hit something hard.

"Perfect," Higginbotham said. "You've got the right club. Just put a good swing on it."

Watching on TV, Brad Faxon heard Higginbotham's comment and thought, that's the right thing to say. Eliminate any doubt from the player's head.

Sure enough, O'Meara's shot landed hole high, 20 feet to the right of the hole. As they walked to the green, their fellow players crowded around TVs in the locker room. They were virtually silent. Everyone knew what was at stake in the next few minutes for all three players who made up the story line.

While Couples was preparing to hit his shot from the bunker, O'Meara looked around at the setting and couldn't help but think about how beautiful this spot was. It was coming up on 7 o'clock and the sun was starting to descend behind the trees on the now empty back nine.

O'Meara snapped out of his reverie as Couples stood over his shot. "I had this thought that Freddie could make this shot," he said. "At that point, we were in match play and in match play you learn to always expect your opponent to do something spectacular. I had to prepare myself mentally to make my putt to tie if he made the shot."

Couples hit a good shot, but it wasn't going in. It stopped six feet below the hole. He marked and the stage was clear for O'Meara. One putt to win the Masters. One putt to fulfill every golfing dream he had ever had. One putt to prove to himself once and for all that he had been right all along about his ability to close the deal on Sunday — regardless of the stakes.

He stalked the putt, seeing less break than he thought was there. He just knew there was more break than the green was showing. Higginbotham believed what his eyes saw — maybe a cup and a half of break. O'Meara was convinced it was more. And so, at 7:02 P.M., right on Rob Correa's schedule for CBS, he stood over the putt, drew the putter back, and held his breath as the ball came off the club.

"I knew right away that it had a chance," he said. "But I was afraid to move. When it got near the hole, I saw it dying left and I thought, please, please hang on."

It did. O'Meara's arms were in the air, Duval's stomach was upside down, and Couples was looking at LaCava and saying, "You know what, that's the right way for it to end."

Lance Barrow had picked the perfect camera angle for O'Meara's last putt, using the camera behind O'Meara. It showed the line of the putt perfectly and, as a bonus, the viewers could see the fans behind the hole starting to stand in unison as the ball closed in on the cup. It was a great moment of television.

At that same instant, Barrow made another decision. He had a camera rolling on Tiger Woods, who was sitting in Butler Cabin waiting to present the green jacket to the winner. As soon as the putt dropped, Woods was out of his seat, arms in the air, cheering for his pal. Barrow could have called for that shot, but he decided not to. This was O'Meara's moment and he didn't want anything — even Tiger's reaction — intruding. When O'Meara heard what Barrow had done, he was gratified and touched.

Couples congratulated O'Meara, who was trying to apologize because Higginbotham, in his excitement, had winged his cap onto Couples's line. Couples couldn't have cared less. He made the six-footer — "I honestly believe I would have made it if it had mattered," he said — and at 7:04 the Masters was over. As long as O'Meara signed his scorecard correctly.

Coming off the green, O'Meara looked for his family. They were nowhere to be found. Alicia O'Meara had tried to get inside the ropes with her two children, but they had been stopped by security people. A year earlier, those same security people had cleared the way for Earl Woods and Hughes Norton (an agent, for crying out loud) but now they blocked the O'Mearas. It wasn't until after O'Meara had signed his card and walked behind the scorer's tent that he got to see his family. They cried. He didn't. "I was still in shock," he said.

While O'Meara was whisked to Butler Cabin for the televised green jacket ceremony, Duval was taken to the interview room. His stomach and head were pounding. But he handled himself remarkably well, especially when someone asked him if he felt he had lost the Masters, having a three-shot lead with three to play.

"Pards," Duval said evenly, "I shot sixty-seven on Sunday at the Masters. The guy who won birdied three of the last four holes. I feel I gave it everything I had to give."

That didn't lessen the pain. The same was true for Couples. He knew that only two players before O'Meara — Art Wall in 1959 and Arnold Palmer in 1960 — had birdied the last two holes to win the Masters. He had seen O'Meara make putt after putt down the stretch. But until the moment that O'Meara made his putt on 18, losing had never really occurred to him.

Everyone was drained. Furyk walked into the men's grill just outside the locker room, sat down, and asked his dad to get him a beer and four Advil. He sat there, saying nothing for a long time. "You played great," Mike Furyk said. "Everyone is outside waiting for us."

"Not yet," his son answered. "I'm not ready yet."

He needed time to think about what had happened, how close he had come. "In a way, I would have been more heartbroken if Mark hadn't made his putt," he said. "Because then I would have been that two inches on 18 from being in a playoff. Mark's birdie softened it a little. Even so, I was just exhausted, drained, and a little sad."

His father was concerned. He had never seen Jim this down after a tournament. But he had never seen him come this close to winning a major.

Duval and Couples both went out to dinner with the people who had been down for the week. Sitting in the quaint restaurant at the Partridge Inn, Couples felt a little bit like the widow at a funeral. Everyone was on eggshells. "I finally told them all to quit worrying about me, that I was fine. I mean, I felt awful. I played well but I didn't win. There just wasn't anything more to say about it."

Duval's friends kept trying to cheer him up by reminding him how well he played. He put a hand up. "Guys, I know what you're trying to do and I appreciate it," he said. "But you know what? There's nothing you can say that will make me feel better. Not a single thing."

While the others tried to gather themselves to move on, O'Meara made his way to the putting green for the real awards ceremony, the one that uses a spectacular sunset as the backdrop with all the green coats and the officials from golfdom around the world inside the ropes. Will Nicholson was the master of ceremonies again and he remembered all the foreign dignitaries without needing a mulligan.

Then he asked Woods to put the green jacket on O'Meara. In the TV ceremony, Woods had struggled, holding the jacket up so high that O'Meara almost pulled a muscle reaching for it. Now he got it just right. The jacket, 44-regular, carried to the putting green as always by Arthur Williams, the club's maître d', felt absolutely perfect as Woods slipped it over O'Meara's shoulders.

"Mark," Nicholson said, "what a birdie that was on eighteen. What a finish."

Mark O'Meara looked around him at all the people, felt the green jacket on his shoulders, and said the most eloquent thing he could think of at that moment in his life:

"Wow."

II

Agony and Ecstasy

12

Square One

The PGA Tour is a little bit like that sickening bunny on TV that pitches the battery: it just keeps going and going. And so, while a lot of people take a deep breath when the Masters is over and don't pay a lot of attention to golf until nine weeks later when the United States Open begins, the tour simply picks up and moves to the next location, which happens to be Hilton Head Island, South Carolina.

Hilton Head has been the post-Masters stop for more than twenty years now, in part because it is a reasonable drive (about three hours) or a very short plane ride from Augusta, but also because it is a good place for players to take their families and such a good golf course that it can attract a strong field even in the wake of the Masters.

"It's a perfect place to go and depressurize," Brad Faxon said. "It's a good place for families, and the golf course is so good it gets your attention back on the game. But it always takes a couple of days — at least — to get any focus at all back on your golf. You just feel too drained."

David Duval was so drained by what had happened at Augusta that he withdrew from Hilton Head, convinced he would be making a mistake to go there, face all the inevitable post-Masters questions, and almost certainly play poorly, "which just would have made my mood even worse," he said. "I had to get away from it all for a little while."

Jim Furyk went but readily admitted he wasn't there mentally, his mind still jumping back to the last day at Augusta. "I played nine holes of practice on Tuesday," he said, "and to be honest I don't even remember being on the golf course."

Jay Haas, who had met his wife, Janice Pruitt, during the tournament at Hilton Head in 1977 (she had been there on a family outing and had taken him in a friendly betting pool because he was the youngest player in the field, then wandered out to watch him play a few holes), arrived at the resort feeling bittersweet about the week at Augusta. The good news was that he had finished tied for twelfth, which wrapped up a spot for him in the 1999 Masters. The bad news was that he had gotten himself into serious contending position on Saturday afternoon, hit one awful shot, and never really recovered.

Scott McCarron had left Augusta on Sunday evening with steam still coming out of his ears. He had gotten to three under par that day after making an eagle-three at the 13th hole and had walked to the 14th tee harboring hopes that he could still win the tournament. It was a long shot, but he figured if he could eagle the 15th and birdie at least two of the other four holes and get to the clubhouse at seven under, he had a slim chance. If he could birdie three of the other four and get to eight, he had a real chance. All those thoughts went by the boards when his second shot at 14, which he thought he had hit perfectly, spun back off the green. "I knew I had to get it on the back tier," he said. "I hit it, saw it bounce and disappear over the ridge. I thought it was perfect, maybe real close. I looked down to fix my divot, and when I looked up I saw the ball rolling back off the green. I felt sick."

From there he made bogey. End of fantasy. He ended up tied for sixteenth, also good enough to clinch a return ticket, but not nearly as high as he thought he should have been. "We were almost in Atlanta before I calmed down enough to have any kind of conversation with my wife," he said. "I guess that shows progress. Two years ago I finished tenth and thought it was the greatest thing that ever happened to me. This year I contended and finished sixteenth and could not have been angrier."

As might be expected, Mark O'Meara all but floated into Hilton Head. He had gone home for two days after Augusta and was still sleep starved when he got to Hilton Head. He hadn't slept much on Sunday night — too hopped up by it all — and he had awakened at 4 o'clock in the morning. He waited until 6 before he called his parents because in all the commotion the night before he had never gotten a chance to call them.

On Tuesday night, his friend Joe Louis, who had made more than a few dollars on his 33 to 1 bet, threw a victory party at his home in Isleworth. O'Meara, wearing the green jacket, pulled up the driveway and was greeted by a twenty-piece mariachi band that serenaded him through the house to the pool area in the back where about two hundred of his closest friends had been invited to celebrate with him. O'Meara loved every minute of it.

"Winning something like the Masters hits you in stages," he said. "I was in shock at first, then I was running around all night Sunday. When I got home Monday and saw all the messages and telegrams from friends and other players, it began to hit me how big a thing it was. Then, when I walked into the party at Joe's house and saw how happy all those people were for me, it really hit me. That was the best thing about the whole deal, being able to share it with all those people."

O'Meara was telling the party story to Tiger Woods on the phone the next day, describing the mariachi band and all the people who had been there. "Two hundred people?" Woods asked. "Gee, what a pain that must have been."

O'Meara laughed. He thought it was absolutely wonderful. All Woods could see was a horde of people coming at him saying the same thing over and over again. O'Meara couldn't get enough of it; Woods had already had too much. He had ended up tied for eighth on Sunday, never making any kind of move, and was on his annual post-Masters vacation with friends in California. He was genuinely happy for O'Meara but simply couldn't fathom the notion that he was actually enjoying all the attention and notoriety that came with the victory. O'Meara was never going to be bombarded the way Woods had been, but his life was most surely going to be different.

"So, how do you like having the whole world looking at you?" he asked O'Meara.

"Tig," O'Meara answered, "I'm having a blast."

On tour, Hilton Head becomes Greensboro which becomes Houston which becomes Atlanta. The players keep playing and the money keeps coming.

But in golf's netherworld, the place all those who aren't on the PGA Tour are consigned to, the places and stakes are very different. In 1998, the official dates of the U.S. Open were June 18 through June 21 at the Olympic Club in San Francisco, a historic site that had hosted three previous Opens. For sixty-seven players, Olympic was a certainty, the next major on their schedule. For everyone else, getting to Olympic meant qualifying.

Getting into the qualifying stages of the U.S. Open is not all that difficult — assuming that you have a handicap of no higher than 1.4 or are a professional golfer and that you have $100 to pay the entry fee. Until 1998 the maximum allowable handicap was 2.4, but the U.S. Golf Association decided to drop the number because they were getting far too many entries.

As a result, there were 7,117 entries for the '98 Open — 114 *more* than in 1997. "Which just proves that it's just as easy to lie about being a 1.4 as being a 2.4," one USGA official said. With sixty-seven players already qualified for the Olympic, the other 7,050 would have to deal with qualifying.

There are two stages of Open qualifying: local qualifiers played at ninety different locations around the country over a twelve-day period in May and sectional qualifiers played at twelve different locations during a two-day period the week before the Open. The local qualifier used to be 36 holes but was reduced to 18 holes five years ago because the sheer volume of entrants made it impossible to finish 36 holes in one day, and two-day local qualifiers were out of the question. The sectional qualifiers are still 36 holes, often in overheated weather. Players who have been through the sectionals — and that is almost anybody who has ever played in golf's top echelon — call it the single toughest day in the sport.

"It just drains you completely both physically and mentally," said Jay Haas, who had to go back to the sectionals in order to get into the Open in 1997. "When I came through that sectional in '97 I was about as proud of myself as I can remember being in a long, long time."

The sectionals are played at a very high level. To get to a sectional you must either be good enough to play on the PGA Tour — meaning you are very good — or have gotten through a local qualifier somewhere around the country. Very few imposters slip through those cracks.

The locals can be an entirely different story. They produce a broad cast of characters, ranging from amateurs who simply don't belong or get so nervous that they play as if they don't belong, to club pros who may or may not have had time to prepare their games to play, to rising young players who are on the Nike Tour or the Hooters Tour or a foreign tour someplace or on a mini-tour, to old pros who may have had a few moments in the spotlight but have slipped back to the point where they must slog through the local with all the various wannabes and never-weres who pay their 100 bucks for one shot at glory.

The USGA assigns a certain number of qualifying spots in the sectionals to each local. It bases those numbers on how many players sign up for a given location and the quality of each field. When players fill out their application, they must designate where they will play the local and where they will play the sectional. To avoid confusion with similar-sounding cities — like Hanford, California, and Hartford, Connecticut — or identical ones — like Springfield, Massachusetts, and Springfield, Illinois — the entrant writes in numbers. Someone playing the local qualifier at Pinehurst, North Carolina, in 1998 and the sectional in Rockville, Maryland, would fill in Site No. 18 (local) and Site No. 5 (sectional).

Locals can be assigned as few as one sectional spot (Anaconda, Montana) or up to a dozen or more. The top number varies from year to year. In '98, Pinehurst was assigned the most slots — sixteen — in large part because the Nike Tour had stopped about ninety minutes away in Cary, North Carolina, the previous weekend and quite a few players had opted to play their local there. At the locals, Nike Tour players are at the top of the pecking order. The locals and mini-tour players call them "big-bag guys" because they work regularly with caddies and use the forty-pound bags that are common on the pro tours. Many players who participate in the locals carry their own bags or take a pull cart or use an electric cart and have someone drive the cart for them since USGA rules specifically prohibit riding — unless you are Casey Martin.

The field at Pinehurst Plantation, a relatively new Arnold Palmer–designed course in the world-famous Pinehurst area, was dotted with players who had not only been on tour, but had been successful on tour: Woody Austin, who had beaten out David Duval and Justin Leonard for the rookie of the year award in 1995 after winning the Buick Open, was in the field. Now a Nike Tour player, Austin was searching for the game that had made him nearly $750,000 three years earlier. Vance Heafner and David Thore were both Wake Forest graduates and longtime players on the big tour. Thore's main claim to fame in golf lore may have dated back to 1975 when he convinced his Wake Forest roommate Curtis Strange to crawl back to his girlfriend at the start of his junior year. A year later Curtis and Sarah Strange were married.

"I told him, 'Curtis, there's no way you're going to find anybody else that nice who is going to put up with you,'" Thore said, laughing. "I said, 'You better *run* back there and hope she'll take you.'" Fortunately for Strange, he listened to Thore.

Other players who had won on the tour but found themselves back playing in a local included Mike Sullivan, Barry Jaeckel, and Mike Heinen, although Heinen withdrew at the last moment.

As it turned out, Jaeckel should have withdrawn too. He would have saved himself a lot of time and grief. Jaeckel had won on tour in 1978 and had been a part of the famous five-way Kemper Open playoff in 1983 that had produced Fred Couples's first tour victory. Jaeckel was waiting for 1999, when he would be eligible for the Senior Tour, and was playing an occasional Nike Tour event to prepare for next year. Jaeckel arrived on the first tee for his 1:24 P.M. tee time, hit his tee shot, jumped in his cart, and started driving in the direction of his ball.

Whoops.

Both the entry form that the players fill out and the local rules sheet each player was handed on the first tee had a very specific note about "auto transportation." The local rules sheet, which Jaeckel had been given, said, "Automotive transportation is prohibited except between nines. Penalty is two strokes for each hole at which a violation occurs, maximum of four strokes. If a violation is not discontinued upon its discovery, the player shall be disqualified."

Jaeckel was standing in the first fairway when the starter approached him and told him he was sorry but he would have to take a two-stroke penalty for riding in a cart. Jaeckel was stunned and furious. He hadn't even thought to hire a caddy. He now had two options: take his bag (a big one) off the cart and carry it (or get a hand cart) the rest of the way, beginning the day two strokes behind the field, or quit.

Jaeckel quit. He got into his cart, rode back to the clubhouse, and told Ray Novicki, who was running the qualifier for the Carolinas Golf Association (CGA), just what he thought of the rules. He said he was going to call Tom Meeks, the chairman of rules and competitions at the USGA, and tell him what he thought about the USGA, U.S. Open qualifiers, the CGA, and Novicki. He stormed through the tiny eating area inside the clubhouse grumbling loudly about the injustice of it all, slamming the door on the way out.

A few minutes later, he was back. "I need to use a phone," he explained as he was pointed to the only phone inside the clubhouse. Riding a cart, as it turned out, hadn't been Jaeckel's first mistake of the day. He had locked his keys inside his car. He called for help, then stood outside by himself for the next twenty minutes looking about as miserable as a human being can look.

Jaeckel wasn't the only player burned by the no-riding rule. Ryan Gioffre, a young pro from Greensboro, misunderstood the starter's instructions on the first tee. "He said to us, 'Gentlemen, keep your carts on the paths, don't drive them on the fairways,'" Gioffre said. "I thought he was talking to the players."

The starter had been talking to the caddies. Gioffre hadn't read the local rules closely enough, so after a few holes he began riding. When a rules official saw him riding, he informed him that he had broken the no-riding rule. Since Gioffre had already ridden for two holes, he was penalized four strokes. He ended up shooting 73 — with the penalty strokes. Without them, he would have qualified.

Even pared to 18 holes, the local qualifiers are always in a race to beat sundown. At Pinehurst Plantation, there were 148 players entered and 146 left after Heinen withdrew and Jaeckel drove himself into oblivion. Tee times were assigned the same way they are assigned at a regular PGA Tour event, half the players going off in the morning from both the first and tenth tees and the other half doing the same in the afternoon.

That meant the morning players had to sit around and wait for the afternoon players to finish before they would know if they were in, out, or in a playoff.

Of course some players knew their fate long before they finished their round. Locals always produce some very high numbers, and this one was no exception. There were twenty scores of 80 or higher, topped by the 89 shot by Brian Ketchem, who had driven over from Hillsborough to torture himself for five hours. At least Ketchem posted his score. Six players in the field didn't even bother. Anyone who shot in the 80s, unless he had some past history of playing better than that, was a candidate to receive a "Prove It" letter from the USGA. In other words, before they would be allowed to enter the Open again, they would have to show some proof that they were capable of playing better than they had played in 1998.

No one knows at the start of the day what kind of score will be needed to qualify. Everyone guesses. "I'm thinking three under [69] at least gets into the playoff," Jay Williamson said, walking down the ninth fairway. "There's some wind, the course isn't playing that easy, and there are sixteen spots. Maybe two under will do it. Or maybe it will be four under. Who knows?"

That's the beauty and the torture of qualifiers. No one knows. This was the third straight year a local had been played at Pinehurst Plantation. Even though the development around the golf course was still in its early stages — the clubhouse consisted of a small pro shop and a snack bar — the players liked the golf course, so the USGA had come back to it.

Williamson, who had played on the PGA Tour in 1995 and 1996 and was now on the Nike Tour, had missed the cut in Cary and had arrived in Pinehurst a day early to play a practice round. To the club pros and amateurs in the field, Williamson was one of the "big-bag guys," someone who had (gasp!) been on the PGA Tour and was now making decent money one level down on the Nike. Williamson had finished 145th on the big-tour money list in 1995 and 175th in 1996, contending a number of times, but never cashing the big check he needed to stay exempt. His best chance had come at the Kemper Open in '96, where he actually led the event for three rounds before a 79 on the last day had sent him spiraling down to a tie for twenty-third.

Williamson was not the least bit troubled to be on the Nike Tour at this point in his life. He had played hockey, not golf, at Trinity College in Connecticut and had turned pro in 1989 more as an experiment than anything else. He had always been a good player without working all that hard at the game, and he wondered how good he might become if he put time and effort into it. "I was arrogant enough to believe I could be good just by spending more time on the game," he said. "I found out it wasn't quite that simple."

Just now at the age of thirty-one was he starting to feel as if he understood how to play and how to compete and how to live life on the road. "When I was on the Tour those two years, I really didn't get it," he said. "I had some ability, so there were times when I played okay. But when I really needed to dig in and figure out how to score on days when I didn't have it, I couldn't do it. That day at the Kemper was a perfect example.

"Being back on the Nike is good for me. I'm learning about having to score and having to go low to make a check. When I get back on the big tour the next time, I'll be a lot better prepared."

He and his wife, Marnie, were traveling from event to event in their car along with their cat, Sherwin. As Williamson headed down the first fairway at 8:40 A.M. with playing partners Lane Smith and Gabe Southards, they had a gallery of one: Marnie. Sherwin was asleep back at the hotel.

Williamson didn't know either of his playing partners. Southards was a club pro from Goldston, North Carolina, who was carrying his own bag. Smith was an amateur, a year out of Appalachian State, who had played very little golf in the year since he graduated. "Last year I shot seventy in the local in Atlanta," he said. "But back then, I was playing every day. Now I haven't played at all. I'm not even sure I should be here."

In many ways, this was a classic local qualifier threesome: a young touring pro trying to find his way as a player; a pro who spent a lot more time teaching than he did playing; and an amateur who had no idea what kind of game he would show up at the golf course with.

Smith's concerns proved to be legitimate almost from the start. He was spraying the ball all over the golf course, and the group spent a fair amount of time tracking down his golf balls. At one point, after a lengthy search for another wild tee shot, Williamson and Southards went off to play their own second shots. A moment later, Smith found his ball and, not wanting to hold play up any longer than he already had, he picked up a club and thrashed his way out of the trees. Williamson was in the fairway standing over his second shot when he heard a thud a couple of feet to his right. He looked up and saw Smith's ball. "Wow," he said. "I never knew qualifying for the Open could be dangerous."

Smith ended up shooting 85, as did Southards, who tired on the back nine and began losing balls too. Williamson kept plugging away, turning in 33, then getting to four under when he rolled in a 10-footer for birdie at the 13th. "Four under isn't bad," he said. "But five or six would be better."

Five or six would have been better, but no matter how much a golfer tells himself to keep playing for birdies when he is playing well, the protective instinct is a hard one to fight, especially in a qualifier where winning means nothing. The last qualifier advances to the next stage with the exact same status as the first qualifier.

Williamson had to work to save par at the 15th hole when he pushed his drive into a tree, and he bogeyed the par-three 17th when he pulled a four-iron left of the green to a spot where an up and down was almost out of the question. He tapped in for bogey and walked off the green with a frown on his face. "I'm playing prevent defense," he said. "Which is the perfect way to blow the whole deal."

Williamson parred the difficult, overwater 18th and signed for a 69. Watching the other morning scores come trickling in, he was confident that 69 would be good enough. The wind had started to kick up on the back nine, and he thought the afternoon players would have a tougher time with the golf course than the morning players had. Marnie had gone back to the hotel to get Sherwin in the hope that they could get on the road to Richmond — the next Nike stop — right after lunch.

Williamson was sitting on the back patio of the clubhouse where Novicki had set up headquarters. He had written the names of all 148 players signed up for the qualifier and posted the scoring sheets on the wall of the patio. Players milled around the scoring sheets, staring at them, analyzing them as if they were hieroglyphics. There had been a couple of 68s among the morning players and four 69s. If that pattern repeated in the afternoon, 69 would easily qualify. Patrick Lee, another

Nike Tour player who had just finished his round, sat down with Williamson.

"Do any good?" Lee asked, speaking pro-golf speak.

"Three under," Williamson answered. "You?"

"Two under," Lee answered. "Three's good. At worst you'll play off."

Lee's analysis rocked Williamson. He had thought three under was a lock to qualify. Lee didn't see it that way.

"I was thinking two might play off," he said.

Lee, a twenty-six-year-old from Oxford, Mississippi, who was in his third year on the Nike Tour, smiled. "Well, I certainly hope you're right because that's my only chance," he said. "But it'll be close."

Williamson groaned. He didn't want close, he wanted in and out — in the sectional and out of Pinehurst on his way to Richmond. By now, Marnie had returned, ready to hit the road. Sherwin was waiting in the car. Williamson updated her on the situation. "Your call," she said, knowing that Jay had to do what was going to make him comfortable.

Williamson looked at Lee again. "What would you do?" he asked.

"Put it this way," he said. "Are you going to feel worse if you stick around and find out you wasted a few hours because sixty-nine was safe or if you get up the highway and you call back here and find out sixty-nine played off?"

Williamson knew the answer to that question. At that moment Perry Moss, another former PGA Tour player now on the Nike, walked by. "How'd you do, Perry?" Williamson asked.

"Three under," Moss said.

"You staying or leaving?"

Moss looked at him as if he was from Mars. "Are you kidding?" he said. "I can't leave. I'd miss the playoff."

That settled it. Williamson stood up and looked at Marnie. "There was a barbershop at that little mall we were in yesterday," he said. "Maybe I can get a haircut."

Marnie looked at her watch. It was a little after two o'clock. The last afternoon group had just teed off. "I hope there's a line," she said.

Williamson and Lee and Moss weren't the only ones playing the waiting game. Anyone who had shot 71 or better still had a chance, although the 71s weren't feeling all that optimistic. Some players went to the range to hit some balls, others sat in the snack bar and waited.

David Havens, a twenty-five-year-old graduate of Virginia Tech, who had been playing on the South African tour, and Kirk Junge, a thirty-four-year-old who had been playing in Europe for a number of years, shared a table and stories about life overseas as a golfer. Havens had shot 70, Junge a 71. Havens was thinking he would be in a playoff; Junge was hoping for one.

"You never know when the breakthrough is going to come," he said softly. "I know it's getting late for me, but I've played pretty well overseas at times. I'd like to come back home and have a shot to play here. If not . . . "

He didn't finish the sentence. Havens was thinking he was almost ready to come home too. He was considering trying the Q-School in the fall, hoping to at least make it to the Nike Tour. For both players, reaching the Open sectionals would represent a step forward and a chance to compete with a higher level of players than they had associated with in the past. "If I got into the Open, wow, that would be something," Havens said. "But even if I didn't, the experience of going 36 holes with that kind of pressure would be good for me."

It was getting late in the day by now, and the afternoon players were starting to come in. The Williamsons had walked out to the steps leading to the 18th and ninth greens (which adjoined one another) to watch players finish. Lee was on the patio staring the board down as if the low scores would go away if he looked at it long enough. Havens and Junge looked up and saw a rangy, blond-haired player approaching, scorecard in hand. He had what amounted to an entourage for this event: caddy, girlfriend, and a couple of friends.

"Uh-oh," Havens said. "Big-bag guy with a smile on his face."

Havens was right. Joey Snyder III was coming off his best week on the Nike Tour — a third place finish in Cary. He was a month shy of twenty-five, in just his second year as a pro. He had shot 67, the low round of the day. As a result, Snyder got to do what every player in the field craved doing: hand in his scorecard and have Novicki hand him a card with instructions on the sectional. "You bring that with you to the sectional," he told him.

Snyder nodded, still smiling. Havens and Junge had walked outside to look at the board again. Vance Heafner — whose father, Clayton, was runner-up behind Ben Hogan in the 1950 Open — had posted a 68. He too got his sectionals card and information sheet. The afternoon scores were proving to be lower than the morning scores. Two more 68s went up. There were now ten players at 69 or better. A sixth 70 was added to the list. Junge knew what that meant. He shook hands with Havens.

"Nice talking to you," he said. "Good luck. I hope you make it."

"Thanks," Havens said. "There will be other days."

Junge shrugged. "I had fun. I played pretty well. Just not good enough. Maybe another time."

He knew, though, that he was starting to run out of other times.

When the last group was finally in, it was 7 o'clock and the air was crisp, the sun beginning to fade. In all, twelve players had broken 70. Williamson's 69 had been safe as it turned out, but he didn't mind waiting. "I'd have been miserable the entire time in the car if we'd left," he said. "Now we can enjoy the trip, break it up with dinner."

He smiled. "The funny thing is one of the reasons I didn't want to stay was that I was worried about Sherwin being in the car for a long time. Imagine what it would have been like if I had to tell my friends I missed making the sectionals because I left too soon worrying about my cat."

The Williamsons stopped on their way out to wish Lee good luck. He would be joining nine other players in a twilight playoff for the last four spots. Only one of the ten players in the playoff had ever played in an Open: Roy Hunter, a club pro from Greensboro, who had qualified for the Open in '97 and found himself playing a practice round at Congressional with Tiger Woods.

Novicki sent the players off in two threesomes and a foursome. "Just keep playing until we tell you to stop," he said, fully aware of the fact that darkness was going to be a factor very soon. It was 7:25 when the first group went off with a gallery of three — members of the club who had wandered out to watch.

Maybe it was experience, but the only player to birdie the first hole was Hunter, who rolled in a 10-footer and threw a tired fist into the air. The bad luck award went to Jay Patterson, a young club pro from Durham whose older brother Lee worked on the PGA Tour as a media official. Jay Patterson hit a perfect drive that landed squarely in a divot and could barely get his second shot airborne. He and Press McPhaul, another young pro from North Carolina, made bogeys and were eliminated.

Everyone else made par. That meant there were now seven players left playing for three spots. The most disappointed of that group was Havens, who had hit a gorgeous second shot to within six feet only to miss the birdie putt that would have given him a spot in the sectional.

"Oh God, that hurts," he said, walking to the second tee.

He was in more pain after bogeying the second hole. That eliminated him. Mark Slawter birdied the hole to win the second spot. The other five players made par. Now it was five players for two spots as they played the par-three third hole. It was after 8 o'clock and starting to get dark. Novicki had told his assistants to hold the players after the third hole since the fourth hole was a par-five. The third hole eliminated one more player, George Bryan, who made a bogey while everyone else made par.

Novicki, who was in the clubhouse, sent word out by walkie-talkie to have the four remaining players play the third hole again. "And put 'em in carts to save some time," he said. Since the playoff was not part of the official round, Novicki was no longer worried about the no-carts rule. He just wanted a conclusion. Somewhere down the road, one could imagine the look on Barry Jaeckel's face when he received this bit of news.

The contenders were playing in virtual darkness by now. Only one of the four, Robert Conrad, could par the hole on the second time through. He got the third spot. Patrick Lee was furious with himself because he had missed a makable six-footer after hitting a gorgeous recovery from the bunker.

It was 8:35 and completely dark. Lee, Chuck Tickle, and Michael Walton, who had made a 30-foot putt on the 18th hole just to get into the playoff, were left. One spot remained. Novicki was on the walkie-talkie again. "Tell the players they can keep going if they want or come back here at 7:30 tomorrow morning."

Lee, Tickle, and Walton looked at each other. No one wanted to come back in the morning. Back to the third tee they went. Lee hit first, using the same five-iron he had used the last two times he had played the hole. It was so dark that the ball disappeared the instant it came off the club face. Lee's gut told him he had done something right. "Fellas," he said, "I think I hit that one perfect."

Up at the green, Havens, who had lingered to see who would end up with the final spot, confirmed Lee's gut feeling. "Great shot," came the sound of his voice.

Whether great meant on the green or 10 feet or really close, no one knew for sure. Tickle and Walton both missed the green again. When the three players got to the green, they saw just how good Lee's shot was: he was 18 inches from the cup. Tickle and Walton both played the hole out, making four. That meant Lee could two-putt. He tapped in and breathed a huge sigh of relief. It was 8:45.

Back in the clubhouse, Novicki was waiting. He now had his sixteen players, but he needed a first alternate just in case someone got sick or for some reason couldn't play in the sectional. "What did you guys make the last time you played the hole?" he asked Tickle and Walton. "Four," they both answered.

Novicki took a coin out of his pocket. "Call it, Chuck," he said.

"Tails," Tickle said.

Everyone looked at the carpet. The coin had come up tails. "Congratulations, Chuck, you're first alternate," Novicki said.

As he turned out the lights on his way out, Novicki sighed. "I can't wait," he said, "to do this again next year."

13

The Men of the USGA

In all, 580 players advanced from the ninety locals to the twelve sectionals. They were joined by 170 players who were exempt from local qualifying, meaning that there were 750 players left to compete for the eighty-nine nonexempt spots available at Olympic.

On the Thursday before the sectionals would be held, exactly two weeks before the Open would begin, David B. Fay sat down at his desk at USGA Headquarters in Far Hills, New Jersey, with the names of the sixty-seven exempt players. His job on that morning was to begin making the pairings for the ninety-eighth U.S. Open.

Fay is the executive director of the USGA, a job he has held since Frank Hannigan stepped down from the job in 1989 to become a full-time journalist and TV commentator, working then for *Golf Magazine* (now for *Golf Digest*) and ABC. Although he does wear the occasional bow tie, Fay is hardly what you would expect in a man who runs the day-to-day operations of an organization that has long had an image of being both patrician and conservative.

Fay is forty-eight, a cancer survivor, and the father of two teenage girls who readily admits his favorite sport is baseball. "You don't have a soul if you don't love baseball," he often says. Fay grew up in the tiny New York City suburb of Tuxedo, New York, but he was a long way from being a rich kid. Fay was introduced to golf working as a caddy at the tony Tuxedo Club. He started playing golf there on Mondays, the one day of the week caddies were allowed to play, teaching himself the game. His parents knew nothing about golf even though his father had been a very good athlete growing up in New Jersey, excelling as a pitcher in high school.

"My dad was a renaissance man in his own way," Fay said. "He played baseball and he boxed and he never went to college. But he was also a pretty good actor. One year in summer stock he was in a show opposite Mae West."

Fay went to Colgate, where he joined the golf team as a walk-on, grew his hair long, and went to Woodstock in the summer of '69. "I wasn't your typical concertgoer though," he said. "I went to the concert one afternoon, to the races that night at Monticello, and played golf at the Concorde the next day." Another renaissance man.

One summer his father, a steamship captain, got him a job working on the SS *United States*, which at the time was the largest passenger ship in the world with accommodations for 1,900 people. Fay had what may be the worst summer job in the history of college students: "When someone got seasick, I went and cleaned up after them."

One particularly busy night, Fay was called to one of the larger staterooms on the ship. When the door opened, he immediately recognized the face, even though it was somewhat green. "The Duke of Windsor," Fay said. "He always traveled the Atlantic by ship and he always went on American ships after his abdication. I guess he wasn't comfortable on Cunard under the circumstances."

He wasn't comfortable that night either. Fay did what he had to do and left. When the ship got back to New York he told his father that he appreciated the help finding a job, but enough was enough. He went back to the Tuxedo Club, where he worked in the pro shop taking care of carts and clubs. About a month after he had returned, one of the members, Stanley Mortimer, showed up with a special guest: the Duke of Windsor. As Fay was putting the Duke's clubs on his cart, the Duke kept staring at him.

"You have seen me before," Fay finally said. "It was on the SS *United States*."

The Duke stared for another moment and then his eyes widened in recognition. "Oh yes," he said without a hint of a smile. "I *do* remember you."

After college, Fay worked as an investment counselor in a New York bank, a job he found very dull. When his roommate at the time, a man named George Peper, quit his job as communications director for the Metropolitan Golf Association, Fay thought, I can do that job, and applied. He was hired, and two years later the USGA offered him a job across the river. By 1979, he was the advance man on site for most USGA events.

In fact, he spent his honeymoon in Toledo, advancing the 1979 U.S. Open. "I got married, had one day with [new wife] Joan, and then went to Toledo," he said. "Back then part of my job was to set up the ropes around the golf course. If nothing else, it got you in shape."

That U.S. Open was the year the famous "Hinkle Tree" was planted. Several USGA officials became very upset when Lon Hinkle, one of the longest hitters on tour, decided the best way to play the par-five eighth hole was to aim way left and hit his ball down the 15th fairway. Hinkle was a prominent player at the time — he would win twice that year and finish third on the money list — and some of the USGA muck-a-mucks thought his strategy was making a mockery of the golf course. So, after Hinkle had made his second straight birdie on Friday, they ordered Inverness officials to go out and buy a tree and plant it to the left of the tee so Hinkle couldn't hit the ball in that direction.

The officials returned with a black spruce tree and a bill for $120, which they dropped on Fay's desk. "I thought they were joking," Fay said. They weren't. It was the USGA that wanted the tree, and the USGA that paid for the tree.

Fay became the starter for the Open when Hannigan became executive director in 1982. Since ABC televised all 18 holes of the Open on Saturday and Sunday, the network wanted to give the viewers an idea of what it was like on the first tee of a major championship. Fay figured this would be his fifteen minutes of fame. He would be on camera as he introduced the players in the last several groups and also introduce the walking officials with the groups.

"It was almost as if they wanted it to be like boxing with a microphone being lowered from the ceiling," Fay said. "It wasn't really a big deal, but I had never been on national TV before. I didn't want to take a chance on ending up standing there doing a Ralph Kramden, you know, humana . . . humana . . . humana."

Fay brought little note cards with him to the tee and smoothly introduced all the players and officials. That night he called his father to see if he had watched.

"I watched," Don Fay said. "Can I ask you a question?"

"Sure."

"Why is it that a reasonably intelligent college graduate needs note cards to read a total of ten lines?"

"Well, Dad, I didn't want to make a mistake and . . ."

"Can I ask another question?" Don Fay said.

"Sure."

"Did I really pay all that money for college so you could be a starter?"

Fay never used notes again.

Late in 1985, Fay began experiencing stomach pains. His doctors ran a number of tests and came back with a frightening diagnosis: cancer, a form known as Burkitt's lymphoma. Burkitt's lymphoma is a very aggressive form of stomach cancer that is found most often in children and, for some reason, very often on the coast of West Africa. "Gee," Fay said when his oncologist explained all this to him, "this would certainly be a strange way to find out I had ancestors from the Ivory Coast."

There weren't a lot more laughs during the next six months. The doctors told him that because the lymphoma had been discovered early, there was a good chance he could beat it but only with very aggressive chemotherapy. Fay was in the hospital, most of the time in isolation, for the next six months. "After a while I was convinced that if the cancer didn't kill me, the chemo would," he said. "I looked at it like a poker hand I had been dealt. One way or the other, I had to play it."

Fay's major concern during those six months was his family. His daughters, Katie and Molly, were four and two. "My thought was, okay this is tough on me, but what if they have to deal with my not being around. That was what worried me most."

The chemo worked. Fay had made it his goal to get out of the hospital in time for the U.S. Open at Shinnecock. He did — leaving the day the championship began — but landed right back there with a fever. A month later, he left for good. He was completely bald and had lost forty-five pounds. A week later, he ran the girls' U.S. Junior Championship in

Marysville, California. "I bulked up on Mexican food and ice cream," he said. "I gained sixteen pounds in nine days."

Three years later, completely cancer free, he replaced Hannigan. Like Hannigan, Fay approaches his job of putting the pairings together with both a sense of history and a sense of humor. Before he sat down to start his work, he always looked up the pairings from the last time the tournament had been played at that site. The Open had been played at Olympic in 1987 with Scott Simpson beating Tom Watson by one shot to win his only major title. Fay noticed that Simpson had played the first two days that year with Nick Price and Don Pooley. So he made an "if" pairing. Simpson and Price were both exempt. Pooley was in the sectional in Rockville, Maryland. If Pooley qualified, he would be reunited with Simpson and Price at Olympic.

Fay did that for one other pairing. In 1987, Hannigan had paired three U.S. Amateur champions: John Cook (1978), Mark O'Meara (1979), and Scott Verplank (1984). O'Meara and Cook were exempt; Verplank was also in Rockville. If Verplank made it, he would play with O'Meara and Cook again.

One pairing was automatic: Ernie Els, Justin Leonard, and Matt Kuchar — the defending champion, the British Open champion, and the U.S. Amateur champion. After that, Fay could get creative. Each year Fay put together his version of the BPNTHWAM threesome. In 1997 at Congressional the group had consisted of Davis Love III, Phil Mickelson, and Colin Montgomerie. Love had made himself ineligible for the pairing with his victory at the PGA. That left Mickelson and Montgomerie. Fay put Montgomerie in the group and then added David Duval, who had won at Houston three weeks earlier, his fifth victory in eight months, not to mention his near miss at the Masters. But he left Mickelson out, replacing him with Jim Furyk.

"I did it because I honestly thought on this particular golf course, right now, based on recent play, Furyk had a better chance to win," Fay said. "In fact, I wouldn't have been surprised if the winner had come from that threesome."

What's more, Fay doesn't like to be predictable. He then put together a couple of groups for fun: the "three-Ws" pairing — Tiger Woods, Lee Westwood, and Tom Watson. This was actually a wonderful threesome: the old Stanford man (Watson) and the young Stanford man

(Woods), and the hottest young player in the U.S. (Woods) playing with the hottest young player in Europe (Westwood). He also came up with a "God Squad" pairing: Steve Jones, Bernhard Langer, and Tom Lehman, all born-again Christians, the first two very vocal about it. Fay then created his "old men" pairing: Senior Open champion Graham Marsh, Jack Nicklaus (limping on a bad hip), and Ben Crenshaw (limping after foot surgery). "They can push each other along," Fay said.

Years ago, Hannigan had taken an opposite tack with a threesome that involved Crenshaw. He had been convinced for years that Tom Shaw, a very solid player during the 1970s, was fibbing about his age, making himself a couple of years younger than he really was. So, in 1971, Hannigan paired him for the first two rounds with nineteen-year-old Crenshaw and twenty-four-year-old Johnny Miller, both very good and very fast getting around the golf course. The weather was hot and Hannigan couldn't resist sneaking out Friday afternoon to watch Shaw come up 18. "He looked as if he had played 36 that day," Hannigan said. "He was the portrait of Dorian Gray."

It turned out Hannigan was right about Shaw. For years, he listed his birth date in the PGA Tour media guide as December 13, 1942. But in 1988, he produced a birth certificate listing his DOB as December 13, 1938. The reason: being fifty meant he was eligible for the Senior Tour.

Fay had followed in the Hannigan tradition of trying to be imaginative in making pairings. But he had toned down in recent years. "I decided I had gone too far one year at the Women's Open when I put three players together because they were all in therapy," he said.

He had not, however, given up one of Hannigan's more hallowed traditions: the prick pairing. Hannigan swears he did not give the pairing its name, but he admits that each year he would put three players together he didn't like or who were generally disliked in the golf world. Insiders loved guessing the prick pairing each year, although more often than not it wasn't that difficult.

For 1998 Fay's prick pairing was Mark Brooks, Scott Hoch, and Andrew Magee. Brooks and Hoch were easy to figure: both were known as complainers, although to be fair, Hoch always softened what he was saying with a tangy sense of humor. He just had a way of saying the wrong thing at the wrong time. Brooks wasn't the least bit mean, he just seemed perennially unhappy, even after winning the PGA Championship in 1996. Neither was likely to be voted man of the year in the locker room.

By contrast, Magee was well liked in the locker room. The only real complaint about him from other players was that he tended to be very slow on the golf course. Fay's complaint was different. Sometime after President Clinton had taken his fall in Greg Norman's house in 1997, he had seen Magee quoted as saying that if Clinton had been at his house, he might have kicked him down the stairs himself.

Like his predecessor Hannigan, Fay is a liberal Democrat, someone who readily admits that his politics are well left of most people in golf and certainly far to the left of almost everyone who plays on tour. But he says he would have been just as offended by the comment if a liberal Democrat had made it about a right-wing Republican. Thus Magee would join Brooks and Hoch.

Once he had finished placing all sixty-seven exempt players into threesomes, Fay forwarded copies of his work to Mike Butz, his assistant executive director; to Larry Adamson, the man in charge of tournament entries; and to Tom Meeks, the director of rules and competition. It would fall to Meeks to make any changes and fill in the remaining players after qualifying was over. Fay had assigned a specific starting time to two groups: the three Ws at 9:02 Pacific Time on Thursday and the group of Nick Faldo, Tom Kite, and Corey Pavin at the same time Friday. The reason: television. NBC, which had wrested the Open's TV rights from ABC beginning in 1995 at a price of $13 million a year, had asked that Woods be on the golf course during the time they were on the air on Thursday (3 to 5 P.M. Eastern time) and the same for Faldo on Friday.

Fay was surprised by the Faldo request. "The only thing I can think is that's prime time in Europe," he said. "But the way he's playing you would think Montgomerie or Westwood would be a higher priority." Nonetheless, if TV wanted Faldo in Euro prime time, TV would get Faldo in Euro prime time.

As soon as he saw Fay's pairings, Meeks had two problems: there were four groups that included two foreign players. Meeks believes that at the U.S. Open there should be at least two American players in every group — especially among the exempt players — unless it is impossible to do so. Second, he thought Fay hadn't left enough exempt players unassigned. He didn't want the pairings to look as if they were tiered: exempt players together and qualifiers together. Fay agreed on both points. Meeks was the detail guy. He would have the job of filling in the entire bracket on the morning of June 10 after all the qualifiers had been completed.

"David gets to have the fun," Meeks said, laughing. "I get to do the work."

Meeks was a perfect alter ego for Fay. He was fifty-five and had worked for the USGA for twenty-three years. Although he was a devout St. Louis Cardinal fan and, being from Indiana, a basketball junkie, there was no doubting the fact that his first love was golf. He was a good player — his handicap fluctuated between six and eight — who liked to say that he was one year away from being a very good player. "And next year," he would add, "I'll be two years away."

Meeks is the point man for the USGA at every Open. It is his job to finalize the pairings and, more important, work with the staff to get the golf course into as close to perfect shape — USGA style — as possible. He had already made several trips to Olympic and would arrive in San Francisco on the Friday before the tournament began to see what kind of shape it was in. Then, on Sunday, the day before most of the players arrived, he would tour the golf course and select the pin positions for the week.

"Hole locations," he corrected. "There's no such thing as a pin, it's a flagstick. That means there's no such thing as a pin position. You pick a spot to locate the hole — a hole location."

The Masters had its patrons and its first nine and second nine; the USGA had hole locations. No one on NBC would be caught dead uttering the dreaded words "pin position."

But there would be an awful lot of talk about hole locations before Tom Meeks's week at the Olympic club was over.

14

Return to the Open

It was shortly after 7 A.M. on Monday, June 8, and the driving range at Woodmont Country Club looked as if the Member-Guest was just about to start. Every inch of turf was being used, golfers squeezing together so that everyone could get a few swings in.

These swings, however, had little in common with the ones seen at anybody else's Member-Guest. These were the swings of 165 players who had come to Rockville, Maryland, a Washington, D.C., suburb, hoping to get into the U.S. Open. Among the twelve sectional qualifiers being played around the country — nine on Monday and three more on Tuesday — this was easily the largest and the most competitive. Since Woodmont is about a fifteen-minute drive from the Tournament Players Club at Avenel, the site of the just-ended Kemper Open, it had drawn the most full-fledged members of the PGA Tour. Mindful of that, the USGA had awarded Woodmont the most spots in the Open — thirty-two.

Each year there are two qualifying sites that the USGA unofficially calls "tour qualifiers." One is played on Monday in or near the city where the prior week's PGA Tour stop was, and the other is played on Tuesday near the location of the next week's tour stop. That gives players the option of staying where they are to play on Monday or traveling on Monday, settling into where they are staying for the week, and then playing on Tuesday.

Most opt for Monday. "It's just easier to stay in the same place and worry about where you're going next after you play the qualifier," Steve Stricker said as he finished his warm-up. He smiled. "If I didn't play today, I'd just spend all day worrying about playing tomorrow."

Stricker's presence in the qualifier was a textbook example of the fragile nature of Life on Tour. From 1993 through 1996 his career had pulled into the fast lane and zoomed past most of the best players in the world. In the summer of '93 he had been the leading money winner on the Canadian Tour. Then he earned a spot on the PGA Tour at Q-School that December. He finished fiftieth on the money list in '94, fortieth in '95, and fourth, with just under $1.4 million in earnings, in '96. He won twice in '96, first at the Kemper Open and then a dominating eight-shot victory a month later at the Western Open.

He was twenty-nine years old, a member of the Presidents Cup team that year, almost a lock to play on the Ryder Cup team in '97, and clearly a player-on-the-come on tour. He was also exactly what corporate America was looking for: tall, blond, handsome, and unfailingly polite with a quick, easy smile. His caddy was his wife, Nicki, just as attractive and charming and polite, a good player in her own right who could often be seen analyzing her husband's swing on the practice tee.

Taylor Made, one of the newer players in the booming golf club business, threw huge numbers in his direction. Play the clubs, wear the hat for three years, and we'll pay you a little more than $2 million. Stricker had been playing Arnold Palmer clubs with a great deal of success, but the money Palmer was offering for a renewal wasn't even close to what Taylor Made was offering. Stricker faced a decision a lot of young players face when they have had great success: take the money staring you in the face or take less money to continue with the golf clubs that have helped you become so successful.

"You go out on the tour with one thing in mind: winning," Stricker said. "But sooner or later you realize that it's also your business, the way you make your living. If the money had been close, I would have stayed with Palmer. But it wasn't even close to being close. I would have been crazy to say no."

The golf world is littered with sad stories about players who changed equipment at a moment in their career when they appeared to be peaking and all of a sudden couldn't find a fairway, a green, or the hole. Corey Pavin, Payne Stewart, Davis Love, Lee Janzen, and Nick Price are a few of the better-known names who took the money and eventually found themselves running from the equipment they were being paid to use.

Stricker knew those stories and knew there was risk involved. But he also knew that Taylor Made would work very hard to make certain it came up with clubs he was comfortable with. But it didn't work. Maybe it was a mental block or maybe it wasn't, but Stricker never once got comfortable during 1997. The big problem was the driver. Stricker had played with a small-headed driver his whole life, often playing with a driver that played more like a two-wood. Taylor Made wanted him to play its new bubble-shafted driver, the one it had unveiled to compete with the big-headed drivers that were making Callaway rich.

The harder Stricker tried to feel comfortable with the driver, the less comfortable he felt. The more he struggled with his driver, the tougher it became to do anything else well. He had to hit perfect iron shots because he was in difficult spots off the tees. He was constantly trying to get up and down, and that wore on him mentally. As soon as he hit his first bad drive of the day, he started thinking, here we go again. He began disliking golf. He didn't want to be on the golf course or in a tournament. "I played only twenty times all year and it felt like forty," he said. "It just stopped being fun."

In 1996 he had finished in the top three on seven different occasions. In 1997 his highest finish was a seventh in the Quad Cities Classic in July. Prior to that, he hadn't finished higher than twenty-seventh all year, and that had come in the thirty-player field for the Mercedes Championships (tournament winners from the previous year only) in January.

In short, Stricker was awful. He took time off in May to rest and try to find a driver he could play with. It didn't work. The seventh place at Quad Cities gave him some hope, but he was sixty-second at the British Open the next week and missed the cut at the PGA three weeks after that. After the tour came through Milwaukee at the end of August, Stricker decided he'd had enough. Even though he had his second-best week of the year — finishing T-12 — he decided to stay home in Madison while the tour moved on to the fall events. He had made $167,652 for the year; his two victories the year before had been worth $630,000 all by themselves.

Curtis Strange, who has been an unofficial mentor and adviser to Stricker almost since he arrived on tour because he took an immediate liking to his game and his personality, told him he was making a mistake. "You aren't going to figure out what's wrong sitting at home," he told him. "You need to be out here playing until you turn this thing around."

Stricker understood what Strange was saying, but he felt he had to get away from the tour. He had gotten snappish on the golf course and when he snapped at his caddy that meant he was snapping at his wife. "It's a wonder that she put up with me," he said months later. "I was brutal."

Stricker stuck to his decision not to play again after Milwaukee. He had the luxury of not having to worry about his spot on the money list — he finished 130th — because the two wins in '96 had made him exempt through 1999. He wanted to start the new year fresh, find a driver he could hit straight, and act as if 1997 had never happened.

It proved not to be a completely lost year for the Stricker family. Early in December, Nicki found out she was pregnant. Everyone was delighted. Nicki's initial plan was to continue caddying for the first couple of months of 1998, and then when the doctor told her it was time to stop lugging a forty-pound bag several miles a day she would retire. That would give Steve time to figure out who he wanted to have caddy for him.

By Christmas week it was apparent that plan wasn't going to work. Caddying and morning sickness are not a good mix. Nicki's retirement was moved up from sometime in 1998 to right away. The question then was who to call about caddying for Steve.

Actually the question had only one answer: James Earl Walker. Jim Walker — Earl to those who know him best — had been been on tour for a dozen years, having chucked the tire business in his thirties to see the rest of the world through golf. He had worked with a number of players, but most recently had spent four years with Jeff Sluman. Sluman and Stricker were friends, and Walker and Nicki had become good friends too. Sometimes they shared a house on the road, and when the Strickers talked about the day when they decided to start a family they agreed that Walker would be one person they would feel comfortable with if he was available.

Surprisingly, he was very much available. Sluman and Walker had decided at the end of 1997 to go their separate ways. This was a surprise to a lot of people on tour because the two had seemed so compatible. Both had gone to Florida State, and they were capable of boring companions to tears talking for hours on end about the vaunted Seminole football team. The only way to shut them up was to mention basketball.

But player-caddy relationships are always tenuous. Mike Hicks, who has caddied for Payne Stewart for most of the last eleven years, once explained it this way: "When something goes wrong, the player has to blame someone. He isn't going to blame himself and, more often than not, he isn't going to blame his wife. Who does that leave?"

Sluman and Walker had enjoyed a good deal of success together, but things had gotten tense between them at the end of the year. After the last tournament of the year in Las Vegas, Walker went home to Louisville and decided to stay there at least until the tour came back east from California in March. He figured he could use a break. But when the phone rang Christmas week and it was Steve and Nicki telling them that Nicki was giving up caddying in favor of mothering, Walker couldn't say no. He liked the Strickers too much not to say yes and he was convinced that '97 had been an aberration. He told Steve and Nicki that he would see them in Palm Springs.

"I was so relieved when he said yes," Nicki said. "I knew it was going to be hard going outside the ropes. But with Jim there, I felt better about it. I knew he was good at what he did and that Steve could trust him completely."

For an outsider it might be difficult to understand just how difficult it was for Nicki to — caddy parlance — give up the bag. She and Steve had met when both were in college — Steve at the University of Illinois, Nicki at Wisconsin. Nicki's father, Dennis Tiziani, was the golf coach at Wisconsin. He had recruited Stricker coming out of high school but had lost him to Illinois in large part because Stricker wanted to go to a school that was more than thirty miles from Edgerton, the small Wisconsin town where he had grown up. When Stricker called Tiziani to tell him what he had decided, Tiziani said to him, "Look, if you ever need any help, don't hesitate to call."

Two years later, he called. He had just completed his sophomore year at Illinois and had enjoyed great success, tying for the Big Ten Championship as a freshman, making the NCAAs as a sophomore. But he wasn't thrilled with his swing or the way he was hitting the ball. He knew Tiziani's reputation as a top teacher, so he called and asked if he could drive over to Madison. He and Tiziani spent about an hour on the practice tee on a warm June day. When they were finished, they were sitting on a cart talking when one of the lifeguards from the pool at the club where Tiziani taught came walking in their direction.

"Whoa," Steve said, elbowing Tiziani. "Who's *that?*"

Tiziani smiled and said, "Steve, that's my daughter."

Stricker turned about a hundred shades of red, never once looked up when Tiziani introduced the two of them, and fled down the road back home a few minutes later, wondering if he could ever look Tiziani in the eye again. The next day the phone rang. It was Nicki asking him if he wanted to go to a movie. Apparently Tiziani had mentioned to her that Steve might not be averse to the notion of going out with her and Nicki hadn't thought it was such a bad idea either.

"I didn't have the guts to call her," Stricker said. "Thank God she had the guts to call me." They went to see the movie *La Bamba* on their first date — "July 2, 1987," Stricker says without prompting — and Stricker soon knew the route from Edgerton to Madison blind.

By the time Steve graduated from Illinois in 1990 and headed for the mini-tours, he had a girlfriend and a caddy all wrapped up in one person. The only time the relationship ever ran into trouble was when they played golf together. Nicki was a very good and very competitive player, and when things didn't go well she was capable of flying into a rage.

"Stop it!" Steve would yell. "You can't act like that. It's no fun being out here if you act like that."

"Italian temper," Nicki told him. "Sorry. Can't help it."

The worst part, according to Stricker, was that for a while he started acting more like her instead of her acting like him. "Gosh, for a while, I started getting crazy out there," he said.

It is difficult to imagine Stricker being crazy on the golf course or anyplace else. But there is an intensity about him that isn't always visible. Part of the problem in '97 had been the fact that he was beating himself up so often for not playing better. Nicki tried to help but nothing was working. Now, with Nicki going off the bag, Steve felt as if he had lost an important part of his game.

"Remember, I'd never really had anybody else caddy for me for any length of time," he said. "She'd been with me a lot on mini-tours, all the time on the Canadian, and when I had my success on tour. We were very much a team. It was never my success, it was our success. We shared it all. I knew it was going to be hard on both of us for her to be outside the ropes."

That was no reflection on Walker and he understood that. Early in the year when Steve would walk over near the ropes to talk to Nicki or when Nicki would come out on the range to talk about his round or his swing, Walker understood. This was a major adjustment period for both of them.

The Strickers were married in the summer of 1993. The only reason it took that long, according to Steve, was that he wanted to have some money in the bank before he asked Nicki to marry him. Finally, after failing to get through the second stage of Q-School for the third straight time in 1992, he said the heck with it and asked her. She said yes, they set a date, and his golf improved markedly after that.

"It was as if I stopped putting so much pressure on myself," he said. "Instead of feeling I had to make money or had to be a success, I just went out and played."

At first Nicki absolutely hated being outside the ropes. People kept coming up wanting to chat or congratulate her on the impending arrival of the baby or ask how she was feeling. Nicki understood why they were asking and knew people were just trying to be friendly. But she didn't want to wander around the golf course chatting about the weather and morning sickness and baby names. She wanted to be as close to the ropes as she could get, analyzing every shot Steve hit. She had been doing that from inside the ropes for too many years to just quit cold turkey.

"I don't want him asking me about a shot or a decision he made when the round is over and find myself saying, 'Oh gee, I wasn't watching or I was talking to so-and-so,'" she said one day in San Diego. "I want to feel as if I can still help him as much as possible. I know when the baby comes, I won't be able to be out here as much. I'm excited about that and how it's going to change our lives. But until it happens, I want to be as involved as I can be."

Stricker played better on the west coast, making all five cuts and finishing seventh in Hawaii. He added a sixth at Bay Hill, and by the time he got to the Players Championship he had already made almost $200,000, more than he had made in all of 1997. Nothing spectacular, but better. The driver still wasn't as consistent as he wanted it to be. He was hitting three-wood off the tee a fair amount and that seemed to help.

The worst part of the disastrous 1997 season had been where it had left him in terms of the majors in 1998. At the start of the year, the only major he was in was the British Open and that was because he was still thirty-ninth in the world golf rankings, thanks to the fact that the rankings are calculated over a two-year period. Even so, he hadn't clinched a spot in the British, since he had to remain in the top fifty in the rankings through late May. If he didn't play better than in '97 that wouldn't happen.

Stricker had played in nine straight majors, dating to the '96 PGA. Now, he wasn't going to play in the Masters unless he won a tournament during the first three months of '98, and he wasn't exempt for the U.S. Open or the PGA. "You get used to the idea that you're in the majors," he said. "Then, all of a sudden, you're on the outside looking in. It's a shock to your system."

Stricker's last chance to get into the Masters came at the Players. He was never in serious contention there, making the cut on the number and finishing tied for fifty-first. He had toyed with the thought of playing in New Orleans — the last tournament before the Masters — to give himself one last shot to get in at Augusta. He remembered how Davis Love had won at New Orleans in 1995 to get into the Masters and then had finished second the following week.

But he decided against going there for two reasons: he didn't want to start changing his schedule this early in the year and, at least as important, Nicki had a doctor's appointment that week and he wanted to be there with her for that. "I feel like I won one," Nicki said during the Players.

Stricker had mixed emotions about missing the Masters. As much as he wanted to be there, the fact remained that he hadn't yet figured out how to play in Augusta. He had missed the cut both times he had played there and felt totally frustrated by the eccentricities of the golf course. "This way at least when I get back there, I'll appreciate being there more and maybe I'll go in with a better attitude," he said.

Even so, watching was no fun. Once you have been at Augusta it is very hard not to be there. But, Stricker kept telling himself all weekend, he would come back to Hilton Head refreshed from two weeks off. Maybe he would sneak up on all those guys worn out from the Masters and have a big week.

Not exactly. He shot 76–70 and missed his first cut of the year. The driver was starting to spray again. Still, it was just one bad week. Greensboro was next. He made the cut. That was the good news. The bad news was an 81 on Sunday, when he had no idea where the ball was going. After yet another wayward tee shot on the 13th hole, Stricker walked off the tee, looked at Walker, and said, "Earl, I'm starting to feel like it's last year all over again. I'm sliding backward and I don't know what to do about it."

By the next day he had decided what to do about it. He called the Taylor Made people and told them he was sorry but he just couldn't play the bubble-shafted driver anymore. He wanted them to come up with something with a smaller head, the kind of driver he had used when he had been winning golf tournaments.

"I knew it wouldn't make them happy," he said. "After all, if I won something, they couldn't use me in their ads saying I had won playing the bubble shaft. But on the other hand I sure wasn't doing them any good shooting eighty-one out there. They had signed me to get exposure for their products. How can I give them any exposure if I'm not playing on weekends or in any of the majors?"

The Taylor Made people told Stricker they would work with him. Stricker was relieved they felt that way. "If they had said I had to play the bubble shaft or else, I would have told them to stop paying me," he said. "I was that desperate."

Two weeks later at the Byron Nelson Classic, playing with a new driver, Stricker shot 65–65 on the weekend and finished fifth. It was his highest finish since '96, his best two back-to-back rounds in memory. Suddenly, he was excited to be at the golf course again. He had played reasonably well at the Memorial and very well at the Kemper, closing with a 69 on a day when only three players broke 70, to finish eighth.

He arrived at Woodmont brimming with confidence, almost looking forward to the grueling 36-hole day. The weather was cool and windy, a break, considering how hot and humid Washington can be in June. The night before, Stricker had reminded himself that it had been a U.S. Open qualifier in 1993 that had jump-started his career. He had qualified in Chicago and finished as co-medalist to get into his first Open. He went on to make the cut at Baltusrol, which convinced him he was good enough to play with the big boys. That had led to his solid summer in Canada, which had gotten him an exemption into the Canadian Open. Totally unknown at the time, he led the Canadian for two rounds and ended up finishing fourth. Then he made it through all three stages of Q-School to get his PGA Tour card.

"I went from nowhere going into that Open qualifier in '93 to being on the tour in six months," he said. "It was amazing. I remember the fourth day at the Q-School finals I knew I had to shoot sixty-nine to make the cut and I did it. After that, everything seemed easy. I came out loose as could be the next day, shot sixty-five, and went from there."

And now he was back in an Open qualifier. He was a long way removed from '93, though, now one of the name players in the Woodmont field. He was not, by any means, the only "name" teeing it up that morning. There were no fewer than forty-six players in the field who had won on the PGA Tour at least once. There were five players entered who had won a major championship — Sandy Lyle ('85 British, '88 Masters), Larry Mize ('87 Masters), Craig Stadler ('82 Masters), Hal Sutton ('83 PGA), and Lanny Wadkins ('77 PGA). Wadkins never made it to the first tee, withdrawing with a shoulder injury. None of the other four survived. The next day in New Jersey, two past major champions — Jeff Sluman (PGA '88) and Fuzzy Zoeller (Masters '79, Open '84) — did qualify.

Wadkins's withdrawal allowed another name player into the field — Lehman. But it wasn't '96 British Open champion Tom Lehman, it was his brother and agent, Jim, a fine amateur player who had been the first alternate coming out of his local qualifier. Jim Lehman had decided to turn Kemper Open week into a business/pleasure trip, seeing friends, getting some work done at the tournament, and then making his way to Woodmont on Monday morning on the off chance that someone might withdraw. His chance came, courtesy of Wadkins, and he managed to shoot a respectable 73 in the morning before fading in the afternoon. Then he put his agent's hat back on and walked the playoff with Larry Mize, a client.

"One of the great thrills of my life," he said later. "For someone like me just to be in a sectional is something I'll cherish."

Stricker's threesome had just about every element one could hope to find in an Open qualifier: there was Stricker, the successful tour member fallen on hard times; there was Howard Twitty, seven months shy of turning fifty and joining the Senior Tour, a twenty-five-year veteran who had won three times in his career; and there was Jeff Thorsen, six months older than Stricker but a lifetime removed from him in golf experience. Thorsen played part-time on the Nike Tour, part-time on the Hooters Tour, and had never been in a major championship. "I lost in a playoff to get into Pebble [the '92 Open]," he said. "I'm not sure I'm completely over that yet."

The pairing was a good one for all three men. Thorsen knew Nicki's brother, Mario, from the Nike Tour, and all day long he could feel Stricker quietly pushing him along, giving him words of encouragement when he needed them most. Twitty, one of the Tour's extroverts, was delighted to be with two players who enjoyed his stories.

"My first Open was in '71 at Merion when I was still in college," he said during a delay on one of the par-threes. "I played the first two rounds with Lou Graham. I still remember taking a car with him back to the hotel after the second round and hearing him say, 'You kids are so lucky. You're coming into the game just when the money is starting to get really big.'"

That year, the Tour offered a record $7.1 million in purses. In 1998 the total prize money would be more than $94 million, and it would jump to $130 million in 1999.

"What do they play for in the Tour Championship?" said Thorsen, referring to the season-ending event that the top thirty money winners qualify for.

"Four million," Stricker said.

"One event," Twitty added.

Money was not the issue on this day. The threesome teed off at 7:57 on Woodmont's South Course. One of the reasons Woodmont has been a qualifying site for so many years is that it has two courses, meaning the field can be split easily since a playoff is almost inevitable and, even in June when the days are long, daylight will likely become a problem.

If Stricker felt any pressure, he certainly didn't show it in the morning round. He birdied the first four holes, draining putts from 22 feet, 25 feet, 8 feet, and 10 feet. The greens had been aerated a couple of weeks earlier and a number of players would complain about their bumpiness. Stricker never saw a bump all morning. "They feel like glass to me," he said, grinning. He made two more birdies on the front side, turning in a sizzling 29. Twitty and Thorsen were both hanging in, Twitty at one under par and Thorsen at even, but both were awed by what Stricker was doing.

"Steve was making it look so easy I thought I was in trouble," Thorsen said. "I mean, he's six under through nine and I'm even. I figured I had to do a lot better than that."

Not that much better. The qualifying score at Woodmont had been as low as five under in past years, but it didn't figure to be that low on a breezy day with bumpy greens (except for Stricker) and thirty-two spots available.

On the 10th, Stricker hit a 129-yard pitching wedge a foot from the hole for his seventh birdie. He finally missed a green at 11, but blasted from a bunker to within eight feet and drained the par putt. Then, after a par at 12, he almost holed a five-iron second shot at 13. He tapped in to go eight under.

The 13th hole on the South Course ends up right next to the road that leads into the club. As he putted out, Stricker spotted Nicki, well into her seventh month by now, walking up the road in the direction of the clubhouse. She had slept in, knowing what a long day it would be, and had just arrived at the course with some friends from Wisconsin.

"Where's she going?" Stricker asked Walker. "And why's she walking?"

Walker pointed at the field across the way where cars were being parked. Woodmont doesn't have a lot of parking, and with players and caddies and friends and relatives and members and a couple hundred fans showing up for the qualifier, the overflow at 11 o'clock was almost to the front gate.

Stricker and Walker began yelling to get Nicki's attention. She couldn't hear them. Finally, Walker ran up the road a few yards and let out a whistle, which Nicki heard. She saw Walker, turned, and walked back to the 14th tee. Steam was coming out of her ears. "If they're out of room, they're out of room," she said. "But if they're going to make you park a mile from the clubhouse, they have a lot of nerve charging you five bucks."

Stricker couldn't help laughing. "I told you, Earl," he said. "Italian temper."

Stricker finished the morning round with a stunning 62 — nine under par. He was four shots ahead of the field and, unless he broke a leg, was going to qualify easily. Thorsen had shot a solid 69 and Twitty a 70. Thorsen was shocked to find only eight golfers ahead of him. He knew he still had a long way to go, though, since the South is the easier of Woodmont's two courses. The players call it "the little course."

The break between rounds is always chaotic. Everyone wants something to eat and there is usually about forty-five minutes to do so. At Woodmont, the clubhouse is closed for the day, so the staff sets up a cookout for everyone, with players — who still have to pay $5 for a hamburger and $1 for a soda — given priority in terms of waiting on line. Then everyone finds a seat or a spot under a tree, wolfs their food, and returns to the golf course after checking the scoreboard.

In all, there were thirty-one players at 70 or better. That made a target score of 140 or 141 — since a majority of the best scores were on the little course — seem reasonable.

Dudley Hart had shot an even-par 72 in the morning on the North (big) Course and was telling himself to stay calm because he still had the little course left to play. Hart was another of the past tournament winners who found himself back in qualifying. Like Stricker, he had missed the Masters in April, but instead of sitting at home, he had gone to play in the Argentine Open. He wanted to be distracted and the $20,000 appearance fee made the trip worthwhile, especially since he was getting married in July and figured the extra cash couldn't hurt.

"I wanted to be busy," he said. "Sitting around watching would have killed me."

Hart would turn thirty in August. He had been a full-fledged tour member since 1991, having made it through Q-School on his first try after finishing at the University of Florida. He had been considered one of the better young players on tour, moving steadily up the money list his first three years, from 120th to 61st to 52nd. He also earned the nickname "Mini-Volcano," a tribute to his temper and to the fact that "Volcano" had been taken years earlier by Steve Pate.

He hit the skids in 1994 after leading at Pebble Beach through three rounds and blowing up in the last round. He ended up making just twelve out of thirty-one cuts and had to grind through Q-School again in December. Then, midway through 1995, he jammed his wrist when he hit a root during the Greater Hartford Open. He was in a cast, he went through rehab, he tried to come back too soon, and when it was all over he had to undergo surgery to repair torn ligaments that hadn't shown up on the initial X rays. At that point, his career appeared to be in jeopardy.

He struggled through most of 1996 but found his game in Canada and, almost from nowhere, won the Canadian Open. Suddenly, he had a new life on tour. The victory put him into three of the four majors in '97 (all but the Open) and he responded by missing all three cuts. One of his goals for 1998 had been very direct: play in the majors; play *better* in the majors.

He was zero-for-one when the day began at Woodmont and needing a rally after 18 holes. He was paired with Paul Goydos and Mark Jansen, a club pro from nearby Fort Belvoir, Virginia. Goydos, whose nickname among his fellow pros is "Sunshine," because of his ability to find a dark cloud in every silver lining, was going through one of the worst slumps of his career. He had shot 79 in the morning, and as the afternoon round began he was hating golf, hating the Open, and hating life. Four holes into the round, standing on the 14th tee (they had teed off on number 10), Goydos looked at Hart and said, "You know, I can see my car from here."

He paused for a minute. "I think this is an omen." He shook hands with Hart and Jansen, wished them luck, took his clubs from caddy Brendan Woolley, and began walking toward his car. "At that moment, if I could have seen *my* car I might have gone with him," Hart said laughing. "I was one over for the afternoon and things weren't going too well for me either. But I kept telling myself, hang in, hang in and something will happen."

Something did. Hart managed two birdies on the back nine to get to one under at the turn, then exploded on the front nine — much as

Stricker had in the morning, making five birdies in six holes to shoot 30. When he added them up after 36 holes he had shot 72–65 for 137, six under par. For the first time since 1992 — when he had tied for twenty-third — Hart was back in the Open. "What a relief," he said, collapsing on the grass after turning in his card. "A few years ago, I might not have been patient enough to stay with it on a day like this. I would have done the mini-volcano thing. But I kept grinding. I'm proud of myself for that."

He was holding in his hands the coveted entry card and instructions on what to do when he arrived in San Francisco. The officials were handing them out at that point to anyone who had shot 139 or better among the early finishers, since they were a lock to be among the top thirty-two. Stricker had been given his entry card as soon as he finished even though he had slogged his way to a 75 in the afternoon. "I just never could get going," he said. "It was as if I knew I'd done the job with the sixty-two, and even though I kept telling myself to keep making birdies, I knew deep down I really didn't have to and I got kind of sloppy."

Still, his 137 was easily good enough to qualify, and that had been the point of the day. Perhaps the most shocked person to receive an entry card in return for his scorecard was Jeff Thorsen. He had bogeyed his last hole of the afternoon round, missing an eight-foot putt, and had walked off the green with an awful feeling in the pit of his stomach.

"Great playing," Jim Walker told him.

"I don't know," he answered. "I think I may have killed myself with that bogey."

Walker looked at him like he was crazy. "Didn't you shoot two under this afternoon?"

"Yeah."

"That's four under for the day, right?"

"Yeah."

Walker patted Thorsen on the back. "Son, I've been through a dozen of these. You got nothing to worry about."

Walker knew what he was talking about. Thorsen had shot 139, which would put him in a seven-way tie for seventh place with, among others, Twitty, who had shot 69 in the afternoon, making him the oldest player to qualify. Thorsen thought he had died and gone to heaven.

Craig Smith, the USGA's public relations man, asked him to fill out a bio form as a first-time Open entrant. Under the question "Greatest thrill in sports?" Thorsen's answer was succinct: "Today."

As it turned out Stricker, Hart, and Scott Verplank tied for medalist honors at 137. Medalist is a literal term in a sectional: all three players would receive a gold USGA medal for their efforts. Verplank would be reunited with O'Meara and Cook. Don Pooley also qualified and then reminded USGA officials that he had been paired with Simpson and Price at Olympic in '87. Tom Meeks smiled at him and said, "It's already taken care of." In all, twenty-six players had shot 141 — two under par. They were all safely on their way to Olympic. Thirteen more players had tied at 142. They would play off for the six remaining spots.

Except that one of the thirteen wasn't there. John Morse, a five-year tour veteran who had won the Hawaiian Open in 1995 and finished fourth at the Open in 1996, had looked at the board after posting his score and decided that the playoff would be at 141. So he had left for the airport.

"I was a little bit hot at myself because I shot 38 the last nine holes," he said later. "When I looked at the scores I didn't think 142 would do anything except maybe play off for an alternate's spot. I wasn't going to wait around for that."

Other players were stunned by Morse's decision. After all, what was the big deal about waiting around for an hour to have a shot at playing in the Open? In Morse's case it was a tournament he had played well in — very well — in the past. Shortly after he arrived at the airport, Morse ran into another player who told him that 142 was playing off at that very moment. He was surprised but, he insisted, not stunned.

"No regrets," he insisted. "I made my decision and moved forward."

The other twelve players moved forward to the par-five 10th hole on the North Course just before 7:30. There were about two hundred people waiting for them on the tee. Many Woodmont members had made the qualifying an annual habit, enjoying the idea that they could literally stand within a few feet of golfers as famous as Stadler and Mize and Lyle and Sutton (among others) while they tried to fight their way into the U.S. Open. They were all aware of the fact that it was not unheard of for a qualifier to win the Open. In 1996, Steve Jones had survived a playoff in the sectional and ten days later became the Open champion. Some members came straight from work to the golf course just to see the playoff. They also knew that one of the men standing on the 10th tee hoping for a spot in the tournament might be the next Steve Jones. Even those who had seen multiple playoffs appreciated their inherent drama: "I'd drive a hundred miles through a blizzard to watch a playoff at an Open qualifier," Meeks said, smiling.

There are no ropes at qualifiers. That meant that as the players headed down the fairway, the fans walked shoulder to shoulder with them. Given the pressure the players were under at this moment, it could be disquieting. "You have to try and block it out," said Larry Mize, who found himself in a bunker with a dozen fans standing on the edge peering down at him as he lined up his shot. "It isn't the way we're used to playing. But you better adjust quickly."

The players went off in three foursomes. When the first group finished, the players waited for the other two groups. Four players knocked themselves out on the first hole with bogeys, including local hero Fred Funk, the one-time golf coach at the University of Maryland who had gone on to be a very good tour player. The day before, Funk had started the final round of the Kemper Open with a four-shot lead and proceeded to shoot 77 and finish fourth. He had then played 36 holes in qualifying, waited around, and played a 37th hole. He walked back up the 10th fairway, head down, a sad and solitary figure.

One player clinched a spot at the 10th: Ted Oh. In 1993 Oh had qualified for the Open as a sixteen-year-old phenom. Back then, he was mentioned in the same sentence with Tiger Woods. Some people even thought Oh, eight months younger than Woods, might have more potential. So far, it hadn't panned out that way. Oh had gone to UCLA for two years and turned pro in the summer of 1997. He was playing minitours, trying to work his way up the golf ladder, and was a long way removed from his phenom days.

But a little of the magic came back for him in the gloaming at Woodmont. After hitting his second shot into the right rough under a huge oak tree, Oh took a long time selecting a club. Finally, he lofted a wedge shot over the bunker guarding the right side of the green. It took two hops, rolled about 10 feet, and disappeared into the hole for an eagle-three. Oh threw his arms into the air, but it was his father, who had been seated almost *on* the green on one of those little folding chairs people sometimes carry with them on the golf course, who went crazy. He threw his arms into the air, screaming, "Yes, yes," and raced back to his son to give him a hug.

Oh was in. Funk, Mark Wiebe, Rafael Alarcon, and Ed Pfister were out. That left seven players competing for five spots. A full moon had risen by the time the players moved to the 11th tee. "How many spots are we playing for?" Trevor Dodds asked Mize.

"Seven for five now," Mize said.

"Wow," Dodds said. "I thought it would be more like twelve for one."

Dodds and Mize went in opposite directions on the 11th. Dodds hit a perfect drive, wedged to 20 feet, and made his birdie putt. Next stop, Olympic. Mize hit his drive into a fairway bunker, had to lay up, and then, after hitting a superb chip to four feet, he rimmed the putt. In 1987, Mize had gone to Olympic as the reigning Masters champion. In 1998, he wouldn't get to go at all.

The last player eliminated was Robin Freeman. He pulled his tee shot at the 11th way left and, trying to hack his way onto the green, knowing he needed par to stay alive, he ended up making double bogey. That meant that the par makers at 11 — Steve Pate, Brandel Chamblee, Jim Estes, and David Kirkpatrick — joined Dodds and Oh as the survivors. Pate, the man known for years on tour as "Volcano" because of his temper, never raised a peep when he missed a six-foot birdie putt at the 10th that would have clinched his spot. "I was too tired," he said.

The most surprising of the survivors was Chamblee, who had broken a toe three days earlier when he had dropped a packed suitcase on it. He had decided to withdraw on Sunday afternoon but changed his mind that night while watching the NBA Finals on TV. "I just decided, what the heck, let's pop some Advil and go out there and see what happens."

He hobbled through 38 holes and, as dusk closed in, he was rewarded for his effort.

"Now, I get to go to Olympic," he said. "There, if my foot doesn't kill me, the golf course probably will."

15

Casey and the Cart

The Woodmont thirty-two would join fifty-seven other players who had made it through sectionals at eleven other sites. During the course of the long day at Woodmont there had been as many as seven members of the media on the grounds. That same day, at the qualifier in Cincinnati, where a total of five spots were at stake, the number of media was closer to a hundred. The USGA even set up a press room, the first time it had ever taken that step at a sectional qualifier.

The reason was Casey Martin.

Martin had become a national celebrity and cause célèbre when he had sued the PGA Tour for the right to use a golf cart. Martin was born with Klippel-Trenauney-Webber Syndrome, a rare circulatory disorder that forced him to wear a strong support stocking on his right leg at all times to keep the swelling in it down. Walking any distance at all was difficult for him. Even so, he had become an excellent golfer and had played at Stanford with Tiger Woods. Although he had walked golf courses throughout his amateur and college careers, the condition, which was progressive, had worsened to the point where, by the time he turned twenty-five in June 1997, walking 18 holes was extraordinarily painful for him.

That meant that the only way for him to pursue a pro career was to ride in a cart. The PGA Tour said no, that walking was an integral part of the game. That position was correct, but was undercut by the fact that the Tour allowed players on the Senior Tour to use carts. If being fifty was enough of a handicap to be allowed a cart, then a disease like this one was surely worthy of an exception to the no-cart rule.

The Tour understood that. Its concern was that if it gave Martin a cart without a fight, then other players would show up with doctors' notes saying they needed carts. "If he gets a cart, I'm next in line," said Fred Couples, who had been forced to limit his schedule for four years because of his back problems. There were numerous other players with varying afflictions who might make a claim for a cart. Clearly, riding in a cart would be an advantage, especially in hot weather. That meant that if some players were allowed carts, eventually all players would have to be allowed carts. The Tour didn't mind the idea of the over-fifty set tooling around in carts, but the idea of seeing players on the regular tour lurching down the fairways in carts was a disturbing one.

"Kind of sucks the drama out of the walk up eighteen if the guys come *riding* up, doesn't it?" asked Davis Love, a member of the Tour's Policy Board. "We're going to lose in court, but we still have to fight the idea that riding is okay. It may be okay for Casey because his case is unique, but it shouldn't be okay for anyone else."

What really bugged people on the Tour was the fact that many non-golfers kept insisting that walking was no big deal, that riding a cart was either no advantage at all or a negligible advantage. "If you think walking is as easy as riding, then next time you go to the grocery store, walk there instead of taking your car," Couples told one skeptic. "I'm not saying it's running a marathon because it's not. But walking four or five miles a day every day, five days a week [including the Wednesday pro-ams] is a lot different than riding those four or five miles five days a week."

The issue divided the locker room. Some players thought it was foolish of the Tour to fight Martin, that clearly his case was unique and that fighting him made everyone associated with the Tour look like Scrooge. "The kid deserves a cart," Payne Stewart said one day, cornering Jay Haas, another Policy Board member. "By fighting him, the Tour is making all of us look bad."

The Tour was certainly taking massive P.R. hits. Martin was a sympathetic character, a bright, good-looking kid, unfailingly polite, and given to saying that no matter what happened he knew the Lord had a plan for him. The fact that doctors testified that he faced the very real possibility of losing his leg completely by the time he was forty certainly didn't hurt his case in the court of public opinion. He also underscored his legitimacy as a player by winning the opening Nike Tour event of the 1998 season. He was riding in a cart because a court had issued a temporary injunction allowing him to do so until his case came to trial.

When it did come to trial in February, it was — as Love had predicted — a slam dunk for Martin. Even though the Tour brought out big guns like Arnold Palmer and Jack Nicklaus to talk on videotape about the importance of walking to the game, no magistrate in Eugene, Oregon (where Martin had grown up), was going to rule against him. Even though the magistrate showed that he knew nothing about golf by saying in his ruling that "walking is akin to breathing," he did help the Tour out by saying his ruling was only for Martin and that he felt his case was unique since he suffered a lifelong affliction that was only going to get worse.

That was about the best the Tour could hope for — give Martin his cart and hope it ended there. Even though Commissioner Tim Finchem said the Tour would appeal, he said it half-heartedly, perhaps knowing that if Martin became a good player he would be another drawing card for the Tour.

David Fay kept a close eye on the trial and all the hoopla surrounding it. He knew that he was going to have to deal with Martin because, like any pro, he would enter the U.S. Open. He had entered the Open three times previously and, walking, had never qualified for the tournament. Technically, the USGA could have forced Martin to take it to court to win the right to use a cart in the USGA event, since it was a completely separate organization from the PGA Tour, but Fay had no intention of doing that. "We probably would lose for the same reasons the Tour lost," he said. "What's more, the public perception would be that we were piling on the kid. Most people don't know the difference between the Tour and the USGA. They would say, 'Wait a minute, this was already decided.' We didn't need to deal with that."

Although Fay agreed with the Tour's position that walking is an integral part of the game, he didn't have any problem with Martin being allowed to ride on the grounds that he suffered from a disability. For that reason, rather than let him ride in a regular golf cart, he decided he should ride in a one-person cart, the kind that people with disabilities use to get around. "Whether he wanted to be or not, he was going to be — is going to be — a role model for the disabled," Fay said. "This will be an example of how a disabled person uses a cart on a golf course. A lot of disabled people who play golf can't even get out of their carts. Casey can get out of his, so a one-person cart shouldn't be a problem for him."

The problem was building a cart that would allow Martin to maneuver up and down the hills of a golf course and in narrow spots between greens and tees. Because he had won a Nike Tour event, Martin was exempt through local qualifying of the Open, meaning that the sectional in Cincinnati would be the debut of his one-person cart (the Tour was allowing him to use a regular golf cart at Nike events) and a media circus, since all of America would want to know how the cart worked and how Casey played.

Like many carts used by the disabled, the cart had only one pedal, meaning that Martin had to lift his foot from the accelerator in order to slow or stop the cart. Certainly not impossible, but at times dicey for someone not experienced at such things. Martin had about thirty minutes to practice with the cart before his round started but struggled with it early in the day. On the third hole, the cart started sliding on him. Martin stopped it, jumped out of the cart, and began walking with the other members of his threesome. Several employees of Pride Manufacturing, which had built the cart, took it back to the clubhouse, then returned it to Martin on the fifth hole, saying it was in working order. He rode the rest of the way without incident.

His golf was smoother than the cart until his 36th hole. Appearing to have one of the five qualifying spots locked up, he double-bogeyed the last hole. That dropped him into a tie for fifth, meaning that he had to endure a five-for-one playoff. Martin was devastated, thinking he had blown his chance to get into the Open. But he came through with a birdie on the second playoff hole, rolling in a 25-foot putt, and, amazingly, he was in the Open.

One of the other four players who qualified for Olympic in Cincinnati was Patrick Lee. He finished in a three-way tie for second, shooting 66–71. Of the sixteen players who had come out of the local in Pinehurst, only Paul Simson, a forty-seven-year-old amateur from Raleigh, Perry Moss, and Lee, who had waited until it was pitch dark to clinch the sixteenth spot, made it into the Open field.

"Just goes to show you that you never know in golf," Lee said.

Casey Martin could certainly attest to that.

All spring, the USGA had been concerned with how soft the golf course would be when Open week rolled around. San Francisco in summer tends to be damp and foggy, and that sort of weather does not lend itself to the kind of fast, hard fairways and greens that are the mark of a U.S. Open.

As if to prove all their fears correct, the first wave of USGA officials arriving in town were greeted by rain on both Thursday and Friday. But when Tom Meeks toured the golf course on Sunday to pick potential hole locations, some of his concerns were assuaged. Two days of dry weather had already dried the golf course considerably. And the long-range forecast for Open week was for more dry weather. "If that holds up," he said, "we'll be just fine."

Or just miserable, depending on your point of view. One of golf's most-argued-about topics is the way the USGA sets up the golf course for the U.S. Open. Many players and experts insist that the Open isn't a fair or true test of golf. Often, it takes the driver out of the hands of most players because missing the fairway is so penal that players will hit irons off the tee and take their chances with a longer second shot rather than risk a wayward drive. What's more, the thick rough around the greens can turn a missed green into an automatic bogey, even if you miss by a foot.

"They take the skill out of the short game," said Phil Mickelson, who may have golf's most imaginative short game. "I don't have any advantage on people around the greens at the Open because we're all doing the same thing if we miss the green — hacking and hoping."

Always, the question raged: Was the U.S. Open designed to humiliate the world's best golfers or, as then USGA president Sandy Tatum had insisted in 1974 during what was called "the Massacre at Winged Foot," was it designed to *identify* the best golfers?

"You know, I get so tired of the whining," Fred Couples said. "I certainly wouldn't want to play this way every week, but why not once a year? It makes the Open different than the other majors. I don't think that's a bad thing. In fact, I think we ought to do it on tour more often. Why should twenty under win every week?"

Couples was walking slowly down the hill behind the clubhouse at Olympic on Monday afternoon as he spoke. The day was bright and clear without a hint of rain or dampness in the air. Almost all of the 156 players were in town and somewhere on the grounds of the club. Couples had made plans to meet Tom Watson on the seventh green so he could play the last 11 holes of the golf course with him. Olympic actually has what amounts to a front eight and a back ten, since the par-three eighth hole is set right in the shadow of the clubhouse and the ninth goes out away from it.

Couples and Watson almost always play at least one practice round together at the majors. As different as they appear to be on the surface — Watson, the man with an opinion on everything from the Kansas City Royals to Bill Clinton's troubles to the world economy; Couples, the man who can watch an entire hockey game to a 0–0 conclusion — they enjoy each other's company. Couples, who is a far better listener than people give him credit for, likes to listen to what Watson has to say about the golf course and, for that matter, the world economy. Watson, who knows Couples is a lot smarter and more with it than his public persona, enjoys Couples's sly sense of humor.

The two had always gotten along but became closer after the 1993 Ryder Cup. Watson was the captain that year and, in that role, had tried to give Couples a pep talk halfway through a four-ball match in which Couples and partner Paul Azinger were getting smoked. Couples, who hadn't played well all week, snapped at Watson when the captain tried to tell him that everything was okay and the match was still winnable. Other players worried about a rift between the two. It never happened.

"Was I wrong to snap at Tom that day? Absolutely," Couples said. "But was everything okay at that moment? Was the match still winnable? No and no. It was just the timing. I'd had such a miserable year with all the stuff going on about my divorce and not playing very well and all I really wanted to do in the end was make that team and help us win the Ryder Cup overseas. Then we get there and I can't do a thing right. I felt terrible and here came Tom trying to give me a pep talk. Wrong place, wrong time."

Couples later told Watson he was sorry, but the apology wasn't necessary. Being the kind of competitor that he is, Watson actually respected the fact that Couples, who is often criticized for not being emotional, was as upset about not playing well as he was. A friendly acquaintanceship grew into a friendship.

The two months since the Masters had been a roller coaster for Couples. He had taken two weeks off and then had come back to the tour in Houston, his old hometown, playing well on Sunday to finish third. He went back to Los Angeles after that to be with Thais, who was scheduled to go into the hospital on May 12 for a series of tests to see if she was still cancer free six months after she had finished her chemotherapy and radiation treatments.

The twelfth was two days after Mother's Day, always an awful day for Couples, since it was on Mother's Day in 1994 that his mother had died. "It's just a day I try to get through without thinking about anything too much," he said. "Because there isn't anything I'm going to think about that's going to be good."

But the subconscious is a powerful thing. Early Monday morning, Couples woke up in bed screaming and crying. When Thais asked him if he had been dreaming about his mother, he shook his head. "No, it wasn't that," he said. "I was thinking that I couldn't possibly deal with the idea of losing you."

No matter how optimistic the doctors might be, Thais's tests, especially coming so close to Mother's Day, had Couples spooked. He stayed in Los Angeles on Tuesday for the tests, then flew to Dallas, where he was scheduled to play in the Byron Nelson Classic on Thursday. The test results would not be back until Friday. He played in a daze Thursday, surprising himself by shooting 66. The next morning, before he went out to play, Thais called. She had come through the tests clean. No sign of cancer. Couples could have shot 80 that day and he would have been dancing from tee to green. As it turned out, he shot 67, then added a 63 on Saturday to take a three-shot lead on the field.

The lead grew to five early on Sunday, but John Cook went on a back-nine birdie binge and caught Couples. "I didn't get tight until he caught me," Couples said. "He surprised me closing the lead from five to one as quickly as he did, but I don't think I got tight until seventeen."

The 17th hole at the Tournament Players Club at Las Colinas is a par-three over water. Couples hit a six-iron that ended up at the bottom of the lake. His chances to win drowned with the ball. He made a double bogey and ended up tied for second. It was frustrating. Having to answer questions about another blown lead on Sunday was annoying. But deep down, Couples couldn't get that upset. Did he want to win? Absolutely. Did the six-iron make him want to hurl the club into the water after the wayward ball? Sure. But was this the Masters? No. Could anything sully the news about Thais's health? Certainly not.

Couples finished 18th at Colonial the next week and then put together four almost perfect rounds at the Memorial to win for the second time in 1998. He played Saturday with a pounding headache that made him so sick he wasn't sure he would make it to the first tee. He shot 67. The victory put his earnings for the year at just under $1.5 million — more money than he had made in any full year in his career. What was scary was how close he was to having four tournament wins, including a major, instead of two wins, two seconds, and a third.

Couples had thought about playing in either the Kemper Open or the Buick Classic at Westchester before the Open, but he was tired after Memorial. He had played four weeks out of five and had spent the one week he had off worrying about Thais. He decided a rest was the best way to get ready for the Open and he arrived at Olympic confident and happy. He felt so good about his golf he even talked about playing someday on the Senior Tour, something he had vowed never to do.

"What do you think, Tommy, I could play fifteen times a year, don't you think?" he said to Watson as they waited to hit at number eight.

"They won't let you on the Senior Tour," Watson answered. "You're too good."

Couples snorted. "And what are they going to do with you?" he asked. "You're forty-nine and still winning out here against the pups."

"Forty-eight," Watson retorted. "My birthday isn't until September."

Regardless of when his birthday was, Watson was reveling in his success against the pups. He had won at Colonial three weeks earlier, a victory that had moved him to tears because he had honestly thought he might not win again on tour at this stage of his life. It had been a difficult year for Watson. He was going through a highly publicized divorce after almost twenty-five years of marriage at a time when his daughter, Meg, was graduating from high school and his son, Michael, three years younger, was starting to come into his own as a golfer.

That wasn't the only major change in his life. The previous fall, Watson had quit drinking. He had done it, Watson said, for his "overall well-being." In recent years, when Watson had struggled with his putting, particularly short putts, there had been a good deal of whispering on tour that it was tough to make short putts when your hands were shaking. Watson heard the whispers. They didn't necessarily bother him, but the thought had occurred to him that they might not be entirely wrong.

"Maybe I'm a little steadier over the ball," he conceded when Tom Callahan of *Golf Digest* asked him if better putting might be directly tied to no alcohol.

Returning to Olympic was bittersweet for Watson. From 1975 through 1983 he had won eight major titles, including his epic U.S. Open victory at Pebble Beach in 1982, when he had made what might be golf's most famous chip-in at the 17th hole on Sunday to snatch the tournament from Jack Nicklaus. Having lost both the Masters and the British Open to Watson in 1977, Nicklaus had thought he had gotten one back until Watson chipped in from that seemingly impossible spot.

"You did it to me again, you little SOB," Nicklaus said admiringly to Watson that day.

"That shot, that day, that moment with Jack was the highlight of my life as a golfer," Watson said later.

This was no small statement. Watson's victory over Nicklaus at Turnberry in the 1977 British Open is generally considered the greatest mano-a-mano duel in golf history. The two men were tied with one another after two rounds. Nicklaus shot a glorious 65–66 on the weekend. Watson shot 65–65 and won by one.

Watson's memories of that final day are vivid. He remembers standing on the 14th tee with Nicklaus, waiting for the huge crowd to settle so they could hit their tee shots and turning to Nicklaus and saying,

"This is really what it's all about, isn't it?" To Watson, playing the last round of the British Open with the greatest player in history, dueling down the stretch on a wonderful golf course, was as good as it gets. That night, after he had accepted the Claret Jug, Watson was getting dressed to go to dinner with his wife, Linda, when they heard a lone bagpiper playing outside their hotel.

"We looked out our window down on the golf course," he said. "It was probably about nine o'clock. The sun was still shining and the course was dead empty. I heard the piper and looked at the golf course and the jug and thought about the day and I just started to cry. I felt so connected to the game and the history of the game."

Watson still gets a little moist-eyed when that moment comes up, but the chip-in at Pebble Beach remains his most stirring moment. When he was growing up in Kansas City, the U.S. Open had always been *the* tournament to Watson because it was *the* tournament to his father, who taught him the game and the game's history. His father could name every U.S. Open champion, and he would often quiz Tom, naming a year and demanding to know the champion. "I never got them all," Tom said. "He never missed one."

Given all that, the lack of a U.S. Open championship was somewhat galling to Watson, who had emerged as the game's dominant player in the late 1970s. On that Sunday at Pebble Beach, he had led most of the day, but Nicklaus had put on one of his famous charges and was in the clubhouse at four under par when Watson arrived on the 17th tee, also at four under. The 17th is one of the most famous par-threes in the world. It brings the players back to the water, the green sitting on a spit of land a few yards from the beach and the water.

Watson chose a two-iron and promptly pulled it left into the high, gnarly rough next to the green. Walking off the tee, Watson disgustedly flipped the club to his longtime caddy, Bruce Edwards, and said, "That's dead." He was convinced the ball would be buried in rough so deep that he would have almost no chance to get it anywhere close to the hole. But when they walked around the bunker that guards the front of the green and the ball came into sight, Watson felt a glimmer of hope.

"The lie wasn't as bad as I had thought it would be," he said. "I was still going to have a little bit of an awkward stance, one foot below the other and the ball below my feet, but I could get my club on the ball.

That meant I had a chance. It was the kind of shot I practiced all the time getting ready for the Open because you have to play shots like that a lot around those greens."

Edwards, who has worked for Watson for most of the last twenty-five years, had the exact same thought as his boss. So, as Watson prepared to play the shot, he offered a couple of words of encouragement: "Knock it close, Tom," he said.

"Close?" Watson answered. "I'm going to make it."

Was he being cocky? Trying to talk himself into the shot? Not exactly. "The best play was to try and make it," he said. "Because the way the green sloped away, if the ball didn't go in, it probably wasn't going to stop anyplace close to the hole."

And so, in a sequence that has been replayed thousands of times, Watson stepped up, glanced at the hole once, glanced down, and popped the shot into the air. It hit and rolled. By the time it got close to the pin, Watson was running after it. When it went in, he kept on running, turning back to Edwards and saying, "I told you!"

Almost every golfer who has played the hole since that day has thrown a ball down near that spot and tried the shot. Most get the same result — the ball rolls forever, proving Watson's theory that he *had* to try and make it. Watson has tried the shot several times since then himself and never gotten the same result. "I went out there late one night with a bunch of friends a few years ago," he said. "They made me try the shot in the dark. I skulled it."

When it mattered, though, he was perfect. And, by his own admission, even though he won the British Open that year and the next, a little bit of the fire went out of Watson after he won that Open. He had lived his golf dream, and he knew that matching it or topping it would be just about impossible.

"When I was at Stanford, I would get up once or twice a week and drive down to Pebble Beach," he said. "I would be on the road by five o'clock. I'd stop and pick up a dozen little donuts and milk just outside of Monterey, eat them all in the car, and get to the first tee just before seven. The starter would let me off before anyone else and I would play eighteen holes and then drive back to Stanford.

"I always kept score. I wanted to know what I could shoot there because in my mind I was playing against Nicklaus and it was the U.S.

Open and coming down the stretch I was trying to make shots to beat Jack and win the Open.

"And then, I actually did it. I came back to Pebble and made a shot to beat the greatest player in the world and win the U.S. Open. How could anything be better than that?"

Nothing could be. Watson stopped winning regularly after 1984, but at Olympic in 1987 he almost recaptured his magic, beaten only by a remarkable performance by Scott Simpson coming down the stretch on Sunday. Now he was back, hoping he could play as well as he had eleven years ago.

"I think it will be difficult," he said, pointing at the long, gnarly rough. "I'm not as strong as I used to be. Getting the ball out of this stuff will be hard for me. I'll have to drive the ball very straight to have a chance."

Watson and Couples were standing in the ninth fairway waiting for a group to clear the green. Couples walked over with a confused look on his face. "Hey, Tommy, what's this about the fairways being soft? This is like concrete."

"They're all like that," Watson said.

"Wow," Couples said, with a shake of his head. "If it stays dry, this place will be brutal by Sunday."

"Would you take even par if I gave it to you right now?" Watson said.

"What won in '87?"

Watson thought for a moment. "Three under."

Couples nodded. "Give me even par right now and I'll take my chances."

16

Mind Games

While most of the players drifted in throughout the day on Monday —
a few had arrived over the weekend and several stragglers wouldn't show
up until Tuesday — almost all the caddies were at the golf course early
on Monday morning.

The best caddies like to get a look at the golf course before their
player arrives. The first thing they do when they arrive at a tournament
is fork over $15 to buy "The Book," an orange-covered pamphlet that
fits comfortably into a back pocket. Inside is a detailed map of the golf
course, complete with yardages, not only from tee to green, but from
sprinkler heads, bunkers, and other landmarks around the golf course.
Also included are warnings about hidden hazards — like a bush or creek
that might not be visible from the tee — and advice on where to aim
shots and where not to aim shots.

"The Book" is put together at every PGA Tour stop by George F.
Lucas, who calls himself "Gorjus George." He has been surveying tour
courses for twenty-two years and has a language all his own that the caddies must learn as they go. For example, if the letters JICYFU appear,
that is a warning that this is a place your player's ball may land that is not
going to make him happy. The abbreviation stands for Just In Case You
Fuck Up, since players tend to blame their caddies when their ball lands

in such awful places. Couples, for one, can often be heard saying to Joe LaCava, "Jeez, Joey, look what you've done to me." There are also references to the truly dreaded JICYRFU, which, of course, inserts a *Really* mid-phrase. More than one JICYRFU in a day can cost a caddy his job.

Once the caddies have purchased their yardage book, they walk the course themselves, double-checking yardages and landmarks, walking off the yardage from certain key points where they think their player is likely to have to play from. They will also pace off the greens, taking educated guesses on where the hole locations (not pin placements, remember) will be. Most caddies save all their yardage books. Bruce Edwards walked around Monday carrying his 1987 Olympic yardage book, not only making comparisons from eleven years ago but looking for changes. He had also written down the hole locations from that year, which gave him some idea where the locations might be in 1998. "On greens this size," he said, "they only have so many options."

One of the first caddies to arrive on Monday morning was Jim McKay, who had worked for Phil Mickelson since Mickelson had turned pro in 1992. McKay had been on tour since shortly after his graduation from the College of Georgia eleven years earlier. He had worked first for Larry Mize, whom he had known as a kid growing up in Columbus, Georgia, and then for Scott Simpson before hooking on with Mickelson. McKay, known to everyone as "Bones" because of his lean, lanky build, was one of the best-liked people on tour, one of many caddies who could just as easily be working on Wall Street or in a law firm if he chose to but enjoyed life on the road too much to give up doing what he was doing. What's more, having worked for Mickelson for six years, he had made a lot more money than he would have been making as an associate in a law firm. The top caddies make between 7 and 9 percent of their boss's earnings, meaning someone like McKay makes well into six figures annually.

McKay was not in the best of moods when he arrived at Olympic. Standing on the putting green, he waved a copy of the now-completed Fay/Meeks pairings and shook his head. "Look at this," he said, "they've dissed my man."

Very few people on tour are actually aware of the unofficial traditional U.S. Open pairings. McKay, who misses nothing, knew as soon as he looked at the pairings who was in the prick pairing and, more important to him, who was in the BPNTHWAM pairing. As soon as he saw that Mickelson had been paired with Darren Clarke and Jeff Maggert and that Colin Montgomerie, David Duval, and Jim Furyk were playing together, he knew his man had been bumped.

"It's not like he's having a bad year," McKay said. "He's won, he played well until the very end at Augusta, he's fifth on the money list. What do they want from him?"

McKay knew the answer to that question: a performance that would make him ineligible for the BPNTHWAM pairing. Mickelson would turn twenty-eight on Tuesday and had already won twelve times on tour, including once while he was still in college. He had won three NCAA titles at Arizona State and the U.S. Amateur title in 1990. He was the second player in history to win the NCAA and U.S. Amateur titles in the same year. The first player to accomplish the feat was Jack Nicklaus. The third was Tiger Woods. He was a flat-out money-making machine, tall, dark, and handsome with a beautiful blond wife, a dimple in his smile, and enough charm to fill most ballrooms.

Phil Mickelson had it all. Except . . .

"I feel as if I'm a good enough player that I should have won a major by now," he said, refusing to take the "I've won the Amateur so I've won a major" route. "I've had chances and haven't converted. But I feel as if I have a lot of years left to change that."

There was no doubting that. And, given his record, it seemed an absolute lock that Mickelson would do just that. But his phenom days were now behind him. When he had come on tour in 1992 he had been Tiger Woods before there was a Tiger Woods. His college coach, Steve Loy, quit his job to become his agent. He signed endorsement contracts that, pre-Tiger, were unheard of for a player just joining the tour. He never had to worry about Q-School because his victory at Tucson in 1991 made him exempt for two years when he turned pro. He finished second in his third pro tournament in 1992, won twice in 1993, and just kept on winning. His victory in the season-opening Mercedes Championships had meant he would have at least one win six years in a row. No one on tour currently had a streak that long.

And yet, there were those who wondered if Mickelson would win a major anytime soon. Some people believed his long, graceful putting stroke made him inconsistent on the greens, especially on short putts. Others wondered about his mentality. One of the keys to winning a major is avoiding big mistakes; Mickelson seemed prone to them. The double bogey at the 12th hole on Sunday at Augusta was one more example. In 1997 at the PGA, he had pulled within two shots of the leaders on Saturday, then taken a double bogey at the 16th. The year before in the PGA, he had led by three shots after 36 holes before shooting a 74 on Saturday, low-lighted by a double bogey on the short par-four 13th hole when he had knocked his second shot in the water. The next day, fighting to get back into contention late, he went in the water at 13 again and finished eighth.

It wasn't as if Mickelson had been a washout in the majors. He had a seventh and a third at the Masters, a fourth at the Open, and a sixth, a third, and an eighth at the PGA. Only at the British Open had he been unable to make a dent. But thirds and fourths and sixths weren't what Mickelson was after. "My record in the majors is okay," he said. "But it isn't as good as I'd like it to be. What concerns me is not so much seeing guys who are younger than I am winning, but seeing guys who I was pretty successful against in college and as an amateur winning them. It makes me question myself. Am I not progressing the way I should? Have I gone backward? I don't think so — if I had I don't think I could have won twelve times out here. But something is keeping me from playing my best golf at the most important times and I have to figure out what that is."

Mickelson has always been his own toughest critic. When he played in his first Masters in 1991, he arrived at Augusta a not-yet-twenty-one-year-old amateur expecting to win. "I had won at Tucson a couple months before," he said. "I went in there thinking I could win the tournament. I wasn't playing to make the cut, I was playing to get into contention."

As a result, after shooting 69 the first day and finishing forty-sixth, he was disappointed not to have done better. Most first-time amateurs at Augusta would have been jumping up and down about making the cut. Not Mickelson.

The same was true when he started to win on tour. He won twice in 1993 and finished twenty-second on the money list at twenty-three. Not good enough. "I thought to myself, two wins, is that all?" he said. "That meant I was *losing* 90 percent of the time."

Maturity and perspective have helped Mickelson understand that in a *great* year, the best players on tour will lose 80 percent of the time instead of 90 or 95. He understands now that his four wins in 1996 were remarkable. But he still lacks patience with himself and his game. In 1997, he began the year absolutely determined to win a major. He felt he had given away the PGA in 1996 and he was going to make amends. The results were disastrous. He missed the cut at the Masters for the first time in his life, and his highest finish was a tie for twenty-fourth at the British Open. Almost without fail he played poorly on Thursday and never could make up enough ground.

"I wanted it too much," he said. "I had no confidence and no patience. Then I would start missing some putts and everything would go straight downhill."

The first round at the U.S. Open that year was typical: he began the day with a three-putt double bogey, fought his way back into position to have a decent round through 16 holes, then double-bogeyed 17 to shoot 75, which left him 10 shots behind the leader after one day.

Mickelson had made some changes for 1998. He had decided to spend more time on his once vaunted short game. He had spent so much time trying to find consistency in his long game that it had improved greatly but, he felt, at a cost to his short game. "It used to be that I felt I could get anything up and down," he said. "For the last couple of years, that hasn't been the case."

On days when he had late tee times, Mickelson had given up sleeping in, choosing to arrive at the golf course at least two hours — sometimes more — before he was scheduled to play. That gave him time to practice, he felt, with complete focus since he did all his autograph signing after rounds. Mickelson has always believed that signing autographs is a daily part of his job, but he had found that trying to sign and get in practice time after rounds that started late was difficult. "I ended up rushing through one or both," he said. "Sometimes I felt I had stiffed people who wanted me to sign, sometimes I felt I had shortchanged myself on the range. This way, I have time for both."

Additionally, Mickelson had sought out Bob Rotella, the sports psychologist who had worked with many Tour players for years. Mickelson had never been a big believer in sports psychology, but he had noticed how calm Billy Mayfair looked coming up the 18th fairway in Los Angeles when he needed a birdie to tie Tiger Woods and force a playoff. Mayfair made birdie and beat Woods to win. Mickelson knew Mayfair had been working with Rotella after a poor year in 1997. "Seeing the way he handled that made me curious," he said.

He called Rotella during Bay Hill and spent an hour with him on the phone. They met face-to-face for almost two hours the next week at the Players Championship, and Mickelson had liked some of Rotella's ideas. "One thing he emphasized was not thinking I had to play flawless golf every round to win a tournament," he said. "I needed to believe that if I kept playing my game, I'd be in contention on Sunday."

Mickelson felt he had made progress at the Masters. After an opening 74, which might have made him panic a year earlier, he coolly shot a pair of 69s to put himself two shots off the lead going into Sunday. But his old impatience sneaked up on him Sunday. He made the turn even par for the day, knowing his two-stroke deficit was now four. He knew there were birdie holes ahead, but when he parred 10 and 11, he felt he had to make something happen at 12.

"Even though the pin was set behind the bunker, with my left-handed draw, I felt I could get close with an eight-iron," he said. "But I was trying too hard. I pulled it and it hit the bank and rolled back into the water."

End of any chance to win the Masters. Mickelson was crushed. "I needed to be patient one more hole," he said. "No matter what, 12 is not the hole to attack. Thirteen and 15 are. I couldn't make myself wait. Seeing that ball disappear was an awful, sick feeling."

While McKay was walking the course on Monday, Mickelson was home. He had decided not to fly in to Olympic until Tuesday. Like a lot of players, he dreaded practice rounds at the Open. "Six hours of torture," he called it and, since he almost always flew his own plane, he didn't have to worry about commercial airline schedules. Mickelson had learned to fly a few years earlier because flying on commercial airlines was always a little bit scary to him. It bothered him that he didn't know what made the plane go up and come down.

"You come out of a cloud and land," he said. "How does that happen? Well, now I know. Even when I fly commercial I'm not really nervous anymore because I know what's going on."

If only figuring out the last nine holes of a major championship could be that simple.

On Tuesday morning, Casey Martin came to the interview room to meet the media. He had been turning down reporters who approached him in the locker room or on the driving range, saying he would answer all questions at his scheduled press conference. Apparently he was learning a lot about media relations from his old Stanford teammate, Tiger Woods. The difference was that Woods rarely had to tell reporters no on a face-to-face basis since he always had a phalanx of security guards with him on the range and several members of his entourage around him almost all the time.

Hanging out with Woods had some very definite advantages. On Monday, Scott McCarron had played a practice round with him. Tuesday morning, when McCarron arrived at the golf course, he was denied access to the players' parking lot by a security guard because he had left his courtesy car there overnight and was, instead, driving his caddy's car. McCarron had his player badge but the guard wasn't buying his story about the courtesy car. Just as things were about to get ugly, another guard appeared.

"Hey, didn't you play with Tiger yesterday?" he asked McCarron.

"Yes, I did."

"He's okay," the second guard said to the first. "He played with Tiger."

"I guess," McCarron said later, "this means I owe Tiger one."

Before Martin began taking questions from the roomful of media types, Mike Butz, the USGA's deputy executive director, made a brief announcement: Martin would be allowed, "for safety purposes," to use a regular golf cart during the tournament.

The reason for the USGA's change of heart was simple: David Fay had gone for a ride in Casey's cart.

Fay had heard that Martin had been complaining that the cart was troublesome going up and down hills and, rather than wonder about it any further, he decided to take the cart for a spin himself late on Monday afternoon. He pointed the cart over to Olympic's second course, the so-called Ocean Course (even though the ocean was across the street), and began tooling around where he could find holes that weren't being used for parking, concessions, or corporate hospitality tents.

"It didn't drive badly," Fay said. "And it could certainly handle going up the hills, which I had heard was a problem. But there was no question that the one pedal made controlling the cart more difficult. I could see why Casey was concerned."

Fay was still mulling over a decision when he pulled the cart back to the cart barn. He was driving it into an empty spot up against the building when he tried to ease the accelerator so he could pull into the parking space. He couldn't do it. The cart plowed into the wall.

"I consider myself a good driver," Fay said. "And I couldn't get the thing stopped fast enough. At that moment I had this vision of a seven-year-old kid surprising Casey by jumping in front of him and Casey not being able to get the cart stopped in time. That was it for me."

And so Casey Martin got himself a regulation golf cart. "I can see it working at some point," he said. "But it just isn't there quite yet."

Martin then talked at length about all the endorsements — worth well into seven figures — that had come his way in recent months (Nike, Spalding, Ping, Hartford Life Insurance, and *We Magazine*) and, smiling for the cameras, said, "Anybody else who wants me, here I am." By coincidence, he had decided to make his PGA Tour debut at the Greater Hartford Open, home city for Hartford Life Insurance. He was hoping that some day people would want to talk to him just for his golf, but he understood that might not happen. "To most people I guess I'll always just be the guy in the cart," he said.

But at least now, it would be a cart he could control.

The driving range was absolutely packed on Tuesday afternoon. Most players, knowing all about the six-hour practice rounds that were common at the Open, had tried to get out early and then get in some practice. Jeff Thorsen was set up a few yards from where players entered and exited the range, and he couldn't help but glance around at the parade that was passing him by. Thorsen had just walked through the putting green and had been amazed at the number of people hanging over the guard rails just to be near Tiger Woods.

"I don't think I've ever seen so many people gathered in one place for the sole purpose of gawking in my entire life," he said, laughing. "You know, the funny thing is, I'm sure if you are standing outside the ropes, being inside the ropes looks like the best place in the world to be.

"But at my level, it really isn't. Now, if I were to make it on the tour for three or four years, then this would be a great place to be. But for me and a lot of guys like me, this life is a struggle. I was thinking driving in here that I'm going to be playing this week for fifteen times more money than I've ever played for in my life. Do you think it will be possible on Thursday to not think about that or what playing well here could mean? Of course not.

"I mean being here is absolutely great. I'm thrilled. But when I look at all these people it reminds me a little of walking past the White House a few years ago. I remember peering through the bars and thinking, wow, being in there must be great. But I'll bet for most of the people in there, it isn't that great."

Thorsen had been at Olympic for two days and he had heard some of the tour players around the locker room complaining about various things: the length of the rough, the traffic around Olympic, the price of parking at the player hotel (an outrageous $26 a night), the quality of the (free) food in the player dining room. "The saddest thing," Thorsen said, "is a lot of guys inside the ropes who *have* got it made don't understand how good they have it."

There were two major topics of conversation on the range that afternoon: bad backs and golf equipment.

The new most popular man on the PGA Tour, or so it seemed, was back guru Tom Boers. In April, Davis Love's back had tightened on an airplane flight to Japan. He had gone to see Boers. A week earlier, Ernie Els had walked off the course at Westchester (where, as at the Open, he was the defending champion) complaining that his back hurt. He had gone to see Boers. Now Boers was on the range with Fred Couples, who was the reigning expert on living with a bad back.

"Ernie saw Tom on Friday, and on Saturday he wanted to hit balls," Couples said. "Can't do that. Tom told him to wait till Tuesday. I know how hard that is. The hardest thing to learn with a bad back is when not to practice. You have to save yourself."

Earlier that day, Love had walked in after playing eight holes. If it had been a regular tour stop, Love would have withdrawn on the spot and gone home. Because this was the Open, he decided he had to try and play. "These guys are going to have to learn to listen to what their bodies are telling them," Couples said. "It's not easy. Your instinct is, you feel better, let's go play. It isn't that simple."

And how was Couples's back? "Tight," he said. "Boersy is going to work on me tonight."

Boersy was going to have a very busy week.

No busier, though, than the golf equipment manufacturers. Everyone who was anyone in the golf business was in town, buzzing around, standing in corners, whispering in hushed tones, looking over their shoulders to see who might be eavesdropping. Everyone was girding for the USGA's annual U.S. Open press conference scheduled for 11 A.M. on Wednesday.

Most years, the USGA press conference was attended by about forty-three USGA employees and nine or ten reporters. This year, it would play to an overflow crowd of more than three hundred, and everyone would be paying rapt attention to what new USGA president F. Morgan (Buzz) Taylor had to say.

The reason: spring-like effect. Or something like that.

"My wife says that between golf clubs and Viagra all she's heard about all year is spring-like effects," Fay joked.

To the equipment people this was anything but a joking matter. Shortly after taking over the USGA, Taylor had appeared to throw down the gauntlet, saying it was his considered opinion — and that of others on the USGA executive board — that technology in golf clubs had gone too far, that the distance players were getting with all the new giant-size club faces was more than most golf courses could handle. Perhaps it was time to scale back. Perhaps some of these clubs — which were making a mint for the equipment manufacturers — might be declared illegal.

If he had said that he wanted the teenage daughters of all the equipment people sold into slavery to Colombian drug lords, the reaction might have been more muted. The equipment people went crazy, tak-

ing out full-page newspaper ads urging their constituents to call someone — anyone — the USGA, Congress, the DEA, the FBI, the CIA, the
DAR, the League of Women Voters, and anyone else who came to mind
to tell them, "Don't let the USGA take away our golf clubs!"

They threatened lawsuits, they hired big-name lawyers, they prepared to go to war. And then, on Wednesday morning, they listened
while Fay read a carefully prepared statement which said — when trans-
lated into English — that while the USGA was concerned with spring-
like effect (how far the golf ball traveled) it saw no reason to scale back
the current equipment but wanted to call a meeting for the fall with the
equipment companies to discuss the possibility of limiting technology
in the future.

Oh.

Not since Geraldo Rivera opened Capone's vault has more been
made of less. All that screaming and yelling and the USGA had stepped
up and said, "Hey, let's talk."

Clearly, it was time to start the golf tournament.

17

Let the Suffering Begin

At 3 o'clock on Wednesday, the first tee was closed so the preparations could begin to get the golf course ready for play at 7 A.M. Thursday.

A little more than an hour later, in order to give the last groups to tee off some space, Tom Meeks and Trey Holland set off down the first fairway in a cart. Their job was to set up the golf course: place the tees and, most important, select the hole locations. Like Meeks, Holland, who was forty-eight, was from Indiana, a urologist from Zionsville. He was also the USGA's first vice president and chairman of the USGA championship committee.

Three men waited for them on the first green: Tim Moraghan, the USGA's championships agronomist for twelve years; Pat Gross, who ran the western section of the USGA; and John Fought (rhymes with vote), the 1977 U.S. Amateur champion who had played on tour for a number of years and was now an up-and-coming course designer. He and Moraghan were friends, and Moraghan had invited him to come along to get an idea of how a U.S. Open course was set up.

Meeks had already put together a list of tentative hole locations for the entire week. The mission this afternoon and evening — as would be the case at the end of play each of the next three days — was to test the locations to make sure they would be fair. Meeks, Holland, Moraghan, and Fought all had putters with them so they could putt to each location and see how the ball reacted. They would spend several minutes on each green, putting at the proposed locations from several distances and angles. Once they decided the location was okay, Meeks would take a can of spray paint and mark the spot where the hole was to be cut with a small green dot.

The holes would not actually be cut until early the next morning when the grounds crew, armed with a hole location chart, would find the dot and cut the hole. Why was it done that way? "We don't want anyone [read caddies] sneaking out here at night or first thing in the morning and checking the locations so they can get a jump on everyone," Meeks said. "Unless you have the hole chart in hand, you'll never find these dots."

It is commonly thought that hole locations get more difficult with each passing day of the tournament. When someone refers to a "Sunday flag," they mean that the hole has been put in the toughest possible location on a green. But that's not how it works. When Meeks picks his hole locations on a given green, he assigns a number to each. The most difficult gets a one, the easiest a four. Then he will mix the numbers up each day. On Thursday and Friday four of the locations would be ones; on Saturday and Sunday five would be ones. If each day's difficulty was exactly the same, the total difficulty each day would be 45. Meeks had broken the four days down to 47–47–44–42. Sunday's locations would be the toughest, but not by nearly as much as people might think — including the players.

Going through his round the next day, Payne Stewart would shake his head about the hole location at number seven and say, "I thought that's where that pin would be on Sunday."

At each hole, Meeks would look at his notes and tell the others where he wanted to go. At the par-five first hole, he had written down 17 front, 8 right. In golf vernacular that meant the hole would be located 17 yards from the front of the green and 8 yards from the right. Someone would step off the yardage, usually from both sides, to make sure they had it exactly right. In other words, knowing the first green was 25 yards deep, Meeks stepped off 17 from the front and then 8 from the back to make sure he ended up at the same spot.

Moraghan had stimped the greens shortly before joining the rest of the group and said they were already 11+ on average. "We don't want them getting a whole lot quicker than that," he said.

Some greens concerned the group. There was no location on the front right portion of the fourth that could be used because the green was contoured there in such a way that any ball putted in that direction would roll right off the green. In 1987, the fifth green had been so sloped it couldn't be stimped. The location Meeks had chosen for that hole on Thursday gave the group some concern. "It's all right," Holland finally concluded after several softly hit putts had rolled several feet by. "But there aren't going to be a lot of one-putts."

They moved along at a leisurely pace, enjoying the cool that was descending on the course and each other's company. At the sixth, Fought hit a perfect putt to the proposed location and said, "You guys are too nice." By the 11th, his tune had changed. Rolling a putt from the top level of the green to the lower, he watched his putt go way past the location and said simply, "Oh my."

Often, after deciding that Thursday's location was acceptable, one of the others would ask Meeks what he had planned for the rest of the week. One major concern for the group was spreading the locations out as much as possible on Olympic's small greens. Placing them too close together would mean a lot of foot traffic in the same area and that would beat up a portion of the green. "One thing you don't want is the U.S. Open being decided by some kind of fluky bounce off a spike mark," Moraghan said.

It was close to 7 o'clock by the time they reached 18. The 18th at Olympic is one of the shortest par-four finishing holes in championship golf. It is 347 yards straight downhill from the tee to a narrow landing area and then straight uphill to a green protected by several deep bunkers. For almost everyone in the field, the hole would be played with an iron off the tee and a wedge second shot. The only thing that protected the hole from being a pitch-and-putt hole was the slope of the green. Any shot that landed above the hole put the player in jeopardy of making bogey. In 1993, trying to birdie the hole to win the Tour Championship, Greg Norman had fired his second shot at the flag and watched it sail 20 feet past it. His second putt — for par — had also been a 20-footer. He missed and lost by one.

While Meeks paced off Thursday's location, Moraghan stood with his arms folded and shook his head. "This is the one green on the golf course that really scares me," he said. "It's the only green we haven't touched because it's so steep back to front. I'm not sure there are four reasonable locations here. It's bumpy because we haven't done anything to it, haven't cut it or rolled it. You have to spread the locations out. I'm not sure we can do that."

Meeks was aware of Moraghan's concerns. He had already told Fay that if and when the Open came back to Olympic the USGA should insist on a clause in the contract that guaranteed that the 18th green would be modified. It was too late to do that this year.

"We'll do the best we can with what we have to work with," Meeks said. "My goal is to have 72 fair hole locations out of 72. Anything less will be disappointing."

Steve Pate had left a wake-up call for Thursday morning at 4:30 A.M. But he didn't need the call. He was already up. Pate had drawn the honor of being first on the tee that morning, which meant he was expected to have his ball in the air a few seconds after 7 A.M. Since the hotel had lost his car two days earlier, Pate had left some extra time to ensure arriving at the golf course to warm up by 6. That would be a few minutes after sunrise.

Ron Read had set his alarm for 5. He was up at 4:50. It was Read who would introduce Pate and the rest of the field on the first tee. He had been the starter at the Open since 1989, succeeding Fay after Fay's ascendancy to executive director. Read was a serious sort, though he had a dry sense of humor. He knew that the opening moments of the tournament could be the most difficult because the first tee tended to be a bit chaotic, especially when the first group arrived, because most of the early arrivals at the golf course — fans, volunteers, media, officials — tended to congregate on or near the tee so they could watch the tournament begin.

Read's worst moment had come in 1993 at Baltusrol. The first tee at Baltusrol is quite small and there were far too many people crowded onto it as far as Read was concerned. He was standing near the small grandstand, microphone in hand, several yards from the players when

Jay Don Blake launched his tee shot way left, apparently out-of-bounds. Read assumed he would hit a provisional. His view blocked by all the people standing between him and the players, Read was shocked when, standing on tiptoes, he saw that Jim Thorpe was teeing his ball up.

Thorpe was one of the quickest players on tour — both in terms of playing his shots and one-liners. "Jim, what about a provisional?" Read asked, referring to Blake.

"Provisional?" Thorpe said, backing away from the ball. "Damn, I haven't hit a single shot yet and already the USGA has me playing a provisional."

The first tee at Olympic wouldn't be quite as bad as Baltusrol. There was more room and, it seemed, fewer hangers-on. Grant Waite was the first player to arrive at the tee, six minutes early, and Read handed him a scorecard — each major has special scorecards made up just for the event — and a hole location sheet and wished him luck. Pate and Olin Browne followed two minutes later. Pate was smiling. "They had my car waiting for me," he said, referring to the hotel. "I think I scared them the other day."

Even with more room to work, life wasn't going to be simple for Read. A marshal came charging up to complain about a USGA cart that had been parked next to the tee. Read said he would take care of finding out who it belonged to after the first group got off. There was also no microphone. So, to make himself heard, Read walked over in front of the small grandstand set up behind the tee and read (no doubt Don Fay would have been horrified) his opening lines:

"Welcome to the 1998 United States Open championship. The championship will be conducted over 72 holes of medal play. There were 7,117 entries for the championship and, based on player performance, 156 players have qualified. Steve Pate of North Ranch, California, has the honor. Play away please."

And so, at precisely 7 A.M. Pacific Coast Daylight Time, Pate, wearing a green pullover to stay warm on the cool, cloudy morning, became the first player to put a ball in play in the 98th U.S. Open. He also became the first player to find the rough, pushing his drive to the right.

Read then introduced Grant Waite. "From northern Australia, Grant Waite."

Waite's caddy, Graham Counts, sidled over to Read. "He's not from Australia," he whispered. "I'm from Australia. He's from New Zealand."

Read turned slightly pale. He looked down at his starter sheet. Waite was listed as being from northern Australia. "Do you think I should say something?" he asked.

Counts nodded. "Might not be a bad idea."

Waite had hit his tee shot down the middle. After he introduced Browne without any hitches and Browne hit his tee shot, Read ran a few steps down the fairway to catch up to Waite.

Waite laughed at the apology. "No worries," he said, in perfect Australian.

Read smiled. Then he sent someone to double-check and make sure the hometowns for the remaining 153 players were correct on the starter's sheet. "The tournament is one minute old," he said, "and we've already made the first bogey."

The tournament was a little more than an hour old when Dudley Hart decided he was overmatched.

Playing in the second group of the day, Hart had gotten off to a shaky start, missing a short birdie putt at number one, then making a double bogey at number two after hooking his tee shot into the left rough. He managed pars at the next two holes, then hit what he thought was a perfect three-wood at the long par-four fifth hole. Standing on the elevated tee, Hart watched the ball bounce in the fairway and start rolling to the left. The ball rolled and rolled and rolled. It finally came to a stop after it had reached the rough.

Hart stood on the tee staring at the ball as it disappeared. "Are you kidding?" he said rhetorically. He flipped his club to caddy Craig Cimarolli and said, "I guess I'm just not good enough to play this goddamn golf course."

It didn't get any better for Hart. Five holes later, he jammed his surgically repaired left wrist trying to dig a shot out of the deep rough. He had hurt the wrist during a practice round but tried to ignore the pain because he had gone through too much trying to get back into the Open to withdraw. But now the pain shot through him and brought back memories of 1995 before the surgery. He struggled in with 78 and knew there was no way he would be able to play the next day. "If I had somehow shot 68 that day I don't think I could have played the next day," he said. "I thought about playing just because I didn't want people to think I had quit because I shot a lousy score. But then I realized I had to think long term. One more swing in that rough and I could be out for the year."

Feeling as discouraged as he could ever remember feeling during a golf tournament, Hart told USGA officials he was withdrawing.

Hart wasn't the only one feeling down. As the morning wore on, there were a lot more players with green numbers (over par) next to their names than red ones (under par). On the range, players warming up could see the numbers players were posting thanks to a giant screen that had been set up in the far right corner.

Glancing at the screen, Justin Leonard could see that there weren't many scores under par. That suited him fine. A golf course that took patience and the ability to be creative around the greens played to his strengths.

Especially the patience part. Leonard had turned twenty-six on Monday, but his maturity level, on and off the golf course, was closer to thirty-six. Or forty-six. He was so organized, so prepared that everyone who knew him, including his older sister, Kelly, joked about it. Leonard constantly protested that people exaggerated, but then would admit that, yes, he did line up his clothes in the closet according to the day of the week that he planned to wear them. "How else would you do it?" he asked.

Leonard was Larry and Nancy Leonard's second child, four years younger than Kelly, born and raised in Dallas without even a trace of a Texas accent. He could, though, on command, lapse into a Texas drawl that would have made J. R. Ewing proud. Larry Leonard was a microbiologist with degrees from SMU and Texas. According to Justin his competitiveness comes from his dad, his organizational zeal from his mom. "My dad will sometimes go on the road for three days on a job where he doesn't sleep the whole time he's gone," Leonard said. "Then he'll come back and play golf and the first time he makes a bogey he can't figure out what in the world can possibly be wrong."

Nancy Leonard was still her son's unofficial travel agent and executive assistant. When Justin returned home after his British Open victory in 1997, he expected to be buried in mail. He was. But getting through it wasn't that hard since his mom had laid it all out on the dining room table with little notes — "sign these"; "read these"; "make sure this answer is accurate," and so on. There were envelopes lined up so that Justin could sign, read, check — whatever — and then pop the reply into the envelope. "She saved me at least a week of work," he said.

Justin started playing golf when he was tiny, squeezing into the cart on Sunday between mom and dad and dropping his ball in the fairway while they were playing. He would knock the ball around until they were finished with a hole, pick up, and do the same thing on the next hole. He loved it. He also played soccer — "too small to even think about football," he said — and was very good. But at thirteen he had to decide between full-time soccer or full-time golf, and he chose golf.

He was a very good junior, not Phil Mickelson or Tiger Woods, but very good. He was never bothered by his lack of size or his lack of length off the tee because he had grown up playing with older kids and was used to giving away yards off the tee. He learned early that you didn't have to be long to succeed, that getting the ball into the hole was a lot more important than getting it way down the fairway.

He did well enough in junior tournaments as a high school junior that he might have dominated as a senior. Instead, much to the surprise of his friends, he decided to play in amateur tournaments against adults. "I always wanted to try and play up," he said. "I figured it was the only way to get better."

He chose the University of Texas, not because his father had gotten his master's degree there, but because he thought it was the school he would enjoy most over four years. "All the schools I visited had good golf programs," he said. "I finally decided to make my choice as if I wasn't going to be playing golf. Where would I like to be most just as a college."

If that sounds like an unusual way for a recruited athlete to choose a school, that's because it is very unusual. Leonard's approach to life is relentlessly methodical. At eighteen he had no idea whether he would be good enough to play professional golf or if he would want to play professional golf. He had always been a good student — A's and B's — and that didn't change in college. He graduated in four years (also a rarity for a varsity athlete) with a degree in business administration.

But while he was going about getting his degree, he was also becoming a world-class amateur player. At the end of his sophomore year, he changed equipment, going to forged blades for the first time in his life, and found that the new clubs made him a much more accurate player. That summer (1992) he won the U.S. Amateur and now turning pro after graduation became something to think very seriously about.

It became even more likely after he had played in seven pro tournaments the next year. He made the cut in five of them — including the U.S. Open — and began getting rave reviews from some of the pros he had played with. He still wasn't very long, but he had this knack for getting the ball in the hole. And pressure didn't seem to bother him. At the Open, paired the first two rounds with defending champion Tom Kite and British Open champion Nick Faldo, he outplayed them both and found himself in the top twenty after 36 holes.

"Playing in those tournaments that year was important," he said. "For one thing, they made me a better player. But more important, I didn't feel overwhelmed. It wasn't as if I had absolutely no chance on those golf courses."

By now it was a foregone conclusion that he would turn pro. He chose Vinnie Giles, one of the greatest amateur players never to have turned pro, as his agent. He had played for Giles on the Walker Cup team in 1993, and Giles represented players like Kite and Davis Love, whom he had come to know, so it was a comfortable fit. But there was another reason he chose Giles. "I asked all the agents we interviewed [about seven different groups] where they thought I should play after graduation," Leonard said. "Some hemmed and hawed. Some said I should play the Nike Tour because they could help me with exemptions there. Vinnie just said flat out that I should play as many PGA Tour events as I could get into and if I didn't do well in them I could go play the Nike Tour and get ready for Q-School. His attitude was the Tour was where I wanted to be, so why not go straight there if I could."

Leonard took that advice. He wrote to five summertime events asking for sponsor exemptions (five being the maximum he could receive in a year) and got them. But actually getting into his first tournament in Hartford wasn't as easy as getting invited to play. Leonard had just turned twenty-two and, at 5 feet 9 and 160 pounds with a baby face, he looked more like the son of a player than a player. He showed up at Hartford the first day and told the guards at the entrance to the club that he was there to play in the tournament.

Sure you are, son, they replied, so where's your player badge?

Leonard didn't have a player badge because he hadn't played in a tournament yet as a pro. He hadn't brought the letter inviting him to play with him because he didn't think he'd need it. Sorry, son, the guards said, you'll have to go park in the public lot with everyone else. Nice try though.

Leonard ended up in a public lot about a mile from the front gate. He pulled his clubs out of the trunk and began walking to the clubhouse. A courtesy van stopped and picked him up and he managed to get by the guards this time without buying a ticket.

Welcome to the PGA Tour.

Things got better quickly. He missed the cut at Hartford, but made the cut the next week at the Western Open and his first check, for $8,800. A week later, in Williamsburg, he played brilliantly and finished third in only his third pro tournament. That performance was critical because it earned him enough money to put him into the top 150 on the 1994 money list. That gave him status as a "temporary member" for the rest of the year, meaning he could get an unlimited number of sponsor exemptions. That meant he had a shot to make enough money to earn his playing card for 1995 without going through the torture of Q-School.

The rest of the year was a roller coaster. He finished sixth in Boston and thought he was a lock to make the top 125, then missed six straight cuts and thought he had no chance. He played well in his last two events of the year, Callaway Gardens and Texas, but couldn't get into either Disney or Las Vegas, meaning he had to sit at home and see how many guys passed him the final two weeks.

"On the last day in Vegas, my father had sat down at his computer and figured out exactly how much money each guy behind me needed to pass me," Leonard remembered. "He wrote it all down on a yellow pad and he and mom sat in the basement and watched. I couldn't do it. I just sat upstairs and watched a football game."

When the day was over his parents came upstairs with the news: he was on the PGA Tour. He had ended up 126th on the money list, but in those days if a nonmember (read European Tour player) finished in the top 125, he didn't count. There were four Europeans in the top 125, extending the list of exempt players to 129th.

"I've never felt like I ducked something not going to Q-School," he said. "I went through my own thirteen-week Q-School and survived it."

Once he had a spot on tour for the following year, his longtime teacher, Randy Smith, suggested that he sit down and set some goals. Not obvious ones, but reachable goals that might help him focus. Leonard sat down one night and made a list. One of the first things he wrote down was "Play in all the majors." He had gotten to play in three of them as the Amateur champion, but he entered 1995 not qualified for any of them. Later he wrote, "Learn to enjoy spike marks on the weekends." This was a way of reminding himself that his Thursday-Friday goal each week should be to get a late tee time for the weekend. That would mean more spike marks, but it would also mean he was one of the leaders.

He met most of his goals that first full year, earning just under $750,000, putting him twenty-second on the money list. He didn't get into the Masters and he missed qualifying for the U.S. Open, but he did get into the British Open at St. Andrews. That was a thrill and, as it turned out, an important step in his career.

"When I played at St. George's ['93 British Open] I had the feeling that this kind of golf would be very good for me," he said. "I flight the ball low from having played in the Texas winds all my life and it doesn't bother me to take out a five-iron from 120 yards if that's the play. I loved the way golf felt over there, the whole deal. The fans, the weather, the bounces, all of it."

That was why he made the decision — unusual for a young American player, especially at that point, when British Open money didn't count on the U.S. money list — to fly to Scotland to play qualifying in '95. "If I'd been struggling on the money list, I might not have gone," he said. "But I wasn't. So there was no reason not to go."

Not only did he qualify, he made the cut easily, shooting 67 on Friday. He played poorly on the weekend but came away from the experience convinced that the British Open was a tournament he could contend in in years to come.

The following year he lost a playoff to Phil Mickelson in Phoenix. Playing against Mickelson in Phoenix is a little bit like playing a Ryder Cup match against Seve Ballesteros in Spain. Since Mickelson went to Arizona State, he is an adopted son there and the huge crowds that attend the tournament pull fervently for him. Leonard remembers standing over his ball on one tee and hearing someone in the crowd yell, "Hit it in the bunker!"

He lost the playoff on the third hole, but came out of the experience a tougher player. The next time he was in position to win, that summer at the Buick Open, he blew the field away on Sunday, winning by five shots. He finished the year with $943,000 in earnings (eleventh on the money list), eight top-ten finishes, and a burgeoning reputation as one of the best young players in the game. Tiger Woods got the headlines; Ernie Els had a U.S. Open under his belt; Mickelson was already a star. But Leonard and David Duval were on the next plateau.

That winter when Leonard sat down to write out his goals for 1997, he had two new ones: "*Contend* in the majors" and "Learn Spanish." He now knew he would get to play in all four majors. That was progress. In fact, he had finished fifth at the PGA the previous summer and the only cut he had missed in a major had been at the British Open. "That was a shocker," he said. "I had to qualify again and I shot 68–64 and easily won at the course I was playing. I went into Lytham full of confidence and somehow shot 78 the first day. I think my expectations got too high, too fast."

Now, his expectations were to be in contention on the four Sundays that mattered most.

And the Spanish? "The Ryder Cup was in Spain," he said. "I wanted to be there."

By the time he got to the British Open that summer, he was well on his way to meeting his goals. He had chipped in for birdie on the 17th hole at Augusta on Sunday to jump into the top ten — T-7 — and he had won his second tournament, the Kemper Open. He had become one of the last players on tour to give up his persimmon-headed driver for a metal driver and felt he added about 15 yards off the tee as a result. A good performance at the British would all but lock up a berth on the Ryder Cup team. Of course he still didn't speak a word of Spanish.

The Open championship in 1997 was played at Troon, a classic Scottish links. The front nine goes straight out from the clubhouse, the back nine comes right back to it. That meant that when the wind blew, the golf course changed radically from front nine to back. On Thursday, the front nine was straight downwind and players were routinely going out in four and five under par. Coming back was quite another story. With the wind right in their faces, many players had trouble reaching the par-four greens in regulation even playing a three-wood second shot.

The back nine that day could not have set up worse for Leonard. He had shot a modest two-under-par 34 on the front nine, and when he turned into the wind, he knew he was in trouble. A bogey at the 10th hole confirmed his fears. But he stuck his jaw out and put on one of the great grinding acts ever seen over the next eight holes. He hit exactly one green — the par-five 16th — in regulation. On two of the holes he couldn't even reach the fairway with his driver because the wind was so fierce. He was hitting five- and six-iron *third* shots into par-fours. But when he walked off the 18th green, he had played the last eight holes in one under par, shooting an even-par 35 on the back nine. Only two other players in the field shot even par on the back nine that day. His 69 left Leonard two shots off the lead.

The next day, with conditions much milder, Leonard shot 66, which left him still two shots off the lead, which was held by Darren Clarke. Two years earlier, Clarke and Leonard had been paired together during qualifying for St. Andrews. Now they would be paired together in the final group on Saturday.

Both played like players in contention in a major for the first time. The conditions were mild again and scores were low. Leonard struggled with his putter all day and felt as if he was giving away his chance to contend on Sunday. But as he walked onto the 17th green, having hit his tee shot to 15 feet, he looked up at the scoreboard. Jesper Parnevik, who had shot 66, was in the clubhouse at 11 under par. Clarke was at eight under. Fred Couples was six under, and Leonard was in a gaggle of players at five under.

Leonard had a thought: "If I can make this putt and get to six, I'll be paired with Freddy tomorrow. That would be good for me."

Almost everyone in golf likes playing with Couples. Leonard has particularly fond memories of Couples because at his first Masters, Couples, as the defending champion, was his playing companion the first day. "I could barely get the club back on number one," he said. "Fred was great that whole day. Supportive, easy to be with. He didn't know me from Adam and he couldn't have been nicer."

Spurred by the thought of a Sunday pairing with Couples, Leonard rolled in his birdie putt. "It was the only putt I made all day," he said. He parred 18 to finish at six under, earning his tee time with Couples.

Even so, Leonard wasn't in a very upbeat mood that night. He had dinner, as he had throughout the tournament, with his caddy, Bob Riefke. Leonard's parents hadn't made the long trip and Leonard had found himself in a tiny room at the Marine Hotel. He didn't really mind, he knew full well that the big rooms in the hotel were taken up by big-name players. But he didn't really feel like lingering in the room any longer than necessary, so he and Riefke took their time over dinner that night, especially with a 2:50 P.M. tee time.

Jack and Barbara Nicklaus stopped by the table. Nicklaus had made the cut on the number and had played early on Saturday. That meant he had been able to watch most of Leonard's round. "I really gave away a lot today, didn't I?" Leonard said.

Blunt as always, Nicklaus said, "You know, it's really tough to make putts when you don't reach the hole."

Leonard knew he was right. "I hope I get a few of them to the hole tomorrow," he answered, still feeling fairly miserable.

It was Barbara Nicklaus who responded, no doubt to the look on his face as much as the words. "You know, Justin, you can still win the golf tournament," she said. "Five shots is far from impossible, especially when there are only two players ahead of you."

Leonard thanked her for trying to cheer him up. Back in his room a little while later, he started thinking about what Barbara Nicklaus had said. Perhaps she had been trying to make him feel better, but she was right. He had been five shots back after three rounds at the Kemper and won. Parnevik and Clarke, the players ahead of him, were good players, but they had never won a major title. If he could get off to a good start and get some putts to the hole, he could win. He went to bed excited instead of depressed.

The next day on the range, he knew he had a serious chance. The Click, that little sound that golfers hear in their head when their swing is exactly right, was there. At one point he hit eight straight one-irons off a slight sidehill lie and hit each one perfectly. "Now that," said Riefke, not one given to hyperbole, "is pretty good."

All day long, his putts got to the hole. On the back nine, he started making everything. Parnevik, who had seemed to be in control early on, began to falter. When Leonard rolled in a 30-foot birdie putt on the 17th hole, he had the lead for the first time. "That was when the hairs on the back of my neck stood straight on end," he said later.

Couples, who was going through a miserable day, was there rooting him on just as Leonard had thought he would if he wasn't in position to win himself. Leonard was walking on the 18th green when he looked at one of the giant yellow scoreboards that flank the green and saw that Parnevik had bogeyed 17. He had a two-shot lead. Two putts from 25 feet and the British Open would be his. Calmly, he got his first putt to about 18 inches and tapped in. Unless Parnevik holed out from the fairway, he had won. He had shot 65 on a day when none of the other contenders broke 70. He had made every critical putt, needing only 25 putts for the entire round. This was not the Buick Open or the Kemper Open, this was the British Open, and he had played the round of his life.

To top it off, his speech during the awards ceremony was memorably gracious. He not only thanked all the right officials, he made a point of talking about how well British amateur Barclay Howard had played, he complimented the fans, and he talked emotionally about his friends and family back home. When he got choked up thinking about his parents, he said simply, "Moment please," stepped back from the microphone, and gathered himself while the crowd waited for him. When he was finished, he received the kind of ovation usually reserved for Nicklaus or Watson or Palmer or local heroes like Faldo and Montgomerie. If he hadn't already won them over with his golf, he certainly won them over with his speech.

"When we watch the tape," he said later, "the speech is my mom's favorite part."

The way he handled himself that day both during and after the golf tournament launched him to another level of stardom. Giles was swamped with offers for endorsements and guarantees for playing overseas. Leonard's groupie quotient skyrocketed. When he came back three weeks later and finished second to Davis Love in the PGA, not winning only because Love put on a record-setting performance, there was no doubt that he had arrived as a star.

Now when the twenty-something names of the tour were talked about, Leonard came shortly after Woods and Els, but very shortly. Winning a major title changes your status considerably.

After a slow start in '98, he had pulled out the British Open tape before the beginning of the Florida swing, to give himself a pep talk but also to look at his swing and his putting stroke and see if anything had changed radically. He made some minor adjustments working with Randy Smith and two weeks later won the Players Championship — coming from five shots back on the last day of course — meaning he had won a major and a significant in a nine-month span. Players refer to a handful of tournaments that aren't majors but stand out from the other weekly events as "significants." The Players ranks at the top of the significant list.

The win at the Players sent Leonard into the Masters brimming with confidence. He knew Augusta favored the longer hitters and always would, but he also knew he had finished seventh a year earlier and that a hot putter could make up for any lack of distance off the tee. He played well, especially on the back nine on Sunday when he shot 33 for a closing 69 that got him into eighth place.

But the last day pairing with the Kuchars left him feeling very uneasy. Peter Kuchar's constant jumping up and down and cheerleading had distracted him on several occasions. "If he's outside the ropes, he should cheer and jump up and down all he wants to," he said shortly before the Open. "But if he's inside the ropes, there is a certain decorum that is part of the deal. You have to be aware of the other players. Shaking a fist or high-fiving after a great shot is one thing, but going crazy every time Matt hits it on the green is a little much."

Leonard wasn't alone in this feeling. Other players and caddies who had been exposed to Peter Kuchar's act were concerned too. At the tournament in Atlanta, Lee Janzen had been paired with Kuchar, who had a sponsor's exemption into the event. Bruce Edwards was caddying for Janzen that week since Watson was off and Janzen's regular caddy, Dave Musgrove, was home in England with his wife, who was ill. Edwards walked off 18 that day with steam coming out of his ears. "He just doesn't know the etiquette of caddying out here," Edwards said. "Which isn't that bad, if you're willing to learn. He isn't willing to learn." Janzen was also upset. "He distracted me as I was about to hit at least twice," he said. "That's twice too many times for that to happen. He should know better."

Leonard was concerned enough about the impending pairing at the Open that he called Bruce Heppler, the golf coach at Georgia Tech, to ask him if he would have a quiet word with the Kuchars. He also suggested to Riefke that it might not be a bad idea for him to talk to Kuchar, caddy-to-caddy, before Thursday's round began.

On Wednesday, Riefke had found Peter Kuchar on the putting green. Quietly and politely he told him that he had some concerns about the pairing the next day because of what had happened at Augusta. "What happened at Augusta?" Peter Kuchar asked.

"Well, to be honest, there were five or six occasions where you distracted Justin," Riefke answered.

"Really." Peter Kuchar said, "why don't you name them for me."

Riefke did. In detail.

Peter Kuchar folded his arms and said, "Well, that's certainly very interesting, isn't it?" Then he walked away. Riefke suspected it was going to be a long two days.

The group teed off at noon, followed by what was probably the largest non–Casey Martin gallery of the day. (Tiger-mania appeared to have waned somewhat, at least in San Francisco. His gallery was sizable but not the kind of mob scene that had been the case so often in the past.) From the beginning it was apparent that Peter Kuchar hadn't listened to Riefke or anybody else. He was cheering every good shot — and Matt hit plenty of them — with his arms in the air, shouting things like "Did you see that? Was that a great shot or what?" in the direction of the fans outside the ropes.

Leonard, who was playing solidly, kept his composure most of the day. Neither he nor Els was thrilled when the entire group was put on the clock for slow play on the 14th hole. When official Mike Shea specifically told Kuchar that he already had one bad time (playing too slowly when the group was on the clock) Matt nodded and said he would try to pick it up. A moment later his dad asked him what Mike Shea had said to him. When Matt told him, Peter Kuchar shook his head and said, "That's wrong, that's just wrong. You aren't slow."

The son understood. The father did not.

The only thing approaching an incident occurred at 17 when Leonard had to back off a two-foot par putt because Peter Kuchar was still moving and he saw him out of the corner of his eye. He backed off, lined up again, and missed. After the round when reporters asked him why he had backed off at 17, Leonard, trying desperately not to get into a P.R. battle he knew he couldn't win, said, "I saw some writers moving behind the green."

It was a very inside joke. There had been exactly two writers behind the green and neither one of them was anywhere close to being within Leonard's vision. But the writers behind 18 who hadn't been there bought the story.

Leonard walked to the range, where Randy Smith was waiting. "What do I do?" he asked. "Being polite doesn't work, giving him looks doesn't work. Nothing works." He had shot 71, a reasonable score, very much in contention. But he was distracted and upset. It was only going to get worse.

18

Payne and Pain

The leader on Thursday was a familiar name but not one that had been atop a major leader board for a long time: Payne Stewart. Or, as his father had always insisted he call himself when filling out his U.S. Open application form, "William Payne Stewart."

"Dad always said, 'This is the United States Open, your national championship, you write down your full name,'" Stewart said.

By any name, Stewart had become a star on tour in the late '80s and early '90s when he had transformed himself from a talented money-maker, best known for wearing knickers on the golf course as an attention-getting device, into a big-time player who didn't need anything but his golf swing to get attention. After winning three times during his first eight years on tour, he won five times during the next three years, including the 1989 PGA and the 1991 U.S. Open. He had almost won another Open in 1993, only to watch Lee Janzen birdie two of the last three holes at Baltusrol, including a chip-in at 16, to beat him.

Stewart was now forty-one and he had won only once on tour — in 1995 at Houston — since his Open victory. There were all sorts of reasons for his drop from one of the world's most consistent players to a good but no longer great player. He had changed equipment and golf balls and that had affected his game. Beyond that, though, Stewart had changed radically as a person between 1991 and 1998.

Once upon a time he had been one of the tour's prima donnas, a bright, charming guy when things went well, an honest-to-goodness pain when they didn't. "I blew off the media so many times I can't even keep track anymore," he said. "I had to learn the hard way."

In truth, Stewart has learned a lot of things the hard way, perhaps because he was so gifted when he was young that he always thought things would come to him the easy way. His dad was a traveling furniture salesman who lived in Springfield, Missouri. Bill Stewart had two passions in life: his family and golf. He was on the road every week from Monday to Thursday but always home for his son's football games or golf matches and always there for his two daughters.

He taught Payne the game the way he taught many people the game. He was an excellent player, good enough to qualify for the 1955 U.S. Open (which was held at Olympic) and someone who loved to help other people with their games. "He was always giving people tips and lessons," Payne remembered. "It got to the point where the pro at our club hung a sign up in the shop that said, 'Bill Stewart, teaching professional.'"

His prize pupil was always his son. Payne had a long, fluid swing almost from the beginning, and by the time he was sixteen he was making the trip to Kansas City with his father twice a year to play in qualifying for the U.S. Amateur and the U.S. Open. His dad knew he wasn't ready to make it into those events yet, but he thought the experience of playing would help him down the road. And he wanted to make sure he filled out those applications correctly.

Payne went to Southern Methodist, fully intending to become a pro when he graduated, although it was made clear to him that he had better not leave school without a degree. He did graduate but there was never any doubt in his mind that he was going to play golf for a living. "I just knew I was going to be good enough," he said. "I'm not sure why, whether it was arrogance or ignorance, but I never had any doubts."

When he came home at Christmas during his senior year he was caught off guard when his father asked him what he planned to do after graduation. "Play golf," he answered, surprised that his father even thought it was an issue.

"Play golf?" his father said. "How do you plan on playing golf for a living when you haven't done anything but have a good time for four years?"

Come to think of it, Payne thought, he hadn't done much for four years. He went out in the spring and won four tournaments, including the Southwest Conference title, beating Fred Couples in a playoff. That victory gave him an exemption to play in the Colonial, which was scheduled for the same weekend as SMU's graduation ceremonies.

"I guess I'll have to miss graduation," Payne told his father.

"We'll see," Bill Stewart answered. "Make the cut and we'll talk."

As it turned out, there was no need to talk. Payne was at graduation on Sunday.

He did turn pro, though, going to Asia to play the tour there after flunking Q-School in his first attempt. That proved an important turn of events because it was there that he met Tracey Ferguson, an Australian whose brother was also playing the Asian Tour. They were engaged in late 1980, a few months before Payne qualified for the PGA Tour at the spring Q-School in 1981. One person who wasn't thrilled about Payne's decision to get married was his dad.

"It had nothing to do with Tracey," he said. "He just thought being married would distract me from golf. What he didn't know was that Tracey was going to be one of the reasons I became successful as a golfer."

Being the sister of a pro and a player herself, Tracey understood golf intimately. She walked almost every round with Payne, charting his drives, his chips, his putts. She critiqued his play, his decision making. "She helped make me a better player, no doubt about it," Stewart said. "When I lost my dad, she became the person I talked to the most about my game."

Payne's father died in 1985. Bone cancer. Even now, it is difficult for Stewart to talk about his father's death. The words come but his voice gets very soft. "You know what they say about the Lord working in mysterious ways," he said. "Early in 1984, Peter Jacobsen found out his dad had cancer. That March, he beat me in a playoff at Bay Hill. When we shook hands, I said to him, 'That one was for your dad.' Two months later, I found out my dad had cancer."

Bill Stewart died nine months after he was diagnosed. He was sixty-four. Payne came home to see him near the end and all his dad wanted him to do was get back on tour. When he did finally decide to go back and play, Payne had just learned from Tracey that she was pregnant. He was sitting with his dad in the living room at 6 o'clock in the morning getting ready to leave for the airport. Bill Stewart was propped up in his favorite chair, sitting in about the only place where he could be comfortable. Quietly, Payne told him that Tracey had told him he was going to be a father.

Bill Stewart looked at his son and said very softly, "Don't buy expensive baby furniture."

A smart salesman and a concerned dad right to the very end. Two days later, he died. Payne didn't cry at the funeral, which his mother and sisters found upsetting. "I wasn't sure if I was trying to be strong for everyone," he said, "or if I was in denial."

He learned the answer a year later. Chelsea was born that November and when Payne and Tracey brought her to Springfield that spring, Payne drove to the cemetery, put Chelsea in her stroller, and went to sit at his father's grave. He started telling his five-month-old daughter about the grandfather she would never meet and, as he did, the tears started. It was a long time before they stopped. A year later, when he won at Bay Hill to break a four-year victory drought, he donated the entire winner's check to a local hospital in his father's name.

Golf wasn't as much fun without his father. Bill Stewart had been his son's biggest supporter and his sternest critic. Payne played very well the next few years, consistently finishing in the top ten — an amazing thirty-five times from 1986 through 1988 — but almost never winning.

"I had gotten comfortable," he said. "I was making a lot of money, I was almost always on the leader board or near it, life was good. I had a nice house and a nice car. I was making a good living for my family."

He had contended in majors a couple of times, finishing second at the British Open in '85 with a late rush, though he never really had a chance to catch winner Sandy Lyle. A year later, playing the U.S. Open at Shinnecock, he had a one-shot lead with six holes to play. He was paired that day with Raymond Floyd. When Floyd birdied the 13th hole Stewart had his first close-up experience with "The Look," the wide-eyed, nothing-will-stop-me-now expression that Floyd became famous for en route to twenty-two tour wins that included four majors. Stewart saw "The Look" and, without knowing it at the time, lost his focus.

"He got to me," he said, years later. "I saw those eyes go wide and I thought, My God, look at him. Instead of just worrying about me and my shots I was thinking about him. I started guiding the ball, swinging a little scared, and the next thing I know, it's all over." Floyd won. Stewart finished tied for sixth.

Two years later, after yet another top-ten finish, Stewart and Tracey pulled their car out of the Tournament Players Club in Ponte Vedra, heading back down the highway toward Orlando. Stewart had finished tied for eighth and collected a healthy check for more than $36,000.

"Well," he said to his wife, "another good week."

Tracey exploded. "Another good week?" she said. "You didn't win did you? You know what you are, you're complacent. You're satisfied to finish in the top ten and make a good check. Why don't you try to win?"

Stewart was shocked. Just as his father had surprised him that Christmas his senior year in college, his wife had caught him off guard now. If the criticism had come from anyone else, he probably would have rejected it. But he knew Tracey wouldn't say those things unless she honestly thought he wasn't playing up to his capabilities.

He began to work harder at his game, focusing on contending to win rather than just cashing a check. He lost a playoff that summer to Phil Blackmar but he thought he was getting closer to winning again. In 1989, he did, winning at the Heritage Classic in Hilton Head. Then, at the PGA, he found himself on the leader board Saturday, but was still six shots back of leader Mike Reid going into Sunday. The front nine was aggravating because he was hitting the ball superbly, but couldn't buy a putt. He shot 36, but noticed that Reid was struggling. As he walked to the 10th tee, he turned to Jerry Pate, who was walking with his group for ABC, and said, "You know, if I can shoot 31 on the backside, I could have a chance."

He did something players almost never do in the middle of a major — changed his putting stance — standing up taller to the ball while trying to envision Ben Crenshaw's long, fluid stroke. He had nothing to lose, he figured. Another top-ten finish would mean little, and he couldn't putt worse than he had on the front nine. Suddenly, the putts started dropping. When Stewart birdied the 18th hole, he had his 31. It was still Reid's championship to win, with a two-shot lead on the 16th tee. He couldn't hold it. One of the straightest drivers on tour — his nickname is "Radar," in part because of that and in part because he looks a little bit like the character in *M*A*S*H* — Reid hit his tee shot in the water on 16. He made double bogey. Then he bogeyed 17.

All of a sudden, Stewart had won his first major. By his own admission, he didn't handle the dramatic turn of events very well. While Reid was struggling home, he sat in the scorer's tent and, with a TV camera on him, he clowned around, showing off his logos and, in his words, "acting very immature." When it was over, he appeared to some to be reveling in Reid's failure. The media, which had spent a lot of time being blown off by Stewart in less happy moments, couldn't resist pointing out that when he finally won a major title he had to back into it, sneaking up the leader board with minimal pressure on him and then lucking out when Reid collapsed.

"They weren't entirely wrong," he said. "It was Mike's tournament to win. But you have to play seventy-two holes, especially in a major. I called a number with nine holes to play, I shot the number, and I won. And then they didn't want to give me credit because I'd been arrogant in the past and I wasn't very mature that day."

Even though the victory at the PGA did little for his relationship with the media, it did help his golf. Stewart finished second on the money list that year and third the next year after winning twice more. Then, in 1991 at Hazeltine, he led the U.S. Open for three days, fell behind Scott Simpson on the last day, caught him to force a playoff, then won the playoff the following day on a golf course that was, by Stewart's description, "completely out of control, almost unplayable."

Winning the Open did a number of things for Stewart. It clearly established him as one of the elite players of his generation with two majors, including an Open. It made him a very wealthy man. It gave him a feeling of completeness as a golfer since the Open had been the tournament his dad revered most. It forced the media to acknowledge that, arrogant or not, he had become one hell of a player.

And, it stole some of his hunger. At the age of thirty-four he had, for all intents and purposes, done everything he had set out to do in golf. Sure, there was the Masters and there was the British Open, which Stewart says is his favorite tournament — "because it's the original" — but if he had retired that day at Hazeltine there wouldn't have been many regrets. He had made big money and won big championships.

He played less the rest of that year than at any time in his career. The next year he slid to forty-fourth on the money list, his lowest finish ever in eleven full years on tour. He bounced back in '93 with the close call at Baltusrol and a sixth place finish on the money list. But the next year was a disaster, by far his worst year in golf. He finished 123rd on the money list. There was talk then that the equipment change was killing him, that he missed his caddy, Mike Hicks, who had gone home to North Carolina to start a business, and that he was distracted because he and Tracey were building a home in Orlando that was only slightly larger than the Parthenon.

All of the above was probably true. And, with a son, Aaron, having joined the family in 1989, there were now two children for him to miss when he was on the road. Even though he played better in 1995 and did win again, Stewart was ready to quit by the end of 1996. He wasn't even close to winning, his mediocre play meant he wouldn't be in the Masters in '97 unless he turned things around and won a tournament, and he wasn't enjoying himself.

"I told Tracey one night, 'I'm gonna quit. We don't need the money and I don't need the aggravation.' She said to me, 'Oh yeah, what are you going to do instead? You're a golfer.'"

So Stewart kept playing golf. He went to a media seminar in Dallas at the urging of Tracey and his agent, Robert Fraley, to work on his problems with the media. He cut back on his schedule so he wouldn't get so homesick, and he decided to focus more squarely on the majors. "At this point in my life, they're what's going to motivate me," he said. "I'd love to win every week, but realistically, that's not happening. So if I'm going to peak my game a few times a year, that's when I want to do it."

His game didn't come roaring back but people sensed changes in him. The snappishness was gone. He would stand around and talk about a round whether it was 67 or 77. When a reporter mistakenly asked him a couple of weeks before the '98 Masters if he was looking forward to the week, he said quietly, "I'm looking forward to spending it with my family, but to tell you the truth I'd rather be playing. Unfortunately, I'm not in the tournament."

Once, the question would have earned the reporter a lecture on knowing what he was talking about or, perhaps, a diatribe on how he didn't really care if he played the Masters or not since he had never been a big fan of Augusta anyway. Not anymore. When Stewart talked about missing the Masters two years in a row, he said, "If you think of yourself as a world-class player, you have to play all four majors. It hurts not to be going."

It also hurt to pick up the Players Guide at Olympic and find a reference in his bio to the fact that he had been known through much of the '80s as a choker. A couple of years earlier the USGA had included that in his Open bio and Stewart had gone ballistic. When Marty Parkes, the USGA's senior director of communications, saw that the old choker label had somehow slipped into the guide again, he was horrified. He went and found Stewart to apologize, figuring he would get the screaming and yelling over with earlier rather than later. He came away from his talk with Stewart pleasantly surprised.

"He wasn't happy and I don't blame him," Parkes said. "But he said he knew mistakes happened and that we didn't do it on purpose. He was very reasonable."

Stewart hadn't finished in the top twenty in an Open since Baltusrol and he very much wanted to reverse that trend. But he wasn't sure that Olympic was the place for him to do it. He had missed the cut there in the '87 Open and finished twenty-sixth in a thirty-man field in the '93 Tour Championship. But the week before the tournament, he took a working vacation with the family in Aruba, taping a Shell's *Wonderful World of Golf* match in which he played Nick Price. He lost the match but felt he had hit the ball as well as anytime in recent memory. The week in San Francisco would be different than most: Tracey was staying home because the kids were starting camp, and Stewart invited his mom to come with him to the place where his father had played in his one and only U.S. Open.

Tuesday, as he stood on the range with Hicks, hitting ball after ball, someone reminded him of his record at Olympic and asked if that would be a factor. "You know, if you'd asked me that last week, I'd have said yes," he said. "But right now, I feel like I can play this golf course. I have a game plan and if I stick to it, well, it could be a fun week."

Stewart was having fun and sticking to his game plan — don't go for too much off the tee or on the greens — when he arrived at the 16th tee on Thursday morning. Stewart and his playing partners, Curtis Strange and Hale Irwin, had been the ninth group off the first tee, so there weren't a lot of scores posted. But there were very few red numbers on the leader board and, by now, half the field was on the golf course.

Stewart had one of those red numbers, a very comfortable −1. The 16th was one of the two par-fives for the Open (normally there are three but, as usual, the USGA had converted one of the par-fives, the 17th, to a par-four) and wasn't reachable in two for anyone — even Woods or Daly. Stewart hit a perfect layup, spun a nine-iron to eight feet, and made the birdie putt to go to two under.

At that moment, Stewart would have been thrilled to finish par-par and post a 68. It would put him, if not in the lead, then close to it — and leading on Thursday didn't mean much anyway.

The 17th was the most controversial hole on the golf course. Most players insisted it could not be played as a par-four because the green wasn't capable of accepting long irons and fairway woods. Everyone had agreed before the tournament that five wasn't going to be a bad score on the hole and four was a great score.

Stewart hit a driver and a two-iron, his second shot skipping between the two bunkers in front of the green and stopping 40 feet below the hole. That was just fine with him. He would take a two-putt par and run to the 18th tee. Instead, to his amazement, his birdie putt dropped right into the center of the hole and he was three under par.

He practically floated to the 18th tee. His two-iron off the tee also floated — into the right rough. Annoyed with himself for losing concentration, Stewart stalked down the hill and was surprised to find that he had caught a good lie in the rough. He hit a knockdown eight-iron from there, got it to within 12 feet, and made that putt too.

Just like that, a very good 68 had become a remarkable 66 and there was little doubt, even though only twenty-seven scores had been posted, that Stewart was going to be the leader. He was happy because the 66 would give him some room to work with the next day. But he also knew that leading the U.S. Open after 18 holes and $4 would buy you a cappuccino in downtown San Francisco.

His score raised eyebrows around the golf course. There weren't going to be a lot of 66s all week long. And everyone, including Stewart, knew there weren't going to be very many red numbers in anyone's future.

It was almost 8:45 by the time the last threesome of the day trudged up the hill to the 18th green. Every golf tournament establishes a time par for speed of play and the USGA had picked four hours and twenty-five minutes for threesomes at Olympic. As was always the case, the early groups were able to maintain a pace at or near the time par, but as the day wore on and the greens quickened, play got slower and slower. Getting everyone in by dark was, in itself, a victory.

Tom Meeks, Trey Holland, and Tim Moraghan weren't far behind the last group, wanting to get the hole locations finished before dark. Everything had gone as smoothly as could be hoped the first day. Most of the grumbling had been about the rough — which was to be expected — about the speed of the fairways — Dudley Hart's experience at number five was something that happened often — and about the 17th, which only 35 percent of the field had been able to reach in regulation. Holland had predicted on Wednesday night that at least 60 percent of the players would reach the green in two. The number would continue to drop all week.

In all, not a bad first day. The group worked more quickly on Thursday than on Wednesday because they were trying to beat sunset. Darkness was closing in when they reached 18. Meeks had planned all along to save the two "front" locations on 18 for the weekend because birdies would be harder to come by there since getting a wedge to stop below the hole when it was on the front of the green would be very difficult.

But as he and Moraghan and Holland putted to the planned Friday location — 18 yards from the front and 8 yards from the left edge — Meeks didn't like what he was seeing. Any putt that went below the hole couldn't stop. The area was just too slick. If a player was below the hole, putting uphill, he was okay. But if he was hole high or above, almost any miss was going to lead to a long second putt.

"Maybe we should go up front," he suggested.

Moraghan was against it. Using three front locations would mean so much foot traffic in the area on Friday and Saturday that the green might be almost unplayable by the time the late groups — the ones contending for the title — showed up on Sunday. There was no place else to go that wasn't up front either.

"Look, Tom, we'll put a lot of water on it tonight, water it again in the morning before the first group tees off, and we won't cut it," he said. "If we do that, it'll still be dicey, but it should be fair."

Meeks was torn. He didn't like the hole location. Water or no water, it was risky. But he also knew Moraghan was right about using three front locations. If he was going to face potential disaster, he would rather face it Friday than Sunday. "Okay," he said finally, "we'll chance it. But let's get water on it right away."

There had been nine rounds under par the first day. Only one player, Mark Carnevale, had come within a shot of Stewart's 66. There had been four 68s and three 69s. Included in the 68s were three players who had won majors: Tom Lehman, the '96 British Open champion, who seemed to almost win the Open every year; Bob Tway, the '86 PGA champion, who was also a perennial Open contender; and José María Olazabal, the '94 Masters champion, whose lowest previous score in an Open had been 69. Joe Durant, the only player who had ever reached five under during the day, also finished at 68.

The group at 69 was also intriguing: Jesper Parnevik, the goofily dressed Swede who had almost won the British Open in both '94 and '97; Jeff Maggert, who had been part of the four-way shootout a year earlier at Congressional; and John Daly, golf's prodigal son.

It was Daly's round that created the most stir. Exactly one year earlier, he had walked off the course midway through his second round at Congressional with a bad case of the shakes. He was only a few weeks removed from alcohol rehab and had tried to come back too soon. Daly hadn't told his playing partners, Payne Stewart and Paul Azinger, that he was leaving and had been roundly ripped for his sudden departure. But he looked back on that decision now and said, "I'm proud of myself for what I did that day. I knew I was in trouble and I got out of there. I didn't drink over it and I understood what I had to do and I did it."

Figuring out what to do in difficult situations and not drinking over them is a battle Daly has waged since he was a teenager. He has often told stories of how much he drank as a kid and in college and in his early years as a golf pro. He was a binge drinker because he has an addictive personality. Daly never likes anything, he loves it. He loves to gamble, loves to smoke, loves to eat, loves chocolate, and he loved alcohol. He also loves people. There are as many stories about his acts of generosity as there are about his drinking.

"John Daly doesn't have a mean bone in his entire body," Fuzzy Zoeller, his longtime friend and confidant, has often said. "He just needs some people to tell him when he's messing up."

If there was anyone in Daly's life who will do that, it was his wife, Paulette. When Daly went on a drinking binge in March 1997 that landed him in a Ponte Vedra, Florida, hospital, she left him and filed for divorce. A little more than a year later, when Daly had been sober since that infamous night, she came back to him but with a warning: "If you have one drink, I'm out of your life forever."

Daly understood. "I know now that if I drink again I will lose my wife and my daughters [he has a six-year-old, Shynah, from his second marriage and three-year-old Sierra with Paulette] and there is a good chance I'll end up dead," he said two weeks before the Open. "I know how lucky I've been. I've had support from people I probably didn't deserve. I hope I'm going to get it right this time."

Daly had first gone to alcohol rehab in December 1992, ordered there by then–PGA Tour commissioner Deane Beman. This came at the end of a turbulent sixteen months during which he had burst into the golf world's consciousness with a stunning victory at the PGA Championship in 1991 and then proceeded to have a series of problems, culminating when his (then) wife called police to their house one night, claiming Daly had tried to beat her. She dropped the charges, but there wasn't any doubt in anyone's mind that Daly had a drinking problem.

Off he went to rehab. "But I didn't want to be there," he said. "I listened to what they were saying, I knew I needed help, but I didn't think a lot of it applied to me. When I came out of there, my attitude was

'Okay, I took care of that, it's behind me.' I didn't think I needed to go to meetings or get any help. The most amazing thing about it all really is that I didn't drink a drop for three and a half years."

He didn't drink, but not drinking made him terribly unhappy. He went through an ugly divorce, then married Paulette, whom he had met at the Bob Hope Classic in 1992. He was so talented that he often made cuts when he wasn't even trying to and, on occasion, he would go on a brilliance binge. He won in Atlanta in 1994 and then, in one of the most remarkable upsets in golf history, he won the British Open at St. Andrews in 1995.

"The golf course was perfect for me," he said. "I knew that from playing over there in the Dunhill Cup in '93. I could hook the ball as much as I wanted to and the ball was just going to end up in the other fairway. I felt comfortable playing there right from the start."

Daly appeared to have won the tournament when he finished at six-under-par 282 with only two golfers left on the course: Costantino Rocca, who was one shot back, and Michael Campbell, who was two shots behind. At the short, par-four 18th, Rocca's drive came up short of the green in the swale known as the Valley of Sin. Needing to get the ball close to have a chance to make birdie, he hit an absolutely sinful chip, an amateurish chili-dip that left him 70 feet short of the pin.

At that moment, Paulette Daly hugged her husband and said, "You did it!"

"Not yet," Daly said. "It's not over."

That brief give-and-take was on camera, and most people assumed that Daly was urging his wife to be cautious because Rocca technically still had a chance to make birdie. That wasn't it. Daly didn't think Rocca could make birdie from where he was. But Campbell had driven the green and had a 35-foot eagle putt that would have tied him with Daly. "At that moment," Daly said, "it was Campbell I was worried about."

Campbell proved to be no concern. His putt came up four feet short. But Rocca's 70-footer, up the hill through the Valley of Sin and across the green, rolled right into the hole as if on an invisible string. Rocca went to his knees, stunned and overjoyed, while Daly just stared in disbelief. Now he and Rocca were in a four-hole playoff.

Daly had to regroup — in more ways than one. When his caddy, Greg

Rita, went to get his clubs, his yardage book had disappeared. Mark Brooks, standing nearby, ran into the locker room and got his. Brad Faxon, Corey Pavin, and Bob Estes, all of whom had seen Rocca's shot from the locker room, came out to give Daly a pep talk. Daly was touched. It had been only a year earlier that he had earned the wrath of many players with a wild claim in a tabloid about drug usage on tour.

"I've made some mistakes, and my big mistake in '94 was talking to that guy [from the tabloid newspaper *The Sun*]," Daly said. "But it was really nice of Mark and Brad and Corey to kind of rally behind me there. I needed it."

He got more help from Rocca, who bogeyed the easy first hole. Then Daly birdied the second for a two-shot lead, and when Rocca triple-bogeyed the infamous road hole, Daly strolled home with a four-shot victory in the playoff.

Even then, he felt little joy. There was satisfaction, yes. A feeling of vindication, certainly. But joy? "Not much," Daly said. "Not much at all."

Throughout that period he talked often to Paulette about how much better he would play if he was drinking again. At other times he told her he was going to commit suicide, once going so far as to get in his car and drive toward a cliff intending, he said, to keep right on going. He would call her from hotel rooms saying he was thinking of jumping out the window.

"I was miserable," he said. "I was dry, but I certainly wasn't sober. I wanted to drink in the worst way."

A year after winning the British Open, he did drink. He was in Holland, playing in a European Tour event for a six-figure appearance fee the week after the British Open. Defending his title at Lytham, he had finished a miserable sixty-sixth and was on his way to a year that would include exactly one top-ten finish (a tie for tenth at the Kemper Open). Paulette was at home, and Daly was with Rita and his longtime agent, John Moscatello. They were sitting in Daly's hotel suite when, without saying a word, Daly went to the mini-bar, took out a beer, opened it, poured it, and sat staring at it.

Neither Rita nor Moscatello wanted to say anything, hoping that the idea would pass. Fifteen minutes went by. Finally, Daly picked up the glass and took a drink. Then another. He finished the beer, picked up the phone, and called Paulette. Her memory of the conversation is vivid.

"I said, 'Hi honey, what are you guys up to?' He said, 'We're just sitting around having a beer.'"

Unamused, Paulette said, "That's not funny, John. Don't play games with me."

"I'm not playing games," he said. "I'm drinking a beer."

She then demanded to talk to Moscatello, who confirmed what Daly had told her.

The rest was almost inevitable. Daly began drinking more and more. When the word got out that he was drinking again, Moscatello tried to wave it off, saying, "He's having a beer or two. That doesn't mean he's fallen off the wagon."

Of course it meant exactly that. He had fallen and, as is always the case with Daly, the fall would be a hard one. As his drinking escalated, his relationship with his wife deteriorated. "I started verbally abusing her," Daly said. "At times, it was pretty bad."

Bad enough that Paulette threatened to leave on more than one occasion. Bad enough that she began pleading with him early the next year to reenter rehab. "I wanted to," Daly said. "I needed to. But I didn't want to miss the Masters. I figured I would play till then and then go into rehab."

He never made it to Augusta. On opening day of the Players Championship, Daly played in the morning and shot a miserable 76. He came back to the villa where he and Paulette and Sierra were staying and announced he was going to lunch. It was well after midnight when he came back. If you believe the stories that were told later, every single person in the state of Florida encountered Daly during the fourteen hours he was gone from the villa. Most said they either bought him a drink or saw someone else buy him a drink.

By the time Daly made it back to the villa, Paulette was asleep. She heard him come in, then she heard some kind of a thud in the bathroom. "I fell into something," Daly said. "To tell you the truth, that's about the last thing I remember."

According to Paulette, when she got to the bathroom, Daly was picking himself off the floor and screaming incomprehensibly. "I had never before been afraid of what John might do physically," she said. "He had never hit me and I had never felt as if he was going to. But now I had no idea what he was going to do. I went and got my baby and tried to get out of there."

Daly didn't want her to go. He screamed that she couldn't go, blocked the door and wouldn't let her go. Eventually, Paulette talked her way out of the room and went and pounded on the front door of the villa next door. There was no answer. She ran back to the lobby of the hotel and found Mark Brooks and his wife, Cynthia, there. They took her back to their room. From there, she called Fuzzy Zoeller, Daly's best friend on tour and the one person he seemed willing to listen to in times of crisis. She asked him to go to the room and talk to John. Then she called Moscatello, who was staying in a nearby hotel, and told him she was taking Sierra and leaving. Before she could make any kind of move to do that, there was a knock on the door. It was the police. Someone had heard the screaming and had called them.

Paulette didn't want her husband going to jail. "All I wanted was to take my baby and get out of there," she said.

Zoeller and the police went to the villa. Daly was subdued and strapped to a stretcher. He was still screaming at everyone and anyone as he was loaded into an ambulance. Zoeller, who was tied for second place in the tournament, went with him. What he saw frightened him. "He was a very sick boy," he said the next day when the story made the rounds at the tournament. In one of its sillier gestures the Tour announced that Daly had withdrawn from the tournament because of an injured shoulder — despite the fact that everyone within a hundred miles of Jacksonville had heard about what had happened at the hotel.

Paulette flew back to Palm Springs that day and began making plans to file for divorce. "I couldn't believe what my life had become," she said. "That night was like something out of a bad movie. I kept thinking, this can't be happening. People told me I needed to go to Al-Anon. I couldn't even think about it. I didn't want to hear the words *alcohol* or *alcoholic*. I couldn't deal with it."

Once he was sober enough to leave the hospital, Daly, who almost never flies, got into his car with lifelong friend Donnie Crabtree and drove to his home in Memphis. After a two-hour stopover to pack and rest, the two of them got back in the car and drove straight through to California. By Monday morning, Daly was checked into the Betty Ford Clinic. When he went through his physical there, doctors told him that he had severely damaged his liver, that it would never be fully functional again, and that if he did not stop drinking it was only a matter of time until he destroyed it completely.

Daly got the message. This time he was in rehab because he wanted to be there and knew he had to be there. "I was lucky," he said. "I didn't kill myself and I didn't kill anyone else. But I knew that it had just been luck and nothing else."

Daly was allowed to register as an outpatient so he could continue to do the one thing that he enjoyed: play golf. He was up every morning before dawn to attend a 5:30 A.M. Alcoholics Anonymous meeting. Then he would play golf and hit balls for a while before going to the clinic late in the afternoon. The AA meetings proved to be a godsend. Daly listened intently to what he was being told at the clinic. He went through all the programs there. But it was in those 5:30 A.M. meetings that he found new life.

"The people in that group saved my life," he said. "There's no doubt about it. They were like me, people who were fighting alcoholism every day. They understood me and I understood them. I fell in love with all of them and with the morning meetings."

When Daly's rehab was over he began making plans to return to the tour. During his absence, two of his major sponsors, Reebok and Wilson, had canceled their contracts with him. But Ely Callaway, the founder of Callaway Golf, thought Daly could come back and believed his story could be inspirational and could sell golf clubs. He signed Daly to a long-term contract, agreed to help him pay off large chunks of his debts (most of them from gambling), and began planning an advertising campaign that would be launched at the U.S. Open with the slogan "Keep It Straight, John."

All of which was fine. Except that Daly's friends in his AA meeting were urging him not to play in the Open. "They told me it was too soon," he said. "They thought I needed to go through the summer, take it easy, and not play in the majors. They thought I should play in tournaments with less pressure, not the ones with more."

Daly knew the advice came from the heart. He also knew he wanted to play golf and, even though Callaway wasn't pressuring him directly to play, he knew they would be very happy if he was at the Open. He decided to go play.

Not wanting to go directly to the Open, he entered the Memorial Tournament and the Kemper Open. At Memorial he shot 76–71 to make the cut on the number and then, after the tournament was reduced to 54 holes by rain, shot 80 on the final day to finish last. Daly thought things would get better the next week. He would be less nervous and the Kemper was being played at the Tournament Players Club of Avenel, a course where Daly had had his one top-ten finish of 1996. Daly knew he was in trouble before the weekend was over. He was still having serious problems with the shakes. Again, he made the cut. Again, he shot 80 in the final round to finish last.

That day, he was in the car with Buddy Martin, another one of his agents, when the shakes hit him. Martin was frightened. He had never seen anything quite like it.

"I should have gone back to California right then and there," Daly said. "But I was right there where the Open was being played. I had missed the Masters. And I honestly thought I was going to get better each day. He shot 77 the first day, but by the second hole on Friday, he knew he was in serious trouble. He felt queasy and shaky. It was hot and he was pouring sweat. That he shot only two over par on the front nine was a near miracle. But as he walked up the hill to the ninth green, Daly knew he was cooked. "I felt I had no choice," he said. "I had to get out of there."

He was in the car headed to Memphis — and then back to California — within thirty minutes of walking off the ninth green. His departure caused an uproar. Same old Daly, everyone said, quitting on his playing partners, leaving his caddy, Brian Alexander, standing on the 10th tee waiting for him to show up.

Callaway pulled its "Keep It Straight, John" ads scheduled for the weekend. The only good news was where Daly went after he pulled away from Congressional: not to a bar, but back to his AA meetings in California. This time, he would wait until the group told him he was ready before he tried to come back.

From that day forward, Daly finally seemed to turn a corner. He came back to the tour — this time urged on by his AA group — late in the summer and seemed to be a different person. He began traveling from tournament to tournament in a huge motor home and even invited some of his fellow players to come over in the evenings so he could cook for them.

His golf wasn't great, but it wasn't awful. He finished tied for twenty-first at Hartford and actually tied Davis Love for the lead after an opening-round 66 at the PGA. He faded to twenty-ninth, but it was progress.

More important, it was clear to those listening to him that he was facing up to his problem. He was an alcoholic and he knew it wasn't curable and that every day was a battle for him. Every time he talked to the media he talked at length about what he was going through and how much the support he was receiving from the public meant to him. "Talking to the media became like having a meeting for me," he said. "I just talked about how I felt."

He began 1998 playing as well as he had played in years. After missing two of the first three cuts, he had three straight top-twenty finishes (two more than he had in seventeen starts in 1997) and then finished tied for fourth in Los Angeles and Fort Lauderdale in back-to-back starts. Those were his two best finishes since his win at the British Open almost three years earlier. He was putting as well as he ever had, and the thought crossed his mind that with his newfound peace of mind he might have the patience to be a factor at the Masters.

The next week at Bay Hill, he played solidly again. But a disaster, the sort that could happen only to Daly, dropped him to fifty-third place. The players were playing 36 holes on Sunday because of rain earlier in the week. When he reset the tees for the afternoon round, Mark Russell, one of the tour's top rules officials, decided to give the players a different look at the par-five sixth hole. He moved the tee way up, meaning that more players might be tempted to cut off a large chunk of the lake that cuts across the hole to try and reach the green in two.

No one loves a potentially reckless play more than Daly. When he and his playing partners, Tom Watson and Paul Goydos, got to the sixth hole (they had played the back nine first in the afternoon) he took one look at the tee, pulled out his driver, and started aiming way down the fairway, cutting off a huge chunk of the lake. He hit the ball solidly, and the crowd oohed as the ball took off. But he had tried for a little too much and the ball splashed a few feet short of dry land.

Unperturbed, Daly walked to the drop area at the front of the tee, took out his three-wood, and tried to clear the lake again. Splash. Then another splash. And another. In all, six balls splashed. Daly was down to his last ball — "other than a couple of shag balls" — when he finally got a ball onto the bank of the lake where he could at least attempt to play a shot. By this time, the crowd was yelling, "Tin Cup," a reference to the final scene of the Kevin Costner movie where the hero keeps hitting balls into the water at the final hole of the U.S. Open.

Daly took it all in stride. "The difference was, the shot I had was makable," he said. "I just kept toeing the thing. I was trying the whole time, but by my seventh swing I was pretty wasted."

Nonetheless, he plowed ahead, smacked his fourteenth shot from the mud to the fairway, hit his fifteenth into a greenside bunker, then blasted his sixteenth shot onto the green. As he was lining up his 20-foot putt, Watson couldn't resist. "Knock it in, John," he said.

Daly and Goydos almost fell over laughing. Daly missed and tapped in for an 18. Watson was still there to offer encouragement. "Don't feel bad," he said. "You're not even close to the record for one hole. It's twenty-two."

Daly actually did feel better hearing that and, at the seventh hole, he hit a five-iron to 12 feet and made the putt. He had gone from an eighteen to a two. "Now *that* may be a record," Watson said.

Daly shrugged. "Tom, that's what I'm out here for," he said. "To set records."

He parred the last two holes and then willingly discussed what had happened with reporters behind the green. This was a far cry from the old Daly, who would have been off the grounds of Bay Hill about thirty seconds after holing out — if he hung around that long. He made fun of himself, said he had been trying on every shot, and had no trouble taking the kidding he received in the locker room.

The next day, he stood on the practice tee at the Tournament Players Club and retold the story to anyone who asked. He was back at the scene of his crime a year earlier but didn't seem the least bit uncomfortable. He was very much looking forward to celebrating one year of sobriety and receiving the sobriety coin that AA members receive on every anniversary. Already, fans were offering him coins as he walked around the golf course. He was proud of what he had done and said so.

"The difference between now and the last time is that now I'm happy to be sober, I want to be sober, I can't imagine not being sober," he said.

Paulette Daly had watched her husband go through these changes. They still saw each other because of Sierra and she was amazed by what she was seeing. He was different with the girls, so much happier, so much more into being a father. He had always loved his daughters, now he clearly enjoyed them. She and John began spending more time together and, just before he left to play in Houston, Paulette called and suggested they try a reconciliation and see how it went. Daly was thrilled.

He arrived at the Open feeling better about his life than he had felt in years. Maybe better than he had ever felt. He had Sierra with him all the time, Shynah some of the time. He was a family man again. And, even though he knew Olympic would take the driver out of his hand and force him to stay patient, he thought he could do it. He didn't hit a single driver on Thursday. The club wasn't even in his bag.

"Not using the driver sucks," Daly said. "I don't like to play golf that way. But if I'm going to have a chance here, this is the only way to play."

John Daly talking about patience. That was news.

19

Over the Edge

As was his practice throughout every Open, Tom Meeks was at the golf course on Friday morning by 5 A.M. There was always work to do to check the setup of the course and, on this day, he wanted to be certain that the 18th green got as much water as possible. When the first groups began approaching 18, Meeks perched on the hill overlooking the green and watched closely to see how his gamble was going to work out.

"After four or five groups," he said, "I knew I was a dead duck."

Even with all the water that had been poured onto the green overnight and in the morning, there was no way to get a putt to stop anywhere near the hole unless you were putting straight uphill. Watching the putts pick up speed as soon as they went anyplace below the hole, Meeks knew he was in trouble. As the day warmed and the green continued to dry out and harden, it was only going to get worse.

"I've always made it a policy that if I have any doubt about a hole location, I don't use it," he said later. "But because we had so few options on that green I went against my own rule and against my instincts and I got burned."

He would not know just how badly until much later in the afternoon.

Friday at the Open is a long, wild day under any circumstances. Everyone is trying to guess where the cut will come and doing so isn't easy because the USGA cuts to "the low 60 and ties or anyone within 10 shots of the leader." That means everyone has to be aware of where the leader is because his score can be what determines the cut.

Early in the afternoon it looked as if Payne Stewart was going to make certain the cut would be the low sixty and ties because he was trying to run away with the golf tournament. Having birdied his last three holes on Thursday, he promptly birdied his first three on Friday. That put him at six under par and, at that moment, he was four shots clear of the field. No one, including Stewart, expected it to last.

"The golf course is going to get you sooner or later," he said. "But getting out fast like that gave me some cushion. I bogeyed four and five but even so when we got to the seventh tee, I was one under for the day and through the toughest portion of the golf course. [Caddy Mike] Hicksey said to me, 'Hey, one under through six on this golf course is a good score any day.' He was right."

Once again the golf course was winning the golf tournament. It was a little drier, a little faster, and a little tougher than on Thursday. By the time the entire field slogged home only seven of the 154 players (Dudley Hart and Tommy Tolles had withdrawn with injuries on Thursday) were even par or better. Once again, the lowest score of the day was a 66, and once again the person shooting that number was someone with serious U.S. Open history: Lee Janzen.

At thirty-three, Janzen was known as a money player. He was so good at closing on Sundays when he was in contention that he had earned the nickname "Terminator." His record in his first five U.S. Opens was testimony to that: Cut–Cut–Cut–Win–Cut. The only time he had ever played the weekend from 1990 through 1994 — 1993 at Baltusrol — he had won. He was also known as a player who played his best golf under difficult conditions and nowhere were conditions going to be more difficult than at a U.S. Open.

Janzen liked it that way. "You play a lot of negative golf at a U.S. Open," he said. "You're trying not to make mistakes. You come to the Open expecting nothing to be fair. If you hit it in the rough, you can't hit it out. Put it above the hole, you can't two-putt. Hit it in the bunker, you don't have a good shot. If you don't hit good shots, you don't make the cut. I know that from experience. It's a test of wills to find out who overcomes adversity the best and who has the most patience. I don't mind that at all. A true champion is not just the guy who hits good shots, but the guy who perseveres."

Janzen had certainly persevered throughout his career. He graduated from Florida Southern in 1986, turned pro, and spent four years on mini-tours trying to grind out a living. He didn't make it to the PGA Tour until 1990. He barely kept his card his rookie year, finishing 115th on the money list. He improved quickly after that, winning for the first time in 1992, then winning the Open a year later. It was his third victory on tour and catapulted him very quickly and suddenly from being thought of as a nice young player to a big-time star.

Janzen had trouble with that. Like a lot of players who wake up one morning carrying a title that people tend to put in capital letters — U.S. OPEN CHAMPION — he felt pressured to play up to that title. "I felt as if a lot more people were watching me," he said. "And when I didn't play well, I could almost hear them saying, '*He* won the U.S. Open?'"

Janzen changed equipment in 1994, then changed again in 1995. That year was his best in golf. He won three times, including the Players Championship under tough, windy conditions, and seemed to confirm his status as a big-time player. The Open hadn't been a fluke; the slump after the Open had been. And then, just as quickly, he stopped winning again. He played well at times, particularly in 1997 when he top-tenned seven times and made the Ryder Cup team. But no wins. Then, early in '98, he led the Players after three rounds and collapsed the last day, shooting 79, then led at Houston on the back nine on Sunday before another poor finish dropped him to fourth. Hardly the stuff Terminators are made of.

"The Players was just ridiculous," he said. "My thumb came right off the club on my tee shot on number one, the ball went straight right, and it just got worse after that. It was one of my most frustrating days in golf."

At Houston, he missed a couple of critical short putts on the back nine, which aggravated him because he had struggled in the 5-to-10-foot range all year. He spent a good deal of time prior to the Open working on his putting from inside 10 feet and saw improvement. He came to the Open in a good frame of mind. He had played Olympic in the 1993 Tour Championship and he liked the golf course. The tougher the better as far as he was concerned. Every time he heard a player whine about the speed of the fairways or the greens or the thickness of the rough, it was music to his ears. As disappointing as his finishes at the Players and Houston had been, he honestly believed that he was going to win again soon. "I just kept telling myself that," he said. "It almost became a mantra. I *will* win again, I *will* win again."

His week in San Francisco did not get off to a good start. He had a 9 o'clock date for a practice round on Monday and, wanting to get to the golf course in time to have breakfast and hit balls, he left his downtown hotel at about 7:15. Looking for signs to Route 101, he went too far and, knowing he had to get back to where he started, he made two right turns, intending to circle the block and try again. "After my second right, I got to a corner where I could either make an illegal left turn, go straight in the wrong direction on a one-way street, or bear right. There were no signs. I went right. The next thing I know I'm on a ramp leading onto the Bay Bridge and there's no way off. I have no choice but to go to Oakland."

It is 4.4 miles across the Bay Bridge to Oakland. It takes about five minutes to get across — at 2 o'clock in the morning. At 7:30 on a Monday morning it is closer to thirty minutes. "I was so angry, so frustrated, that I was screaming in the car," Janzen said. "I mean, there were people three lanes over who could hear me and I had the windows rolled up. In a matter of seconds I became Steve Pate."

When he finally got across the bridge, Janzen didn't want to go back across because the traffic going in that direction was worse. So he kept going down Route 880 hoping to find another bridge that would take him back to San Francisco. "After ten miles, I gave up."

Turning back toward the bridge, Janzen had a talk with himself. "Calm down, it's Monday morning and you are here to play in a major championship. Don't let this ruin your day or your week. You aren't going to get to the golf course when you planned to. It's all right. Don't overreact. Overreacting is for the weekend, not Monday."

Later, when he thought back on the whole thing, Janzen decided that his wrong turn had actually been a right turn. "The most frustrating thing about a major are the practice days," he said. "It takes six hours to play eighteen holes, people are swarming everywhere. You can't take a step without signing an autograph. Instead of letting all of that build, I got it out of the way at once. After that, nothing was going to bother me."

He wasn't thrilled with an opening 73, but not panicked either. It was much too early to do that. "Whoever wins this tournament is going to have at least one round where he shoots two or three over par," he said. "I honestly think I'm going to be somewhere in contention on Sunday. I just have that feeling."

His goal on Friday was to break 70. He figured that a 69 would put him well within striking distance of the lead. He was right. But he didn't shoot 69. For sixteen holes, he played as well as anyone could play. He was six under par for the day, having birdied three of the four par-threes, an almost impossible feat. He finally made a mistake at the 17th. He missed the green right, misjudged his chip shot, and knocked it into a bunker, leading to a double-bogey six. Even that didn't frazzle him. He parred the 18th for 66 and wasn't just within striking distance of the leaders but was one of them at one-under-par 139.

Janzen finished a little more than an hour after Stewart, who had come to the 18th hole even par for the day and four under for the tournament. Stewart had hit a solid second shot, a pitching wedge that ended up hole high, 10 feet right of the pin. He had that putt for a birdie, a 69, and a three-shot lead. As he walked up to the green, Colin Montgomerie was being asked behind the green if he thought anyone could run away with the U.S. Open.

"If Payne makes this for five under, that's great golf for two days," Montgomerie said. "But no one runs away with the U.S. Open."

Looking over the putt, Stewart and Mike Hicks both recognized the fact that if the ball went below the hole it was going to have a hard time stopping. "I made a mistake right there," Hicks said later. "I should have told him to try and make the putt. There was no sense being careful because if you missed, you were dead no matter what."

Obviously, golfers try to make every putt they look at. What Hicks meant was that he should have told Stewart to be aggressive, not try to cozy the ball up close, because it wouldn't stay close. Stewart understood that. He rolled the putt at the hole, waiting for it to break right to left, hoping to curl it into the hole. The ball curled, but it was a couple of inches short. It dove to the left and then started rolling. Stewart watched it for a few seconds as it went two feet past the cup, then four feet, then six feet.

"By then, I knew it was gone," he said.

He walked to the bottom of the green, 35 feet below the hole, and stood, arms folded, chewing his gum so hard it looked as if his jaw might break, and waited for the ball to stop. It finally came to a halt 25 feet below the hole. He had gone from a 10-foot birdie putt to a 25-foot par putt. "I knew it wouldn't stop if I missed," he said. "But I never dreamed it would be that bad."

From there, he had a routine two-putt for bogey. Walking off the green, Stewart turned to Pete Richter, the walking rules official with the group, and said, "Doesn't that border on ridiculous? I mean, come on. I just hope I don't lose the Open by one shot because of this."

Stewart was far more polite than several other players. Earlier, Tom Lehman had come to the green needing a two-putt par for a 73 that would have left him one over par for the tournament. He walked off the green with a four-putt double bogey after watching his par putt rim the cup, come out, and roll 10 feet below the hole. Under most circumstances, Lehman is one of the most gentle souls in golf, a born-again Christian who thinks gosh-darn is pretty borderline when it comes to bad language. At that moment, Lehman was, as he said later, "as angry as I've ever been coming off a golf course."

He screamed at his walking official, Tom Loss, and then screamed at USGA official Jeff Hall in the scorer's room. "That was a fucking joke," Lehman screamed. "There's no excuse for it."

He stormed up the stairs to the locker room, slammed the door so hard that people standing outside the building heard the door shut, and then stalked around the locker room yelling at anyone within earshot about what a joke the hole location was. Later, Lehman was so embarrassed by his performance that he sought out both Loss and Hall to apologize. "I lost it," he said. "I used the f-word, which was wrong, and I yelled at two guys who didn't deserve to get yelled at that way no matter what."

Kirk Triplett didn't even wait to finish to express his disgust. After he had missed a putt and watched the ball just keep on rolling, he actually stopped his ball with his putter while it was still moving. He knew he was violating a rule and would be penalized — two shots — but he didn't care. He was going to miss the cut anyway (he finished +12 after the penalty) and was simply trying to make a point, the same point every other player in the field wanted to make.

David Fay watched all this from the NBC TV tower behind the 18th green. Meeks had warned him early in the day that there was going to be trouble, and now he could clearly see that what he had on his hands was a full-blooded fiasco. He sent word to the media tent that he would come in when the round was over to field questions about the hole location. By then, everyone was ripping the location and the USGA. "Why don't they test the holes to make sure this can't happen?" Fred Couples asked on TV. Meeks groaned at that one. They had tested the location, just as they tested them all. "Worst I've ever seen," John Daly chimed in. The worst part, of course, was the constantly replayed picture of the man leading the golf tournament standing there with his arms folded watching his ball roll and roll as if on a miniature golf course.

"This wasn't what we had in mind," Fay told the assembled media. Someone asked him who was responsible for the hole location. "The USGA," Fay answered. Tom Meeks and Tim Moraghan appreciated that answer. But it didn't make them feel any better.

The cut came at 147 — seven over par. That was 10 shots higher than Stewart's score, but it was low sixty and ties that got in. And, as it turned out, there were exactly sixty players on the number — the first time that had happened since 1977. Fifteen players who were at eight over were knocked out of the tournament when Rocky Walcher, playing in the third-to-last group, made an unlikely par from the front collar of the 18th green to finish at seven over. Walcher was a thirty-six-year-old Nike Tour player who had qualified for only one previous Open and had missed the cut. As it turned out, Walcher could have made bogey at 18 and still made the cut, because there would have been fifty-nine players at seven over and everyone at eight over would have tied for sixtieth and played the weekend.

But Walcher, naturally, was taking no chances. "I heard someone yell, 'You have to get up and down,'" he said. "I would have tried to anyway, but when I heard that I really focused in on doing it."

Walcher's par knocked some very big names out of the tournament, including three Open champions — Tom Watson, Hale Irwin, and Corey Pavin — not to mention Nick Faldo, Jay Haas, and John Cook. It also eliminated Paul Simson, the forty-seven-year-old amateur who had come out of the Pinehurst qualifier in what was undoubtedly the unkindest cut of all. Simson would have been at six over par except for the fact that someone had apparently picked up his tee shot at number 10 on Thursday and walked off with the ball. Although two witnesses reported to a USGA official that they had seen someone walk off with the ball, he ruled that there was not enough "verification" that the ball had been picked up. Simson was forced to play the ball as lost, which cost him two shots. That ended up costing him the cut.

Patrick Lee also missed the cut because of Walcher's par. He had played wonderfully for 28 holes, birdieing the ninth and tenth holes on Friday to get to three over for the tournament. But, as often happens to players in that situation, he began thinking about the cut instead of thinking about hitting good shots. He bogeyed 11, 13, and 15. Now he was six over and knew he was close to the cut line. He managed to par 16, but bogeys at 17 and 18 left him thinking he had little chance to survive.

"I thought it would be seven at best," he said. "I went back to my hotel room and didn't even watch. I didn't want to. Finally, my parents called me. They had been watching. They told me what happened."

Lee was disappointed, but not crushed. He knew he had played well until the final few holes, and the way he had played the first 28 holes had confirmed his belief that he had the kind of game to play well on difficult golf courses. "If I've had a problem on the Nike Tour, it's that most of the courses are set up for making a lot of birdies," he said. "I don't play that way. I'm better at grinding it out. That's why I did well in the qualifier in Cincinnati. That was a grinding day. This will help me, I'm sure of that."

Jeff Thorsen missed the cut too, shooting 77–81. He had hoped to play better, but when all was said and done, he still couldn't walk away feeling too badly. "No matter what happens in the future," he said, "I played in the U.S. Open. I think that's something to be proud of."

Justin Leonard was still in the U.S. Open, but he wasn't feeling very proud or very happy as he worked on the range with Randy Smith and Bob Riefke on Friday afternoon. His second round had been a disaster in every possible way. He had finished with a 75, which put him at 146 for the tournament, nine shots behind Stewart in a tie for thirty-eighth place. The day and the week had fallen completely apart for him on the 15th green.

At that stage, he was still very much in the tournament, one over par for the day and two over for the tournament with the par-five 16th still to play. If he could get to the clubhouse at one or two over, he would still be in serious contention. His tee shot at the 15th had landed safely on the green, about 25 feet from the cup. Matt Kuchar had hooked his tee shot into the heavy rough to the left of the green. For the second straight day, Kuchar was playing very well. He had gotten to two under par with a birdie at the 13th, but had double-bogeyed 14 to fall back to even par. Now he appeared to be in more trouble.

Leonard had steeled himself for Peter Kuchar's cheerleading, knowing that nothing anyone was going to say or do was going to get the father under control. He was thinking that all he had to do was get through four more holes and then, if he was lucky, he would never see the father — at least inside the ropes — again.

Then Matt Kuchar pulled off one of the great shots of the tournament. From the deep rough, he lofted his wedge over a bunker and onto the green. It took two hops and rolled right into the hole for a miraculous birdie. Kuchar threw his arms into the air as the crowd — justifiably — went nuts. His father — justifiably — came over to high-five and celebrate. Leonard waited for Kuchar to pick his ball out of the cup and acknowledge the crowd once more. Then he went about lining up his birdie putt. It was a slippery downhiller, one he wanted to just get moving. A three on the hole would be just fine with him. But as he went to get over the putt, Leonard noticed Peter Kuchar over by the ropes still cheerleading and expressing wonder to the fans at his son's wondrous shot. Enough was enough. Leonard backed off the putt and glared directly at Kuchar. For the first time in two days, there was nothing subtle in his action. Everyone watching knew exactly what he was doing and why he was doing it.

Then he went through his routine again to get ready to putt. But he was completely distracted. He was upset with Kuchar and upset with himself for letting his antics get to him. Instead of thinking about par, he was thinking about how out of hand all of this had gotten. He knew he would be asked about the glare and he knew when he was asked about it he would be in a no-win situation. And so, instead of being the calm, clear-eyed, focused Justin Leonard who rarely made mental mistakes on the golf course, he was a frustrated, frazzled golfer whose mind was a million miles from the work he had to do.

His first putt went 10 feet past the cup. Angry with himself, figuring he had now set himself up for a bad bogey, he hit a mediocre second putt and left himself three feet for bogey. Just to make certain the hole and the day could be a complete disaster, he missed that one too. Wham! Four putts, double bogey, and a drop of about forty spots on the leader board. Leonard was fuming when he walked onto the 16th tee and there was nothing he could tell himself, nothing Riefke could say that was going to calm him down anytime soon. He proceeded to bogey 16 and 17, losing four shots in three holes. In less than thirty minutes his chances to win the Open had been flushed.

Leonard was angry with himself for letting Peter Kuchar get to him. He thought it was wrong for him — for anyone — to act that way inside the ropes, that his continuing to do those things showed a complete lack of respect for the other players. He also knew that Matt was one of the main stories of the Open at that moment. Spurred by the birdie at 15, he had shot 69, which left him at one under par for the two days, just two shots out of the lead. Anything negative he said about anyone named Kuchar was going to be viewed as sour grapes from someone who was upset with his own game. He would be seen as a killjoy, someone who couldn't understand how sweet this father-son story was.

And so, when the inevitable question about the glare came up behind the 18th green, Leonard tried to bite his tongue. "Next question," he said. Then he looked at the writer who had asked the question and said quietly, "It does me no good to answer that question, do you understand?"

Almost everyone understood. Leonard could have lied, he could have said that he hadn't really been glaring, he had just been waiting for Peter Kuchar to finish his celebration and that he hadn't been the least bit distracted, that the four-putt had just been a mental mistake on his part.

"I have never lied to the media," he said later. "I didn't want to start then. If I did lie, the guys who were out there would know I was lying and I didn't feel comfortable doing it under any circumstances. So I tried to be polite and not answer the question. I thought that was the best I could do."

It was. But it wasn't good enough for several local columnists who absolutely killed Leonard the next day. As he had predicted, they ripped him for not seeing the joy in the story of the Kuchars, for not having a sense of humor, for taking himself too seriously, for taking out his own bad golf on Peter Kuchar. Of course Leonard had not publicly said one disparaging thing about Peter Kuchar. At the moment that he had glared at him, he had not been playing bad golf, in fact he had been tied for twelfth in the golf tournament. But the glare and the "next question" had made his feelings clear.

The next day, for the first time in his entire life, Leonard was heckled on the golf course. On several occasions, he heard fans yelling at him to find a sense of humor, to learn how to have fun. When John Huston, his playing partner, hit a good shot on one hole, Leonard heard someone say behind him, "Be careful not to clap too loud, you'll upset poor Justin."

It was upsetting because Leonard knew he wasn't the bad guy but there was nothing he could say or do to change the notion that he was. Naturally, his fellow players were there to comfort him. Saturday afternoon, as he stood on the range hitting balls with Smith and Riefke, his old mentor Tom Kite came by.

"Wow," Kite said with a straight face. "Those papers this morning were something weren't they, Justin? You got barbecued, skewered, roasted, and toasted."

Leonard never looked up. "Tom," he said, "you're making me hungry."

"Not to mention sliced and diced with onions and peppers on top," Kite added.

"Now," Leonard said, "you're making me nauseous."

But at least, for the first time in three days, he was smiling.

David Duval was smiling as he sat in the locker room on Friday evening, but it wasn't about his golf — even though he had rallied with a 68 after an opening 75 to get back into contention.

Sitting in front of him was an open FedEx package. The package had contained a book, addressed to him in the locker room at Olympic. The title of the book was *Improve Your Golf, Lower Your Handicap and Increase Your Sales.*

"Hallelujah!" Duval said looking at the book. "Now I can win the U.S. Open. Isn't that great? All I have to do is take this thing home, read it tonight, and I'll win the Open."

He tossed the book into a wastebasket. "What do people think when they send things like this out?" he asked rhetorically.

It had been a strange two days for Duval. He had played horribly during the middle of his round Thursday, unable to make the golf ball do anything he wanted it to do. By his own admission, he felt a little rusty, having hit very few golf balls between the Memorial Tournament and his arrival at Olympic.

"I just had to have a break from golf," he said. "I needed to go fishing. If I just grind and grind, I get bored and then I'm not any good to anybody for a while."

As much as he likes to win, as competitive as he is, Duval isn't as single-minded as some other young players. He could no more live his life the way Tiger Woods has lived his than he could putt standing on his head. Maybe that's because of what his family has been through or maybe it's just in his nature. Like anyone, he wants to be respected and liked, but he's a long way from being obsessed with any of those things.

"Hey, did you see the paper this morning?" he said with a smile. "Guy said I have the personality of a divot. I started to get upset, but then he said a bunch of nice things too. Maybe I ought to thank him."

Another Duval difference. Instead of throwing the story away when he read the divot line in the opening, he read it to the end and decided it really wasn't all that bad. He was actually more confused by pretournament stories that had made him the favorite. "Me the favorite at an Open?" he said. "Any of those guys check my Open record?" His best finish in five starts was a T-28. "I've never done anything here."

He was tied for fourteenth after his 68 on Friday and hoping he could make a move on the weekend. He and Jim Furyk had both been disturbed that day by the way a number of hecklers had treated Colin Montgomerie, who was one shot back of Duval after 36 holes. "It wasn't like it was a lot of people," he said. "But some of them were brutal. I mean it's a little embarrassing because as an American you don't like seeing someone from another country treated that way. It was way out of line."

Duval smiled. "I'll say this, though, I like Colin, I really do. He's a hell of a player and he's entertaining to watch out there, especially when he gets mad about something. But he does bring some of it on himself."

On one hole, Montgomerie had rolled a birdie putt to about a foot from the cup. Someone had yelled, "Why don't you cry about it, Colin?" from the crowd. Instead of just walking up, tapping in, and departing the green, Montgomerie marked his ball, backed away, and waited for quiet. That wasn't going to happen anytime soon. The hecklers knew they were getting to him and they weren't going to stop.

"It got to the point where I was thinking maybe the USGA should put some people out there to identify the hecklers and get them out of there," Furyk had said after the round. "It really was a shame to see that happen."

At one point, a friend of Montgomerie's had sought out Will Nicholson, who was working on the back nine as a roving rules official and demanded that something be done. Nicholson had let the USGA braintrust know what was happening and extra security had been sent out to join the group. But Montgomerie didn't need extra security, he needed earplugs.

"Nothing out there bothered me," he insisted after the round was over, trying, as Leonard had earlier, to defuse a difficult situation. Montgomerie had been heckled in a number of places in the U.S. in 1998 because he had been made into the villain by a lot of Americans in the wake of Europe's stunning Ryder Cup upset the previous September. Not only had Montgomerie played well, he had had the audacity to say before the matches started that he thought the U.S.'s role as the favorite was overblown. He pointed out that the golf course would blunt a lot of Tiger Woods's power (correct; Woods didn't win a single match); he noted that Scott Hoch was a Ryder Cup rookie at forty-one and might not deal with the pressure well (wrong; Hoch went 2–0–1); and he pointed out that Brad Faxon had to be distracted by the divorce he was going through (absolutely correct; Faxon was 1–2 and said later that Montgomerie's point was well taken).

That was Montgomerie, though. He said what he was thinking most of the time and often that got him into trouble even though he was right far more often than he was wrong. As Furyk said, he had done absolutely nothing to deserve the treatment he was receiving. But, as Duval noted, his histrionics on the golf course — the sighs, the faces, the slumped shoulders — made him an easy target. The heckling was indefensible. It was also unlikely to stop.

20

Sleepless Nights

The wind came up Saturday morning, not a blow-you-away British Open wind, but the kind that dries a golf course very quickly. Fred Couples's Monday comment that the golf course would be brutal by Sunday looked quite prophetic as the early groups headed out to start the third round.

The leader board was a typical mixed-bag Open leader board. It included a number of players who had won majors: Payne Stewart, Bob Tway, Lee Janzen, Nick Price, Tom Lehman, and Scott Simpson trying to repeat his Olympic feat of 1987; a group of prominent players who had challenged in majors: Jeff Maggert, David Duval, Frank Nobilo, and Jesper Parnevik; and the unknowns: Mark Carnevale, Joe Durant, Chris DiMarco, and Olin Browne. (Browne had finished fifth at Congressional, meaning he did have some Open pedigree to fall back on.) All those players were within six shots of Stewart beginning the day on Saturday. One shot behind them and still capable of getting into contention with a good third round were players like Colin Montgomerie, Phil Mickelson, Steve Stricker, and John Daly. Daly had followed his 69 on Thursday with a 75 on Friday and had decided to put the driver back into his golf bag for Saturday, a decision most people thought questionable.

One shot back of that bunch and probably a little too far back were names like Tom Kite, Vijay Singh, Scott McCarron, John Huston, and Casey Martin, who had bounced back from a nervous, opening-day 74 to shoot 71 on Friday and make the cut with two shots to spare. There had been no incidents with his cart, and everyone who had watched him play was impressed with his game.

Martin's old teammate Tiger Woods was one shot back of him, having four-putted a green on Thursday while struggling with his putter throughout the tournament. More remarkable was the gallery that followed Woods, Tom Watson, and Lee Westwood on Friday afternoon. It wasn't exactly sparse, but it wasn't anywhere close to the teeming masses that had been a given during the halcyon days of Tiger-mania. There was little doubt that if Woods made any kind of move on the leaders, the crowds would be back in an instant but, at least for the moment, it seemed that some golf fans were taking a wait-and-see approach with the onetime Boy God.

One person who didn't mind the relative lack of attention was Woods. He had talked often about living for the day when he didn't have to make a pretournament appearance in the press room every single week, for a time when his every move and pronouncement weren't considered news. Smaller crowds and less media didn't bother him one single bit. His mediocre golf did.

One of the more excited golfers in the field on Friday evening was Brad Faxon. He had shot 68 in the second round, playing perhaps his best round of golf all year. Putts were finally starting to drop, and he could feel some of his old confidence coming back. The Open had always been the roughest of the majors for him because of what happened to wayward tee shots, but he went home Friday tied for eighth, just four shots off the lead, looking forward to the weekend.

He woke up Saturday morning frustrated and in pain. His back was killing him. Occasionally, when he slept a certain way, he had back pain. It didn't usually last more than a day or two and rest and a few Advil took care of it. But this was a morning when only the Advil was available. The rest would have to wait.

Warming up, Faxon felt better. Maybe the Advil had done the trick and he would be okay. He and Nick Price were paired in the fifth-to-last group, and at 12:05 Faxon walked onto the tee for his 12:09 tee time full of hope. Five minutes later, the hope was gone, replaced again by pain.

"I took my swing on the first tee and the pain came back all over again," he said. "All I could think was, oh no, not now."

His tee shot sailed right into the deep rough. The first hole at Olympic is probably the easiest on the golf course, the closest thing there is to a birdie hole. It is a par-five, reachable in two, and, with an accessible green, even those who lay up have a good chance to get close to the hole and make four. Faxon looked at his lie in the rough and, as if needing to add to his misery, made a horrible decision. Instead of hitting a safe wedge to the fairway to leave himself 150 yards — or less — to the green, he decided to try and choke up on a three-wood, thinking he could slash the ball free and get close enough to the green where he might spin a wedge shot close to the hole.

"I went brain dead," he said later. "I was thinking I *had* to make birdie on that hole, which was silly because there were so many holes left and a par wouldn't hurt me. What's more, from 150 yards, I might still have made birdie."

His caddy, John (Cubbie) Burke, who had worked for Faxon for most of twelve years, was thinking the exact same thing. But he knew his boss was in pain and he didn't think this was the right moment to question his thinking. He asked him, "Are you sure you can get to it?," hoping Faxon might take the hint, but Faxon didn't. He slashed at the ball and advanced it perhaps 30 yards — still in the deep rough. Now Faxon had to play his wedge. He chipped out, then hit his fourth shot to about 20 feet. Frazzled, he missed the putt and walked off the green with a horrendous bogey.

Standing on the second tee, he popped several more Advil. Unfortunately, there weren't going to be enough in the bottle to relieve the pain he was going to feel over the next two hours. While Price was patiently playing himself into contention, Faxon was slashing his way into an early Sunday tee time. He three-putted the third for a bogey; then, feeling another twinge in his back, he hit a hacker's five-iron that led to a double bogey at the fourth. Another three-putt at the seventh put him five over par for the day, and a second double bogey at the ninth meant that he had played the front nine in a see-you-next-week 42.

By then, the Advil had kicked in and his shoulder felt better. He could have used another dose for his aching head.

"What a miserable feeling," he said later. "I was so excited after the 68 on Friday. I thought I really had a chance to do something. Then the first hole just blew me away, the shoulder and then getting brain-lock on that second shot. I couldn't believe how badly I played."

Amazingly, he came back to shoot 34 on the back nine. But it was much too little, much too late. By day's end, he had gone from a tie for eighth to a tie for eighteenth and, more important, from four shots behind the leader to ten shots behind the leader.

Faxon wasn't the only player to blow himself out of contention on Saturday. Phil Mickelson started the day at four over par knowing he needed a round in the 60s to get into contention. That seemed possible when he birdied the 10th to get to one under for the day and three over for the tournament. But once again he couldn't keep the momentum going late in a major. He played the last eight holes in five over and finished the day back in the pack at eight over par. John Daly, claiming he hit the ball better than he had all week, shot another 75 and was tied at nine over par with, among others, Casey Martin.

Tiger Woods, needing a big move to get into contention, made no move, shooting a 71 that left him 10 shots back. "If the conditions are tough tomorrow, maybe I can go out, put up a low number, and see what happens," he said.

That low number would have to be about a 63.

The biggest surprise fader was David Duval. After his 68 on Friday he had spent a long time on the range hitting drivers. His plan for Saturday was to attack the course with his driver, believing that he could hit it straight enough to keep it in the fairway and then take advantage of his length to make a move. "You can win from six shots back starting out Saturday," he said, accurately.

You cannot win, though, from 11 shots back starting Sunday, and that's where Duval was after his second 75 of the week. Perhaps he should have held on to the book that promised to lower his handicap. He had one of those days where nothing goes right and nothing goes in. He came off the golf course discouraged, knowing that his chances of winning had gone aglimmering.

To no one's surprise, the golf course played even tougher than it had the first two days, thanks to the wind and the continuing drying out of the fairways. The good news was no one complained about hole locations. Only three players broke par all day: Tom Lehman, who recovered from his Friday tantrum to shoot 68; Jim Furyk, who also shot 68 after making the cut on the number Friday and declaring, "The way I'm hitting the ball I'm lucky it ends up on the planet"; and Steve Stricker, who shot 69 after a Friday evening putting lesson from his wife.

When all was said and done Saturday evening, the players who still had a realistic chance of winning were, for the most part, players who would be expected to contend for a major championship. Payne Stewart still had control, shooting a 70. That put him at three-under-par 207 through 54 holes. His lead, one on Friday night, had grown to four. Lehman's 68 jumped him into a tie for second place with Bob Tway, who shot 73. Because Lehman finished before Tway he would go out after him on Sunday (the rule when players are tied is, first one in is the last one out), which meant he would be paired with Stewart. "I think that helps me," Lehman said. "I'll know exactly what the guy I'm chasing is doing all day."

It would be the fourth straight year that Lehman started the last round of the Open in the final group. He had finished third in 1995 at Shinnecock, tied for second in 1996 at Oakland Hills, and finished third at Congressional in 1997. "When you've been that close, you feel like you can reach out and touch it," he said.

Tway and Price, who was five shots back of Stewart, would be in the next-to-last group. Right in front of them would be Lee Janzen, who was also five shots back after a 73 that included another aggravating double bogey on 17, and Stricker, who was six behind and had come a long way from sectional qualifying at Woodmont. Jeff Maggert was tied with Stricker at three over, and Stewart Cink and Mark Carnevale were one shot farther back.

Matt Kuchar had finally returned to earth on Saturday, shooting a respectable 76 that left him tied for tenth with Furyk and Lee Porter. Peter Kuchar had been quieter during the third round, perhaps because his son wasn't playing quite as well, perhaps because Reed McKenzie of the USGA, who was assigned to officiate Kuchar's group, had spoken to him about his behavior on Saturday morning. McKenzie asked Kuchar to cool it a little; Kuchar acted as if he had no idea what McKenzie was talking about. The only question was why hadn't the USGA gotten around to chatting with him earlier? They might have saved Justin Leonard, who shot 77 while listening to his newfound hecklers, a lot of unwarranted grief.

With none of the other leaders able to make any kind of move, Stewart appeared to be in control of the golf tournament with 18 holes to play. Everyone agreed that if he shot even par on Sunday, he would walk away with the trophy. But everyone else also agreed that doing that was easier said than done. Stewart was the only one of the leaders who had not struggled at least once. His only over-par round — Friday's 71 — was attributable in large part to the hole location at 18 and there was no doubting the fact that the pressure on the first three days was nothing like the pressure on Sunday. To a man, everyone in contention said that if he could get to the clubhouse Sunday afternoon at even-par 280 for the tournament, he would happily post that number and take his chances.

Janzen made one other point: "Payne isn't going to sleep well tonight," he said. "Sleeping on the lead in a major is hard. I know because I've been there ['93 at Baltusrol]. I stayed up as late as I possibly could the night before and I was still up at 7, which only left me like seven hours to kill before my tee time. The rest of us will sleep better than he will."

Stewart wasn't buying that argument. "I'll sleep fine," he said. "Unless my mother snores."

Deep down, he knew it wouldn't be that simple. This wasn't new for him — he had led the Open at Hazeltine for three rounds. Additionally, he wouldn't have to wait as long as Janzen had at Baltusrol because NBC wanted the golf tournament over by 8 o'clock Eastern Time, which was 5 o'clock Pacific Time. That meant that Stewart and Lehman would tee off at 12:50. There would be less waiting time than on the east coast.

"I've been a champion before," Stewart said. "If I can play the way I have in the past, I'll be fine."

21

Total Control

The last day of the U.S. Open always has an extra bit of emotion because it always falls on Father's Day. No matter who wins, there is always a father-son story of some kind to be told.

Payne Stewart had won the Open in 1991, but he hadn't done it on Father's Day because he needed a playoff on Monday to secure his victory. That didn't mean he didn't think of his dad, who had meant so much to him and to his golf game. "Of all the wins I've had, including the two majors, the one I think about most often is Quad Cities in 1982," he said late one night. "Because that's the only tournament my dad saw me win in person. Sometimes, when I think about what I've accomplished in golf, I get a little sad because my dad didn't live to see me do those things."

Stewart couldn't help but think of his dad a little bit as he got ready to play the last round at Olympic on Father's Day. His mother, who would turn eighty in January, had been with him all week and so had memories of his father. "I remember him talking about playing the Open at Olympic," he said. "All he said was 'Boy was that golf course tough.'"

Forty-three years later, nothing had changed.

Stewart was at the golf course Sunday by about 10:30, wanting to get stretched by the PGA Tour training staff in the locker room, grab a bite to eat, and head out to the range. The one thing that had been unsettling about leading all week was that all the postround media obligations had cut severely into his normal postround practice routine. All golfers like to hit balls after they play, either to confirm the good feelings they had on the course or try to rid themselves of the bad ones. It had been too late on both Friday and Saturday for Stewart to hit balls — "and I was too whipped to go do it anyway" — so he wanted to be sure he got a good warm-up Sunday morning.

It didn't take very long to realize it was going to be a long day. "I just didn't have the same feel," he said. "The ball didn't feel the same coming off the club. Unfortunately, you can't go to the guys running the tournament and say, 'Hey, I don't quite feel it today, how about if we come back and try it tomorrow.' I had to go play."

Mike Hicks, Stewart's caddy for most of the last eleven years, knew just as quickly as Stewart that the crispness that had been there for three days was no longer present. He knew he would have to be in Stewart's ear all day, bucking him up, keeping him confident on a day when confidence might not be easy to find.

"Payne likes me talking to him," Hicks said. "It helps him. Sometimes people think I'm crazy I talk to him so much. It isn't anything brilliant, just little reminders to stay in his routine, what to watch for, not to get down if something goes wrong."

Hicks was thirty-eight. He had left North Carolina State midway through his sophomore year to spend a semester caddying because a friend of his had been doing it and told him it would be fun. That was eighteen years ago. He had been with Stewart for both his major victories and he knew exactly how difficult these Sundays could be, especially without your A game. But he also knew that winning majors often came down to attitude and toughness and making pressure putts. There was no reason why Stewart couldn't be strong mentally regardless of how his swing felt.

Stewart believed there were three players capable of catching him: Lehman, Price, and Janzen. It wasn't that he didn't respect the other players on the leader board, it was just that he knew from experience how tough-minded each of those three players could be. All had won majors, all knew about Sunday afternoon nerves coming down the stretch.

Sunday nerves were readily apparent to anyone standing on the first tee as the leaders began the round. No one in the last three groups could hit the fairway. Stewart, who had played the hole birdie-birdie-eagle the first three days, hit his ball deep into the right rough. Lehman then hit his shot farther to the right. Both managed to get the ball on the green in three, but Lehman missed his four-foot par putt. His shoulders sagged. "Go get 'em, Tom!" his wife, Melissa, walking just inside the ropes, shouted as Lehman walked off the green. Her husband never looked up.

Stewart two-putted from 30 feet for par. The par wasn't thrilling on the easiest hole on the course, but for Stewart, it was just fine. Lehman was now five shots back and, up ahead, everyone else was moving in the wrong direction: Price had blown his birdie chance at the first by three-putting, then bogeyed the second. Janzen had also parred the first, then bogeyed the second and third. That meant the three men Stewart was most concerned about were now five, six, and seven shots behind.

"I kept telling Payne all day, 'Par's a good score,'" Hicks said. "The way the golf course was, no one was going to make too many birdies."

The golf course was now officially at the brutal level that Fred Couples (who had been in the first group Sunday morning and finished tied for fifty-third) had predicted for it on Monday. The fairways were so fast that players were hitting three- and four-irons off the tee at the long par-fours just to keep the ball in play.

Janzen, trailing by seven and knowing he needed something miraculous to get back into the tournament, gambled at the fourth, hitting a three-wood off the tee. He found the fairway, got a five-iron to 20 feet, and made the putt, the first of the leaders to make a birdie. Even so, he still trailed by six. Gambling again on the fifth, he played a four-wood off the tee. This time the ball sailed right. It hit one of Olympic's giant cypress trees and disappeared. The marshals in the area scrambled frantically looking for it. They couldn't find it. Just as Janzen and caddy Dave Musgrove arrived in the area, they heard someone yell from across the fairway, "It stayed up in the tree."

The trees at Olympic are very thick and it is not uncommon for balls to stick in them. Earlier in the year when one of the course's larger cypress trees had been cut down in preparation for the Open, more than two hundred balls had been found lodged in its branches. Janzen, Musgrove, Steve Stricker, and Jim Walker searched a little longer, looking up into the tree to see if they could see a ball. Nothing.

Disgusted, Janzen took another ball from Musgrove, put a towel over his shoulder, and began making the long walk back to the tee. Clearly, his Open — at least as any kind of a contender — was over. "I'm thinking that I now need a great tee shot to get into position to make double [bogey]," he said. "I'm going to be eight shots back with thirteen holes to play. I'm done."

All these thoughts were rattling around in his head when Janzen heard his name being called. A gust of wind had blown up and a ball had suddenly dropped a few feet from where Stricker and Walker were standing. Along with Musgrove, they looked at it and saw that it was a Precept 2 with the black LMJ for Lee Michael Janzen, which is stamped on all of Janzen's golf balls. At that point they all began shouting. At first, Janzen was so muddled that he thought the yelling was encouragement from fans and he kept walking. Then he heard the voices — and Walker's whistle — more clearly and turned around to see them waving at him to come back.

Not sure why they were waving him back, Janzen went back anyway. When they told him what had happened and he saw that, yes, it was his ball, he was relieved — sort of. "Obviously it was an unbelievable break that it fell out," he said. "But I still had a lot of work to do. I had to get out of the rough and then I still had a six-iron to the green and I hit it over."

Fortunately for Janzen, he had a moment to collect himself after he hit his wedge back onto the fairway while Stricker played his shot to the green. Unlike Couples, who didn't take a minute to regroup mentally and emotionally on the 13th at Augusta, Janzen took a deep breath to remind himself that he was back in the golf tournament. "But I knew it wouldn't do me any good if I made bogey," he said.

Janzen was just over the green, close enough to have a good lie rather than punching out of thick rough. Thinking he had to sink the chip, he did just that, the ball trickling down the hill and into the cup. Stricker saw Janzen's eyes go a little bit wide when the ball went in.

"It was as if he thought he had caught the kind of break you need to win a golf tournament like the Open," Stricker said. "That day, I could see the difference experience makes. We both made two bogeys early.

Lee's attitude was 'I have to make some birdies and get back in this thing.' My attitude was 'I've blown it. I have no chance. Let's just try to hang on.'"

Playing the fourth hole at that moment, Stewart had no idea what had happened to Janzen at the fifth. All he knew was that he had just made his worst swing of the week on the tee, pull-hooking a three-iron into the trees. The ball hit the trees so hard that it ricocheted backward and ended up in the deep rough no more than 100 yards from the tee. "One word describes that swing," Stewart said. "Gross."

From there, he actually made a good bogey, chipping out, then hitting a solid five-iron to 15 feet and just missing the par putt. Lehman saved his par at the fourth with an up and down, and the difference between Lehman and Stewart was back to four. Janzen trailed by five. Everyone else was sliding backward.

None of the leaders were scoreboard-watching at that stage. Stewart had decided to play the front nine without worrying about anybody else, then check where he was at the tenth. Janzen didn't think it was even relevant to check the board until and unless he got under par for the day. At the seventh, he got back to even par for the day, hitting a perfect sand wedge to within five feet of the flagstick, tucked in the front right of the long, narrow green. When his birdie putt went in, he was tied with Lehman, still four back of Stewart. By now, it appeared to be a three-man golf tournament, and Lehman was showing no signs of making a move. He was grinding out pars, hanging in, but was clearly mystified by the greens. On many of the holes he stayed behind after Stewart left the green to hit a couple of extra practice putts.

Stewart was doing exactly what he and Hicks wanted, making pars. At the seventh, after a three-iron put him in the left fairway, he chose a pitching wedge, hoping to hit the ball just behind the pin and spin it back. Since the green has two tiers, Stewart figured if he was long by a foot or two, the ridge between the tiers would act as a backboard and feed the ball back down to the hole.

When he hit the shot, his first thought was "perfect." He went so far as to say, "Hicksey, I might have made that one." But when the ball landed, Stewart heard nothing from the gallery. Since the fairway is below the green, he couldn't see the ball or the pin, so he had to depend on the crowd reaction to tell him if he had hit the ball close. Judging by the lack of noise it was pretty clear he hadn't holed the shot. It was almost as clear that he hadn't hit it close. "Could that ball have stayed on top?" he said to Hicks.

The question was rhetorical. There was no doubt that it had. Instead of walking to the green to look over a short birdie putt, Stewart had to walk to the second tier and look down at the hole, 25 feet away, almost straight downhill. He now had a lot of work to do to make par.

"If there was one shot in the golf tournament that threw me, that was it," he said. "I went from thinking I might have made it to being in serious trouble trying to make par. I lost my concentration just a little bit right there."

There was no way to stop the first putt. It went 10 feet past the hole, just as Stewart knew it would. Flustered, he hit a poor second putt, pushing it and leaving it short. Now he was one under for the tournament. Janzen and Lehman trailed by three.

On the eighth tee, Hicks gave him a brief pep talk. Nothing was wrong, he told him. That hole was just a bad break, not a bad shot. Stay in your routine, stay patient, everything will be fine. Stewart nodded. He hit a solid seven-iron hole high at the eighth and made par. Then he parred nine too, while Lehman, who had made seven straight pars after the first, flew the green with his second shot and made bogey.

At almost that precise moment, Janzen was looking at an eight-foot birdie putt at the 11th. He had hit a six-iron for his second shot from 156 yards out and the ball had landed short of the green, taken a big bounce out of the rough, and stopped eight feet away. "Worst-case scenario there the ball stops and I have a fairly easy chip and probably make par," he said. "When I got the hop, though, I had a great chance."

Janzen had been frustrated by his putting stroke for much of the year, particularly at Houston, where he had missed several putts in the eight-to-ten-foot range on the back nine on Sunday. He had worked very hard on putts of that length because he believes that those putts are the ones that make the difference on the back nine on Sunday — especially in a major. The work paid off. His birdie putt was dead center. For the first time he was under par for the day. Walking off the green, he glanced at a scoreboard. Stewart was one under for the tournament, two over for the day. Janzen took a deep breath. Stewart wasn't running away, he was slowly coming back to the field. The field, at that moment, was Janzen — two shots behind. The door was open.

He hit the 12th green in regulation, then, while Stricker was preparing to putt, he walked to the right of the green so he could watch Stewart Cink and Jeff Maggert hit their tee shots at the par-three 13th. He knew that the green would be hard and fast, but he wanted to know just how fast. He wasn't the least bit surprised when he saw both players land what looked like good shots in the middle of the green and then watched both shots bounce right through the green into the deep rough.

"I knew watching those guys that I had to land the ball toward the front of the green. Actually, I wanted to land it exactly twelve paces from the front and roll it up."

By now, Janzen was into the kind of zone players get in when they feel as if they can hit any shot in the bag. He had been flawless from the moment the ball fell out of the tree and he was starting to believe he could win the tournament.

Behind him, Stewart had just made a brilliant save at the 10th, coming out of a bunker to 10 feet and sinking the par putt from there. For the first time all day, he pumped his fist, truly excited about making the putt. Leaving the green, he looked at a scoreboard for the first time. Immediately, he saw Janzen's name in red numbers for the day (-1) and saw that he was +1 for the tournament. Everyone else was over par for the fourth round. It was a two-man game, just as it had been at Baltusrol in 1993. The only difference was that then Stewart had been the pursuer.

Janzen chose five-iron at the 13th and put a smooth swing on it, not wanting to hit it too hard. The ball landed — he later paced it off based on his divot — exactly 12 paces onto the green. It took a hop and spun to a stop four feet from the hole. The putt was dead center, and at 3:20 in the afternoon Janzen was at the magic number — even par for the tournament. He glanced at the scoreboard one more time leaving the green and saw that he was one shot behind. Then he made a decision: "I'm not looking again," he told himself. "If I keep playing like this and don't make a mistake, I have a great chance to win. I don't want to distract myself by looking."

Stricker had just bogeyed the 13th hole to drop back to six over par for the championship. Standing on the 14th tee, Janzen, focused as he was, couldn't help but notice Stricker hanging his head a little. After he had hit his tee shot (down the middle) he stopped Walker as they left the tee.

"He okay?" he asked, indicating Stricker, who was walking a few strides ahead.

"Not sure," Walker said.

"Should I say something?" Janzen asked.

"Couldn't hurt," Walker answered, amazed that someone who had put himself in position to win the U.S. Open would actually be aware of anything another player was doing at that moment.

Janzen walked up next to Stricker. "Hey, are you in next year's Masters yet?" he asked, remembering that Stricker hadn't been in the tournament in '98.

"No, I'm not," Stricker answered.

"Well, why don't you get in today?" Janzen asked.

Stricker smiled. He knew what Janzen was doing. He was telling him that just because he wasn't going to win was no reason to quit playing hard. Actually, Stricker was comfortably in the top sixteen he needed to make the Masters at that moment (+9 made it), but he appreciated Janzen's gesture. He picked his head up and played even par the rest of the way, which was good enough to earn him a tie for fifth, his first top-ten finish ever in a major.

While Stricker and Janzen were going up 14, Stewart and Lehman were on 12. Stewart's lead was now one. He hit his drive in the fairway but, as it had done with Janzen earlier in the day, fate intervened. After four days of a golf tournament, a lot of fairways are absolute divot havens, especially in the landing areas. The USGA and the PGA Tour have taken in recent years to filling larger divots with sand. This has been controversial because many players think playing out of the sand is just as difficult as playing out of an actual divot. Stewart's tee shot rolled into one of the sanded-over divots.

When he and Hicks got to the ball, they were both shocked. But there was nothing that could be done. They went back and forth on club selection, not sure how the ball would fly coming out of the sand. Stewart finally chose a nine-iron and watched helplessly as it came up well short of the green and landed in the front right bunker. He was still standing there, club in hand, trying to regroup mentally when Tom Meeks walked up to him. On Sunday, Meeks was responsible for monitoring pace of play for the late groups, making sure no one lagged. He had already put Janzen and Stricker on the clock earlier in the day. Now Stewart and Lehman were out of position, having dropped a little more than a hole behind Tway and Price, who were on the 13th green. They had been out of position since the 11th tee.

"Payne, I'm sorry but you got a bad time on that shot," Meeks said.

Stewart was stunned. "Tom, they shouldn't be filling those divots with sand," he said.

"That's another discussion for another time," Meeks said.

"You didn't see I had to change clubs?" Stewart asked.

Meeks nodded. He had noticed and he had stopped his watch during that period. Even so, he told Stewart, he had taken a minute and twenty seconds to play the shot. USGA rules allow a player forty seconds when he is on the clock. "I didn't want to give Payne a bad time in that situation and I really did cut him some slack because of the sandy divot," Meeks said. "But it wasn't even close. I had no choice. You can't administer the rules when you feel like it, you have to administer them fairly and the same for everyone."

Stewart, naturally, disagreed. "If the ball was sitting in the fairway and I took that much time, okay, I could see getting a bad time," he said. "But the ball was in a bunker in the middle of the fairway. I'm in the last group at the U.S. Open. Shouldn't I be cut some slack?"

Stewart was now officially flabbergasted. He managed to pull himself together to hit another excellent bunker shot to within 10 feet. But unlike at the 10th, he couldn't make the putt to save par. It twisted left at the last moment. It was 3:26 P.M. For the first time since shortly before noon on Thursday, Stewart did not have sole possession of the lead. He was even par for the championship, tied with Janzen, who was on the 15th fairway.

And, try as he might to put the 12th behind him, Stewart was still fuming on the 13th tee. It was not until later that he learned that Lehman had been practice putting after holing out for much of the front nine. "Do you think that might have been a factor in us being out of position?" he asked.

Stewart pulled a five-iron on the tee and made the same mistake that Janzen had watched Maggert and Cink make, aiming for the middle of the green. He hit the shot well and then watched it run through the green into the deep rough. "Given how pumped up I was at that moment I should have hit six-iron," he said later.

Lehman was slow choosing a club on that tee and, as the players walked to the green, Meeks came through the ropes again to tell him he had a bad time. As he did, Stewart waved him over. He asked Meeks to explain exactly how they stood in terms of bad times.

"You've each got one bad time," Meeks said. "If you get another, it's a one-stroke penalty. Once you get back in position, you're off the clock."

Stewart was still shaking his head over the whole thing walking onto the green. He hit a mediocre chip out of the deep rough — "I had an Olympic Club lie," he said, meaning a gnarly one — then left the par putt woefully short.

At that moment, it seemed the wheels were off and flying in different directions. Janzen had the lead outright, and Stewart had made back-to-back bogeys and looked like he wanted to kill someone — probably Tom Meeks. Once upon a time, Stewart would have been finished. He would have been so angry and so thrown by losing the lead and the bogeys and the incident with Meeks that he would have fumed his way to the finish and then, in all likelihood, would have stormed off without speaking to anyone.

"Your swing is just fine," Hicks told him on the 14th tee. "We're going to make a birdie sooner or later. Stay patient."

Stewart did just that. He hit a three-wood down the middle and a nine-iron 12 feet below the hole and rolled the putt in. He shook his fist as if to say, "Take that," and breathed a sigh of relief. It was his first birdie since the eighth hole on Saturday. He and Janzen were tied again.

Up ahead, Janzen was resolutely hitting fairways and greens, making routine par after routine par. On Sunday at the U.S. Open if you are in the lead or near the lead there is no such thing as a bad par — or for that matter, if truth be told, a routine par. Stricker was so impressed with Janzen's shotmaking, with the absolutely dialed-in look on his face, that he had to remind himself that he was still playing in the golf tournament too. "If nothing else, watching Lee that day is going to help me down the line," he said. "I got a close-up view of what a champion looks like when the pressure is greatest."

Janzen arrived on the 17th tee not certain what Stewart was doing but convinced that two pars would mean no worse than a playoff. Of course that was easier said than done. He had double-bogeyed 17 the last two days. His best score on the hole all week was the bogey he had made on Thursday. So what was Janzen thinking on the tee? "Make birdie and I win," he said. "I knew I had hit two good shots the day before. I was convinced if I did that again, I would have a birdie chance this time."

His drive split the middle, and he hit a near perfect three-iron to the middle of the green, about 35 feet above the hole. Standing a few feet away, Jim Walker watched Janzen hit the three-iron. "He just stood on it," he said. "I didn't even have to look to know it was perfect."

Carefully, Janzen lagged his birdie putt down the hill to within two feet and happily took par. Even if he had been thinking about birdie on the tee, he knew par was a good score. "I knew playing the last four or five holes in even par would be tough," he said.

He now had one more par to make to get to the clubhouse even par for the four rounds. He hit a three-iron off the tee and sailed it down the fairway, although it wasn't hit with the same fluid tempo of the last few holes. Walking off the tee, Musgrove whispered to Walker, "That wasn't the sound I wanted to hear on that one. Bit clunky."

Seeing Walker laugh, Janzen asked him what was so funny. When Walker repeated Musgrove's comment, Janzen cracked up. Later, when he looked at the tape and saw himself laughing, he couldn't remember what the conversation had been about. He had to ask Walker to remind him.

Clunky or not, the ball was right where it needed to be in the flat part of the fairway and not in any of the sandy divots spread out across the fairway. Taking no chances on coming up short, Janzen played a pitching wedge to the green. It flew a little bit farther than he wanted — the hole location was only five paces from the front — and ended up 18 feet above the flag.

"The only problem with that was that I knew if I didn't make the putt I was going to have to deal with at least three feet coming back," Janzen said. "I would rather have been below the hole, but that shot would have been too risky."

He jiggled the putt down the hill, thought for a brief second he might have made it, then watched it slide left and — as predicted — about three feet past the hole. He walked to the side of the green to let Stricker putt out, watching him carefully because his putt — from about six feet — was on almost the same line as his. All Stricker wanted to do at that point was get out of Janzen's way. He had been looking at the scoreboard and he knew exactly what was happening. So did the huge throng ringing the 18th green. If the scoreboard hadn't told Janzen what he was on the verge of accomplishing, the roars of the crowd as he walked up the hill to the green certainly provided a clue.

As soon as Stricker's ball was in the hole, Janzen walked to his ball to re-mark. As he did, a thought crossed his mind: Make this putt and you win the U.S. Open. Every kid who has ever played golf has told himself that standing over putts on the practice green. Janzen had done it his whole life. When he had won the Open at Baltusrol, he had been in such control that all he had to do was two-putt from eight feet on the 18th green to win. Now something in his gut told him this putt was to win the Open.

He checked the line carefully and reminded himself to hit the putt firmly. At this late juncture, the area around the hole had dealt with a lot of foot traffic and was a little bit rough and spiky. Any tentativeness and the ball could easily roll off line. Janzen hadn't hit a bad putt from a short or medium distance all day. This was no exception. It went straight into the heart of the hole. The crowd screamed. He shook hands with Stricker, Musgrove, and Walker and tipped his hat to the cheers. He still hadn't looked at the board. Seconds later, as he and Stricker were walking off the green, Janzen heard another roar. Finally, he turned and looked at the scoreboard to the right of the 18th. A green "1" had just gone up next to Stewart's name in the slot under the 16th hole. Stewart had bogeyed 16.

Oh my God, Janzen thought. It's really going to happen.

He felt himself starting to well over with emotion, so he almost sprinted up the hill to the door leading to the steps where the players went to sign their scorecards. He knew Stewart had two holes to play. But he would have to play those two holes in one under par to force a playoff. It wasn't impossible, but it also wasn't likely.

On the 17th tee Stewart understood just how grave the situation had now become. He had just made an ugly bogey at the 16th, pushing a three-wood tee shot, recovering with a five-iron to within 173 yards of the pin, and then coming over a seven-iron that landed in the front bunker. "I got quick on it," he said later. His lie was thin because the ball landed in a crosswalk, but he couldn't really complain at that point because he had been fortunate that he had an opening to hit his second shot from. He hit another good bunker shot to about eight feet, but the putt was left all the way. In fact, he had to make a testy four-footer coming back for bogey.

It was that bogey going up on the board at 18 that started Janzen's heart racing. From the fifth to the 18th he had been amazingly calm, making four birdies and no bogeys, a stretch almost unheard of on Sunday at an Open. He had shot 68. Later that night, he would tell his pal Rocco Mediate that he had played the last thirteen holes in "total control." No one else who started out within seven shots of Stewart shot lower than 73. Once he had signed his scorecard, the most difficult part of Janzen's day began: the waiting.

The scorer's table was in an auxiliary locker room in the basement of the clubhouse. Janzen was familiar with it because it had been used as the players' locker room during the 1993 Tour Championship. Bev was waiting for him there and NBC asked if the two of them would mind watching Stewart finish from a corner of the locker room where they had set up a chair and a camera. They wanted to wait until Stewart played 17, then talk to Janzen briefly while Stewart was on 18. Janzen agreed.

"That was torture," he said. "Waiting was bad enough, but doing it on camera was brutal."

Stewart played 17 solidly, just missing the green, then hitting a chip that looked for a second like it had a chance to go in before it settled about two feet from the cup. He knocked that in for par and walked to the 18th tee needing a birdie to force a playoff. There had been seven birdies at 18 all day — none from the last thirty players on the golf course. Even so, Johnny Miller pointed out to the NBC audience that in 1955 Ben Hogan had been sitting in the clubhouse thinking he had won the Open when Jack Fleck birdied 18 to tie him, forcing the playoff that Fleck won the next day.

Janzen, listening to the NBC feed in his ear on an IFB, winced. "I said to myself, 'Okay, if he birdies, I'm in a playoff tomorrow and that's great,'" he said later. "If I played the way I did today, I'd be fine."

Stewart hadn't hit the 18th fairway all week. This time, his three-iron drifted left but bounced back into the fairway — almost landing in another sand divot — before stopping safely on green grass. Stewart and Hicks thought about a sand wedge but figured 113 yards was a little too long a shot. So they went with the pitching wedge. "I'd have liked to hit sand wedge there to get the extra spin," Stewart said. "But it was too long a shot for that. I had no choice."

He also had no choice but to try to make three. The ball flew just right of the flag, hit, bounced, and stopped 18 feet away. It looked, at first, like a reasonable shot and a reasonable chance to make birdie.

But when Hicks looked at the putt up close, he almost gagged. The combination of line and speed made the putt, in Hicks's mind, almost unmakable. "If you stood there and putted from that spot a hundred times," he said, "if you are a very good putter you might make it once. With luck, twice."

The problem was that a bold putt was going to race right through the break, not move an inch, and end up 10 feet past the cup. Stewart didn't care how far past the cup he went, but he knew he couldn't try to ram the ball into the back of the cup. But if he finessed the putt, the chances of having it hold its line all the way to the hole were somewhere between slim and none. Hicks finally pointed to a spot six feet above the hole and said, "It has to start breaking right there." The approximate margin for error was an inch.

Stewart knew all that. But he knew crazier things had happened in golf, that great players made one-in-a-hundred putts. He reminded himself that he had hit good putts almost the entire week and he needed to hit one more putt and hope he could get it to that exact spot Hicks had pointed at.

Janzen, sitting with Bev, almost couldn't look. At that moment he was probably more nervous than Stewart, because Stewart had work to do. Stewart went through his routine, got over the ball, checked the spot, and putted.

"For a second, I thought it had a chance," Janzen said.

So did Stewart, but halfway to the hole, he sensed trouble. At that point, the ball was dead center, and he knew it would never stay on that line. "It actually got closer than I thought it would," he said. "With three feet left I was going, can it . . . ?"

No. Just as Hicks and Stewart knew it would, knew it had to, the ball veered left about a foot away. It stopped hole high, six inches below the left edge. That six inches was the difference, after four days and 72 holes, between Janzen and Stewart.

As soon as he saw the ball go left, Janzen lost it. Bev was hugging him and he was crying and she was crying and then he was burying his head in a towel, the tears soaking the towel. Stewart tapped in, shook hands with Lehman, and handed his putter to Hicks.

"Great playing all week," Hicks said softly.

Stewart smiled. "Well," he said, "at least we're back in Augusta."

Hicks almost laughed out loud. If he hadn't, he probably would have cried.

The next hour was a whirlwind for both players. They met briefly in the scorer's area when Stewart came in to sign his card. Stewart congratulated Janzen with a handshake and a "great playing, you deserved to win." Janzen wanted to say something, wanted to tell Stewart that he had played every bit as well, but the words choked in his throat. Stewart understood.

Janzen was escorted onto the 18th green to receive the trophy. Just as he had done at Baltusrol, he cried when they handed it to him. "I do this every time," he said. "I can't help it."

By then, Stewart was back on the green. He had given Bev Janzen a hug and had told NBC that Janzen deserved to win because he had gone out and hit the shots that he needed to hit to win the golf tournament, and he hadn't. Simple as that. No excuses. He said the same sort of thing in the interview room, crediting Janzen again. "A 68 under this pressure in these conditions is a phenomenal round of golf," he said. "That's how you win a major championship. He was the only guy in contention who shot under par today. That's how you win major championships."

This was a Stewart many reporters had never seen before. He answered every question, never snapped at anyone, didn't act rushed or impatient. When Les Unger, who moderates the press conferences for the USGA, asked him to go through his birdies and bogeys, Stewart smiled and said, "Les, the birdies won't take very long."

He did complain about the bad time Meeks had given him, saying that out of position is out of position, but it was the last round of the U.S. Open, he was in a fairway sand trap, and he and Lehman had still finished twenty minutes before NBC went off the air (actually twenty-three). But there wasn't even a hint of the Payne Stewart of the late '80s and early '90s.

"As soon as I missed that last putt, I started girding myself for what was to come," he said later. "I knew I had to do the interviews and answer all the questions. I had a four-shot lead and didn't win, I was going to be asked about that. I understood the questions had to be asked and I needed to answer them. When it was over, I was proud of myself because losing hurt but I found out I could handle it. I lost because I wasn't the Payne Stewart I wanted to be that day."

In a sense, though, he was. Maybe not on the first 18 holes, but certainly on the 19th, the most difficult one of all. When he left Olympic that night, even without the U.S. Open trophy, there was little doubt that Bill Stewart would have been very proud of the way William Payne Stewart dealt with not winning the U.S. Open.

When Janzen came into the interview room a few minutes after Stewart had departed, he looked around the packed room and said jokingly, "Does everyone in here have a press badge?"

"No!" came a voice from the back.

It was his wife.

Janzen admitted he had wondered when he was going to win again after almost three years without a victory, but added that all those frustrations were now erased. He was calm and controlled, by now giving the shot-by-shot analysis that is required of a player after he wins a major.

But ten minutes into the press conference, there was an interruption. Connor Janzen had spent the day away from the golf course with his babysitter because Bev knew that five hours at the golf course would be too much for a little boy who would not be five until October. She wanted to walk with Lee, so she told the babysitter to take Connor out for the afternoon but check back at the hotel around 5 o'clock just in case Lee won. When the babysitter and Connor returned just before 5, turned on the TV, and saw Lee holding the trophy, they flew into a car, raced to the course, and arrived ten minutes into the press conference.

As soon as Connor Janzen saw his dad, he made a beeline for him. "Dad!" he yelled, "I missed you. Happy Father's Day!"

Lee Janzen wrapped his son up in a hug, tears in his eyes again. It was a couple of minutes before he said anything. Everyone waited. And then the 1998 U.S. Open champion said quietly, "There's nothing better than being loved."

III

The Original

22

If It's Nae Wind and Nae Rain, It's Nae Golf . . .

The start of the U.S. Open marks the official beginning of golf's frantic season. While the rest of the year meanders along from tournament to tournament with a one-week break from the merry-go-round to play the Masters, the Majors Season — as it might be called — is sixty frenetic days during which the world's top players run themselves ragged deciding three major championships.

Most players who are exempt into the U.S. and British Opens and the PGA will piece together a schedule so that they play five or six of the nine weeks. For most, that schedule will include one event between the two Opens and one or two between the British and the PGA. Players on the U.S. Tour are more likely to play the week before the PGA than the week before the British because they don't have to deal with a transatlantic flight and a five-hour time change en route to the PGA.

The British Open has always been the major that Americans — some, not all — whine about the most. Without question it is the most difficult to get to, not just because of the long plane flight, but because all the Open sites are a good-sized hike from any major airport and a lot of the drive from airport to golf course inevitably involves narrow two-lane roads and dozens of Great Britain's infamous roundabouts that leave you either dizzy or lost or both.

But that's not all. Americans complain about the food, the showers (or lack of them), the jacked-up hotel prices for Open week, the weather, the bad bounces on the links courses, and the tabloid media.

To which most of the rest of the world replies: quit whining and shut up.

Just as Fred Couples makes the point that there's no reason why golfers can't deal with rock-hard fairways and greens and knee-high rough once a year, there is also no reason why American golfers can't deal with fried food, wind and rain, and paying the same rates as the rest of the world once a year. The shower complaint is legitimate.

In return for their trouble, they get to play in the place where the game was invented, in front of the world's most knowledgeable and appreciative fans, and have a chance to win the oldest and, many would say, the most prestigious title in golf. Most Americans who have made a habit of going to the British Open fall in love with it. It just takes time and a little patience — the latter not being an American commodity.

"When I first came over here I hated it," said Tom Watson, who is now considered an adopted son in the British Isles. "I said, 'This isn't golf; golf is played through the air, not on the ground. And what's the deal with all these bounces?' It wasn't until I'd been over here several times that it occurred to me that *this* was golf, not what we played, that this was the way the game was meant to be played."

Amazingly, Watson says he had already won the Open championship twice ('75 and '77) before this revelation came to him. "It was in '79 at Lytham," he said. "I played one of those rounds where I hit a five-iron 230 on one hole and 130 on another. Real links golf. Something just clicked in me that this was a really fun, challenging way to play." Links golf is completely different from "American" golf. The golf courses are all near water — the term *links* is a reference to the land linking the sea to the rest of the land — and there are almost no trees, few American-style hazards, and very little green grass. Links courses are obviously lacking in glamour but are rich with history.

One doesn't have to be a five-time Open champion to feel like Watson. Payne Stewart, who has won the U.S. Open and the PGA but not the British Open (he was second twice), says now that if he was starting his career again and could win only one major it would be the British, in spite of his father's feelings about the U.S. Open. "It's the original tournament," he said. "Everything golf is began at the British."

Tom Kite, who has played in the event twenty-one times without winning, gets almost apoplectic talking about Americans who are exempt and don't play. "You can't win the tournament," he said one year, "if you don't play in the damn thing. Who wouldn't want to win the British Open?"

The list goes on. Davis Love, Peter Jacobsen, Brad Faxon, and Ben Crenshaw all get misty-eyed talking about the magic of playing in the Open. As much as he loves Augusta, Fred Couples says the one thing he would love to do in golf before he retires is walk up the 18th hole at the British Open on the final day with the lead. He calls it "the best walk in golf," because of the huge grandstands that are built each year flanking the fairway and the green. The ovations that players receive walking up 18 often leave them in tears.

In 1997, Jack Nicklaus walked up the 18th on Sunday at Troon nowhere near contention but nonetheless making the walk for the thirty-sixth straight year. Every single person in the grandstands was on their feet cheering Nicklaus as he reached the green. Stewart, his playing partner that day, stood to the side joining the applause. When he had holed out, Nicklaus signed his card and then stood chatting with reporters behind the green for several minutes. As he was talking, Andrew Magee, who had been playing in the group behind Nicklaus and Stewart, walked up.

"Jack, I don't mean to interrupt," he said, "but I just have to tell you, I was in the middle of the 18th fairway when you walked onto the green and those cheers gave me chills just standing there. You deserved every bit of it."

All the hassles — real and imagined — are worth it if you've ever had the chance to make The Walk.

Like the U.S. Open, the British Open is open to anyone willing to pay 80 pounds (about $125) who can prove he is a pro or an amateur with a two-handicap or better. Because the population of the British Isles is approximately 30 percent of the population of the United States, there are considerably fewer entries than in the U.S. Open — 2,344 for the 1998 event held at Royal Birkdale.

The British Open is also more liberal in handing out exemptions. Anyone ranked in the world's top fifty in late May is exempt, and spots are held for players on all the major tours around the world. In 1998 a total of 102 players were exempt, leaving only 54 spots available for qualifiers. The sectionals for the British — known as final qualifying — are quite different from the U.S. Open. To begin with, they are played over two days rather than one at least in part because questionable weather makes the chances of getting 36 holes and a playoff completed in one day very unlikely. The final qualifying is also held much closer to the start of the actual tournament — the Sunday and Monday prior to the event — so that overseas players who choose to play in qualifying don't have to arrive in the country almost two full weeks before the tournament begins. A number of European players have suggested that the USGA adopt this approach to encourage more members of their tour to take a shot at U.S. Open qualifying.

While the U.S. qualifying is spread out across the continent, the British final qualifying is always played on four courses that are no more than thirty minutes from the championship site. In '98, Hillside, one of the courses used for qualifying, was so close to Royal Birkdale that the Hillside driving range was used for parking during the Open. The first tee at Hillside is a five-minute walk from the first tee at Birkdale — but in the context of the Open, the distance looked like the Atlantic to the golfers teeing it up at Hillside.

The Royal and Ancient Golf Club (the R & A), which administers the Open Championship, assigns players to golf courses for final qualifying. It tries to balance the four fields because, unlike the USGA, which hands out qualifying spots based on strength of field, the R & A divides the number of spots available by four and distributes them to the four sites. When the number is unbalanced, the extra spots are given out by lot: in '98, West Lancashire and Southport and Ainsdale drew fourteen slots while Hillside and Hesketh drew thirteen, with the first alternate spot going to Hillside, the second to Hesketh. Each golf course had 120 players in its field.

There weren't very many Americans to be found at any of the four golf courses. A number of Americans were listed in the original qualifying draw because they had entered the tournament hoping to be exempt and then decided to withdraw rather than play qualifying. Among them were Scott McCarron (who had dropped from the world top fifty list the week before exemptions were handed out), Jay Haas (another late top fifty dropout), Scott Verplank, Steve Flesch, Rick Fehr, Howard Twitty, Rocco Mediate, Russ Cochran, and Craig Stadler. Some considered coming for qualifying — McCarron went back and forth until the last minute — but most had no intention of showing up unless they were escorted directly to Royal Birkdale.

In all, twenty-seven Americans were among the 480 players teeing it up on a wet, windy Sunday morning at the four courses along the Lancashire Coast. Only seven of those twenty-seven were current members of the PGA Tour. The rest played around the world, including a group from the Asian Tour who were there because that tour had encouraged them to play and agreed to pick up their hotel expenses for the week. Two non-Americans playing the PGA Tour — David Frost and Iain Steel — were also playing.

Two names jumped off the pairings sheets. One was Nicklaus — twenty-nine-year-old Gary, son of the legend, a journeyman player on the European Tour. His presence in the qualifying field had extra poignance since his father had announced a week earlier that his injured hip and general frustration with his game would force him to skip the British Open for the first time since 1961. That decision ended one of sport's most remarkable streaks: Jack Nicklaus had played in 146 consecutive major championships, starting at the Masters in 1962. When he had been given an exemption into the U.S. Open by the USGA — and exemptions for both 1999 and 2000 — most people had thought he would keep the streak alive through the PGA in 2000 and then end it at the age of sixty. But his troublesome hip changed that.

Naturally, the romantic notion was that Gary would step into the sudden void created by his father's absence. That sort of notion had been Gary's problem since his days as a teenager when he had been identified as the most talented player among Nicklaus's four sons. *Sports Illustrated* had run a cover story in 1986 on him with the headline "The Next Nicklaus." Jack Nicklaus had gone semiballistic over the story. "I never would have agreed to let Gary (who was seventeen at the time) do it if I had known they were planning a cover," he said, years later. "That was very tough on Gary."

Being named Nicklaus and playing golf was going to be tough on

Gary under any circumstances. Most of the time he kept his sense of humor about it, joking when reporters wanted to talk to him that he had to be the only player at his level in the world who had to hold press conferences. Gary had played in a number of PGA Tour events courtesy of sponsor exemptions provided by tournament directors eager to get the other Nicklaus in their field. He had been to the Tour's qualifying school on several occasions without ever reaching the finals. He had made a breakthrough of sorts at the end of 1997 when he successfully made it through the European Tour's Q-School.

The other name that jumped off the pages of the draw sheet was Mize. In this case it was the real thing — Larry Mize, the 1987 Masters champion. Mize was the only player in the qualifying field who had won a major title. He had played in every British Open from 1983 through 1995 before losing his exemption in 1996. He had thought about trying to qualify that year but decided against it because he was playing so poorly. In 1997, still not exempt, he entered qualifying but also accepted an invitation to play the week prior to qualifying in the Loch Lomond Invitational, which is now the warm-up event on the European Tour the week before the British.

Loch Lomond is played Wednesday through Saturday, meaning it is possible to play there and then be at a qualifying site on Sunday. This was especially true in 1997 because Loch Lomond is less than an hour from Troon — the '97 Open site — and from the four qualifying courses nearby.

But while playing Loch Lomond gave him some guaranteed money (most Americans who play there get an appearance fee) and the chance to make some prize money, Mize also found that it lessened his chances of qualifying for the British, which was his real reason for making the trip in the first place. To begin with, Loch Lomond is an inland golf course, nothing like the links courses used for the Open and for qualifying. Mize had no chance to prepare for links-style golf while playing there. And, because he was at Loch Lomond until Saturday, he didn't have a chance to play a practice round at his qualifying course, get the lay of the land, walk off yardages with his caddy, get comfortable on the golf course.

"When I decided to put this on my schedule this year, I decided to do it right," Mize said. "No Loch Lomond. Come over early, get in a couple of practice rounds, and give it my best shot. Otherwise, why bother."

Mize will always have a place in the golf pantheon because he struck one of golf's most historic shots: the 140-foot wedge shot from off the 11th green at Augusta that went in the hole to stun Greg Norman on the second playoff hole at the 1987 Masters. Mize was only twenty-eight at the time, and the jump to major champion — especially in such spectacular fashion — wasn't always easy for him. He was almost haunted by his Masters victory, feeling that he somehow wasn't worthy of it, that he had to play better to prove to people that he really was a Masters champion. It was another six years before he won again.

He had played solidly on tour since then — although he had dropped to ninety-ninth on the 1997 money list, his lowest finish since 1982, his rookie year — but hadn't won since the 1993 Buick Open. A week before flying to England, Mize had blown a four-stroke lead on the back nine at Hartford and then lost a playoff to Olin Browne. That was the closest he had come to a victory in a long time. It was his first second place finish on tour since 1993.

As much as losing the lead at Hartford hurt, the way he had played for 68 holes was encouraging to Mize and gave him a dose of confidence heading overseas. He arrived on Friday with decidedly mixed emotions. Leaving his wife and three sons for what could be a fruitless effort wasn't his idea of fun. Arriving to find that his hotel reservation had been lost and he didn't have a room made him even more homesick. Finally, getting a room in which he could stand up and touch both walls with his arms outstretched — "Seriously, I'm going to take pictures to prove it," he said — made him wonder if he wasn't just a little bit crazy to be here. But getting out on a links course to practice and knowing the challenge ahead energized him.

"If I make it through qualifying, that will mean I'm playing well and I'll go into the tournament with a lot of confidence," he said. "That's the good news. The bad news is, qualifying isn't going to be easy and if I don't qualify I will have spent a lot of money [about $8,000] to not play in the British Open and spend four nights sleeping in a closet."

Mize didn't like being in qualifying — who did? — and admitted it was especially difficult after years as a player exempt into all the majors to find himself back in the qualifying events. He hadn't had much luck with it either: failing at the British in '97, then losing in the playoff at Woodmont in June. Still, he wanted to play. "I love playing in the majors," he said. "I think the British Open is very special. It's worth the effort for me to give this a shot."

Mize had no idea how much his willingness to take part in the qualifying meant to the British fans. Golfers are revered throughout Great Britain, and those who have won a major championship are put on a special kind of pedestal. What's more, knowing that most Americans, especially ones with any kind of star status, won't make the transatlantic trip without an exemption into the tournament proper, the fans regarded Mize's presence with a little bit of awe, a little bit of wonder, and a lot of appreciation.

Mize had been assigned to Hesketh Golf Club, one of those British courses that tourists would flock to if it were part of the British Open rota. It is located in Southport, about a ten-minute drive from Birkdale, and has a stretch of holes on the front nine that go out to the Irish Sea, then run along the water, then come back inland. On a windy day — most days — Hesketh was a bear of a golf course.

Mize was paired with Frenchman Olivier Edmond and European Ryder Cupper David Gilford. They teed off at 9:10 on Sunday, a windy, slate gray day with rain blowing in off the Irish Sea in squalls that ranged from a shower to a downpour. In other words, a typical British Open day. By the time the group turned back inland after playing the three holes that parallel the water (five, six, and seven), the gallery following them had grown to close to three hundred people, all of them walking down the middle of the fairways with the three players, which made getting from one shot to the next something of a challenge for the players.

"You get used to it after a while," Mize said. "You have to."

Mize was very happy to get back to the inland holes just one over par and even happier when he holed a 25-foot birdie putt at the ninth to get back to even par. He was guessing that anybody that shot close to par (71) was going to be in good position. A birdie at the 12th got him under par, but then British Open luck jumped up and got him at the 13th.

The USGA are not the only ones who believe in turning short par-fives into long par-fours. The 13th at Hesketh is a par-five for the members but was being played as a 471-yard par-four during final qualifying. There is a burn that wanders right across the fairway 275 yards from the tee. Dead into the wind, Mize didn't think there was any way he could get a three-wood to the burn. He was right. But in the instant that Mize drew his club back, the wind let up. You could actually feel it. The ball flew farther than Mize had dreamed it could possibly go and took one hop into the burn.

Mize looked at his caddy, Van Silver, as if to say, how did that happen? Silver had no answer. Mize had to drop behind the burn and still had 220 yards to the green — now dead into the howling wind. He came up 40 yards short, chipped to 10 feet, and missed the bogey putt. Just like that he was one over par.

The 13th green is so close to the third tee that when players walk off the tee they pass so close to the green that they will stop and wait if a player is putting on the green. As Mize was putting, three young British players were walking off the third tee. They all stopped. One turned to his mother, who was walking with him, and said, "Do you know who that is — Larry Mize!"

Mize wasn't feeling very famous as the group walked across the street back in the direction of the clubhouse and set up on the 14th tee. The rain had become an in-your-face downpour by now and the wind was blowing everybody sideways. The 14th tee backs up to the red-brick sidewall of a nursing home. All the players looked as if they might belong there by day's end.

Mize managed to regroup. He birdied 15 and then parred in, somewhat disappointing since 17 and 18 are both par-fives. At 17, playing the hole downwind, Mize had only a nine-iron left on his second shot. But the ball came up well short of the green — again, the swirling wind seemed to blow in a different direction in midswing. Mize stood there staring at the ball. Just as he did, a woman in the gallery walked by and, not seeing that he was still standing there, accidentally caught him on the side of the head with an elbow. Mize, soaked to the bone and shivering, just laughed. "If I had played better, I wouldn't be here," he said. "And I wouldn't have this headache."

As he had suspected, even par put him in good position, tied for tenth place. "That's not bad, but with thirteen spots, it isn't a lock by a long shot," he said. "And it's supposed to blow again tomorrow, so who knows." He was sitting in the locker room now, drying off, relaxing. But a qualifier isn't like a tournament. There's no guard standing on the door to make sure the players aren't bothered. A number of spectators and club members were in the locker room wanting autographs. Most had walked all or part of the 18 holes with Mize.

"Anyone who went out and walked around in that weather deserves an autograph," he said, signing away. "At the very least."

Over at Hillside a little while later, Michael Campbell had also taken refuge from the weather inside the locker room. He had chipped and putted and then signed autographs after shooting 71 for his first 18 holes. The locker room was empty. Most of the players had gone home, looking for a hot shower or bath. Campbell was taking a break from the wind and rain, but he wanted to hit a few more putts before leaving. He didn't want to take anything for granted.

That was the mistake he had made in 1995. That year, at the age of twenty-six, Campbell had emerged as one of golf's next stars. He had played consistently well on the European Tour but became known worldwide when he took a four-shot lead into the final round of the British Open at St. Andrews. Campbell can still remember dreaming that night about winning the tournament and holding the trophy, but he didn't do it. He shot 76 on the last day and ended up a shot out of the John Daly–Costantino Rocca playoff after his 35-foot eagle putt at the 18th — the one that had Daly worried — came up four feet short.

"I misread the putt," he said, lighting a cigarette. "I actually thought it was a little downhill, and it was a little uphill. I'd love to have another go at that one."

Campbell's play in the British Open, his dark good looks, and the buzz among golf people that this was one of the game's next stars made him a lot of money that year. He signed contracts with Nike, Titleist, Callaway, and Oakley. He decided to play both the European and the U.S. Tours in 1996 even though his fellow New Zealander Frank Nobilo, who knew something about trying to play all over the world, pleaded with him not to. "Frank told me it couldn't be done, that I'd wear myself out trying," Campbell said. "Of course I knew he was wrong. I was ten feet tall and bulletproof. Nothing could stop me."

Tendinitis in his wrist could. It first developed late in '95 after Campbell had played in every silly season event imaginable, cashing in on his newfound fame. The doctors told him he needed to take six months off. He took two because no way was he going to miss the Masters. The wrist got worse before it got better. Trying to play both tours, he managed to lose his playing privileges on both continents for 1997. Finally healthy again in '97, he struggled with his attitude. He couldn't understand why the game wasn't rolling over and playing dead for him the way it had early in his career. The world wasn't at his feet anymore. He wasn't a rising star anymore either, just a guy who'd had a good run and had now slipped back into the netherworld of the nonexempt.

"It wasn't any fun, but it taught me a lot," he said. "I always took my golf for granted. Heck, I won my fifth pro tournament. I almost won the Open championship when I was twenty-six. It was easy. I would finish second or third in a tournament and be upset about it. I couldn't understand how anyone could beat me." He laughed. "If I finished second or third in a tournament now, I'd be thrilled."

He had re-earned his playing privileges in Europe the previous fall by surviving Q-School, and he was playing decent, unspectacular golf. He was healthy, though, and his attitude was much better. "I'm happier with myself now than when I was a star," he said. "I appreciate a good round of golf — like today — more than I used to. I understand people better than I did and how this world works. If I get back to that level again, I'll appreciate it more and understand it better.

"The hard part is getting back."

Getting back into the British Open would be a step in the right direction. "Three years ago, I finished third and was disappointed," he said. "Now I feel as if teeing it up on Thursday would be an accomplishment."

Teeing it up on Thursday would be an accomplishment for almost anyone in the qualifying, whether he was a Masters champion, an almost British Open champion, or anyone else. If anything, the weather was worse on Monday than it had been on Sunday. There wasn't as much rain, but the wind was absolutely howling, averaging close to 40 miles per hour, with gusts more than 50. The golf courses had all been difficult on Sunday. On Monday, they were close to impossible. In fact, most of the exempt players playing practice rounds at Royal Birkdale played nine holes or walked in sooner than that, thinking it was pointless to practice in such conditions. "All you do is mess up your swing trying to flail it through the wind," said David Duval. "It just makes no sense. I'm going someplace warm."

The qualifiers didn't have that option. They had to keep on playing regardless of the conditions. Their only consolation was that the conditions were just as brutal for everyone else. Mize had a terrible time on the front nine with the winds, especially on the three holes by the Irish Sea. Out there, it looked and felt as if the players were trying to play through a hurricane. By the time Mize got to the turn, he was five over par for the day and the qualifier, and wondering if he could pull himself together on the back nine. "I wasn't exactly brimming with confidence," he said. "But I figured all the scores were going to be high. I had to hang in there."

Mize wasn't the only one hanging on for dear life. Two groups behind him was the only other player in the field who could claim to have won a major championship. Eric Meeks had won the U.S. Amateur in 1988, and Arnold Palmer, Mark O'Meara, and Tiger Woods — among others — would tell you that meant he had won a major.

Meeks hadn't had a lot of success in golf since that one shining moment. He had played in the Masters, the U.S. Open, and the British Open in 1989 because of his victory in the amateur and had been in exactly one major — the '95 U.S. Open — since then. After turning pro he had started a golfing odyssey, traveling from place to place in search of home — the PGA Tour — only to find his way blocked by all manner of sorcerers, demons, and one-eyed giants, better known to golfers as not making enough birdies. He had been to Q-School for the U.S. Tour eight times and had made it to the finals once. That had gotten him onto the Nike Tour in 1996, but he had made just $12,000 that year and had returned to the Asian Tour, which is where he had spent most of his professional career.

"I'm not where I want to be right now, but I still believe I'm good enough to get there," he said. "It's been a long haul, and now that I'm going to become a father in the fall, I have to start thinking seriously about how much longer I'd want to go on playing overseas if I don't make it to the PGA Tour. But I still believe in myself. I'm thirty-three. It's not too late."

Meeks looks younger than thirty-three. He has brown hair, a slender build, and an easy, friendly smile. He is just under 6 feet tall and doesn't hit the ball prodigious distances, meaning that he has to depend on a good short game and making a lot of putts to have success. He was at Hesketh because the Asian Tour had encouraged players to take a shot at the qualifier. He had flown to England from his home in California on an $800 plane ticket, and the Asian Tour was picking up his expenses for the week. His twin brother, Aaron, who also played in Asia, was doing the same thing. It had never occurred to Meeks when he played at Troon in 1989 as the Amateur champion that he might be playing in his first and last British Open. By now, the thought had occurred to him. "To get back in now would be special," he said. "I'd certainly appreciate it more than the first time."

Meeks had shot a one-under-par 70 on Sunday, which put him in serious contention for a spot at Hesketh. But, like everyone else, he struggled with the wind on Monday. In fact, if he hadn't made almost every putt he looked at inside 10 feet, he would have had absolutely no chance. He hit only six greens in regulation all day. He made zero birdies — "I can't honestly remember the last time that happened," he said when it was over. The wind seemed to grab hold of every shot he hit, and during one stretch he hit just two greens in nine holes. And yet, he played those holes in just two over par, a tribute to his putting.

As Meeks and playing partners Max Lane, a British amateur with a gorgeous swing and a fierce temper, and Edward Goodwin, an English club pro, made their way up the 15th fairway, word came drifting back that it looked like 148 or 149 would play off. Meeks had just made a sliding seven-foot par putt at the 14th hole and was sitting at five over par for the two days. That meant that if he parred in, he would shoot 147, which sounded like a good score based on the whispers around the greens.

Meeks was thinking if he could par 15 and 16, he might have a chance to birdie the two par-fives, 17 and 18, and that could put him in good position. But it wasn't nearly that simple. After another good save at 15, he bogeyed the par-three 16th, then watched helplessly as the wind picked up what looked like a good drive at 17 and pushed it into the hip-high bushes on the right. By the time he was finished hacking and chopping, he had to make an eight-foot putt for bogey. That put him at seven over par. Still, if he could birdie 18 and finish at 148 . . . He couldn't. He made a par and signed for 70–79 . . . 149. As it turned out, the information passed along at 15 hadn't been very accurate. The play-off came at 147 — and that was for the alternate's spot.

Meeks looked at the scores, shrugged, and went inside to get warm. "You know, the bottom line is the very best I could do today was shoot 79," he said. "Looking at some of the other scores makes me feel better, even if I'm not going to qualify."

Some of the other scores were amazing. A number of very good players had shot in the 80s. Quite a few others had simply walked off and refused to post a score. But the most remarkable score of the day was the one posted by José Coceres of Argentina. Coceres was not some amateur who had faked his way into the qualifier. He was a good player, a man who had won six times in Europe and had been a medalist in final qualifying in 1997. He had shot 74 the first day. On Monday he shot 105. The wind just got to him and he couldn't play. To his credit he didn't quit and he posted his score. People reading it in the newspaper the next day probably didn't believe it.

While Meeks sat in the bar drinking a Coke with his brother (who had shot 78–84) and thought about his long trip home and what his long-term golfing future would be, Larry Mize was trying to find a quiet spot while waiting to find out what his short-term future was going to be.

Mize had staged a fierce comeback over Hesketh's final holes. After bogeying the bugaboo 13th, he had been seven over par for the day and the event, and appeared to be going, going, gone. But he rallied, birdieing the 14th, scrambling out pars at 15 and 16, and then, thinking he needed to finish birdie-birdie to have a chance, he did exactly that, reaching both the par-fives in two, just missing a pair of long eagle putts and making birdie on both. That got him to the clubhouse at four-over-par 146.

Would it be good enough?

Mize spent some time staring at the scoreboard, surrounded by his many new friends, quite a few of them Hesketh members who had adopted him over the two days of qualifying. "You're in, look at how high the scores are going," one said. "Too soon to tell," said another. "Might be a playoff," said a third. "I think I'll go wait in the locker room for a while," said Mize.

He did that. Even there, helpful members and R & A officials kept bringing him updates. During one ten-minute period one R & A official came in to tell him there was no way that 146 wouldn't get in, before another came in and asked if he wanted to hit a few balls to prepare for a playoff. Mize rolled his eyes. "Isn't it dark yet?" he asked.

It was 6 o'clock. It wouldn't be dark for another four hours.

As it turned out, Mize had to wait until the very last group came in because there were twelve players posted at 146 or better, and word from the course — and Meeks could certainly attest to how accurate that could be — was that there were two players in the last two groups with a chance. Sure enough, Andrew McLardy came in and posted a 146. Now there were thirteen at 146 or better, five of them at 146. A six-for-five playoff seemed possible. "I do not want to play any more golf today," Mize said, huddling in his jacket against the whipping winds while the final group came up 18.

He didn't have to worry. The player in the last group who supposedly had a chance was Coceres. One look at him walking off 18 and Mize knew he was in, even before Coceres had posted his mind-boggling number. The Hesketh members — the new Larry Mize fan club — crowded around offering congratulations. Mize was delighted — and exhausted. He was back in the British Open, and the next day he would get to change hotel rooms.

"That reminds me," he said. "I have to go buy a camera so I can take a picture of my room. If I don't, no one is going to believe me." He was smiling, really smiling for the first time in two days. He was entitled.

Gary Nicklaus had been smiling for most of the day. But it was shortly past 7 o'clock now, and instead of celebrating his spot in the British Open over dinner with friends, Nicklaus was standing on the first tee at Hillside listening to R & A official Jeremy Caplan explain what was about to take place.

"There are twelve players who have returned a score of 150 or lower," Caplan said. He read the twelve names (one of them being Michael Campbell at 146). "Those twelve players have qualified for the Open Championship. There are seven players tied at 151 and they will play off for the one remaining spot and for the alternate's spot. I should tell you that the first alternate in the tournament will come from this qualifier, so that could be quite significant."

In fact, the word across the street at Birkdale was that John Cook had withdrawn from the Open that day and the first alternate would take his spot. That meant the playoff was actually seven-for-two. For Nicklaus, the thought of seven-for-two couldn't be all that comforting. Earlier in the day, he had walked onto the 16th tee just four over par for the two days, knowing that the conditions were going to drive scores up. If he parred in, he would be a lock for a spot. He had successfully qualified for one major in his life — the '97 U.S. Open — and had spent most of that week answering questions about playing in a major with his dad. Now he could look forward to spending a week answering questions about playing in a major without his dad.

Maybe he looked forward to that too soon. He bogeyed 16. Then he bogeyed 17. And finally, he bogeyed 18. When he finished and signed for a 78, giving him a two-day total of 151, he was fairly certain he had blown himself out completely. But now he had another chance, and he stood patiently on the tee along with the others while Caplan took roll to make sure all the 151s had stuck around. When he sort of heard his name — "Gary NickLOUSE," Caplan said — Nicklaus put his hand up like everyone else. No John Morses in this group. All seven players were still there.

They would play in one group of seven, which was going to make for fairway gridlock, since that would mean seven players, seven caddies, a host of officials, and about two hundred fans. The big challenge was to keep the players from being trampled by fans hustling ahead to get a good view. It also took several minutes to get everyone off the tee, since players twice had to back off as trains rumbled into the Hillside train station that was adjacent to the clubhouse. A large sign to the left of the tee left little doubt about the folly of hitting your ball left on number one: "Danger, The Railway Is Electrified. Do Not Trespass."

The only place currently off-limits that the players wanted to go was in the opposite direction from the tracks — the bleached white Art Deco clubhouse of Birkdale.

Everyone managed to keep their tee shots away from the railroad tracks, except for Mark Davis, whose pull-hook sailed straight at the chain-link fence separating the golf course from the trains. While the other players waited, Davis and several dozen fans searched for the ball. "Wait a minute," one fan said, "I've got it." Apparently oblivious to the sign on the tee, he squeezed through the fence, hopped over a rail, and picked up a ball. "Titleist two," he called, while a number of people stood yelling at him to get the hell away from the rail. Davis said nothing until an R & A official came over to ask if the ball was his.

"I'm going back to the clubhouse," he said, answering the question that way. The fence jumper shrugged, pocketed the ball, and continued with the other six players. There were five pars and a bogey at the first hole, and the five remaining players trudged to the par-five second. It had taken thirty minutes to play the first hole.

At the second, Nicklaus made a bold — perhaps foolish — play, trying to hit a driver off the fairway. He hooked it and the ball disappeared behind a sandhill near the ever-present railroad fence. When he arrived at the ball, it was almost under the fence, directly under a sign that said, "Danger of Death, Do Not Climb." Nicklaus's chances might have died there if not for the fact that the fence was an obstruction, meaning he could move his ball. He had to drop directly into the sandhill. From there, he played a superb wedge to within eight feet. Everyone else missed their birdie putts, and Nicklaus had an open door to the British Open. The putt rolled directly at the hole, then turned right at the last instant. It stopped an inch — one inch — to the right of the cup. Nicklaus looked stricken — with good reason.

They all plodded to the third. One player, Ross Drummond, missed the green. He took out a lob wedge and plopped his third shot onto the green. It bounced, hopped, trickled, and disappeared into the cup. Drummond was forty-one, a lifelong Euro Tour journeyman who had flunked Q-School the prior December and had gotten into only nine events so far in 1998. He had been a pro for twenty-three years and had never won a tournament. Now, though, he won the playoff when no one else could birdie. When American Ken Duke three-putted, Nicklaus, Barry Lane, and Paolo Quirici moved to the ninth tee to continue on for the second spot. Everyone parred nine. By now, it was closing in on nine o'clock. At the tenth — the fifth hole of the playoff — Lane was just off the green, a good 35 feet from the cup. By now there were no more than fifty spectators left. When his putt dropped into the cup for a birdie, they let out a collective shout — Lane is an Englishman — and when neither Nicklaus nor Quirici could match, Lane had the final spot.

The playoff had taken just under two hours. Lane, surrounded by friends, walked back to the clubhouse with a huge grin on his face. Nicklaus and Quirici looked more like Joe Hardy and Lola in *Damn Yankees* — Two Lost Souls on the Highway of Life.

In the morning, both would be back on the road, headed away from Birkdale, where the rest of the golf world was settling in for the week.

23

English Summer

Johnny Carson would have had an absolute field day telling weather jokes during the practice days at Birkdale.

As in, "It was so cold and windy that . . .

- Nick Price and Fred Couples spent several minutes on the practice tee one morning hitting wedge shots that went straight up and then went backward over their heads . . .
- David Duval arrived on the range Tuesday afternoon, hit five balls, and then went and sat in the Titleist trailer for forty-five minutes. "I'm waiting for it to calm down," he told Titleist rep Bill Young. "You may be here until next year," Young answered . . .
- Dudley Hart stood on the practice tee hitting balls, closing his eyes after each shot, tapping his feet together, and saying, "There's no place like home, there's no place like home . . ."
- Payne Stewart finished playing Monday afternoon and said, "If it blows like this all week, the winning score will be 290" (10 over par) . . .
- When Tiger Woods asked one of the members when the weather

might warm up, the man shook his head and said, "You never know. Last year, summer fell on a Tuesday . . ."

Okay, so this was the British Open and it felt like a British Open. In recent years, there hadn't been very much British Open weather at the Open. A year earlier, Troon had been practically balmy the last three days, and Lytham in '96 had been dry and dusty. Turnberry in '94 had been so calm the last two days that the late, great Dave Marr, glancing at all the scores in the 60s on Saturday, had wondered "Is this Tucson or Turnberry?" Only at St. Andrews in 1995 had there been any consistently cold, tough-to-play-in weather.

Clearly, no one was going to confuse Birkdale with the Bob Hope.

No one was happier to see the wind and all the grim faces than Bruce Edwards. "This is what he plays best in," he said. "The more it blows, the better I like it."

The "he" in Edwards's life for most of twenty-five years had been Tom Watson. Edwards had started caddying for him in the summer of 1973 at the age of nineteen and, except for a three-year separation during which Edwards had worked for Greg Norman, they had been together ever since.

"I still remember the day Tom hired me like it was yesterday," Edwards said, pulling a cap tight over his dark hair in the wind. "It was in St. Louis. The temperature was at least 100 degrees and I had worked for several guys during the summer. I was sitting outside the clubhouse on Tuesday, hoping to find a bag for the week, when I saw this guy walking by carrying a green McGregor golf bag. A buddy of mine said, 'Hey, that's Tom Watson. I don't think he's got anybody. Why don't you go talk to him?'"

Edwards vaguely remembered Watson's name. "I remembered he had been on the leader board in Hawaii in February," he said. "I was watching at home on a Saturday and I saw this guy make three bombs. He could really putt."

Figuring he had nothing to lose, Edwards approached Watson, introduced himself, and said he was taking a year off to caddy before going to college and was looking for work. Watson was twenty-three, in his second year on tour. He had just returned from a two-week respite from the tour to marry Linda Rubin, his school sweetheart, and go on his honeymoon. "Okay, we'll try it," he told Edwards, handing over the bag. "Let's get to work."

For the next four hours, they worked — on the driving range. "All I did was go for more balls and more ice," Edwards said. "I remember thinking, this guy will do anything to make himself a better player."

Edwards's instinct about Watson was, of course, completely correct, and a business relationship and a friendship were born. Edwards had told his parents, both graduates of the University of Pennsylvania, that he wanted to take a year off before college to caddy, but he never did get around to pursuing his education. He had been bitten by the tour bug at the age of fourteen. In those days, many clubs that hosted PGA Tour events insisted that their own caddies work the event rather than tour caddies. Edwards worked during the summer at Weathersfield Country Club, which at the time hosted the Greater Hartford Open. In 1968 he was rewarded for a summer of hard work by getting to caddy for Dick Lotz in the GHO. "He made $1,200 for the week and paid me $60," Edwards said. "I still have the check framed at home."

Edwards loved the work, loved being inside the ropes, loved being part of the competition. He caddied in the GHO throughout high school and became friends with Lotz. When he graduated from a Connecticut prep school, Lotz helped him find work that summer. He had been with several different players — including David Graham, who wrote him a check for $100 after his first week and said, "You're much too nice a kid to be doing this" — before he met Watson.

Watson rose quickly as a player, and in 1975 he began winning major titles: the British Open that year, the Masters and the British in '77, the British in '80, the Masters in '81. By then, he was the best player in the world. Edwards loved every minute of it and was making a good living. But he had one frustration: Watson had won five majors; he hadn't been with him for any.

During the 1970s, neither the Masters nor the U.S. Open allowed tour caddies to work their events. When Watson led the Open in both 1974 and 1975, Edwards was outside the ropes on Sunday watching his man go down to defeat. "It really hurt," he said. "I felt helpless."

Tour caddies were allowed to work the British Open in those days, but few did because, unlike today, players didn't pick up expenses when their caddies traveled overseas. Edwards was home when Watson won at

Carnoustie in 1975, having decided at the last minute not to go because a friend he was going to make the trip with had passport problems and canceled. A year later he made the trip only to watch Watson begin the tournament with a triple bogey and miss the cut by one. A year later, he decided not to put himself through the torture — and expense — of the trip. That was the year Watson beat Nicklaus at Turnberry.

Watson's caddy that year was Alfie Fyles, a Scotsman, just as in 1975. Edwards knew that Watson was going to continue to use Fyles in the British from that point on. "Years later, Linda told me that she was the one who insisted on keeping Alfie, that she thought he was a good luck charm."

There was certainly no arguing with that logic since Watson and Fyles won the tournament five times. By 1982 Edwards was beginning to wonder if he was ever going to win a major, just as Watson was wondering if he would ever win the U.S. Open, the title he wanted most. It was that year at Pebble Beach that Watson converted The Chip at 17 on Sunday and made his famous "I told you" point at Edwards after calling his shot.

Of course Watson still had to play the par-five 18th at Pebble Beach with a one-shot lead. He hit two shots to get into position on the fairway and then hit a nine-iron that he caught a little bit thin, 18 feet above the hole. As he handed the nine-iron back to Edwards, Watson said, "Just like Byron says, 'Hit it thin to win,'" remembering one of the many homilies passed down to him from his mentor, Byron Nelson. There was no doubting the fact that thin to 18 feet above the hole was a lot better than fat and in the bunker.

Edwards still remembers how relieved and overjoyed he felt when Watson's last putt hit the hole at 18 and dropped for a birdie and a two-shot victory.

"What I remember about that putt," he said, laughing, "is that it was really moving when it hit the hole."

Watson's memory is the same. "It was moving too fast," he said.

When it dropped, the missed chances at the other majors didn't matter to Edwards anymore. He had been with Watson for the victory that meant the most to both of them, and he could live on that memory — if he had to — forever. "That doesn't mean I wouldn't love another," he said. "And if I could choose one, it would be the British."

Edwards had returned to the British in 1988 after Fyles had become too ill to continue caddying. A year later, he almost won the tournament, but not with Watson. Greg Norman had first approached him at the end of 1987 about working for him, and Edwards had said thanks, but no thanks. He loved working for Watson and, what's more, Watson had just ended a three-year victory drought by winning the inaugural Tour Championship.

But 1988 was a struggle for Watson, and 1989 started off worse. Norman had brought the question up again, and Edwards had continued to turn him down. By early 1989 Watson had told him that if another opportunity came along, he should take it. He was playing less golf because of his family and was no longer close to being the dominant player he had once been. Edwards finally decided to make the jump at the Memorial in 1989. Watson missed the cut by a shot and, for one of the few times in his life, didn't appear upset about it. He told Edwards he was withdrawing from the Colonial the next week and going home for a while. Edwards went to see Norman that day.

"Tom understood completely," Edwards said. "He knew it was hard for me but it was business. Norman was the biggest star in the game at the time. I'd heard all the stories about how tough he could be on caddies, but I really thought with my experience I could handle that. The person who was upset about the whole thing was Linda. She felt betrayed because they had always treated me like a member of the family. I told her I hoped someday she would understand."

Two months after joining Norman, Edwards was with him when he shot 63 on the final day at Troon to make it into a playoff with Mark Calcavecchia and Wayne Grady. Norman birdied the first two holes of the four-hole playoff, meaning that he had played 20 holes in 10 under par that day. At the third playoff hole, the par-three 17th, Norman wanted to hit four-iron. Edwards thought five, but remembered that Norman had hit four earlier that day. He said nothing. Norman hit it over the green and made a bogey, the beginning of his demise.

"A lot of people have questioned Greg for hitting driver on the next hole [18]," Edwards said. "In hindsight, maybe that was a mistake, because he hit in the bunker. The shot I kick myself for is the one at 17. It was 193 to the front and he was all pumped up. I should have told him five."

Whether Norman would have listened is another issue, but Edwards blames himself for not saying anything. After driving the ball in the bunker at 18, Norman ended up making an X, hitting his third shot out-of-bounds while Calcavecchia birdied the hole to win. "It was a bitter pill," Edwards said. "Because he played so well for 20 holes. I still remember walking up 18 during regulation play and the place was going crazy, thinking to myself, so this is what I missed all those years with Tom. Now I'm getting to feel it. But in the end, the feeling was empty."

Edwards enjoyed his first eighteen months working for Norman. He enjoyed the travel, the private planes, the feeling that he was with a rock star. Norman was the opposite of Watson when it came to glitz and glamour — he loved it. Watson just wanted to play golf and go home to Kansas City.

The beginning of the end, from Edwards's point of view, came a year after Troon, when the Open was at St. Andrews. Norman and Nick Faldo were tied for the lead after 36 holes and were paired together during the third round. Faldo shot 67; Norman shot 76. That day is remembered as a turning point for both men, the day Faldo stared Norman down, going on to the second of his three British Open titles the next day.

"We're walking down the 17th hole that day and Greg turns to me and says, 'Well, Bruce, I guess sometimes it's better to be lucky than good,'" Edwards remembered. "I was stunned. Nick had kicked his butt that day and he says that. I just looked at him and said, 'Greg, all I want to do is caddy for someone who plays with heart.'"

He still remembers the look Norman gave him at that moment. Things weren't the same after that. By the summer of 1992, the two were barely speaking to one another, even on the golf course. "I became a 'yes-caddy' the last six months," Edwards said. "I didn't want to say anything to set him off, so I just said what I thought he wanted to hear. I hated that. With Tom, I said what I thought, and when I was wrong, I was wrong, but I didn't worry about it because Tom never tried to blame me if he didn't play well."

The end came in Milwaukee. Edwards knew it was just a matter of time until Norman fired him, so he decided to beat him to the punch, telling him he was quitting. He called Watson that night. "You calling to wish me a happy birthday or to ask for your job back?" Watson asked.

"Both," Edwards answered.

John Daly. Nothing comes easy,
but he never stopped trying in 1998.

(© *Golf Magazine*/Fred Vuich)

Brad Faxon. A long, long year for
a good, good guy. (©*Golf Magazine/*
Sam Greenwood)

Scott McCarron. Life, he has figured
out. Now if he could just figure out
the greens at Augusta a little better…
(© *Golf Magazine*/Sam Greenwood)

Jay Haas. Could be the NPNTHWAM:
Nicest Player Never To Have Won
A Major. (© *Golf Magazine*/Sam Greenwood)

Dudley Hart. The next step is playing
late on Sunday. (© *Golf Magazine/*
Sam Greenwood)

Steve Stricker. Comeback player of the year. (© *Golf Magazine*/Fred Vuich)

Vijay Singh. Comeback player of the
decade. (© *Golf Magazine*/Fred Vuich)

Tiger Woods. He'll be back, very soon.

(© *Golf Magazine*/Fred Vuich)

They had been back together ever since. Watson had played very good golf during that time, but the yips had kept him from winning very often. Even in 1996, when he had won at Memorial, he had still struggled over short putts. The most frustrating tournament had been — naturally — the British in 1994, when Watson led with 11 holes to play before back-to-back three-putt double bogeys knocked him from contention. "That one was hard to take," Edwards said. "Because he really thought he was going to win. He kept saying, 'I'm firing on all cylinders,' and he was. But the putter wouldn't hold up on Sunday."

Watson calls that one of his three most devastating losses, the others being the U.S. Open at Winged Foot in 1974, when he led for three rounds before shooting 79 on Sunday, and the PGA in 1978, when he had a four-shot lead with nine holes to play and lost to John Mahaffey in a playoff. Since the PGA is the one major he has never won, that loss stands out. Turnberry hurt, though, because a sixth British Open title at the age of forty-four would have been sweet, especially at the site of his stirring victory over Nicklaus seventeen years earlier.

Now Watson and Edwards were back at Birkdale, a place where Watson had hit one of his most memorable shots, a two-iron to the 18th green on the final day in 1983 that had clinched his fifth Open victory. Birkdale didn't feel quite the same, though, because Linda Watson wasn't there. As painful as the divorce was for the Watsons, it was also difficult for their friends — and that included Edwards. "It really was like a family for all those years," he said. "It's great that Tom has [15-year-old] Michael with him, because he really enjoys that. But it can't feel the same as it used to feel."

Even so, Edwards was exactly where he wanted to be, working with the player he wanted to be working with. "I remember when I first went to work for Greg, people came up to me and said, 'That bag doesn't look right on you,'" he said. "Now I'm back on the bag that always felt right on me."

The Birkdale weather was keeping players inside a lot more than normal for practice days, but sooner or later, they all made their way to the range because the range is where golfers go when they are at a golf tournament. At Birkdale, the range was almost a half-mile from the club-house, so players and caddies were shuttled back and forth in golf carts. On Wednesday morning, Tiger Woods arrived on the range with tears in his eyes, sneezing up a storm. "All the dust kicking up in the wind," he said. "I'm allergic. I just need to take some more Claritin and I'll be fine."

Woods had already been in Europe for nine days. He and Mark O'Meara had flown to Ireland a week early to play golf and do some fishing before making the short trip from there to England. Woods had brought a girlfriend with him, and the English tabloids were having a field day trying to find out more about her. Of course the great thing about the tabs was that they didn't need to learn that much. What they didn't actually know, they just claimed to know.

None of it seemed to bother Woods, not the wind or the allergies or the tabs. "I feel really good," he said, sitting in the Titleist van near the range. "My game is as good as it's been all year. If the wind blows, that's fine with me. I think I can handle it."

When he arrived at the British Open in 1997, Woods had already won four times on the U.S. Tour that year, one of those wins coming at the Masters. Now, he had won once in the U.S. in 1998 (Atlanta) and had finished eighth at the Masters and eighteenth at the U.S. Open. He talked so often about the fact that he was a better player than he had been in 1997 that some players were joking about it.

"If he gets much better," someone said after the Open, "he could be on the Nike Tour in another couple of years."

That was, of course, a gross exaggeration. Woods was fourth on the money list, first in stroke average, and still formidable week in and week out. He was absolutely right when he said he had improved — in most ways. His temperament was 100 percent better, he was much more consistent week in and week out, and he had improved about 200 percent in dealing with the media and was a completely different person around the locker room. A year earlier, if you had done an anonymous survey in the locker room and asked the question "Do you like Tiger Woods?," the vote probably would have been split three ways: one-third of the players would have said yes; one-third would have said no, and one-third would have said he didn't hang around enough for them to know him one way or the other. Now the same question probably would produce a

2–1 or 3–1 result in Woods's favor. And the dissents would be more on the grounds of jealousy than anything else.

What Woods hadn't done as well as when he first arrived on tour was make putts. When he first turned pro at the end of 1996, Woods was almost like the twelve-year-old kid everyone sees playing on weekends who never misses a putt. He was fearless, completely confident. As Michael Campbell might put it, he was ten feet tall and bulletproof. That was no longer the case. Now, as with most mortals, the putting came and went. Some days, it was awful. He was especially vulnerable on those four-to-eight-footers — "throw-up-zoners," the pros called them. Those were the putts, as Lee Janzen might tell you, that won or lost majors. Woods wasn't making them with any consistency. And so, he wasn't winning majors. In fact, he had not seriously contended in a major since his victory at Augusta.

His pal O'Meara had finished thirty-third in the U.S. Open, disappointing after the Masters, but not devastating. He also had arrived at Birkdale brimming with confidence. O'Meara had always thought his best chance to win a major would be in the British Open because of his relatively low ball flight. Beyond that, he loved Birkdale. He had won a European tour event on the course in 1987 and had been in the last group with eventual winner Ian Baker-Finch on Sunday in 1991. "As soon as I saw we were going back to Birkdale in '98, I remember thinking, that might be my chance," he said. "Coming in already having the Masters just made me feel that much more relaxed. I knew I could play the golf course and, having played in the wind and rain in Ireland for a week, the weather wasn't going to bother me."

Just as at the Masters, Woods and O'Meara had shared a private plane en route to the tournament. On the trip to Augusta, Woods had been thinking the trophy would come home with them on the plane. This time, both of them had that thought.

For Justin Leonard, returning to the Open had a bittersweet feel. Flying over from Dallas, he knew the week was going to bring back a lot of memories from the previous year. He was actually looking forward to going through all the pretournament rituals of being the champion, because they would remind him of just how big a deal it had been to win at Troon. The hardest part, though, would come first: giving back the Claret Jug.

Leonard had a copy — about two-thirds the size of the original — sitting at home. He had paid $6,000 to have it made by the London jeweler the R & A had licensed to produce the copies. Golf is the only sport where the players who win major titles have to pay to have their trophies made. Both Opens and the PGA present their champions with a duplicate of the actual trophy and let them keep it for a year. During that year, they have the option of paying to have a copy made. The copy must always be smaller than the original (apparently, so there is no chance of the copy being mistaken for the original), and the player pays for it himself.

The players don't really mind — after all, winning a major is worth hundreds of thousands of dollars (or more) to them — but Davis Love had carried on a running battle with the PGA of America about the size of his duplicate trophy. The Wanamaker Trophy, which goes to the PGA champion, is huge. The duplicates are much smaller. Love wanted to make one that was the same size, promising to make certain there were markings so that there would be no doubt which one belonged to the PGA. The PGA said no.

Leonard had no problem with his copy, but turning over the duplicate was a little bit like saying goodbye to a friend. He packed it up carefully for his trip to Birkdale and, as soon as he arrived on Sunday, he took it to the R & A office to hand it over. "I sort of hated doing it," he said. "It was like an ending to something that had been very nice."

Of course, the solution would be to win it again the following Sunday. That, however, would be easier said than done. Since World War II four players had won back-to-back British Opens: Peter Thomson (three in a row, '54 to '56), Arnold Palmer ('61–'62), Lee Trevino ('71–'72), and Tom Watson ('82–'83). That was an impressive group. It wasn't that Leonard didn't think he could win. It was just that he knew the odds were against him.

The oddsmakers made Woods the favorite in spite of his "disappointing" year at 8 to 1. A host of players were rated just behind him: Duval, Leonard, O'Meara, Love, Couples, Colin Montgomerie, Lee Janzen. On Wednesday, one of the local papers surveyed the caddies to see who they picked. Their favorite: O'Meara.

24

Nae Wind and Nae Rain

It was about 10:30 on Thursday morning when the first threesome of the British Open arrived at the 18th green. One look at the scoreboard told you all you needed to know about the weather. Two of the players, Fredrik Jacobson of Sweden and Gary Evans, a U.K. homeboy, were under par: Jacobson at minus three, Evans at minus one. Two of the first three in red figures? What had happened to the wind? Where had the rain gone?

Both had, for the most part, taken the day off. It was a bright, breezy day, but the winds were nonexistent compared to the four days leading up to the championship. Everyone took one look at the golf course and said, "This is a day to go low."

And go low they did, led by Tiger Woods and John Huston, who both shot 65. If Woods was looking for an omen, he might have looked directly at Huston. The leader after 18 holes in Augusta fifteen months earlier had been John Huston. But Woods and Huston weren't alone in red numbers by any means. Low scores were everywhere: Fred Couples, who had become engaged to Thais Bren shortly after the U.S. Open, shot 66. So did 1994 champion Nick Price as did Loren Roberts. Davis Love, back miseries seemingly behind him, had 67, and so did

Vijay Singh. Before the day was over, no fewer than twenty-seven players had broken par 70.

"It was a day when you needed to make something happen," said Woods, leading a major for the first time since Augusta '97.

Those who didn't make something happen were shaking their heads about it. Mark O'Meara wasn't panicked but wasn't thrilled with his 72, and Tom Watson was disappointed to shoot 73. "We need the wind to blow tomorrow," Bruce Edwards said. "Bring everybody back a little."

David Duval shot 70, as did Steve Stricker. It took Stricker almost nine holes to relax after he was paired with Watson and Seve Ballesteros. Playing with Watson wasn't a problem for Stricker. He had played with him before and enjoyed his company. But Ballesteros was a different story. Like Watson, he was a legend of the game, the winner of five major titles — three British Opens and two Masters — and was regarded as perhaps the best player ever when it came to finding ways to remove himself from seemingly impossible predicaments.

To a younger player, Ballesteros was an intimidating figure. Even though his game had deserted him several years earlier — he hadn't been a serious factor in any of the majors during the '90s — he was still, at forty-one, one of the most popular players in the world, especially in Europe, where his heroics as a Ryder Cup player and, most recently, as the Ryder Cup captain in 1997, made him ultrapopular.

Stricker had no idea what to expect from Ballesteros. He knew all about his mercurial personality. When he wanted to be, Ballesteros could be utterly charming. On Tuesday, he walked onto the range and, spotting Michael Watson, he stopped dead in his tracks. "Michael," he said, "is that really you?"

He looked at Tom Watson and said, "What happened to," and then he put his hand waist-high to indicate he couldn't believe how much Michael had grown. He and Watson then had a warm chat, legend to legend.

Stricker got none of that. Instead, he got a quick hello on the first tee and then not a single word of conversation for the next hour. "I wasn't intimidated," he said, "but when we were on the first tee I'm thinking, five-time champion Tom Watson, three-time champion Seve Ballesteros, and *who?* Then Seve doesn't say a word to me on the front nine. I felt like I had to prove that I could play. It was silly, but it happened."

Stricker managed to bounce back after his nervous start, and he even made an impression — finally — on Ballesteros. As they walked off the 13th tee, Ballesteros turned to him and said, "So, I hear you are having a baby soon." From that point on, Stricker felt as if he belonged in the threesome.

At least Stricker had some rationale for his start. Phil Mickelson was completely baffled by his. He had a good pairing — Frank Nobilo and Costantino Rocca — but drew a brutally late tee time (2:55). The British Open likes to spread name players out throughout the day because the BBC is on the air for so many hours (9 A.M. to 7 P.M. the first two days) that it can't bunch the stars the way tournaments in the U.S. do. That's why the Watson-Ballesteros-Stricker group could draw a 7:55 tee time. It is also why a group that included Ernie Els, Tom Lehman, and 1999 European Ryder Cup captain Mark James could go off at 2:45 followed by Mickelson's group.

Mickelson managed to par the first hole, but then hit his second shot into one of Birkdale's famous sandhills at number two and made double bogey. Then, at three, he hit his tee shot into a pot bunker, hit a great recovery, chipped to 12 feet, and missed the par putt. "Gosh darn it," he said. (Really, that's what he said.)

At the par-three fourth, he hooked his tee shot left of the green and let out a disgusted "aaargh," as the ball kept going farther and farther off line. Still polite to a fault, he made a point of complimenting Nobilo and Rocca on their tee shots, both within 10 feet of the hole. Then he got up and down himself to save par. That seemed to get the round turned around in the right direction. He made a remarkable birdie at the par-four sixth hole, another converted par five that, on a windy day, was virtually unreachable in two. On this day, with the wind nothing more than a breeze, Mickelson hit a 236-yard two-iron to 25 feet and made the birdie.

Leaving the green, Jim McKay murmured, "Thanks BBC." He and Mickelson had been watching the TV feed earlier in the day and had noticed that the putt broke more right-to-left than it appeared to break when you were on the green — one of the advantages of wall-to-wall TV coverage. Mickelson made another birdie at the seventh to get back to one over par for the round, but the rest of the day was spent scrambling to save pars. When it was over, it was a good news, bad news story: the good news was that 71 was still in contention after a horrible start. The bad news was that it was behind forty-one other players because the conditions had been so mild.

Two other players who shot 71 had similarly mixed emotions. Payne Stewart had arrived in England, after spending time in Ireland with Woods and O'Meara, hoping he had one more big tournament left in him before the summer was over. His U.S. Open loss had been salved by the highly complimentary nature of 99 percent of the stories written about him in the days and weeks following Olympic. Everyone had talked about his grace in defeat and the class he had shown in the wake of it.

He had flown on a private plane that night with D. A. Weibring, Justin Leonard, and his mom to Quincy, Illinois, because the three of them were scheduled to play the next day in a charity pro-am that Weibring put together each year. They had landed well after midnight and checked into the hotel. Stewart had given his mother a kiss and said, "Mom, I'm going out. Don't wait up."

Bee Stewart understood. She didn't wait up.

Stewart's only disappointment that week had come on Tuesday when he saw the pairings for the Western Open. For Thursday and Friday he was paired with Frank Nobilo and Lee Janzen. Any other week of his golfing career, Stewart would have had no problem being paired with Janzen, someone he liked and considered a friend. But not this week. "It was completely unfair to Payne," Janzen said later. "He could have been leading the tournament by ten shots and I could have missed the cut and no one would have given him credit or said he had gotten redemption. It was an absolute no-win situation."

Unlike the majors, the PGA Tour does its pairings by computer. The players are divided into three groups: 'A' players are major champions and players who have won a tournament in the past three years, 'B' players are top 125 players without a recent victory, and 'C' players are everyone else — Q-Schoolers, Nike Tour graduates, nonexempt players. The computer pairs A's with A's, B's with B's, and C's with C's. Then the name players are spread out to accommodate TV.

On occasion, though, humans intervene. That is what had happened in this case. Because the Western was being played earlier than normal and was following the Open, it did not have as strong a field as it normally did. Jon Brendle, the tour's advance man that week and therefore the man responsible for the pairings, was besieged both by the tournament people and by CBS. They needed one really sexy pairing for their cablecast on Thursday and Friday. At that moment, there was no sexier pairing than Janzen-Stewart.

The Tour insisted publicly that it was just a fluke spit out by the computer. Janzen and Stewart knew better. Stewart is a close friend of Brendle's. In fact, Brendle lives in a house adjacent to Stewart's in Orlando that is owned by Stewart. When Stewart confronted him about what had happened, Brendle had to tell him the truth. "I'm sorry, Payne, I really am, but they insisted that they had to have a TV pairing."

Stewart looked at him for a minute. "Well, you know what I'm going to do in that case?"

For a moment Brendle panicked. The last thing he needed was to have Stewart get into a snit and withdraw. "Now Payne . . ." he said.

"I'm going to raise your rent!" Stewart said.

Brendle laughed and breathed a sigh of relief.

Stewart played, made the cut, and didn't raise Brendle's rent. "I like his wife too much," he said.

Like Mickelson, he knew that 71 at the British Open didn't knock him out of the golf tournament by any means. But he knew that he had let a day for low scoring go by without scoring low.

Tom Lehman knew all about the weather conditions, but he also knew that his 71 was almost a miracle given the fact that he wasn't certain he could play until less than thirty minutes prior to his tee time. When he went to the range to warm up, he left word with tournament officials to have first alternate Malcolm MacKenzie ready to take his place if he couldn't play.

Lehman had a back injury. The injury had not occurred swinging a golf club but attempting a handstand. He had been with his wife and children at an amusement park on Tuesday night and had tried to do a handstand. He had failed. As a result, the 1996 British Open champion didn't know if he could bend over to place his ball on a tee Thursday afternoon — much less play competitive golf. That he played and shot a respectable score might have been Thursday's most surprising story.

The least surprising story of the day came as the final groups were making their way up the 18th at 9 o'clock that evening. It was the weather report for Friday. "Windy and overcast," it said. "Rain possible. There may be sunny spells in the afternoon."

You had to love those sunny spells.

The next morning, at a few minutes before 7 o'clock, Ivor Robson walked onto the first tee. He would be there for the next nine and a half hours.

For twenty-four years, Robson has been the starter for the Open Championship. During that time, he has introduced every single group that has teed off, without exception. He has never taken a break to eat, to get some tea, or to go to the bathroom. Not once.

"The starter should introduce each group," he said. "If you miss one, that sends a message that it somehow isn't as important as the others. I try to treat each group with equal importance regardless of who is playing."

Robson, a former golf pro with white hair and a ready smile, was working for a golf shaft company in 1975. On occasion, the company supplied starters for the European Tour. Keith McKenzie of the R & A heard him at a tournament early in 1975 and asked if he would like to be the starter for the Open. Subsequently, Robson was hired full-time by the European Tour, and his cheery, singsong Scottish brogue is familiar to anyone who follows golf in Europe.

His introductions are simple but upbeat. "On the tee," he will say, voice rising, "Tiger Woods!" Every name, whether it is Tiger Woods or Willie Wood, comes out with an exclamation point implied. The suggestion is that Robson thinks this is an important person and those listening and watching should think so too.

On tour, Robson never misses an introduction either, but that is different from the Open because there the players tee off in a morning wave and an afternoon wave, meaning he is on the tee for just under two hours. At the Open, where they go off one tee beginning at 7:15 A.M. and ending at 4:15 P.M. the first two days, it is quite a vigil. "I love the game and I love the people who play the game," he said. "I don't consider it a burden but an honor."

Clearly, Robson means it. To prepare for the first two days of the Open he eats a light dinner, usually just a sandwich, and then has one glass of mineral water for breakfast. That's it. No coffee or tea, and he has nothing brought to him while he is on the tee. He buys a new blazer for the Open each year and will not wear rain gear on the tee regardless of the weather. "It would be undignified," he said.

Robson is unfailingly polite to each player as he comes on the tee, wishing him luck, pointing out scorecards, hole location sheets, and snacks. In Europe, each group is referred to as a "game." So Robson will get the attention of the crowd simply by saying, "Ladies and gentlemen, this is game number one." And then, "On the tee . . ." The only times he will vary his introduction is in the presence of royalty (when Prince Andrew showed up to walk the course on Saturday, he began by saying, "Your Royal Highness, ladies and gentlemen") and when the defending champion is on the tee. Throughout 1998, Robson said, "On the tee, the defending Open champion, Justin Leonard!" Past champions get no such mention nor do those who have won other majors. Just the current champion.

As polite as Robson is, there have been players through the years he has come to know well enough that an occasional barb might be exchanged. One of his favorites was an American named Rick Hartmann, who often teased him about the quality of his blazers. Once, when Hartmann was digging at him about a blazer, he added when he was finished, "Well, Ivor, are we ready to go?"

Peering down the fairway at a group no more than 150 yards from the tee, Robson said, "The way you're playing, Rick, you could go right now."

On most occasions, Robson is much more serious than that. His respect for all the players is apparent. In 1995, when Arnold Palmer walked onto the tee at St. Andrews on Friday to play what would be his last round in the British Open, Robson shook his hand and said, "Mr. Palmer, I just want you to know it's been an honor to watch you all these years."

Friday, as predicted, was cold and windy, the wind blowing off the Irish Sea with rain squalls coming in behind it. Robson stood on the first tee waiting for the first group looking as comfortable as someone sitting in front of a roaring fire. "I have the greatest job in the world," he said. "Every day, I come out here and I can't wait to get started."

It was time to start. At that hour, the crowd was sparse. But if you closed your eyes and just listened to Robson, you might have thought he was introducing the final pairing on Sunday afternoon. "Ladies and gentlemen, this is game number one. On the tee . . . Thomas Levet!"

That was one down and 155 to go.

The morning players on Friday caught a break. They only had to play in bad weather. The afternoon players had to play in weather that bordered on ridiculous. On Thursday there were twenty-seven rounds in the 60s. On Friday, there were seven, and five of those were 69s.

The most amazing round of the day, perhaps of the decade, was turned in by a seventeen-year-old British amateur named Justin Rose. Rose shot 66. That was an astounding round for anybody on the planet under the conditions, but absolutely otherworldly for a seventeen-year-old kid who four days earlier had been playing in the qualifier at Hillside. No amateur had ever scored lower than 66 in a British Open. In 1953, Frank Stranahan had shot a 66 and finished tied for second. In 1996, Tiger Woods had shot a 66 and finished tied for twenty-second. "His 66 is a lot more impressive than mine," Woods said. "Mine was in dead calm conditions. His was in brutal conditions."

As Woods could attest, having shot 73.

Rose's round made him an instant celebrity in Great Britain. One of the difficulties of being a star athlete in the British Isles is that the country is absolutely sports crazed. (During British Open week the national *swimming* championships were also on live, every day, every event. In the U.S. the nationals *might* get thirty minutes on tape delay.) Anyone who shows any kind of potential becomes a household name overnight. Nick Faldo had dealt with this since the day in 1977 when, as a twenty-year-old, he had beaten Tom Watson in a Ryder Cup match. Colin Montgomerie still battled the pressures. Lee Westwood, the up-and-coming young Brit, would get it next.

And now came Justin Rose.

The tabloids went wild, coming up with all sorts of quotes from allegedly love-struck teenage girls about Justin's "dreamy eyes" and "sweet smile" and "lovely walk." The BBC, which would never stoop to such things, opened its Saturday telecast with a huge vase of roses on the set. Faldo and Westwood were no place close to the leaders. Montgomerie had made another early exit by missing the cut. But Justin Rose was in second place after 36 holes and, oh my, was this ever a big story.

The leader, in case you missed it, was Brian Watts. Yes, that Brian Watts.

Brian Watts was thirty-two years old and made his living playing golf in Japan. His parents were English and German; he was born in Canada, lived there six months, grew up in Dallas, and then attended Oklahoma State. He had flunked his one shot at the PGA Tour in 1991 and had gone to Japan. There, he had become a star, winning eleven times and making a very nice living. He hadn't even attempted to requalify for the U.S. Tour since 1992. Now, though, he had a one-year-old son and the commute from Tokyo to Oklahoma City was beginning to wear on him. He wanted to come home and play the PGA Tour. Winning the British Open would be a first step.

"I'm not even thinking about winning the tournament right now," he said on Friday. "I'm just glad to have played well for two rounds. My practice rounds were so bad I never thought I'd have a chance."

Actually, no one really thought he had a chance. Watts had played in five previous British Opens, qualifying because of his status on the Japanese Tour. He had never finished higher than fortieth. He was quiet and polite, so polite that he ended each of his press conferences by saying to the media, "Thanks very much for your time." As he walked the golf course, he acknowledged every cheer or word of encouragement as if he owed the person a thank-you note.

There was only one strange moment in his far-flung résumé. Earlier in the year, playing in a tournament in Indonesia, he had decided that he wanted to miss the cut. This sort of thing happens to some players on occasion. They are tired from too many weeks away from home, their game isn't very good, and they decide that playing the weekend is going to be a waste of time and energy even if they manage to make the cut. So they will miss a five-footer here, a bunker shot there, and go home. It is an infrequent occurrence, but it does happen, especially overseas when a player may be homesick — as Watts admitted he often was — and in need of some time at home.

Watts, however, wasn't the least bit subtle in his pursuit of an exit visa. He blatantly mishit a couple of shots, depositing two balls in the Pacific Ocean on one hole. He had no trouble missing the cut, but the

Japanese Tour was outraged enough by his behavior to fine him and suspend him from the Japan Open, one of its major events, later in the year. What was baffling about the whole thing was that Watts had no prior history of misbehaving in any way.

Naturally, the question came up after Watts's 69 in the second round. It was the only question he didn't handle well. "I made a mistake and it is two and a half months behind us and I'm just going to leave it at that."

Admitting he made a mistake was fine, but explaining what led to the mistake would have been better.

But that didn't really matter at this juncture in Watts's life. He was leading the British Open by one shot over Rose, Tiger Woods, and Nick Price. There weren't five people within a hundred miles of Birkdale who thought that either Watts or Rose had any chance of actually winning the event. They were good Friday stories and they would be paired together in the final group on Saturday. Only a handful of people expected either one of them to still be a factor by nightfall.

The rest of the leader board — in addition to Woods and Price — was filled with people who had to be given serious consideration. Davis Love was three shots behind Watts at even-par 140, as were Fred Couples, Jim Furyk, and Jesper Parnevik, who was becoming the British Open's Tom Lehman — always in contention but never in the winner's circle. One other name at 140 raised eyebrows: Mark O'Meara.

Just as he had done at the Masters, O'Meara had bounced back from a disappointing two-over-par first round to shoot two under par the second and sneak up the leader board. What made O'Meara's second round at Birkdale more notable was that he did it under such difficult conditions. His 72 on opening day had left him in a tie for sixtieth place. By the time everyone made it to the clubhouse on Friday, O'Meara was tied for sixth. He had gone from seven shots behind Woods and Huston to three shots behind Watts. He was just where he wanted to be.

"The way I like to play any golf tournament is to make sure I'm in good position on Saturday and Sunday," O'Meara said. "Leading isn't important to me. Being around the lead is."

He was now around the lead. So were Lee Janzen and David Duval, one shot farther back and seemingly poised to make a move on the weekend. Janzen had come back from his opening 72 to shoot 69. Just as he had done at the U.S. Open, he had moved into contention with a good Friday round. Duval, who had been like a yo-yo at the Open (75–68–75–68), was going the consistent route, shooting 70–71. Brad Faxon and Payne Stewart were also in contention at 141, and Steve Stricker was one shot behind them, at 142. When Tom Watson shook Stricker's hand on Friday afternoon, he pointed to the scoreboard next to the 18th and said, "You're right in this thing. Go out and do some damage on the weekend."

Stricker appreciated the pep talk. It was all Watson had left to give. He had gotten the windy day that Edwards wanted but hadn't taken advantage, shooting 76. There would be no sixth British Open title this year.

There wouldn't be a first one for Colin Montgomerie either. For the fifth time in nine years, the local hero missed the cut. Montgomerie knew he was in some trouble after his 73 on Thursday, and he made matters worse by beginning his day Friday with back-to-back bogeys. When he managed to get his ball on the third green in regulation, albeit a good 40 feet from the pin, one of the ever-optimistic BBC commentators said, "Well, maybe that's a start."

Not quite. Montgomerie had his woe-is-me look firmly in place all day. The cheers and encouraging shouts that had been so loud at the start of the day Thursday were little more than a whimper by the time he reached the back nine Friday. It was almost 7 o'clock by the time he came trudging up the 18th (there had been a thirty-minute weather delay, almost unheard of at the Open, because of a threat of lightning in the area), and he was eight over par for the two days, having reached that number by eagling the easy par-five, downwind 17th.

Until 1996, the R & A had used the 10-shot rule for the cut the way the Masters and the U.S. Open do, but had abandoned it after 103 players made the cut at St. Andrews in 1995. Paying that many players a minimum of 5,000 pounds caused some rethinking. Now, 70 and ties made the cut. As Montgomerie walked up 18, the number was six over, but there was some faint hope among the locals that it might go to seven over before the day was done. After all, when Justin Leonard had trooped in sopping wet and disgusted at six over early in the afternoon, he had mournfully declared his British Open over, had all but publicly apologized for playing so poorly, and had gone off to check on flights home. When someone suggested that the wind and rain might move the cut as high as six over and save him, he shook his head. "No way it will go that high," he said. "I'm done."

He was now preparing to play Saturday.

The only way Montgomerie would have any chance to join him would be to birdie the 18th. He hit a good second shot to 18 feet behind the hole. As he walked on the green, the reaction from the crowd was muted. It was as if he had personally let everyone down by not playing better. Montgomerie understood. He calmly rolled his birdie putt dead center, acknowledged the roar with a grim smile, and headed into the scorer's trailer to see if he had any chance.

When he emerged fifteen minutes later, the look on his face told the story. "One too many, I believe," he said. "I had four three-putts and that did me in. It was thirty-three putts yesterday and thirty-seven to-day. That's ten too many."

Why, Colin, why, the media wanted to know. Why does this always happen to you at the Open Championship? "If I knew the answer, I'd have worked it out by now," he said. "I went south about six years ago in this event and I've never really gotten it back. When I made the putt at 18, I had a bit of hope. My caddy told me on the 17th tee I needed to finish 3–3 to have a chance. Well, I did, and I feel good about that. But it's going to be too little too late."

He spoke calmly, almost without emotion. He had done this before. Occasionally in the past he had gotten snappish when the media asked about his failures, but through the years he had come to understand that they had a job to do too. But the pain he felt was apparent. As he turned to leave, several writers thanked him for his time and patience. "No trouble," he said, smiling. As he walked away, the smile disappeared and the head went down. He would have to wait another twelve months to try the Open again.

If Montgomerie was the most disappointed cut misser, John Daly was the most frustrated. Daly always liked coming back to the British Open. One of the few fond memories he had of his "dry, not sober" period was his victory in 1995 at St. Andrews. He liked the idea of being able to use a driver most of the time, and his strength gave him an advantage over most players in the wind.

But he arrived with a struggling golf game. After his opening 69 at Olympic, he had shot 75–75–78, the last round lowlighted by a five-putt eight on the short par-four seventh hole. On Saturday, after not using it for two days, he had put his driver back in the bag and used it to drive the seventh green. Sunday had been a different story.

Daly was paired with Payne Stewart and Bernhard Langer on Thursday and Friday. He shot 73 on Thursday, but on Friday he played better in the wind and arrived on the 18th tee just two over par for the day and five over for the tournament. A par would put him comfortably inside the cut and, as it turned out, a bogey would have been good enough too. One of the things Daly has always prided himself on is the fact that he rarely misses cuts at majors. He has never missed a cut at the Masters and he had never missed one at the British.

But he drove his ball poorly at 18 and found a fairway bunker. Trying too hard to slash the ball onto the green from there, he knocked his ball into a second bunker, still a good 150 yards from the green. By now, he was starting to panic about the cut. He went into the second bunker and tried to gouge the ball out and get it close to the green, instead of playing a wedge onto the fairway from where he could try to get up and down for bogey. He gouged once and the ball stayed in. Twice. Three times. Four times. Finally, on his fifth attempt, he got it to a greenside bunker. Now he was a dead man. He blasted onto the green and two-putted for a 10.

This was not Bay Hill. There was nothing funny to Daly about making 10 on the 36th hole of the British Open to cost himself the cut. He was almost in tears coming off the green. In the scorer's cabin, Stewart, who was keeping Daly's scorecard, asked him what he had made on 18.

"I don't know," Daly said. "I think it was a nine."

Stewart didn't want to be cruel, but he felt responsible to make sure Daly's score was right. If it wasn't, all the TV replays — and there would be plenty of them — would certainly confirm any error. "John, are you sure?" he asked.

Daly looked up at Stewart. "No, I'm not sure. I don't know. What difference does it make? Put down whatever you want."

"I can't do that," Stewart said. "I have to put down the correct score."

He asked Langer to come over and, together, they pieced together the 18th hole. Langer remembered five swings in the second bunker. They went from there and eventually got to 10.

"Fine, then it was a ten," Daly said.

He signed his card for 78, got up, and stormed from the trailer. He was mad at Stewart, mad at himself, mad at the world. Daly hadn't ducked the media all year, but this was too much. He walked right past reporters waiting outside, tossed a ball angrily against the wall of the clubhouse, and headed for the car park, looking for the quickest exit he could find.

On the surface, it looked like another John Daly meltdown and, to some degree, it was. But the old Daly would have quit trying at some point. Daly didn't. In fact, much of his anger stemmed from the fact that he had given it everything he had and still failed. He was angry about his golf, not about his life. He was upset with Stewart because he couldn't understand why Stewart had to be so damn exact about what he had made on 18. What difference did it make? He was going to miss the cut, regardless. Stewart was just doing what he was supposed to: protect the field. He had a responsibility to see to it that Daly's score was accurate, whether he was leading the tournament or last. Daly knew that, but at that moment it seemed to him that Stewart was twisting the knife he had just put into his own back. He wasn't, but it felt that way.

The good news was that 99 percent of Daly's anger stemmed from the fact that he cared about the way he played. Not long ago, that would not have been the case.

25

Hurricane Birkdale

Everyone was happy to see Friday end, most notably the eighty-one players who had made the cut. Fred Couples was delighted to get away with 74 on Friday, leaving him just three shots behind Watts. "With any luck, the worst is behind us now," he said. "I'm going back to the house and eat there. I don't want to be out for a single extra minute tonight. I'm cold, I'm wet, I'm miserable, and I'm starving."

He spoke for almost the entire field. They would all go home, take hot showers or baths, and start fresh in the morning. Those who were staying at the Prince of Wales Hotel in downtown Southport were raving about it. They were raving angrily about the price: 220 pounds (about $350) a night, minimum stay eight nights. If you missed the cut and wanted to go home, that was fine. You still paid for eight nights. They were also raving, positively, about the quality of the showers: "Best I've ever had over here," Steve Stricker said. "The room is small, but the shower's great."

A lot of players would probably spend almost as much time in the shower as in bed on Friday night.

They all woke up Saturday morning, looked out the window, and groaned. It wasn't raining, but the wind was howling, even early in the morning, even downtown away from the water. "A couple of days during the practice rounds when it was really windy at the golf course, there wasn't much wind in town," Dudley Hart said. "When I saw the wind in town, I knew we were in trouble."

Hart wasn't complaining. He had finally ended his streak of four straight missed cuts in majors (even though statistically his WD [withdrawal] at Olympic didn't count as a missed cut) by shooting five over par the first two days. He had come back after a mediocre 73 to shoot 72 in the wind and rain the second day — all this in an event he hadn't figured to play in. He had sent in an entry form in May even though he wasn't exempt on the off-chance that something might happen to make him exempt.

Something did: a 63 on the last day of the Western Open, which jumped him to third place in the tournament and, unbeknownst to him, into fifth place on what is known as the Little Money List. This is a money list consisting of five selected events beginning with the Players Championship in March and ending in 1998 at the Western. It exists so that a player who gets on a hot streak before the British who isn't already exempt can become exempt. The top five players on the list who are not already in the tournament get in. Hart had no idea that the $149,600 he made at the Western had put him into fifth place on the little list until the next day when his agent, David Yates, told him during an outing that he thought he had made himself exempt for the British.

Hart was shocked. He asked Yates if he was sure. Yates wasn't, but said he would make a phone call and find out for sure. Soon after he reported back: Hart was in the British.

There wasn't any question that he was going, but Hart knew this wasn't going to make things easy for Suzanne Wills, his fiancée. Their wedding was scheduled for July 25 — six days after the British ended. That was one reason why he had never considered going over to qualify if he wasn't exempt. Being away for twelve days would have been just too much. As it was, Hart flew over on Sunday night after spending the entire week beforehand helping with wedding plans. He paid for the eight nights at the Prince of Wales even though he might be staying for as little as five nights. "Everything else was booked like you might expect," he said. "Still, it was the British Open. It was a no-brainer. I was going no matter what."

Making the cut was a bonus that made the trip worthwhile. But when

Hart got to the golf course and began warming up on Saturday, he started to wonder if perhaps he wouldn't have been better off if he had been on a nice warm airplane. If anything, the wind was worse than it had been on Monday during the final day of qualifying. Lee Westwood, the young British star whose 78 was not one of the worst scores of the day, described the day best when someone asked if he had ever played in wind any worse: "Sure I have," he said, "in Iceland."

On Thursday there had been twenty-seven rounds in the 60s. On Friday there had been six. On Saturday there were zero. Two players shot 70 — Costantino Rocca and Katsuyoshi Tomori. Both played early because they had made the cut on the number: six over par. By the end of the day they had gone from tied for sixty-fifth to tied for tenth by shooting even par. In all, twenty-three of the eighty-one players failed to break 80. It wasn't as if these were stiffs either. Among those shooting in the 80s were Phil Mickelson (85), Hart (85), Justin Leonard (82), Nick Price (82 — including 45 on the back nine), Lee Janzen (80), Steve Stricker (80), and Michael Campbell (80). Tiger Woods shot 77 and only dropped from a tie for third to a tie for sixth.

"Hardest day I've ever seen at a major," said Fred Couples, who was disgusted nonetheless with his 78 because it bounced him from three shots back to eight shots back even though he was still tied for sixteenth place. "It just got to a point where all you could do was laugh at yourself."

Justin Leonard came off the golf course laughing after his 82. "What else is there to do after a day like that?" he said. "I'm going to take this score back to my home club, post it, and see if I can get my handicap up a little bit." He smiled. "The good part is that now I can go back to my room, watch the leaders this afternoon, and laugh my head off."

None of the leaders was laughing very much while Leonard watched them. Every hole was torment. It didn't matter if it was downwind, upwind, or sidewind. No one knew where the ball was going. It was all guesswork. Stricker began the day with high hopes, especially when he birdied the first hole. Birdies were like gold on a day like this, and starting out with one was a huge bonus. The second hole, a 421-yard par-four, was playing dead into the wind. Both Stricker and playing partner John Huston hit woods on their second shots. Stricker ended up three-putting for bogey. He made another bogey at the fifth, but at one over for the day was still hanging in contention (three over for the tournament) standing on the sixth tee.

By that point, the wind was so bad that the teenage girl assigned to carry the walking scoreboard couldn't hold it up in the wind. The raker (at the British each group is assigned someone whose sole job is to rake bunkers. This speeds play since the caddies don't have to stop and do it) was doing his best to help her, but the wind was so vicious that Stricker and Huston were afraid she might get hurt.

Stricker asked Michael Tate, the R & A official assigned to the group, if anything could be done. Tate shrugged helplessly and said he would make sure to keep an eye on her. "How much do you guys get paid for this?" Stricker asked the girl.

"One hundred pounds for the week, plus room and board," she said.

"Not enough," Stricker said.

Play was already backed up by the sixth tee because the wind was causing players to back off shots, especially on the green, where they were terrified the ball might move while they were addressing it. The sixth was the converted par-five that on the best of days was difficult to reach. It was now playing dead into the wind and the tee was as far back as possible. The hole was listed as 480 yards, but it was playing more like 550.

Stricker hit a good drive and was about 40 yards behind the huge bunker that comes out from the right side of the fairway. He was 242 yards from the hole, and the only way he had any chance of reaching the green was to crush a driver off the fairway. Pros can pull this shot off, but even for them, it isn't easy. Stricker decided to try. But in his attempt to muscle up, he came over the ball just enough that he hit a low line drive that screamed into the face of the bunker and dropped right into the sand.

He had absolutely no play except to chip out sideways, which he did. He was now lying three and still more than 220 yards from the hole. He hit a third driver, hooked it left into a sandhill, then blasted his fifth shot over the green. Only a gorgeous chip to one foot saved his triple-bogey seven. He walked off the green with the look of a man who has just seen his own ghost.

"It was just a stupid shot trying to hit the driver on my second shot," he said later. "I should have hit a four-iron, laid it up, and tried to get up and down from the fairway. If I didn't and I made five, it wouldn't have hurt me because how many guys made four there today? [Twenty-one, and no one made three]. Until then, I was going along fine. That just knocked me backward. I never recovered."

Before the day was over, the sixth hole had become the focal point for the most controversial story of the round. At the time, it hardly seemed to matter. By the end of the round, that had changed. Mark O'Meara and Fred Couples, reprising their pairing on the last day of the Masters, were playing together in the fourth-to-last group. Both began the day horribly with a double-bogey six on the first hole. "If I play that hole a hundred times and play it a hundred different ways, I'll still make double," Couples said later.

Frustrated, already cold, and wondering what the heck the deal was with playing in a hurricane, Couples went from bad to worse, bogeying three of the next four holes. That brought him to the sixth tee already five over par for the day. "Good solid bogey golf," he said. O'Meara had settled down after the first, but he had just bogeyed the fifth, so he was three over. Of course, with everyone getting blown over par, this was a day where holding on and finishing two or three over wouldn't be a bad round at all.

Both players were a long way from thinking about that playing the sixth. Like Stricker, O'Meara hit a good drive and, like Stricker, he still had a million miles (actually 232 yards to the front) left, dead into the wind. Like Stricker, he made the mistake of trying to crush a driver instead of laying up and playing for bogey. His shot wasn't as bad as Stricker's, but he pushed it. It took off right, got stuck in the wind, and then began blowing right — way right — onto one of the sandhills and into the thick gorse adjacent to the green.

Trouble. Couples had done just the opposite, hooking his second shot into a sandhill left. "I was so far left I couldn't even see the green," he said. "So I had no idea what was going on over there."

Couples and Joe LaCava went over to find and identify his ball while O'Meara and his caddy, Jerry Higginbotham, walked over to search for his ball. The sandhills at Birkdale are thick, tangled masses of high grass and (naturally) sand and weeds and gorse and roots. Walking through them is like trying to walk through waist-high mud. If a ball goes into one, it can easily be lost unless someone is standing almost on top of the spot where the ball disappears. When O'Meara and Higginbotham arrived, they found several dozen spectators and marshals hunting through the sandhill for the ball.

"Oh boy," O'Meara said. "This doesn't look good."

He and Higginbotham joined the search. They looked for just under four minutes, the rules allowing up to five minutes before the ball was declared lost. By now, Couples had hit his third shot onto the green and had come over his sandhill to see what was going on. "It looked like a Keystone Cops thing with all those people," he said.

But still no ball. Finally, O'Meara gave up. He took another ball from Higginbotham and started walking back down the fairway to hit what would now be his fourth shot. "At that point I figured, even if we found it, I was going to have to take an unplayable," he said. "I just thought I'd save some time and start back." He was disgusted with himself. Absolute best-case scenario he was looking at double bogey. He knew he should not have hit the driver. A Stricker-like seven was certainly not out of the question. What would almost undoubtedly be out of the question walking off the hole at five or six over par for the day would be winning the golf tournament.

And then, just as with Lee Janzen at Olympic, fate intervened.

O'Meara was about 75 yards from the green when he heard shouting. He was feeling angry and embarrassed, especially because Davis Love and Thomas Bjorn, playing in the next group, were standing in the fairway, waiting for him. More shouting. O'Meara turned and saw Higginbotham waving his arms frantically. Then he heard Higginbotham's voice: "We found it." O'Meara paused, then kept walking. "My first thought was that I had abandoned the search when I started back, so the ball was lost. But everyone kept shouting so I turned and went back."

Once upon a time, O'Meara starting back would have meant he had abandoned the search. But the rule was changed in the 1970s. Now the ball is not considered abandoned until the player actually plays another ball.

What had happened was this: Since there was still time left, Higginbotham and several spectators continued searching for the ball. Higginbotham, who was just about as depressed by the turn of events as O'Meara, heard someone say, "Hey, I found one." He looked up and saw a spectator holding a ball in his hands. He ran over to him and, sure enough, it was O'Meara's Top Flite Strata 2. Higginbotham immediately called Michael Lunt, the R & A official walking with the group, over to tell him the ball had been found within the five-minute period. Then he began shouting to get O'Meara's attention.

Lunt looked at his watch. There were still about thirty seconds left in the five-minute search period, but O'Meara was now at least 150 yards down the fairway. Even if he were Michael Johnson it was unlikely he could make it back to where they were all standing in thirty seconds, especially in golf spikes and a windbreaker. As a slightly overweight forty-one-year-old he had absolutely no chance.

But there was no doubt that this was O'Meara's ball, Higginbotham had confirmed that. Did that qualify as "finding and identifying" within five minutes? Lunt didn't think so, but he was loath to make a snap judgment, especially with Higginbotham screaming in his ear that the ball had been found and identified and all was well.

Here again, luck came into play. On the last two days at the British Open, the final ten groups are sent out not only with a rules official — in this case Lunt — but with an "observer," a second golf official who is there in case there are questions on rules or if the rules official needs backup in any way. Only the U.S. Open also does this.

The observer with O'Meara and Couples just happened to be Reed McKenzie of the USGA. If it had been anyone else, Lunt almost surely would have ruled that since O'Meara could not return to identify his ball within five minutes it was lost — regardless of what Higginbotham said.

But McKenzie had been involved with the Janzen ruling at Olympic. There, the USGA had decided that once it was confirmed that it was his ball that had fallen out of the tree, he should be given "reasonable" time to return to the ball and identify it, even if he did not do so within five minutes. This very question had been debated back and forth by the USGA and the R & A for two years, and although no official decision was on the books, the USGA had decided that day at Olympic that this was the way to go. McKenzie informed Lunt about the Janzen decision and suggested that he call in David Rickman, the R & A rules secretary, for confirmation.

O'Meara, still not sure what was going on, was now walking back up the fairway. He wasn't sure if the ball had been found in time either, and one of his thoughts was about how embarrassed he was going to be if he had to walk back again and hit a new ball if in fact his original was declared lost. "By then, there was a part of me saying, 'Let's just get out of here,'" he said later. "I mean Davis and Thomas are standing there waiting, Freddie's been standing there waiting. Jeez, it was crazy."

It got crazier. Lunt got on his walkie-talkie and asked for Rickman to come out to the sixth hole. The entire rules cavalry raced to the rescue. Rickman, who had the final word on the matter in an R & A–run event, showed up. So did Mike Shea from the PGA Tour, who was the roving rules official in the area. Almost everyone in the British Isles was consulted. "I think at one point they called the White House," O'Meara said later.

Maybe they could have asked Prince Andrew, who by now was only a hole behind, walking with Justin Rose and Brian Watts.

O'Meara stood and listened for a while, then he went and got into Shea's cart and chatted with Shea. "I'll do whatever they want me to do," he kept saying. "Just tell me what to do and I'll do it."

By now Love and Bjorn had been waved through, and Tiger Woods and Nick Price were in the fairway waiting. Couples, wondering if this miserable day was ever going to end, stood by the side of the green, leaning on his putter. Finally, Rickman decided to go along with McKenzie and the USGA: since the ball had been found in less than five minutes, O'Meara was entitled to the opportunity to return to the ball and identify it even if more than five minutes had passed before his arrival.

Thus, after twenty minutes, the ball was ruled as found. The next question was what should be done with the ball. The spectator had picked it up. He took O'Meara and the cavalry to the spot where he said he had found it in the sandhill. Twice, O'Meara attempted to drop the ball as close to the spot as possible. There was no way to drop a ball onto a hill that steep and have it stop anyplace close by. Twice, it rolled closer to the hole. Now O'Meara had to be allowed to place the ball. The only place flat enough to place the ball and not have it move was next to the sandhill. As a result, instead of trying to slash out of the sandhill, O'Meara was left with a relatively easy chip. Easy, in the sense that he could get the ball on the green. He chipped to about 10 feet, missed the putt, but left the green with a bogey-five that bordered on miraculous.

"I have never in my life been happier to make bogey," he said. "It was like Watergate out there for a while."

Couples and LaCava, seeing O'Meara dropping and then placing his ball, assumed that he had taken an unplayable lie and a one-stroke penalty. Walking off the green, LaCava asked O'Meara if he thought about dropping farther back from the green to have a better angle. "I couldn't," O'Meara said. "It was a free drop."

"A free drop?" Couples and LaCava both said, stunned.

O'Meara explained what had happened with the spectator. Couples and LaCava were amazed. O'Meara had made five on the hole. "To say that was wild," Couples said, "doesn't begin to do justice to it."

O'Meara was still four over par for the day, but that was a lot better than he had thought he was going to be. His rescue from the sixth seemed to rejuvenate him. Over the next six holes he went on a par binge — which on this day was about the same as making six straight birdies — and then birdied 13 and 17 on the way home. He didn't make another bogey the rest of the day. It was as if he understood that someone or something had conspired to give him a giant break and he was obliged to take advantage of it. After playing the first six holes four over par, he played the last 12 in two under, almost impossible to do under the conditions.

But he did it, and the result was he finished the day in a tie for second place with Jim Furyk and Jesper Parnevik, just two shots behind the leader. The surprise was the name of the leader: Brian Watts. Both Watts and Justin Rose had played far better than anyone had expected. Each admitted that he had been helped by the pairing. Watts felt comfortable being with Rose because he was almost invisible to 90 percent of the fans, who were enraptured with everything Rose was doing.

"Everything he did, they were ecstatic," said Watts, who had played in the U.S. Open as an amateur in 1986. "It was actually quite fun to watch. He was happy and they were happy. But could you guys [the media] please print that I'm fifty percent English? Maybe I'll get some of that support tomorrow."

Watts shot 73, Rose 75. By shooting 73, Watts actually extended his lead from one shot to two shots. Rose dropped back, but only to fifth place. It was two shots back from Rose to the group tied for sixth: Tiger Woods, John Huston, Thomas Bjorn, and Brad Faxon.

Faxon was annoyed with himself for bogeying the 18th hole, but overall thrilled to find himself in contention going into the last round.

After his disastrous third round at Olympic, he had been concerned about how he would play under the gun in difficult weather at Birkdale. The answer was just fine. Ordinarily, 74 wouldn't have been a great score but this was no ordinary day.

When all was said and done, there were fourteen players within seven shots of Watts, which, assuming another difficult day on Sunday, meant they were within striking distance. No one really expected Katsuyoshi Tomori to shoot lights out on Sunday and come from six strokes back to win, but if David Duval or Davis Love were to rally from six shots back (Duval) or seven (Love), no one would be stunned.

No one was more aggravated with his day than Couples (78), except perhaps Lee Janzen, who had gone to bed Friday convinced he was ready to make a move after a Friday 69 and then watched the tournament blow up in his face with an 80 on Saturday. "You aren't going to win very many golf tournaments if you can't make two-foot putts," he said, stalking angrily to his car.

Everyone had trouble putting in the wind. Golfers can make adjustments for wind on their long shots, but since standing still over a putt is something that takes complete concentration, the wind makes extra trouble. "The putting was the worst of it, no doubt about it," Woods said. "I never felt comfortable all day. The good news for me is that it's over."

The fact that he was still only five shots back after a 77 was good news too.

Of course, the big story in Great Britain that day continued to be Rose. He hadn't gone away, as all the experts had predicted, and he would now play the last round of the British Open three groups from the end, paired with John Huston. Watts and Parnevik would be in the last group with Furyk and O'Meara in front of them.

The most jam-packed press conference of the day was Rose's. Someone asked him what he would do if he somehow won the Open Championship at seventeen. He smiled the smile that had all the girls swooning and said, "Well, I guess I'd have to win the Masters at eighteen, the U.S. Open at nineteen, and the U.S. PGA at twenty."

Everyone has different goals on the last day of a major championship. For a select few, winning is the one and only goal. For some, finishing high enough to ensure a spot in the event twelve months hence (at the British Open it is top fifteen and ties) is the motivator. For others, it is just to play well the last day and leave with your dignity intact.

For Dudley Hart at the 1998 British Open, it was catching his plane.

Hart had tried as hard as he could on Saturday, but the result had been an embarrassing 85. He hadn't played all that poorly on the front nine — three over — but the back nine had been the worst nine holes of his life. He made three double bogeys and one triple bogey, and when he walked off 18, he had shot 47 for nine holes, something he couldn't remember doing since about the age of twelve. "And I birdied the 17th!" he said.

Amazingly, he wasn't alone in last place. Phil Mickelson, who also shot 85, and Andrew Oldcorn were tied with him at 20 over par. But since Hart was the last of those three to finish on Saturday, he would be the first player off the tee on Sunday morning. It occurred to him that there might be a bright spot in that tee time: he could get home that day. A phone call to Delta confirmed his thinking: there was an 11:50 flight from Manchester to Atlanta. From there, he could easily connect home to West Palm Beach.

The problem was getting to the airport in time. He was scheduled to tee off at 8:00. Since there were eighty-one players in the field, he was technically a single. Getting around the golf course in two and a half hours by himself, then racing into a car for the forty-five-minute trip (under optimum conditions) to the airport was doable. There was one small problem: unlike on the PGA Tour, where players in singles are given the option to play alone or with a marker, the majors believe no one should play alone and almost always assign a marker.

Hart didn't want company.

"I went to this guy from the R & A and asked him if I could play as a single. He said, 'Well, we prefer that you play with a marker.' I said I understood that, but I really wanted to catch this plane because I was getting married in a week and it would help me a lot if I could play as a single. He said, 'We prefer that you play with a marker.' So finally I said,

'Why don't you just say you're going to *make* me play with a marker whether I like it or not and get it over with?'"

Fortunately for Hart, his marker was a young assistant pro from Birkdale who was more than willing to help out by hitting and running all day. Hart didn't rush his shots; he tried on every one of them. But he wasted no time in between shots. The only semicomical scene of the day came at the ninth hole. Hart was moving so quickly that the golf course crew hadn't gotten around to putting the flagstick in when he arrived. His rules official told him it would take only a couple of minutes to get someone out there. Not to worry, said Hart. He looked at his hole location chart and played to the green sans flagstick. "It was the only time in four days I hit that green in regulation," he said, laughing. "My only par there all week."

Playing in nonstop rain, he shot 80, a five-shot improvement from Saturday. He signed his card at 10:15 and was in a courtesy car with his caddy, Craig Cimarolli, ten minutes later. They walked into Manchester Airport at 11:15. There was just one problem: the courtesy car driver had dropped them off at the wrong terminal. Carrying their luggage — including Hart's clubs — they set off on a dead sprint for the international terminal, a good half-mile away. Had it been the next day when the airport was jammed with people heading home from the tournament, they would have had no chance. But this was Sunday and the airport was almost empty. They ran to the business class check-in, tossed their bags onto the conveyor belt, and convinced the woman behind the counter to call the gate to let them know they were on their way. They arrived at the gate at 11:48.

"Made it easy," Hart said. "Two minutes to spare."

For the week, Hart made $9,200, which meant he had just about broke even. That was just fine with him.

If Hart was sanguine about shooting 80 on Sunday, Fred Couples was anything but, after finishing with an 81. After his 66 on Thursday, even after his 74 on Friday, he had honestly believed he could win the tournament. Saturday's 78 had pretty much ended that, and he played Sunday's round in a terrible frame of mind, at least in part because he started out double-bogeying the first hole for a second straight day.

"I hit an iron off the tee because I didn't want to end up in the rough again and get off to a bad start like Saturday," he said. "I hit it just a little right, but it's just off the fairway, so it's no problem. Then I get down there and it's in a bush. I'm like, this can't be happening. So, I make double from there. After that I went south."

He paused in the retelling and looked at LaCava. "I think you'd agree, wouldn't you, Joey, that if I had made par on that hole, things would have been different that day, right?"

"Right," LaCava said. "You would have shot 79."

When Couples finished off his 81, he was so angry he almost couldn't see. Anyone who thinks Couples is laid-back about his golf should have been standing outside the scorer's trailer when Couples exited. The only words he said to anyone were directed at LaCava: "Find Thais and let's get the hell out of here."

LaCava went off to find Thais Bren. Couples cleaned out his locker, tipped the kids in the locker room, and walked to the area outside the locker room where the courtesy cars pulled up for the players, expecting to see LaCava, Bren, and a getaway car. He saw none of those things. Still furious, he sat down on a bench to wait. He was in an area that was off-limits to the general public but not to those holding clubhouse badges.

A couple of fans approached, thinking themselves lucky because, here, sitting all alone as if waiting to chat with them, was Fred Couples.

"Hey Freddy!" they chirped happily. "Did you have a good day out there?"

"I had an awful day!" Couples responded. "And it isn't getting any better right now!"

Later, he felt bad for snapping, but he was so angry at that moment he was a little relieved he hadn't been any worse. As it turned out, Bren had gone to the ladies room after walking 18 holes in the rain and La-Cava couldn't exactly barge in there and say, "Hurry up, Thais, Fred wants to get out of here." Bren and LaCava did show up before Couples snapped at anybody else. It was not the ending — or the exit — that Couples had hoped for.

The rain continued all morning. Phil Mickelson added a 78 to the 85 he had shot on Saturday and came off the course looking shell-shocked. He had been in the twosome directly behind Hart and had finished forty-five minutes later, or about ten minutes before Hart pulled into Manchester Airport. He three-putted the 18th hole for a double-bogey six, then admitted that it had been hard for him to stay interested after the first few holes on Saturday. Mickelson knew that the right thing to do was keep on grinding and try to finish as high as possible but, especially in the miserable conditions, he just couldn't keep his game face on. He would play in Holland the next week for a six-figure guarantee. Life was still good — except, it seemed, during majors.

By the time Mickelson and Andrew Oldcorn walked up the 18th, the rain was slackening. The wind was still in evidence but nothing like Saturday. The huge grandstands were already starting to fill up, especially in the unreserved sections. Each group that arrived at 18 for the rest of the day would receive a warm ovation. One of the warmest came shortly after Mickelson had headed off for Holland. It was for Robert Giles, a twenty-eight-year-old Englishman who was a club pro in Ireland. Giles was the only player in the field who had gone through both local and final qualifying and made the cut in the Open championship.

The crowd knew who he was and how far he had come from his local in Killarney through Hesketh to here, to making the best walk in golf onto the 72nd green at the Open championship. The rain and the wind didn't matter at that moment, nor did the fact that Giles was going to shoot 78 and finish in seventy-eighth place. Seventy-eighth out of 4,000 wasn't bad at all, especially with a standing ovation at the end. Giles finished with a flourish, rolling in a 10-foot putt for par, then doffed his cap to another ovation.

"The whole thing was fantastic," he said a few minutes later. "For me, just getting to Hesketh was an achievement. To play here and play all 72 holes, that's a memory I'll carry with me forever."

Giles had made it to the finals of the European Q-School a year earlier. He was convinced that his experience during the week would help him when he went back to Q-School in the fall. "It costs 850 pounds to enter," he said. "The money I made here [5,600 pounds] will help a lot."

The ovation for Justin Leonard walking up 18 was also long and lingering. In a sense, it was a send-off, a thank-you from the crowd, which appreciated not only the way Leonard had played in winning the title a year earlier, but the way he had handled himself as the Open champion.

The week had been disappointing for Leonard, but he had bounced back to shoot 69 on Sunday, the first round of golf in a major that had left him smiling since the last day at Augusta. He had worked hard on Sunday, almost feeling obligated to try and shoot one good round before he went home.

"I enjoyed a lot of things about this week, about being here as the champion," he said when it was over. "But today makes me feel better about the whole thing. I can smile about it a little bit sooner. Yesterday was almost like a blooper tape the whole day. The ovation coming up 18 was nice."

He smiled. "Of course, last year at 18, I was a little more nervous. I'd like to get that feeling back sometime soon."

By the time those who would be nervous walking up 18 in the early evening began teeing off, the day had become almost pleasant — pleasant being a relative word. The skies were still gray, with scudding clouds overhead, and the wind was noticeable if not howling. But it wasn't raining. Mark O'Meara walked onto the first tee shortly before 2:30 wearing a short-sleeved black shirt and no sweater or jacket. He had the look of a man who believed he had a mission to accomplish and that doing it was just a matter of staying as loose and calm as possible.

"I knew," he said later, "that I had put myself in great position to win the golf tournament with the way I played the last 12 holes on Saturday."

Jim Furyk, his playing partner, had a similar feeling. Furyk had parred the last 12 holes on Saturday to shoot the same 72 that O'Meara had shot and, remembering how close he had come at the Masters after trailing by four going into Sunday, he was also full of confidence.

The first three holes proved to be a harbinger for what was to come the rest of the day. Furyk hit the ball with remarkable precision. At number one, he had an 18-foot putt for birdie — and just missed. At number two, it was 12 feet for birdie — this time he burned the edge. At number three, he was 14 feet away — the putt slid left at the last instant. Furyk is one of the best putters on the PGA Tour. Much of his success and consistency is based on his ability to save strokes on the greens. If he had made all three of those putts, it would not have been surprising to him or anyone else who knows his game. But he missed them all.

Watching Furyk, O'Meara understood what he was feeling. "I've been exactly where he was that day," he said. "Before Augusta I had gone out on Sundays in several majors thinking I had a chance to win and all of a sudden I can't make a putt. I'm a good putter. Jim is a very good putter. But making putts on Sunday in a major championship is a lot different than making them on Sunday anyplace else."

Now O'Meara had the confidence he had earned by winning at Augusta. His first three holes were a lot different than Furyk's. He had to make a five-footer for par at number one — and did. He was 35 feet from the hole at number two and made a routine two-putt. He did the same thing at the third. At no time did he have a serious chance to make a birdie. Furyk had three. But they walked onto the fourth tee dead even. Then O'Meara hit his seven-iron to 12 feet and swished the putt. Furyk pulled his seven-iron left of the green and made bogey. Two-shot swing. Momentum to O'Meara.

The game was on all over the golf course. Tiger Woods, having almost gotten himself into serious trouble at the first hole, was hanging in contention, scrambling to make pars and still lurking just three shots back as he made the turn. On number one, Woods missed a short par putt and, frustrated, appeared to push the ball into the hole from a foot away. If he had pushed it, he would have incurred a two-stroke penalty. R & A officials decided to look at the TV tape in the BBC truck. When they did, they ruled that Woods hadn't pushed the ball, that it had left his putter before it dropped into the hole. Others who saw the tape, including the BBC's Peter Alliss, thought the ruling might have been generous.

The weather worsened as the players approached the turn. Furyk finally made a birdie, hitting a wedge to within six feet at the fifth, and O'Meara bogeyed the sixth, again pushing his second shot right off the green into a sandhill. This time finding the ball was no problem, but he had almost no chance to get the ball onto the green much less close to the hole. He and Furyk were again even for the day, two over for the tournament. They still trailed Brian Watts by two shots after Watts had birdied the fifth to balance a bogey at the fourth. Everyone kept waiting for him to go away. He didn't seem interested in that idea.

Standing on the elevated seventh tee, Furyk and O'Meara watched Justin Rose and John Huston putt out 177 yards away. To the left of the green they could see the scoreboard. Rose had slipped to five over par, and it was pretty clear he wasn't going to be a factor when the winner was decided. But that hadn't lessened Justin-mania one bit. Next to the scores, in the area normally reserved for messages, the kids working the scoreboard had put up letters that read: "Go Justin Rose. You Are Doing England Proud."

Rose's gallery was as huge on Sunday as it had been on Saturday and again included Prince Andrew. Security for royalty in Great Britain is a quirkish thing. When reporters had attempted to walk on the first tee on Saturday, they were told that the gate at the back of the tee had been secured because of the presence of the prince. They were instructed, as an alternative, to walk around the tee to the right, up a hill, then down a hill, where they would end up near the front of the tee. One reporter followed the roundabout route, came down the hill, and found a spot. Glancing at the person standing next to him, he noticed a familiar face: Prince Andrew.

"Bit windy," said the prince, proving that royalty is fully capable of understatement.

Rose hadn't let Andrew or anybody else down on Saturday, and he was doing his best to hang in on Sunday. A press conference to announce that he was turning pro had already been scheduled for Monday. When he and Huston holed out on seven, O'Meara launched his tee shot a good 20 yards over the green. From there he made bogey. Now, for the first time all day, Furyk was alone in second place behind Watts. O'Meara promptly responded by birdieing the eighth after his second shot, from the deep rough on the left, kicked over a bunker and bounced to within 18 feet. From there, he made the putt.

Everybody then parred the ninth and, with nine holes left, little had changed: Watts was still even par for the day and the championship; O'Meara and Furyk were two shots back. Parnevik had dropped one shot and was three back, and Woods, a couple of holes ahead, was four behind. No one else was making any sort of move.

The wind was little more than a whisper by this point but the rain was steady. On the ninth green, Jerry Higginbotham pulled out an umbrella and O'Meara's windbreaker and said, "We're really having fun now."

As it turned out, the fun was just beginning.

Brian Watts was performing a miracle. On the biggest day of his professional life, he was somehow keeping himself in the present, not thinking about what winning the tournament would mean to him or picturing himself holding the Claret Jug. He was playing steady, almost mistake-free golf, knowing that if he stayed at even par — just like at Olympic — he was going to have a great chance to win the golf tournament. The rain didn't bother him and, for that matter, he wouldn't have minded a bit if the wind had continued to howl. When it slackened, it meant his pursuers could attack the golf course.

And attack they did.

O'Meara started it with a birdie at 11. Then he and Furyk both birdied the 12th. For the first time all day, Watts didn't have the outright lead. He and O'Meara were both even, Furyk was one shot back. Up ahead, Woods made great saves for pars at 13 and 14, then birdied the 15th to creep to within three. Still, he appeared to be running out of holes.

Nerves were starting to fray. O'Meara hit perhaps his worst shot of the day at 13, pulling a three-iron into the left bunker from the middle of the fairway. He bogeyed the hole at almost the same moment that Watts, after a miserable tee shot way left of the green, was bogeying 12. Now it was a three-way tie at one over: Watts, O'Meara, and Furyk, with Woods only two back.

O'Meara was now officially angry with himself. He hadn't looked at the scoreboard all that often, but he knew exactly where he was. It was no knock on Watts or Furyk for him to think that he should emerge from that scrum on top, based on experience, past record, and his memories of Augusta. The bogey at 13, he told himself, was silly. There were five holes to play. He had won the Masters coming down the stretch; there was no reason he couldn't do it again here.

O'Meara had some time to give himself that pep talk because he and

Furyk had to wait briefly on the tee at the par-three 14th. The hole was playing 201 yards into the wind. O'Meara figured he would need every bit of a three-iron to get there. "I really laced it," he said later. The ball bore through the wind, bounced onto the green, and rolled to a halt three feet left of the pin. If his second shot at 13 had been his worst of the day, this was clearly his best. When he made the putt for birdie, he was back at even par and, for the first time in four days, in the lead by himself. At the Masters he hadn't led until the 72nd hole.

Furyk had to make a good up and down at 14 for par, and then he butchered — and bogeyed — the par-five 15th, driving his ball into the rough and never really recovering. O'Meara now led Watts by one and Furyk by two. Seconds later, he also led Woods by two. Trying desperately to birdie the par-five 17th because he knew he needed a birdie-birdie finish to have any chance, Woods knocked his third shot over the green. He had a 30-foot downhill chip for birdie, the kind he had often holed in those halcyon days of old (1997). Woods popped the chip up, and it rolled down the hill, gathering speed. If it had missed the hole, he would have had 10 feet coming back for par. But it didn't. It went straight into the middle of the cup and, for an instant, the good old days were back. There was Woods, pumping his fist, saying, "Come on!" while the crowd screamed.

He was still going to need a birdie at 18 and some help to have a chance. He got both. First, O'Meara hit his second poor iron shot of the back nine, a six-iron that he pulled left of the 16th green. With a down-hill lie he couldn't get any closer than 10 feet, and when he missed the par putt he was back to one over. Furyk had a putt of almost the same distance that would have tied him for the lead again, but, as had been the case all day, he couldn't get the ball to go in when it had to. He was still one shot back. Watts parred 15, leaving him tied with O'Meara, and then they were joined at that number by Woods, who drained a 25-foot birdie putt on 18. He had shot 66, birdieing three of the last four holes à la O'Meara at Augusta.

O'Meara was playing the par-five 17th at that moment. Standing in the fairway, he heard a roar come from 18 and wondered if it was Woods. A moment later, after he had hit his third shot onto the green, O'Meara looked up at the scoreboard and saw the answer to his question: Woods had birdied. He was in the clubhouse at one-over-par 281. O'Meara looked at his 18-foot birdie putt and couldn't help but smile. I'm going to do it to him again, he thought, remembering all those matches at home when they would often walk off 18 with Woods a few dollars ahead for the day and O'Meara would suggest they go to the putting green.

"Tiger can never resist," O'Meara said later. "And I always get back even or ahead before we're done."

Furyk actually had the more makable birdie putt, having put his third shot 10 feet from the pin. O'Meara checked the break in the putt, got over it, and for a split second actually found himself visualizing Woods sitting in the locker room thinking, please Mark don't do it to me again.

He did it to him again. "It was funny, because I just felt so confident over that putt," O'Meara said. "I just knew it was going to be just like home. I needed to make it, I was going to make it."

He was now back at even par. Furyk's only real chance was to also make birdie. But this wasn't his day. He missed one more time and walked grim-faced to the 18th tee, trailing by two. As Furyk and O'Meara were walking up the hill to the 18th tee, they heard an absolutely earth- and bone-shattering roar come from the green. They had no idea what it could be. The only other player still in contention — Watts — was playing 16. Later they heard what had happened: Justin Rose had holed a 45-foot wedge shot for birdie to finish the championship at two over par. The shot had been a near miracle: from high rough left of the green, over a bunker, and into the cup.

"I figured I had nothing to lose, so why not go for it," Rose said later.

Michael Bonallack, the chairman of the R & A, who has seen only forty Open championships, later called the crowd reaction the loudest roar he had ever heard at any golf tournament anywhere. The shot was Rose's last as an amateur. He didn't even wait until Monday to announce he was turning pro; he announced it in his postround press conference.

All O'Meara wanted to do now was hit one more fairway, one more green, and two-putt for par. He knew that Watts, playing behind him, still had 17 to play and would have a birdie chance there. But, like Lee Janzen at Olympic, he wanted to post even par and see if that would be good enough.

His three-wood found the fairway, his four-iron was 20 feet right of the flag. Shortly after 6 o'clock, O'Meara marched between the grandstands, enjoying golf's best walk but knowing he still had work to do. He could look left or right at the giant yellow scoreboards on either side of the green and know exactly where he stood. Watts had parred 16 and was playing 17 at one over par. Woods was in at that score. A par would close Woods out and force Watts to birdie to tie.

O'Meara is as good as anyone in the game at controlling his emotions when there is still work to be done. But the sight of the overflowing grandstands, the sun (which had broken through finally in the last hour) working its way westward over the clubhouse, and the notion that he might be on the verge of winning a second major in the same year, got to him just a little bit. It wasn't as if he broke down or even got misty-eyed. But when it came time to putt, his concentration wasn't what it normally is. The guy with the magic putting stroke put one of his worst strokes on one of his most important putts.

"Absolute de-cel," he said, meaning he had decelerated through the ball. A de-cel is almost always caused by nerves and almost always causes an ugly, short putt. That's what this was, stopping a good four to four and a half feet shy of the hole. O'Meara marked so that Furyk, who had missed the green, could finish. He had 10 feet for par. Just as he got over the ball another roar went up — this one from 17. Everyone knew it had to be Watts and he had to have made birdie. Steve DuPlantis, Furyk's caddy, who was just as frustrated as Furyk at that point, looked up when he heard the roar and said, "Quiet please." That was a little bit pointless, since the noise he was attempting to quiet was coming from 450 yards away.

Furyk made his par putt — finally — to shoot an even-par 70 and finish at two-over-par 282. That left it up to O'Meara. While Furyk was putting, O'Meara had given himself another talking-to, aggravated that he had hit such a poor first putt. But as he walked up to place his ball and line up his putt, he was amazed at how calm he felt. "For some reason, it occurred to me that making this putt wasn't life and death," he said. "Obviously, I wanted to make it, but I said to myself, 'If you miss this, you aren't going to die; just go through your routine and knock it in.'"

He then did exactly that. As he and Furyk shook hands, the scoreboard confirmed what everyone knew: Watts had made birdie at 17. If he birdied 18 — unlikely — he would win. If he parred, he and O'Meara would play off. If he bogeyed, O'Meara was the champion.

O'Meara and Furyk went into the trailer to sign their cards. The officials asked O'Meara where he wanted to watch Watts play 18 from. O'Meara knew that Alicia and his two children, Michelle and Shaun, were out by the 18th green. Unlike at Augusta, they had been allowed inside the ropes to watch O'Meara finish. "I'd like to go out to the green and sit with my family," he said. That was fine with the R & A. O'Meara walked back to the green, while Furyk headed in the direction of the locker room, stopping first to go through his birdies and bogeys with an R & A media official. He wore a pained look on his face, the look of a man who knows a great opportunity has slipped through his fingers.

When the R & A man was finished, he thanked Furyk for his patience and said, "Well, Jim, fourth place last year, joint [tied] fourth this year. You should feel quite proud."

Furyk almost smiled. "Right now I could not be more miserably angry with myself," he said. "I'm just absolutely furious."

He never raised his voice when he spoke, but the anger and the exhaustion were evident.

While O'Meara and Furyk were finishing their cards, Watts had driven his ball in the left rough. Returning to the green, O'Meara could see that he had what looked like a difficult second shot. He was right. "I had such a bad lie I wasn't even sure I'd be able to get a club on the ball," Watts said. He slashed at a six-iron, and the ball hopped into the front bunker, left of the green. When Watts got to it, he could see that he had again caught a poor lie. He was in the front of the bunker and to the left, so close to the bank that there was no way for him to stand with both feet in the bunker and get a swing. When O'Meara saw Watts setting up with one foot in the bunker and the other one out of it, fighting to hold his balance, he knew there was a chance he might not have to play another shot.

"He obviously had a difficult shot," he said. "My thought was, if he hit a good shot, he was going to be between six and eight feet from the hole. I told myself to expect him to hit a good shot and make the putt. I had to prepare myself mentally to go to a playoff. If that didn't happen, well, that was fine. But I had to be ready."

He came a lot closer to not playing off than he could possibly have bargained for. In golf's greatest theater, Brian Watts pulled off one of the most spectacular shots anyone had ever seen and almost hit a shot that would have gone into golf's pantheon in the same paragraph — perhaps sentence — as Sarazen's four-wood at Augusta, Watson's chip at Pebble Beach, and Larry Mize's wedge at Augusta. His shot came out of the bunker, hit the green to the left of the flag, and began rolling toward it. "I thought it was left all the way," O'Meara said. "But it did keep creeping to the right."

It rolled hole high, then, as O'Meara said, it spun right as the noise got louder and louder. It finally came to a halt no more than a foot from the hole. O'Meara, sitting several yards away with his family, clapped as loudly as anyone. "One of the great shots under pressure I've ever seen," he said later.

Ken Lindsay, the President of the PGA of America, was standing by the green waiting for the awards ceremony to begin. "I would have given you a thousand to one odds against him holing that shot," he said. "And I might have lost."

Watts tapped in and waved his white visor at the crowd he had now won over, not only with his extraordinary shot but with the way he had hung in through the last two days when no one expected him to. He was walking off the green when the announcement was made: "The playoff will commence in precisely ten minutes time at the 15th tee."

The R & A has the best playoff system in golf. It does not put people through the torture of returning on Monday for what is often an anticlimactic 18-hole playoff, the way the USGA does. It also does not use sudden death, where one lucky shot can decide a major championship, the way the Masters and the PGA do. Instead, knowing there will be plenty of light when the tournament ends at 6:30, it stages a four-hole playoff. No fluke shots decide, and the champion is still crowned on Sunday evening.

O'Meara walked onto the 15th tee at 6:45 — ten minutes after Watts had holed out. He then had to wait several minutes for Watts, who had paused to get a sandwich before making his way to the 15th. If that bothered O'Meara, he didn't show it. As soon as Watts walked onto the tee, he grabbed his hand and said, "Brian, what a great bunker shot at 18, that was awesome."

Gordon Huddy of the R & A produced a pound coin and suggested that O'Meara drive first if it came up heads, Watts if it came up tails. "I've got tails?" Watts asked, still clearing his head from what had been going on in the last twenty minutes.

"Exactly," Huddy said.

He flipped the coin and heads came up. O'Meara had the honor.

As it turned out, the first hole decided the playoff. Both players hit two good shots, laying up short of the green. Watts hit a gorgeous third shot to within five feet. O'Meara's wedge was about a foot outside of Watts, which proved to be an advantage. "I knew I had to make that putt," O'Meara said. "I didn't want to give him a chance to get ahead and build some confidence. I felt I had been in this sort of position in majors more than he had and I had to exert control right away."

He did, making his putt. Watts then missed his.

That was all the edge O'Meara needed. Both players parred 16 and 17 — Watts making a superb up and down at 17 to make his par — and they returned to the 18th tee with O'Meara still one shot ahead. The only added suspense on each hole came from the crowd. The officials had pretty much given up on keeping people behind the ropes once the players teed off on each hole, and the players and caddies had to keep up a lively walking pace to keep ahead of the surging crowds. No one — not even Sean McDonough — would have called these people patrons.

O'Meara hit three-wood at 18, just as he had the first time, and again found the fairway. He was between four- and five-iron for his second shot, but felt just enough breeze in his face to go with the four. He hit the ball straight at the flag. It hit and rolled just through the green, no more than 12 feet from the cup. Watts's only chance was to make birdie. He aimed his second shot at the flag, but pulled it just enough to find the left bunker — the back one as opposed to the front one he had been in a little more than an hour earlier. "I knew I had to hole the shot from there," he said. "I went for it."

The ball flew directly at the flag, but it was too strong. He was left with 25 feet for par and missed. That meant O'Meara could three-putt and win. He looked at Higginbotham, a wide smile creasing his face. "What a great feeling," he said. "Three putts to win the Open championship."

He needed only two. At 7:42 P.M. his three-foot par putt went into the hole and his arms went into the air. This was different from the Masters, though. This time he had had a few minutes to savor the walk to the green knowing he was going to win, the beautiful setting with the sun beginning to go down, the smiles on the faces of his family members a few yards away. After a handshake with Watts and a hug from Higginbotham, they were all there: Alicia, Michelle, Shaun. The man who couldn't win majors had now won two in a little more than three months.

The British Open awards ceremony is golf's best. Unlike the Masters, where half the golf officials in the world have to be recognized, it is simple and dignified. Bonallack, who has been the R & A's chief executive for fifteen years, carries the Claret Jug onto the green and the runner-up and low amateur join the champion there. There are no PGA Tour–style corporate executives and no giant checks. The applause for Rose was thunderous; for Watts very warm. And then Bonallack introduced the champion the same way the Open champion has been introduced for as long as anyone can remember:

"And the champion golfer of the year, with a score of two hundred and eighty . . . Mark O'Meara!"

That's it. The champion golfer of the year. Who could ask for a more flattering description?

O'Meara had held the Claret Jug before when his friend and neighbor Ian Baker-Finch had invited him to his house in Orlando in 1991 for a post-Open celebration. "I drank champagne from the jug that night," he told the crowd. "But I always thought that was as close to it as I would ever get."

He said all the right things about all the right people, stumbling only when he referred to the Claret Jug as "the Clariot Jug." Later he admitted he was fighting nerves, even more so than at the Masters.

But he recovered quickly. "I can't tell you what this means to me," he said. "This is the championship I dreamed most about winning, because this is the most special championship there is."

He meant it too. No knock on Augusta, but O'Meara, having played around the world, has always felt the Open championship (he never calls it the British Open) is golf's greatest event. "Maybe," he said, "it had a little to do with the fact that I thought it was the one I had the best chance to win."

Either way, there was no doubting the fact that this was an extraordinary moment in an extraordinary year for O'Meara.

The capper to the day came much later, when the O'Mearas, exhausted and elated, returned to the house they were renting in Birkdale. Shortly after they arrived, the phone rang. O'Meara was a little surprised because it was late and not many people had the number. When he picked it up, he heard a familiar voice.

"Why," Tiger Woods asked, "do you keep doing this to me?"

IV

The Final Chapter

26

High Heavenly Ground

To the men who run the PGA Championship, Mark O'Meara's victory in the British Open was a godsend because it meant that there would be an honest-to-goodness big-time story unfolding when their championship began.

The Masters doesn't need a story line. Neither do the Opens. Just by happening they become a story, whether the winner is Tiger Woods or Charles Coody, Ben Hogan or Orville Moody.

The PGA isn't quite the same. It isn't fair that this should be so. After all, the PGA has a distinguished history, and the list of players who have won the event includes most of the game's great names: Hagen, Sarazen, Hogan, Nelson, Snead, Nicklaus (five times), Player, Trevino. Two of golf's most important players, Arnold Palmer and Tom Watson, would each tell you his greatest regret in golf is never having won the PGA.

The week has the feel of a big-time event: the extra nerves on the first tee, the suffocating media coverage, the wall-to-wall TV coverage, the presence of most of the important people in golf. To win the PGA has great meaning, right up there with winning a Masters, a U.S. Open, a British Open. John Daly became a star — and a very wealthy man — by winning the PGA in 1991. Paul Azinger's playoff victory over Greg Norman in 1993 was easily the most dramatic finish to a major that year.

And there have been few endings in golf history that topped Davis Love's walk up the 18th at Winged Foot in 1997 with a rainbow on his left and memories of his dad on everyone's mind.

But the PGA *is* different from the other majors. It comes at the end of the summer, when everyone is a little bit burned out, when a lot of top players are looking forward to a fall respite from the game and from the road. If there are four major championships, one of them has to be number four.

"Would I be thrilled to win the PGA?" David Duval asked. "Of course. It is a major championship and it would be a great honor. It may have the strongest field of the four majors. But would it mean as much as the Masters, the U.S. Open, or the British Open? No offense intended, but no. It's the fourth most important tournament there is. Period."

The PGA has three significant problems: dates, venues, and personality. The first probably isn't going to change, the second has changed but not enough, and the third is unchangeable unless something radical is attempted.

The PGA is traditionally played in mid to late August, which means it is often played in brutally hot, humid weather. It also comes not only last on the majors rotation, but at the conclusion of nine intense weeks of golf that often leave the best players running on fumes. It is probably not a coincidence that eleven of the last thirteen PGAs have been won by players who had not won a major title in the past. Of those eleven, three — Payne Stewart, John Daly, and Nick Price — have gone on to win at another major after their PGA wins.

In 1971, the PGA was played in February, making it the year's first major. There would be two problems if that early date became permanent: it would limit the golf courses available because of weather constraints, and perhaps more important, the Masters would raise hell about being displaced as the opening event on the majors calendar. Once was okay; every year would not be. Chances are, the PGA will stay where it is for the foreseeable future.

The PGA's venues have improved in recent years. It has come a long way from the not-so-long-ago days when, in consecutive years, it was played at PGA National on dead greens in 100-degree heat: at Oak Tree in Edmond, Oklahoma; and at Kemper Lakes, near Chicago. The latter two were considered good golf courses by most players, but they lacked history and pedigree. During the '90s the PGA has been played at Inverness, Southern Hills, Riviera, and Winged Foot, and its 1999 location is Medinah. These are classic courses with history and pedigree.

Of course, thrown into the mix in 1996 was Valhalla, outside Louisville, Kentucky. Valhalla is strictly a business deal. The PGA of America was given the option to buy the club after the '96 PGA, and it did just that. Then it announced that the tournament would return to Valhalla in both 2000 and 2004 and that the Ryder Cup would be played there in 2007. Most players, having played Valhalla in '96, are aghast at this move.

"I think Valhalla is a perfectly nice golf course — for a Nike Tour event," Duval said. "But a major championship? You have to be kidding."

Justin Leonard, who played well at Valhalla, finishing fifth, is more diplomatic than Duval. "I would say with the work they're doing to fix it up it's good enough for a regular tour event," he said. "It's not a bad golf course. But is it comparable to Winged Foot? Come on."

Fred Couples, who is rarely critical of those who run golf, just shook his head after the Valhalla-Valhalla-Valhalla announcement was made. "They go to places like Winged Foot and Medinah and that's great," he said. "And I don't personally object to trying new golf courses every now and then. We went to Sahalee this year and I don't think anyone would say it's Winged Foot. But I think everyone thought it was better than Valhalla."

And no one is planning to return to Sahalee for major events three times during the first eight years of the new millennium.

Jim Awtrey, the CEO of the PGA, who has played a critical role in turning the organization into a success, defends Valhalla on two levels: first, that it will be worthy of major events before the PGA is done with it, and — as Couples points out — it is part of the PGA's mission to search for new venues. No one argues with that. They just argue with going back to a new venue that was greeted with — at best — mixed response from the players, when it is clear to everyone in the sport that money is the driving force behind the decision.

Personality is probably the PGA Championship's biggest drawback. Not player personalities, but the personality of the event. The other three majors have clearly defined personalities: the Masters is all about the golf course, the setting, and all the traditions associated with the event. Say "green jacket" and everyone even vaguely familiar with golf knows exactly what you are talking about. The U.S. Open is defined by the difficulty of the golf courses and the unfairness of the whole week. When the late Tony Lema wrote his autobiography, he titled his chapter on the Masters "Fun at the Summit." The chapter on the Open was called "Fear at the Summit." The British Open is, as Payne Stewart says, "the original golf tournament." It has the most history, the unique atmosphere, and the links golf courses that make it entirely different from the majors played in the U.S.

And then there is the PGA. What can it do different? Use the same golf course every year? Been done. Tight fairways and fast greens? Done. Go play on a links like Pebble Beach or Shinnecock? Done and done. Once upon a time (until 1958) the PGA was a match-play event. There has been talk through the years of returning to match play to make the PGA unique. But that isn't going to happen. TV wouldn't stand for it. There are too many pitfalls. Suppose two no-names make the final? Suppose the match ends on the 12th hole and the network is left with 90 minutes of fill time? As it is, even if no stars are on the leader board on Sunday, the telecast can still show them during the course of the day. They can't be shown on Sunday if they've lost in the quarterfinals on Friday. Match play isn't coming back.

And so, the PGA must do the best it can with what it's got. What it has is the cachet of a major championship and an excellent field. That isn't all bad. In 1998, the PGA was taking one of its gambles, going to a new site. Sahalee Country Club is about thirty miles east of Seattle. Sahalee is Indian for "High Heavenly Ground," and in terms of aesthetics, the name is apt. The golf course is beautiful, every hole framed by giant trees. "It may be the most vertical course I've ever seen," Tom Watson said one morning standing on the first tee. "Every hole, you feel like you're driving right down a chute in between the trees."

The PGA had a number of concerns about Sahalee. Many of them were logistical. *Seattle Post-Intelligencer* columnist Art Thiel wrote one morning early in the week that he believed that Sahalee really meant

"No parking available," because there simply wasn't any within walking distance of the golf course. That meant creating a shuttle bus system to bring in almost all the spectators. And of course weather was always a concern in the northwest. Would it rain all week? If it did rain a lot, what kind of condition would the golf course be left in?

The range was also a problem. It was, quite simply, too small to accommodate 150 players. One morning Bob Estes and Fred Couples, normally two of the most pleasant men on the tour, got into an argument on the range over the question of spacing. Estes thought Couples was too close to him. Couples disagreed, pointing out that everyone was practicing in tight quarters. They ended up agreeing to disagree.

Most important to Awtrey and his people was the golf course. They knew everyone would rave about the way it looked. The question was how it would play. They had been surprised in 1997 by Davis Love's ability to shoot an 11-under-par 269 at Winged Foot. But Winged Foot had enough tradition that most people simply wrote Love's score off to an extraordinary week of golf, noting that only four players in the field had broken par.

If par got hammered at a new venue, the golf course would lose people's respect. Mark Brooks's winning score at Valhalla had also been 11 under par, but forty-six players had broken par there. The PGA didn't want a repeat of that at Sahalee. So it did two USGA-like things: it took two par-fives (number six and number 18) and made them into par-fours, turning the course from a par 72 into a par 70. And it grew the rough to four-to-six inches on most holes and narrowed the fairways in the normal landing areas for the pros' drivers. Just as at Olympic, most players would use the driver rarely, if at all.

The players were more concerned about the landing areas than about the par-fives becoming par-fours. Whether they agreed with that move or not, they knew it was going to be done, especially after the PGA had watched Steve Elkington win at Riviera at 17 under par in 1995. But most felt that narrowing the fairways was going a little too far. "Why not cut the rough short and let balls roll into the trees?" Duval asked. "That way, the golf course *is* different from a U.S. Open. I think that would be healthy for them to try to be different."

In truth, they were different. The greens weren't as fast or as tricky as at a U.S. Open, and the fairways weren't nearly as hard. On most holes, if you hit a ball in the fairway, it would stay there. That made Sahalee quite a bit different from Olympic. Even so, the PGA needed a story to tell. It needed Jack Nicklaus winning for the fifth time at the age of forty or Lee Trevino winning at forty-four or John Daly winning as the ninth alternate or Davis Love winning as everyone's sentimental favorite.

Mark O'Meara tying to become the second player in history to win three professional majors in the same year — and the first since Hogan in 1953 — was certainly a good place to start.

There was also the story about the hometown kid, his head filled with memories of his mom and dad, coming home to try and win a major title as the returning hero.

Fred Couples had originally planned to get to Seattle at least a week before the championship began. But when he thought about it, he changed his mind. "I thought that if I went up there and played the golf course for a week and then started on Thursday with a bogey I'd probably freak out. I decided it was better to get there on Sunday night, the way I usually did for a major, and try to prepare as close to the way I usually do as possible — even though I knew it wouldn't be possible."

It wouldn't be possible because Couples is the pride of Seattle. His parents were from Seattle, he had grown up in Seattle, and now he was coming back to Seattle as one of golf's great names. It was a week he had looked forward to for five years, ever since the PGA had announced during the 1993 championship at Inverness that it had selected Sahalee for the 1998 tournament.

There was, though, a large element of sadness in the week. One of the reasons Couples had been as excited as he was about a major coming to Seattle was knowing how much it would mean to his parents to be able to come out and watch him and bring all their friends and neighbors. Now, many of those friends and neighbors would be out there, but without his parents.

"Of course my dad wouldn't have been watching me anyway," he said, smiling. "He never watched me. It made him too nervous. He'd go off and watch my buddies like Jay [Haas] or Davis [Love]. The only tournament he ever really enjoyed was the World Series [of Golf] because there was no cut and he didn't have to worry about me missing it."

It would be especially difficult for Couples to put the loss of his parents behind him during this week — not only because so many people would want to talk about them, but because his uncle Pete Sobich would be there. Uncle Pete was his mother's brother and now he, too, was dying of cancer. Couples had made arrangements with his pal Jim Nantz to have Uncle Pete sit in the tower behind the 18th green the first couple of days of the tournament.

Even though there were sad memories to deal with, Couples was very much looking forward to the week. Thais was going to be there with her two children and they had rented a house on the 13th hole at Sahalee, meaning it would be an easy commuting week. The best part was that he would be close to his new family.

Couples had mixed emotions about how his summer had gone. There was a part of him that wished he had played more after his win at Memorial. He had been locked into the best golfing groove he had been in since his back had gone out in 1994, and the chance to really do some serious damage during the summer was right there.

But he had told Thais that he would take time off in the summer to be with her and the kids. He wanted to play a lot before the Masters and keep on playing, if things were going well, until the kids were out of school. Once school was over, he would make a serious attempt to be at home.

He had kept his word. "In terms of being with Thais and the kids I never regretted not playing for a second," he said. "I had a ball. Loved every minute of it and never missed the tour or playing one bit when I was away. The only time I regretted it was when I got back out on the golf course."

Even someone as blessed as Couples isn't going to stay in a groove not playing. He had decided that he would play only four events in June, July, and August: the U.S. Open, the British Open, the PGA, and the World Series of Golf. That was it. He was off for two weeks before Olympic, for three weeks before Birkdale, and for three weeks before Sahalee. That was not a schedule likely to keep your game sharp and he had paid the price. He had never been in serious contention at Olympic and had played one good round — 66 on Thursday — at Birkdale. His description of his British Open was succinct: "I went from good to bad to worse to worse than worse."

He wanted very much to play well at Sahalee. He knew what the week would have meant to his parents. He knew what it was going to mean to all his friends and relatives and Uncle Pete. And he knew it was going to mean a lot to him. But he also knew his game wasn't as sharp as it could have been. He asked Paul Marchand to come to Los Angeles the weekend before the tournament and then on to Seattle to work with him. Extra work with Marchand had helped going into Augusta, maybe it would help now.

"I had started the year not having any idea how much golf I was going to be able to play or how well I could play," he said. "Then I won the Bob Hope and played well right through Memorial. If I had kept going, who knows. But I was thinking if I could get to playing well for one more week, well then it could just be an unbelievable finish to a great year."

If anyone can go to the on-switch without hours and hours on the range, it is Couples. He felt good playing his practice rounds. The only problem was the adoration. Being adored is not an awful thing, but when there are thousands of people who all want a few seconds of your time — sign an autograph, pose for a picture, shake a hand, kiss my daughter, give my son a few words of encouragement — it adds up.

If Couples had wanted to, he could have demanded a Tiger Woods–style security phalanx to escort him from each green to each tee during the practice rounds and from the clubhouse to the putting green to the driving range. But he didn't want to do that. He wanted to shake the hands, sign the autographs, pose for the pictures, and give the words of encouragement. He was never going to have another week in his life quite like this and he wanted to savor it.

During his Tuesday practice round, played with Tom Watson (naturally), Craig Stadler, and a local club pro Couples had grown up with named Scott Williams, Couples walked around with a huge grin on his face. He was relearning Sahalee, since he hadn't played it for years, but also enjoying all the hoopla around him. Standing just off the eighth green, he turned to his caddy, Joe LaCava, and said, "Tell you what, Joey, let's have a chip-off here, let everyone see how caddies play golf."

LaCava, a decent player, was willing. "What are the stakes?" he asked.

"Easy," Couples said. "All the pressure's on me. You win, I carry the bag on the ninth hole."

LaCava was certainly willing to play for those stakes. His chip stopped about six feet from the hole. "Pressure," Couples said.

"Yeah right," LaCava said, knowing his boss's talents. Couples' shot stopped about a foot from the hole.

The crowd cheered his victory wildly. Couples smiled at LaCava. "Too bad they don't know what they just missed seeing."

Watson shook his head and laughed while the crowd kept cheering as if Couples had just wrapped up the title with his chip. "It's a shame you haven't got any fans out here, Freddie," he said.

"They're only out here because I'm with you, Tommy," Couples said.

There were also a lot more people who wanted some of Mark O'Meara's time. Whatever he had been in the past or might be in the future, this was his week to be a star. At least to most people.

On Monday morning, O'Meara and Tiger Woods pulled up to the front door of Sahalee to go and check in for the tournament. As soon as the car pulled up one of the attendants was there to open the door for golf's young god.

"Mr. Woods, welcome to Sahalee," he said. "We're so glad to have you. If there's anything at all you need this week, please don't hesitate to ask."

Woods thanked him. In the meantime, O'Meara had gotten out of the car on the other side and was walking around to head into the clubhouse. The attendant stepped into his path. "Excuse me, sir," he said. "Is there something I can help you with?"

O'Meara laughed. Maybe if he had worn the green jacket the guy would have recognized him.

"It's all right, though," he said later. "By Wednesday, things were much better. As I was leaving the locker room one of the members working in there said to me, 'Good luck tomorrow, Mr. Lehman.'"

O'Meara *had* come a long way from Augusta. Back then he had been mistaken for Mark McCumber. Lehman has won the British Open. The best McCumber has ever done in a major is tie for second.

Golfers are often misidentified by fans, in part because they look different away from the golf course without their caps on. Payne Stewart can walk through hundreds of fans on a practice day and not be recognized because he is dressed in normal clothes and not his knickers and hat. Earlier in the year, Jim Furyk had been walking out of a bathroom at Doral when a fan stopped him. "Hey, Tom Lehman, wow, it's a thrill to see you," he said.

"Well thanks very much," Furyk said, "but I'm not Tom Lehman."

The man looked at him closely and said, "Are you sure?"

O'Meara was also sure he wasn't Lehman, but he knew he wasn't the same person who had once been the King of the B's. At least to the public and the media he wasn't the same. He had finally made the cover of *Sports Illustrated* after winning the British Open. He had been genuinely miffed when *SI* hadn't put him on the cover after the Masters. This made up for it. Jaime Diaz sent him two hundred extra copies and O'Meara asked him if he would sign one for him. The inscription he asked for was simple: "To Mark O'Meara. An 'A' player."

Like Couples, O'Meara hadn't played since the British. But that had been a golf decision. He was exhausted when he got home from Birkdale, and he knew his instinct was to overpractice and overplay. Rest, a few days of practice at home, and a chance to unwind from the pressures of the British were probably the best way to get ready for the PGA. He had played the two weeks after the Masters and had been a shadow of himself. There was no sense forcing it and no need to.

He felt confident when he saw Sahalee. He knew he would have to keep the ball in the fairways off the tees because of the high rough, but the two major victories had left him so confident that he wasn't going to be thrown by very much. He knew his pal Woods was dying to win so he could quiet the critics who were wondering what had become of the golfing messiah who was going to win a hundred majors. Woods had played consistently well all year but he had not been brilliant. Brilliance was expected of him. Instead, it had been produced by O'Meara.

O'Meara knew what was at stake for him during the week. "To have a chance to do what only Ben Hogan has done," he said, leaning on a club on the range one afternoon. "If I think about that very much, it will be intimidating." He smiled. "Maybe I just won't think about it."

Of course if he did equal Hogan, people might start to recognize him.

While O'Meara's quest and Couples's homecoming were being talked about early and often by fans and the media, the player most often discussed in the locker room was Stuart Appleby.

Appleby was one of the game's up-and-coming players, a twenty-seven-year-old Australian who had won twice on tour and appeared to have the swing and the mindset needed to become a big-time winner on tour. He and his wife, Renay, a very good player in her own right, had moved to Orlando and become a part of the golfing community there, friends with people like Payne Stewart, Lee Janzen, Mark O'Meara, Tiger Woods, and many of the other tour players who lived in the area.

The Applebys had planned a vacation after the British Open, a second honeymoon of sorts. They were going to Paris for a week, to forget about golf and the pressures of the summer, and just enjoy some time together away from it all.

They were getting out of a cab at a London train station when they realized they had left something in the back of the cab. While Stuart got the rest of their luggage loaded on a trolley, Renay went back for the bag in the cab. Apparently, the cab driver didn't see her walking behind his cab. He put the cab in reverse with Renay Appleby standing right behind it. While Stuart stood watching in horror, his wife was driven backward into the front of another car that was pulling up behind the cab.

"As soon as I got to her," he said later, "I knew it was a very serious situation." Appleby tried to keep his wife alive while help was called for. Paramedics arrived in a matter of minutes, but it was too late. Renay Appleby died on the way to the hospital.

When the story reached the tour, the overwhelming reaction was one of disbelief. "I've been on tour for close to twenty years, and something like this has never happened, this kind of shocking tragedy," John Cook said during the PGA. "Several years ago Willie Wood's wife died, but she had cancer, and when it happened, as tragic as it was, it wasn't a complete shock. This is one of those situations where you go over it again and again and you still can't believe it happened."

Stuart Appleby had taken Renay home to Australia to be buried and then come back to play in the PGA. He knew Renay would have been furious with him for not playing, and that sooner or later he had to face the rest of his life.

In a sense, he was the most composed person in the locker room on the subject. He had been crying for most of three weeks and was just about cried out. He had steeled himself to the fact that everyone was going to need to say something, and he knew that he couldn't break down every single time they did. Time and again, players came up to tell him how sorry they were and, time and again, it was the other player who ended up in tears.

"I walked up just to give him a hug and tell him how much we were all thinking about him and the next thing I know I'm crying on *his* shoulder," Payne Stewart said. "It's just so awful. There's absolutely nothing you can say and yet you feel as if you have to say something."

Even the media, which understands that some days the job calls for asking questions no one wants to ask, wasn't sure how to deal with Appleby. Amazingly, he was the one who stepped up and removed the burden. As soon as he arrived at the golf course on Monday, he asked Julius Mason, who ran the PGA's press operation, if he would schedule a press conference for him. That way, he could face all the questions at once. "It was something I had to do sooner or later," he said. "I figured it might as well be sooner."

And so, on Tuesday afternoon, while most players were on the golf course or the range or the putting green preparing for the start of the championship, Appleby walked down the hill from the clubhouse to the media tent to answer questions. He looked — predictably — horrible. His eyes were vacant and hollow, his shoulders sagged with exhaustion. He looked like a man who had been to hell and back, which he most certainly had been.

Mason, moderating the press conference, said what everyone was thinking. "Stuart, most of us don't know what to say . . ."

Appleby understood. "I want you all to feel as if you can ask any question you want to," he said. "Don't be shy. Fire away."

Gingerly, they did. And for close to thirty minutes, Appleby answered. His courage was evident, his words heartbreaking and stirring. He cried at times, and so did some of the people in the room and many of those watching on the Golf Channel, which was televising all the pre-tournament press conferences live.

John Cook was watching while he talked on the phone to his wife, Jan. They both had to put the phone down because they both started to cry. Jeff Sluman walked away from a TV set in the locker room. He couldn't bear to watch.

Appleby described the accident, patiently going through details that had to make him want to scream. He talked about holding his wife and understanding right away that something horrific had happened. And he talked about going on.

"It's the little things you miss the most," Appleby said softly. "Getting through the nights is the toughest part. Being alone. Not having her there to talk to . . . I feel as if I won some kind of lottery in life when I met her and married her." He talked about driving to the golf course and turning to Renay to ask for directions because she was always the navigator. Now he had to get his own directions. "Turning to talk to her and not having her there, that's when it really gets to you," he said.

He knew his life would never be the same. He knew going back to the house in Orlando that she had designed was going to be especially difficult. He hadn't been there yet and he really wasn't looking forward to it.

When most press conferences finish, there is a scramble at the front of the room. Invariably, several reporters have questions they want to ask without all the TV lights on. Or they need to ask the player when they can sit down with him one-on-one for ten or fifteen minutes. Players call it the postconference scrum. When Stuart Appleby finished, there was no scrum. Just applause.

27

From String Bikinis to Sahalee

For Jim Awtrey, the first few days at Sahalee were a huge relief. Although he had become an eloquent defender of Valhalla — somebody had to do it — he certainly didn't want the PGA to be played on another new golf course that the players spent the week dissing.

"When you go to new places, you never know how people are going to react," he said. "We think part of our mission is to find new places to play major championships. But when you do that, there is some risk involved."

Awtrey had been running the PGA of America for eleven years, and a lot had changed during that time. One of his first jobs had been to get the PGA Championship back to a rotation that included more of the country's classic golf courses. During the '70s and '80s it seemed as if the PGA was being played every other year at a golf course no one had ever heard of. Awtrey and his board knew that had to change.

"The venue is a very important part of a major championship," he said. "We weren't playing the classic golf courses enough. We need to play new courses, but we had gone too far in that direction."

Part of the problem was that a lot of the classic old clubs in the country didn't think it was worth giving up control of their club to host a PGA.

The U.S. Open, sure, but the PGA — why? "When I first sat down with the people from the Country Club [in Brookline, Massachusetts] they had hosted the U.S. Open every twelve years or so for most of the century," Awtrey said. "But the PGA? They didn't know anything about it. I had to educate them as to who we were, what we were, and where we were going."

The PGA also had to come up with an incentive for the clubs to go into business with them. Hosting a major championship is no small thing for a golf club. It means giving up control of your golf course for close to a year so that it can be transformed into a test for the world's best golfers. It means moving out of your clubhouse and your locker room for two weeks during a peak time of the golf season. It means seeing your rough torn up and trampled by thousands of spectators, grassy areas destroyed because they are used for parking lots, and the spectre of terrible traffic tying up your entire community for a week.

In other words, if you are going to do it, there had better be a reason that goes beyond prestige. Of course there is: money. The PGA went to the clubs and offered the kind of deal the USGA doesn't need to offer: partnership. The club would share in all revenues — ticket sales, corporate sales, souvenir sales, concessions, parking — everything but television. That meant making the sacrifices necessary to host a championship could be very lucrative. It also gave the clubs an extra incentive to do a good job as the host, which could only benefit the tournament.

The strategy worked. The rotation of clubs improved, as did the management of the tournament. In 1986, when Awtrey joined the PGA as director of tournaments, he had a staff of four. In 1998, the PGA's tournament staff had twenty-two people on it. Awtrey came to the PGA from a job as a club pro in Oklahoma. He had grown up there in the town of Shawnee and dreamed of playing on the PGA Tour. He did, briefly, in 1970 thanks to a sponsorship offered by a member at Siwanoy Country Club in Bronxville, New York, the club that had hosted the first PGA Championship in 1916. Awtrey was twenty-six at the time; he was the pro at Siwanoy and very comfortable there. He was also a new father, but he saw this as his chance. He and his wife packed their infant daughter into their car and spent the year driving through America.

"I knew I was in trouble on the west coast playing in Monday qualifiers," he said. "I didn't play badly at all. In fact, I was right around par almost every week. And I never came close to getting into a tournament. It seemed like three or four under was playing off every week."

Awtrey finally did get into a couple of events and make a little money — "less than $5,000" is as close to a specific dollar figure as he can remember. At the end of the year, he went to his sponsor, who had committed to pay his way on tour for three years, and asked out of the deal. "Probably not many guys have done that," he said. "Asked off the tour. But I just felt realistically my game wasn't good enough to really compete on the tour. I had a young family, no place to live, and a lot more travel ahead. I thought it was time to go home."

He did, to club pro work back in Oklahoma. He became involved with the PGA of America through work he did on the rules committee. That relationship led to the offer of full-time employment in 1986. When he took the job, he asked for a year to evaluate all the championships the PGA runs — PGA Championship, Ryder Cup, PGA Seniors, PGA Club Pro, and a number of sectional events — so he could see what was needed and recommend changes. The following spring, Lou King resigned as executive director of the organization and Awtrey was asked to take over his job. "I went from being a club pro to being executive director of the PGA in less than a year," he said. "It was quite a change."

Not an easy one either. Shortly after Awtrey had been given his new title, he got a call from the superintendent at PGA National, the PGA-owned golf course that is right next to the organization's headquarters in Palm Beach, Florida. PGA National was scheduled to host the PGA Championship that August. When the golf course had been built, part of the contract had called for it to host the PGA. In 1971, the original PGA National had hosted the tournament, but that was the year the PGA had held the championship in February. No one wanted to find out what it would be like to hold a golf tournament in Florida in August. "I think when the contract was signed, everyone figured an agreement would be reached not to hold the tournament at the new course," Awtrey said. "But it never got done."

Now, it was early July and the superintendent was calling to say that the greens were dying. Something had gotten into the chemical system and the grass was literally dying before everyone's eyes. Awtrey now had the spectre of a tournament being played in 100-degree heat with 100 percent humidity and dead greens. There was nothing to do but grit his teeth and get through it. "My only consolation," he said, "was that I figured things couldn't get a lot worse."

Of course they could. The weather wasn't bad, it was worse than bad. "Record heat the entire week," Awtrey remembered. Players were wobbling down the fairway. The golf course was in bad shape, the greens even worse. And then, as he sat in the clubhouse on Thursday watching a little bit of the telecast with several PGA board members, he noticed that the camera had turned its attention away from the golf.

"There was a scoreboard floating in the lake near the 18th green," Awtrey said. "All of a sudden, they go to a shot of the board and there's a woman standing in front of the scores wearing a white string bikini."

This wasn't supposed to be World Championship Wrestling. This was supposed to be the PGA Championship, a major championship that the world's golfers hungered to play in and win. Awtrey called the local organizers to ask them why in the world there was a woman on the 18th green scoreboard in a white string bikini and to get her out of there immediately.

They said they couldn't do that. Apparently, one of the club members who had been on the organizing committee had a girlfriend who ran a modeling agency. He had made a deal with the agency to have a model rowed out to the scoreboard each day wearing a volunteer's uniform. Once she reached the scoreboard, she would go behind it, take off the volunteer's outfit, and reappear in her bikini.

"I realized right then," Awtrey said, "that this was a championship in serious trouble."

Of course he didn't know what real trouble was until three years later. That was when Shoal Creek hit the PGA like the tornado hit Dorothy's house in *The Wizard of Oz*. In late June, Awtrey first got the phone call advising him about Shoal Creek owner and founder Hall Thompson's comment that a black person would be an unlikely candidate for membership in a country club in Birmingham, Alabama.

Awtrey knew he had a problem, but he didn't realize right away how serious it was going to become. "My first thought was that the best resolution was for Shoal Creek to invite a minority to join the club right away," he said. "But Hall wasn't willing to do that. He said his club wasn't going to be told what to do."

While Thompson wasn't being told what to do, the PGA was facing a crisis. "Shoal Creek stopped being a sports story very quickly," Awtrey remembered. "It became a front-page story."

The Southern Christian Leadership Conference was threatening pickets at the tournament. Corporate sponsors were pulling ads from the ABC telecast left and right. At one point, ABC, which was a lame duck anyway, since Awtrey had sold the rights to the tournament beginning in 1991 to CBS, threatened not to pay its rights fee. Awtrey and his staff and several board members went to New York to meet with crisis management counselors from Burson-Marsteller. A decision was made that Awtrey, as the day-to-day leader of the organization, would be the spokesman on Shoal Creek rather than PGA president Pat Rielly. At one point, there was talk about moving the championship. Awtrey spoke to Jack Nicklaus about moving it to Muirfield Village in Ohio. Nicklaus, a friend of Thompson's, was reluctant. If the tournament moved, litigation was virtually guaranteed.

Finally, Thompson and Shoal Creek agreed to compromise and invite Louis Willie to join immediately as an honorary member, with full membership to come in the future after the normal waiting-list period that any applicant went through. That soothed the waters just enough that the event was played, although it was a complete disaster for everyone except perhaps Wayne Grady, that year's winner.

Shoal Creek forced everyone in golf — not just the PGA — to take a hard look at minority access, not just to country clubs but to the sport. It brought about rules changes in terms of the membership criteria for a club to host a PGA Championship, a USGA championship, or a PGA Tour event. One club scheduled to host a PGA — Aronomink in Newtown Square, Pennsylvania — decided to drop out of its 1993 commitment rather than change its procedures on membership. Another, Oak Tree (which was in serious financial trouble), dropped out of hosting in 1994 rather than deal with questions about being an all men's club.

"It was easily the most difficult thing I've ever been through professionally," Awtrey said. "But in the long run, Shoal Creek was good for the PGA and good for golf. It forced all of us to take a hard look at what was going on in the sport. None of us had ever really dealt with the issue. Now all of us are involved in minority programs, and Tiger [Woods] coming to the game has given us a great platform to build from."

Awtrey and his key staff members now make an annual trip to Burson-Marsteller to be put through a crisis management seminar. One of the reasons the PGA wanted to purchase Valhalla was to have a backup venue in case of a future crisis, whether it is caused by a hurricane, dead greens, or foolish comments made by the founder of a club. Awtrey can even smile about the events of 1990 a little bit now. "That was one year when no one questioned our status as a major championship," he said. "We were as front and center as any championship has ever been."

The PGA has come a long way since those days and the days of models on the scoreboard in string bikinis. It is still number four and probably always will be, but it is now a respected number four. And a profitable one.

The PGA has a field of 150 players. Twenty-five of the 150 are PGA of America club pros.

Every year, there are complaints from tour players about the presence of the club pros in the PGA. Most of those complaints usually come from players whose position on the money list would have gotten them into the championship if the club pros were left out. What those tour players fail to understand — or choose not to understand — is that the PGA Championship belongs to the club pros. They are who the PGA is and has been since the touring pros broke away from the PGA of America in 1968 to form the PGA Tour. The president of the PGA — in 1998 Ken Lindsay — is always a club pro. So are most of the board members. The men who rotate on the first tee making player introductions are club pros, and so are the members of the rules committee — much as Jim Awtrey once was.

Once, there were forty club pros in the PGA. That number was dropped in 1995 as a means of getting a stronger foreign contingent into the event. "We felt we needed those fifteen extra spots to make sure that we had the ability to invite any top players who slipped through the cracks in terms of qualifying criteria," Awtrey said. "It was a difficult decision and our members were very unhappy with it. They felt as if we were taking their championship away from them. But we thought it was something that needed to be done to improve the strength of the field."

Most of the extra slots were used on foreign players, but exceptions were made for American players who were ranked in the world's top one hundred but not exempt off the PGA Tour money list. In 1997, Fuzzy Zoeller had been invited to play at Winged Foot because it was there that he had won the U.S. Open in 1984. In 1998, Jay Haas and Paul Stankowski, both top one hundred players in the world rankings but not otherwise exempt, were also invited. The PGA seriously considered inviting Rick Fehr, a longtime tour player who lived in Redmond, Washington, just a couple of miles from the front gate of Sahalee. In the end, Fehr didn't get invited. He was tenth alternate to get in off the money list and was on his way out of town with his family on Wednesday when he got a call from the PGA. They said he had moved up to number two on the alternate list because of withdrawals and there was a decent chance that David Ogrin — number one on the list — wouldn't be able to get there. Fehr turned the car around and drove back to Sahalee. He was on the putting green the next morning when he saw Ogrin, who had arrived just before midnight.

"Sorry, Rick," said Ogrin, who knew how much Fehr wanted to play in his hometown.

The twenty-five club pros in the field secured their places during the PGA Club Pro championship. To play in the PGA is a major perk — one that has to be earned — but then comes the question about how you will play. The best-case scenario for most of the club pros is to make the cut. "It's a tough thing because you want to come in playing the best golf possible, but the summer is your busiest time and you get very little time to work on your game," said Ed Terasa, a pro from Waukesha, Wisconsin, who was playing in his fourth PGA. "My goal has always been to make the cut, but if you don't come in at the top of your game, you don't have a chance."

For the club pros, the setup for a major championship was considerably more difficult than anything they had experienced in their golfing past. They had played tough courses but none that were set up with fairways as tight and fast as they were now seeing, rough as thick, or greens as firm and quick.

"When I got into the tournament a lot of my friends back home were saying, 'Hey, maybe you'll get out there and something crazy will happen and you'll win the PGA,'" Jim Schuman, a first-timer from Gaylord, Michigan, said. "I got out here, took one look at the golf course, and said, 'No way.' The kind of scores some of these guys are shooting I can't even relate to. It's like a different sport."

Terasa and Schuman and Gene Fieger, like Terasa in his fourth PGA, were assigned the first tee time — 6:40 A.M. — on Thursday morning. Needless to say, the club pros were not put into the glamorous, midday TV slots. They played early and they played late. The biggest gallery any club pro would have was the one that followed Scott Williams, a local pro from Redmond, during his practice round on Tuesday. The fact that Williams had family and friends out to see him certainly increased the crowd. The presence of Fred Couples, Tom Watson, and Craig Stadler in his foursome may also have added a few people.

Terasa had his taste of glory on the range Tuesday afternoon. He was off to the right side, trying to hit balls quietly when he heard a commotion behind him. He turned and saw Tiger Woods and entourage (caddy, teacher, ball rep, shoe rep, security reps) approaching. Woods set up next to him and began hitting balls. A few minutes later he heard another commotion and saw Mark O'Meara approaching with his entourage (caddy). O'Meara walked to the other side of him and began hitting balls.

"I would hit a ball, stop and watch Tiger, hit another, stop and watch O'Meara," Terasa said. "I was in absolute awe of what they were doing."

Terasa, Schuman, and Fieger had no objection to their Thursday tee time. All of them knew they were going to go early or late, and they figured it would help to get on the golf course early when it was still a little bit wet and the greens hadn't been spiked up. Schuman was up at 4:15, keyed up and ready to go play. He drank some coffee and was on the road to the golf course by shortly after 5. "The only thing I saw between my hotel and the golf course was a milk truck," he said. Given the horrific Seattle traffic, that was another advantage of the early tee time.

All three players were on the practice tee by 6 A.M., which meant they had the chance to watch the run rise over Sahalee. They were amazed when they walked on the first tee to see the small grandstand to the left of the tee packed at such an early hour. Schuman walked onto the first tee and saw the Wanamaker Trophy, which goes to the PGA winner, sitting on the back of the tee glistening in the early morning sun and felt his knees starting to knock. He gave himself a pep talk. "There are no obstacles out there except trees and rough," he told himself.

Sure, no problem. He bogeyed the first hole. So did Fieger. Only Terasa managed par. But all three of them ended up playing very respectably the first day. Schuman, the rookie, shot a one-over-par 71, which put him in a tie for forty-sixth place, very much in contention to make the cut to low 70 and ties. Terasa was one shot back at 72, and Fieger was at 74. Schuman was low club pro that day. Some of the club pro scores were surprisingly high. Bruce Zabriski, a former tour player who had tied for thirtieth place at Olympic and who was one of the best club pro players in the country, shot a disappointing 77. Mike Burke Jr., who had won the club pro championship in June, shot 75. Burke had dedicated his victory to his late father, Mike Sr., a lifelong club pro who had died three years earlier. His brother Pat had played on the PGA Tour for a number of years and was trying to come back to the tour after a serious wrist injury. For this week, Pat and Mike were in reverse roles: Mike played and Pat watched.

Pat Burke was one of the funniest people on the PGA Tour, a young curmudgeon who had a wisecrack for almost any situation. After he had walked around with Mike on Thursday, someone asked him if he enjoyed watching or playing more. "Are you kidding?" he answered. "I don't like either. If I ever won the lottery, not only would I never play golf again, I wouldn't have friends who played golf."

Burke was kidding . . . sort of.

The club pros were all rooting for each other, hoping that one or more of them would make the cut. None of the club pros had made the cut at Winged Foot a year earlier, and given the grumbling by some of the tour pros about their presence in the field, making the cut was one way to quiet the critics who said they didn't belong. A number of them were in position to make the cut when Friday began, including Schuman, Terasa, Bob Ford, the veteran pro at Oakmont who had made the cut in the past, and Stephen Keppler, a pro from Atlanta who had once finished fourth in the Bell South Classic in Atlanta playing on a sponsor's exemption.

Schuman and Terasa didn't have the benefit of an early start again on

Friday. This time they teed off at 10:52, which meant they got to sleep later, but also meant they were looking at a very different golf course from the one they had faced on Thursday. The weather was similar to Thursday's — surprisingly warm and humid — but even so the golf course that the three club pros started out on at midmorning was running fast and hard because the morning dew they had started their round in the day before was long gone.

What's more, the golf tournament was now well under way. The wide-open golf course they had played in those dewy early hours on Thursday was now a packed golf course, backed up by slow play, crawling with spectators, and overrun with scoreboards that told them who was leading, who was falling back, and what the other players in the field were doing.

Even before they teed off they knew that the cut was probably going to come right around 144 — four over par. There was some chance it would be three over, but it was also possible as the golf course got tougher in the afternoon that it would go up to five over. In all likelihood, four over was a pretty good target.

That certainly didn't seem out of reach. To shoot 144, Fieger would need to shoot 70, Terasa 72, and Schuman 73. But shooting that sort of number when you know you have to is a lot tougher than going out in the first round and just playing. All three players wore serious expressions starting out and they didn't change much as the day wore on. Birdies were hard to come by; the bogeys seemed to pile up. By the time the players reached the turn, 144 had gone from reasonable to difficult. Terasa and Fieger had both shot 38, and Schuman, who had made it look so easy the day before, turned in 40. That meant all of them would have to shoot under par on the back nine to have a chance.

"You could feel it slipping for all of us," Terasa said. "We all got on a roll the wrong way quickly. I was walking off the tenth tee thinking, gee, I wish we could have had another 6:40 tee time. I think we all got a taste of what it must have been like at Olympic during the Open."

Schuman had caught himself lying awake in bed the previous night dreaming about making the cut and playing on the weekend. He could sense that those dreams were fading quickly. "It's funny how a couple of bad swings can get you going in the wrong direction, and then you have a lot of trouble getting it back," he said. "There's just no margin for error at this level. Those guys at the top of the leader board look at the golf course and they see flags to fire at. I look at it and all I see is rough I want to stay out of."

The back nine wasn't going to be any easier than the front, especially with the greens hardening by the minute. Terasa did have a glimmer of hope when he rolled in a 10-foot birdie putt at the 10th to get back to four over for the championship, but he immediately gave that shot back when he bogeyed the par-five 11th, an unforgivable sin when you are fighting to make a cut.

Still, no one could accuse him of losing his sense of humor. After he had pushed his drive into the thick rough on the 11th, he walked over and found his ball sitting way down in the rough. "Oh gee, look at that," Terasa said.

"I tried to fluff it up for you," one of the marshals said jokingly, "but there were too many people watching."

"I can fix that," Terasa said, laughing. "Hey look!" he yelled, pointing behind the spectators toward the 12th fairway. "Isn't that Tiger Woods?"

A few people turned their heads until they got the joke. "Can't blame me for trying," Terasa said, still grinning. Then he gouged his ball out of the rough and moved on. Bogeys at 13 and 15 pushed him to seven over and pretty much ended any hopes of making the cut. Schuman had gone into full reverse and would end up shooting 79. He did get one last thrill, though, getting up and down from a bunker to the left of the 18th green for a par to avoid the dreaded snowman — 80. Terasa also got up and down at 18 to shoot 76. Fieger, high man on Thursday, was low man on Friday with a 73. That left him with the best two-day score in the group: 147, one shot lower than Terasa and three less than Schuman. All three of them walked the 18th fairway, up the narrow chute that led to the packed grandstands to the left of the green and behind them, knowing the week would be over for them as soon as they finished the hole.

"I felt a little bit like a guy who goes to a wedding and has a great time, then looks up and the night is over much too soon," Schuman said. "When we were walking up 18, I made sure to stop and take a good look around because who knows if I'll ever get this chance again. I wanted to be sure I remembered everything. It would have been great to make the cut and I wish I had played better today, but in a sense, having been here is what it was all about. When I look back at this, I won't remember the score, I'll remember that I was here."

Which is why the club pros should always be a part of the PGA. In 1998, for the second straight year, none of them made the cut. Certainly, the long-ago days when some club pros were good enough to actually compete with the touring pros are never going to come back. The life of a club pro is the exact opposite of the life of a touring pro: a club pro makes his living by ignoring his own golf game so he can make others' golf games better. A touring pro makes his living by ignoring almost everything else in the world so that he can make his game better.

There will always be those who will complain that those twenty-five spots could be used for players with a lot more game than the club pros. They're right. But every major has quirks that leave some good players out of the field. The Masters invites fewer than one hundred players and that includes five amateurs and all the old champions, meaning that some of the world's best players — witness the absence in 1998 of Payne Stewart and Steve Stricker — get left out. The U.S. Open has the tightest exemption system going, leaving many good players to deal with the one-shot test of qualifying. In 1998, Bob Estes was eleventh on the PGA Tour money list in June and didn't get to play in the Open. The British Open invites more players from more tours than any other major, meaning that a number of quality players — Scott McCarron and Jay Haas are prime '98 examples — are left out unless they want to fly transatlantic like Larry Mize to give the qualifier a shot. The PGA exempts more players from the U.S. Tour than any of the four majors. But those twenty-five club pro spots still bother some people.

The fact is, the strongest field of the year is the one at the Players Championship. There is no qualifying, there are no amateurs, no senior champions, no club pros. Just the best 144 players that can be rounded up. Some players — especially those who have won the title — have campaigned through the years to try and get the Players status as a fifth major. It won't happen. The Players will always be a significant — tops on the list — but there will always be four majors and no more, and each will have quirks when it comes to who plays and who doesn't play.

It was a shame in 1998 that Rick Fehr and Brian Henninger, alternates one and two when play began on Thursday, didn't get into the field. Both are good players and good guys and, as it happened, both are from the Pacific Northwest (Fehr from Redmond, Henninger from Portland). But the truth is, their absence didn't diminish the quality of the championship nor did the absence of those below them on the money list. And the presence of the club pros *does* add something. It adds tradition, it keeps the event in touch with the roots of the organization that puts it on, and it gives guys like Schuman, Terasa, and Fieger something to work toward and the chance to create memories that will stay with them forever.

28

Tears, Cheers, and Jeers

To most who made their way to Sahalee on Thursday for the start of the championship, there were three groups to watch: at 8:10 A.M. — Tiger Woods, Nick Price, and Jeff Sluman (two past champions paired with the man the media liked to call FOG — Future of Golf); at 9:04 A.M. — Mark O'Meara, Lee Janzen, and Davis Love III (the Masters and British Open champion, the U.S. Open champion, and the defending champion; normally this threesome consisted of the winners of the first three majors, but since O'Meara had won twice, Love was added); and, at 11:55 A.M. — Fred Couples, Lee Westwood, and José María Olazabal (local hero plays with two European stars).

The largest galleries would follow those three threesomes. Most of the fans would even be aware of the fact that O'Meara wasn't Tom Lehman. To many players, though, the group going off at 1:16 P.M. was as significant as any. That was Stuart Appleby's group. He was paired with Vijay Singh and Phil Blackmar.

Almost every player in the world follows the same routine before a round: get something to eat, warm up on the range, then walk to the putting green to hit some putts before heading to the tee. At Sahalee, the putting green is adjacent to the first tee.

By the time Appleby, Singh, and Blackmar finished their preround routines and began to walk onto the first tee, a number of players who had morning tee times had finished their rounds and were on the putting green practicing. Others were there getting ready to tee off. And others were crossing from the clubhouse to the range or vice versa. Under most circumstances, when players walk onto the tee to be introduced, no one on the putting green looks up. They have heard players introduced a million times in a million places.

But this was different. Players stopped what they were doing. Tony Navarro, longtime caddy for Greg Norman, who was working for Jeff Sluman with Norman out injured, yelled, "Go get 'em, Stu!" from across the green. Sluman, who had not yet seen Appleby during the week, walked onto the tee to wish him luck. Like almost everyone else, he gave Appleby a hug and, like almost everybody else, he was crying when he walked away. "I didn't mean for that to happen," he said later. "I just hadn't seen him and I wanted to say something to him before he teed it up. The next thing I know, I'm losing it. I just started to think about what he must be feeling and I couldn't handle it."

That was the thought on everyone's mind when Stan Marshaus, a club pro from Chautauqua, New York, said in what almost sounded like a whisper, "Ladies and gentlemen, please welcome Stuart Appleby." The starters at the PGA do not use a microphone, and different club pros rotate on the tee throughout the week. Marshaus didn't need to add anything to his introduction. Everyone knew what was going on, and Appleby had to wait through a long ovation — including applause from his fellow pros standing on the putting green — before he could go through his routine. He somehow managed to coax a two-iron down the fairway, and off they went for what his caddy, Joe Dimiano, would later call "the longest round of his life."

Appleby tried. He tried to shut off his emotions and, as he put it later, "get back to doing my job." But it couldn't possibly be that simple. He was wearing one of Renay's pins on his shirt and, on several occasions, he caught himself looking for her outside the ropes. He wouldn't have been human if he hadn't. Dimiano, who had worked for him for most of two years, could tell Appleby wasn't all there. "Believe it or not, it surprised me a little," he said. "He's been so strong, I almost thought he could come out, get away from everything being inside the ropes, and focus. But there was no way. He wasn't there all day. He was in a daze."

He did manage to get up and down to save par at the 18th after another long, warm ovation. But that par still left him with a 77. "The good part was that it felt very familiar being out there again," he said. "The crowds were wonderful all day. I just wish I could have lived up to their enthusiasm. I had very good intentions but I just couldn't hit the shots I wanted to."

Someone asked about the ovation walking up the 18th. Appleby smiled sadly. "I just wish," he said, "they had been clapping for my golf."

About an hour before Appleby teed off, Tiger Woods walked up the 18th, and the ovation *had* been for his golf. He had played superbly. He finished off a 66 — breaking the course record of 67 that Jack Nicklaus had set in an exhibition years ago — with a par four and walked off the green with a two-shot lead on the field. He had done something he had rarely done during 1998 — putted like the wizard of Augusta, circa April 1997. He had needed only 27 putts for the day and had made seven birdies.

He still wasn't thrilled with the way he was hitting the ball — he almost never was — so after he had finished talking to the media and had some lunch, he made his way out to the range to hit some balls while waiting for his teacher, Butch Harmon, to finish with his commitment to Great Britain's SkyTV, to join him.

Woods hadn't been on the range for more than five minutes when he was shocked to look up and find a young man he had never seen before standing right in front of him as if he was preparing to render judgment on his next swing. Woods looked at him quizzically as if to say, who are you?

The young man, who was holding a legal pad, held it out and said, "Tiger, sign this for me."

Woods was flabbergasted. "I don't sign autographs on the range," he said.

"Hey!" a voice said a few feet away. It was the suddenly-alerted-to-a-possible-crisis Fluff Cowan, who had been conversing with a couple of other caddies while his man warmed up. "What do you think you're doing?"

"I'm just asking for an autograph," the young man said, still very calm, still holding the pad and pen out as if he thought Woods might change his mind.

"You get out of here right now," Cowan said. "How'd you get in here?"

That was the $100 million question. The young man had no credentials of any kind. He had simply walked under the rope at the far side of the range and proceeded unimpeded until he reached Woods. This was no less shocking than someone walking up to the president of the United States in the Rose Garden without going through any kind of security check.

As the young man was herded by the huffing and puffing Fluff to the exit, someone asked Woods where his omnipresent security coterie had been.

Woods shrugged. "I don't know," he said, "lunch?"

Up and down the range, everyone got a chuckle. The subject of Woods and his security people had graduated from being a touchy one among the players to being a running gag. When he first came on tour, Woods had tried to use the extra security he was always provided with to shield himself from just about anyone and everyone. Once, after he had blown a tournament on the back nine on Sunday, he had allowed his security people to keep the media out of the locker room. He didn't have the authority to do that, and the PGA Tour told him that in no uncertain terms. They also told him that in the future the security people were to stay out of the locker room.

As Woods grew more comfortable in his role as a star and with day-to-day life on tour, he became much more approachable for everyone: other players, reporters, tour staffers. The only place he was still uncomfortable was in crowds, and that was understandable. He was still swarmed in many places and he had never grown comfortable with doing lengthy autograph sessions. What's more, like other pros, he knew that no matter how many he signed, someone would end up getting stiffed and that would be the person telling the story about what a bad guy Tiger Woods was.

Even with the calming of Tiger-mania, he still remained the most visible player on the tour — just ask Mark O'Meara — and he still had all sorts of security with him as he moved from clubhouse to range to putting green to golf course and back to clubhouse. Some players pointed out that he would probably have much less trouble getting through the crowds if he just had one or two security people with him to clear a small path rather than having the entire cavalry with him at all times. There was no way Tiger and company could sneak from one place to another. They were like the guys chasing Butch and Sundance: you could see them coming from miles away. At the British Open, the swoosh people had thoughtfully provided caps to the gang, knowing they would be photographed and filmed following in Tiger's wake all week. Perhaps by 1999 some of the more clever security types would be making their own deals: for a certain fee, they would wear your company's logo and make certain to push enough people out of Tiger's way during the week to ensure lots of camera time.

Butch Harmon arrived on the range a few minutes after the autograph seeker incident. He was still dressed for TV in a multicolored shirt with a dangling IFB earpiece wrapped around his belt. Spotting Harmon and the shirt, Jeff Sluman said, "Hey, everybody, look, it's Doug Sanders!" Sanders, who had won twenty-one tournaments in the '60s and '70s, was the Payne Stewart of his day, wearing clothes that were gaudy beyond belief. The entire range cracked up as Harmon tried to ignore Sluman and get to work.

But Sluman, who sees the range as a place to entertain and be entertained, was on a roll. Spotting Justin Leonard and his teacher, Randy Smith, working a few yards away from Woods, Sluman put a goofy-looking grin on his face, walked up to Tom Watson, and said, "Hey, Mr. Watson, my name's Matt Kuchar. Gee, I think you're a great player, Mr. Watson. Do you think if I turn pro I can play with Justin Leonard someday?"

By now, the entire range was rocking with laughter. Woods was doubled over, and Watson, who usually brings his game face to the range, was cracking up. The only one not laughing was Leonard. "They just won't let me up, will they?" he said.

He knew the other players were only teasing him because they thought he had been treated unfairly in San Francisco. But even two months later, Matt and Peter Kuchar still weren't funny to him.

Fred Couples wasn't in a laughing mood himself when he reached the 18th green late Thursday afternoon. He had struggled all day long but still came to the final hole in position to post a respectable score. He was two over par for the day, and an opening 72 would leave him in position to make a move on the leaders on Friday.

The 18th was the one hole at Sahalee that had drawn criticism from the players. It was normally a par-five and the green was better equipped to handle wedge shots than long irons and fairway woods. It wasn't as severe as the 17th at Olympic had been, but it was going to be a very challenging — in the eyes of some players unfairly so — finishing hole.

Couples hit a good drive and had a four-iron left to the green. But he tried to do too much with the shot, came over it, and hit an ugly hook that took one big hop, bounced onto a platform set up for wheelchairs, and came to a stop right beneath a spectator's wheelchair. Couples walked up with a stricken look on his face. While he was being introduced to the crowd around 18, he was apologizing to the man in the wheelchair, making sure he was okay and asking for a ruling on where he could drop his ball. He barely heard the thunderous ovation he was receiving.

"Last thing on my mind at that moment," he said later. "I was embarrassed. Here I am playing not great but with a chance to get away with a halfway decent score, and I hit a shot like that. It was ridiculous."

That wasn't all he was thinking about. As planned, his uncle Pete had been sitting in the CBS tower behind the green most of the afternoon. Now he was sitting right outside the broadcast booth and Couples could see him. He wouldn't, not even for a second, blame his uncle's presence for unnerving him, but he played the hole as if unnerved. After getting his drop, he flopped a mediocre wedge onto the green a good 20 feet short of the hole. For a split second it looked as if his par putt might drop, but the ball slid three feet past the hole. Couples was now completely flustered. He was thinking about his uncle, about his four-iron, about disappointing the crowd, about the lousy wedge he had just hit. Everything but the three-foot putt he had left.

He missed.

"Nice finish," he said a few minutes later in the locker room. He was completely disgusted with himself. His entire group had played poorly: Westwood had also shot 74, and Olazabal had shot 75. "We were all pathetic," he said. "Seventy-two would have been decent after the way I played, very decent. Seventy-four is not decent. I'm exhausted right now. I feel like I've already played 72 holes."

That was the risk Couples had known he would run during this week. It hadn't helped that he had gone to dinner with a group of friends on Monday night at one of Seattle's most popular restaurants and then spent the whole night being sick. "Steak," he said. "Must have been something wrong with it."

He was taking no chances the rest of the week. "I'm stopping at Safeway right now," he said, "and going home."

There would be no trip to the range, no late practice. Couples had to play very early Friday — 7:53. What he needed more than anything was some rest. And some birdies.

The first round ended with Woods leading eight players by two shots. There were eleven more players at 69, meaning that twenty players had broken par. O'Meara was one of those at 69, his best opening round in a major all year. He was happy and confident as he headed home that evening. Davis Love was one shot further back at even par along with Nick Price, Brad Faxon, Dudley Hart (playing his second tournament as a newlywed), Colin Montgomerie, Vijay Singh, and Phil Mickelson.

Mickelson had arrived at the golf course that morning and been presented with a copy of *Golf World*, the weekly magazine that is widely read by everyone associated with the tour. He was on the cover. The cover read: "Does Phil Mickelson Have What It Takes To Win A Major Championship?"

Jim McKay groaned when he saw the cover. "Why," he asked, "do they have to do this to him this week?"

McKay was smart enough to know the answer to his own question. The PGA was the last major of the year, a year that had started with Mickelson winning the opening tournament of the year and vowing publicly to change his luck in the majors in 1998. It hadn't happened. He had been close until the 12th hole on Sunday at the Masters, in contention until the back nine on Saturday at the U.S. Open, and never in it at the British.

When McKay read the story, he had to admit that it was fair, that the points raised were legitimate. His concern was how his man would react to it. Mickelson didn't read it until that night, but when he did he didn't have any serious argument with it either. Mickelson is not one of those athletes who expects constant adulation. "There's only one way to stop people from writing stories like this one," he said. "And we all know what it is."

Mickelson wasn't thrilled with 70, but he wasn't upset with it either. The three most upset people on the grounds that day were probably Lee Janzen, who had been full of confidence earlier in the week and then had gone out and shot 76; David Duval, who had also shot 76; and John Daly, whose lost summer continued with an 80. Even though a lot of players — including Woods — hadn't hit a single driver all day because of the narrow fairways in the driver landing area, Daly had decided to go for broke with the driver. "I might knock down two thousand fir trees before it's over," he said on Wednesday.

He came close. He was all over the lot all day long, his day summed up by the triple-bogey seven he closed his round with. Still using the driver that had gotten him into trouble all day long, he hooked his drive at 18 way left and had to be given a drop between two TV trucks. He chopped his ball back to the rough, then onto the fairway, into a bunker, and finally onto the green. Two putts later he walked off with an 80. He wasn't as angry as he had been after the second round at the British Open, but he was just as defeated. When several writers approached him in the locker room, he held up a hand and said, "I can't, guys, not right now. I just can't."

Steve Stricker would have been more than happy to talk to reporters after his round. Not that he was a media hog — anything but — but he was very pleased with his opening 69. "It didn't start out too well," he said. "But it ended up okay."

It started poorly because Stricker made a mess of the par-three fifth hole, hitting his tee shot into the water that fronts the green. That produced a double bogey that put him in an early hole. He was angry with himself for making that kind of mistake but rallied on the back nine to shoot 33. That left him just three shots behind Woods and pleased that he hadn't let one bad hole ruin the day.

Like a lot of players, Stricker was a little bit tired and a little bit burned out. Even though he had played well, it had been a difficult summer for him because the impending birth of the baby — due date August 30, two weeks after the end of the PGA — had kept Nicki off the road. Adjusting to not having her inside the ropes had taken a while; now he had to adjust to her not being there at all.

The latter was more difficult. He had become very comfortable with Jim Walker, his new caddy, on the golf course. Each had needed some feeling-out time, but now they were working well together. Walker was a more conservative caddy than Nicki had been. There were times when he counseled a layup when Nicki might have said go for it. There were times when he wanted to make par and get off a hole when Nicki might have been thinking birdie. Stricker had gotten on him on occasion for being too conservative, and Walker had learned to understand that there were times when Stricker didn't want to know what the safe play was. He wanted to fire at the flag, and if something went wrong, he would take the blame for it.

Just as important as feeling confident with Walker was enjoying himself with Walker. That was never a problem. The two men got along very well away from the golf course and, in Nicki's absence, spent a lot of time together at night, often going out to dinner. But as much as Steve liked Walker, he wasn't Nicki.

"It's hard sometimes," he said. "Talking on the phone just isn't the same. I understand it and I'm excited about the baby, but I still miss having her with me." He shrugged. "But I better get used to it. From now on, she won't be able to be with me all the time. In a way, this is good practice for me."

Stricker had arrived in Seattle feeling a little bit tired and discouraged. He had played very well for three days at the Buick Open and had gone into the last round tied for the lead with Vijay Singh. But he (and Singh) had gone backward on Sunday and Billy Mayfair had ended up winning the tournament by shooting 66. Stricker shot 72 to drop back into a tie for sixth on a golf course where anything over 70 is mediocre golf at best. He had been angry with himself for not holding up better under Sunday pressure.

"I never got anything going," he said. "I guess it had been a while since I had that good a chance to win and I didn't react well to it."

He had flown home to Madison that night so he could see Nicki for a few hours before flying to Seattle on Monday afternoon. He had gotten a jolt of energy and adrenaline Tuesday morning when he saw the golf course. Not only was it beautiful but there really wasn't any need to hit a driver. If there was one player on tour who didn't mind the notion of not hitting a driver all week, it was Stricker. He decided not to even carry it with him. "I don't want to be tempted," he said. "I like my three-wood, and on this golf course that's plenty. The driver can only get me into trouble."

Shooting 69 after a poor start confirmed his notion that he could play well at Sahalee. The next day was further proof. After turning in even par, Stricker got hot. He birdied 10, 11, 13, and 16, hitting a three-iron to within six feet at the 16th to set himself up. When that putt went in, he was five under par for the championship, and a glance at the leader board to the right of the green told him he was doing something he had never before done in his life: leading a major.

The 17th at Sahalee is a dangerous par-three. A lake fronts the green and wraps around it to the right. To the left is a long, narrow bunker. The hole was playing 215 yards, and Stricker and Walker took a long time selecting a club. The tee is elevated but, as is the case on many of the tees, it is surrounded by trees, which can make gauging the wind a guessing game.

Walker is one of the tour's leading wind experts. He studies the wind the way a political pollster studies trends. At most courses where the tour goes annually, he can tell you what percentage of the time the wind will blow from the north, the south, the east, or the west. On occasion during the year Stricker had told him he had heard enough about wind tendencies. Now, though, both men were baffled. They weren't certain if the wind was across, across-against, or perhaps across and slightly with them. Even Walker wasn't certain what the wind — which had kicked up considerably during the afternoon — was going to do.

They finally agreed to go with a hard five-iron to make sure to get the ball safely across the water. A par would be just fine on this hole and 18. Two pars would give Stricker a 66 and the lead. Stricker pulled the five-iron. One of Walker's strengths as a caddy — as with all good caddies — is making sure his player has absolute confidence in what he is about to do. The two words caddies are most likely to say to a player when a decision has been made on a club are "that's perfect." Even if they feel some doubt, they want to be sure their players don't.

Now, though, Walker wasn't certain that was the way he felt. Stricker, looking for that boost of confidence, stood behind the ball for a second and said, "This it, Earl?"

Walker didn't answer. He was looking at the trees, searching for a clue from the wind. "Yeah, I guess," he said finally. "I'm not absolutely sure it isn't a six, though."

Stricker almost gagged. The last thing he wanted to hear was doubt from Walker. He had the club in his hand, he was ready to play. Now he had two choices: he could back off and discuss it some more, or he could play the five, the club he had felt certain was right just five seconds earlier.

"I decided to play the five," he said. "I figured if I was going to make a mistake I would rather make it long than short."

By his own admission, he was distracted by his doubts. Instead of getting over the ball and simply focusing on putting a good swing on it, he was over the ball wondering if he was doing the right thing. The result was his worst swing of the day. He caught the ball thin and, almost as soon as it took off, he knew it was in trouble. "That's wet," he said, disgusted.

He was right. The ball splashed into the lake — Stricker's second water ball of the week — and Stricker was walking down the hill off the tee a moment later with steam coming out of his ears. "I was hot," he said. "I was hot at myself for a bad swing and not thinking clearly and I was hot at Earl for being uncertain."

The indecision, the poor swing, and the drowned golf ball led to a double-bogey five. Stricker managed to right himself on 18 to make par, but a potential 66 had become a 68. "Still a good round," he said when it was over. "But I'll probably think about 17 tonight more than all the good shots I hit."

As unhappy as he was with what had happened at 17, he wasn't at all unhappy with his position. Vijay Singh had gone out early and matched the 66 Woods had shot on Thursday and was now leading at four under par. Stricker, Colin Montgomerie (69), and Scott Gump (67) were a stroke back at three under. Then, at two under, came Woods (72 on Friday), Davis Love (68), Brad Faxon (also 68), Steve Elkington (69), and David Fay's favorite golfer, Andrew Magee (68). Lurking three shots back in the group at one under was Mark O'Meara, who seemed to have mastered the technique of hanging in the pack and then charging on Sunday. He had been five shots back after two rounds at the Masters and three shots back after two rounds at the British. Now he was three shots back again.

As it turned out, the wind and drying out of the greens did push the cut higher than anticipated, to five-over-par 145. It was that extra stroke that saved Fred Couples. He had shot 71 on Friday morning and walked off the course convinced his week was over. Like Justin Leonard at the British, he was distraught and didn't really want to hear it when people tried to tell him that scores would go up in the afternoon and he might survive at 145. "I just didn't play well enough," he said. "I feel like I let a lot of people down."

He left with Thais and her children to spend the afternoon with a friend who lived about eighty miles away from the golf course. Couples was scheduled to play an exhibition match against Ernie Els in Canada on Monday, so he figured he would spend the weekend hanging around and then make the trip north. Everyone went out on his friend's boat that afternoon, and Couples tried to forget about the golf tournament. Late in the afternoon they got back to the house and turned on the TV. Looking at the scores, Thais said, "Fred, I think you're going to make it. It looks like the cut is going to five over."

Couples wasn't believing until he was seeing. But by the time TBS went off the air, he knew Thais had been right. There were fifty-nine players at four over or better and sixteen more at five over. Those seventy-five players would play the weekend. Normally, making the cut on the number is not something that sends Couples into paroxysms of joy. He would always rather play the weekend than not play it, but playing it without being in contention is often difficult for him. At 11 shots back on a golf course where a low, low score was almost out of the question, the odds of his being in contention were somewhere between slim and none, leaning strongly in the direction of none.

But he didn't care. The week had not been a golf washout. He would get to play all four rounds and he had a chance for some kind of redemption on the weekend. He was thrilled. "I was really and truly excited when I made it," he said. "I just didn't want to leave my hometown feeling the way I felt at the end of the round on Friday."

His tee time was 7:46, which would mean leaving the house by 5:30 the next morning to make the drive back to Sahalee, but that was okay too. All he wanted to do was show all those fans who had come out to cheer for him that he was better than what they had seen on Thursday and Friday. Now he would have that chance.

A number of big-name players weren't as lucky as Couples. John Daly added a 76 to go with his opening 80 and was long gone by nightfall on Friday. Lee Janzen tried to fight back but never could get anything going. His 72 for 148 left him three shots outside the cut.

David Duval never even threatened to get close to the number. He started the day figuring he would need a 68 to play on Saturday and Sunday and got the 8 part right — he shot 78. Unlike a lot of the other players, Duval hadn't liked Sahalee from the first time he laid eyes on it on Monday morning. He thought it was wrong of the PGA to create such a U.S. Open–like setup, to take the driver out of everyone's bag, to grow the rough as long as they had.

Duval knew that disliking the golf course was not the way to go into a major championship. He spent most of the week trying to talk himself into a different attitude. He reminded himself that the only way for him to steal the player-of-the-year award from O'Meara was to win the last major and then make such a runaway on the money list that one major title and the money title might outweigh winning two majors. "Probably a long shot," he said. "But it's my only chance."

On Tuesday afternoon he had a long talk on the putting green with Bob Rotella, brain guru to the stars, about his negative attitude toward Sahalee. Rotella has known Duval since he was in high school, and he said nothing as Duval vented. Finally he asked him quietly what he thought he could do about it.

Duval thought for a moment. "Nothing, I guess," he said. "No matter what I think of the golf course, they're going to give someone the Wanamaker Trophy on that 18th green Sunday afternoon."

Rotella nodded. Duval had answered his own question about attitude. His approach had to be "I'm here to win the PGA," not "Why do they have to play the PGA on a golf course I don't like?" Duval tried mightily to flush the negative thoughts from his mind but couldn't do it. He started poorly, played poorly in the middle, and finished poorly. Other than that, it was a good week. It was the first cut he had missed since February.

Scott McCarron had no problems with the golf course or with attitude. In fact, he went to bed on Thursday night thinking he had a real chance to contend. He had finished his first round with a birdie at the almost un-birdieable 18th and had shot 69. He had been struggling to find some consistency in his game all summer. Maybe it was going to come together just in time.

Or maybe not. Even though he had played well on Thursday, McCarron's confidence was still shaky, especially on the greens. A week earlier, flying to the Buick Open, he had arrived in Michigan, opened his clubs, and found that the shaft on his putter had somehow been snapped during the trip. For some players, a snapped putter is no big deal. For McCarron, it was a disaster. He had used the same putter during his entire time on tour and, making matters worse, the company that made the putter no longer made the kind of shaft he had in his.

More than any aspect of the game, putting is psychological. McCarron, having gone through his yips period, knew that better than anyone. Intellectually he understood that a new putter and a new shaft wouldn't make very much difference in how he stroked the ball. Emotionally, though, he felt as if he had been left on a deserted island with no food, no water, and — most important — no putter.

On Thursday, he had made a few putts. On Friday, he started out missing them. He shot 39 going out and wasn't happy. "I went from looking at the leader board to looking at the cut line," he said. "I got discouraged. And when I got discouraged, I got careless." A bad round became an awful one when he double-bogeyed 11, double-bogeyed 12, and bogeyed 13. Now, he was nine over par for the day, eight over for the tournament, and very much on the outside looking in when it came to the cut. He was disgusted not only with his golf but with his attitude.

"For a few holes there I actually stopped caring," he said. "I'm not sure the last time I let that happen to me, but that is definitely not who I am as a golfer. The second double bogey was a direct result of the first because I was pissed off and pouting and feeling sorry for myself. There's no excuse for that. Not ever."

To his credit, McCarron gave himself a lecture after the not-caring stretch and played better from that point on. He even birdied 16 and 17 — making a 70-foot putt across the green at 17 — and stood on the 18th tee needing a birdie to make the cut. Knowing that, he tried to kill his drive and hooked it into the left rough. From there he had no chance to get on the green and ended up making bogey to miss the cut by two. But at least he had fought back into position where he had a chance. That gave him a glimmer of hope, although he left Sahalee with his game, his putter, and his smile all missing.

The most surprising cut misser had to be Jim Furyk. Mr. Consistency — he had been fourth, fourteenth, and fourth in the previous three majors — was running on fumes by the time he got to Sahalee. He had flown straight from the British Open to Sutton, Massachusetts, to play in the CVS Classic. Normally, he wouldn't have even thought about playing the week after the British, but the CVS event was going out of business after 1998, swept away by PGA Tour politics, and Furyk felt he should go and play as a show of respect to the tournament organizers, even if he was tired and in need of a rest.

Although he said he didn't regret going to play (and missing the cut), it threw off his preparations for the PGA. "It was more mental than physical," he said. "I didn't feel great about the way I was hitting the ball going in, and maybe there was some leftover disappointment from the British. I wanted to play well, I really did, but I just never got anything going. I actually hit the ball a lot better than I did at the U.S. Open, but there I made putts to keep myself alive. At Sahalee, I never made any putts. Even when I'm hitting the ball well, I'm not going to do well if I don't make putts."

Furyk shot 72–74, missing the cut by one. Even though he knew he wasn't playing well, missing the cut was a shock to his system. He always expected to make cuts, especially at the majors. He had played in thirteen majors prior to Sahalee and had never missed a cut. In fact, he had played the weekend in every major since the 1995 PGA. The only players with longer streaks than that were Mark O'Meara and Ernie Els, who had made every major cut since the 1995 British Open, one tournament before Furyk's string began.

Making the cut in all four majors is not nearly as easy as it looks. In fact, in 1998 only seven players accomplished the feat: Tiger Woods, Fred Couples, Brad Faxon, Phil Mickelson, John Huston, O'Meara, and Els. That's a small and elite group. Jim Furyk had been in the group in 1997. It never occurred to him until late on Friday at Sahalee that he wouldn't repeat the feat in 1998.

"It was a sad way to end the year in the majors," he said when it was over. "As disappointing as losing was at the Masters and the British, I at least felt as if I was part of the golf tournament. At the PGA, I never felt as if I was there."

He was gone by dusk on Friday. So was Justin Leonard, who, like McCarron, played well on Thursday (70) but had a disastrous Friday (77). Perhaps the most disappointed man to miss the weekend was Tom Watson, who shot 72–76. For Watson it would be the first time in his twenty-seven-year professional career that he failed to make the cut in at least one major. He was three weeks shy of his forty-ninth birthday. One thing was certain: Tom Watson would not go gently into the night or onto the Senior Tour. He would be back at the majors in 1999 — playing practice rounds with Fred Couples no doubt — determined to wipe away the memories of 1998.

29

Vijay Day

If Sahalee had done nothing else the first two days, it had produced a tightly bunched field. After two days at the U.S. Open there had been thirteen players within five shots of the lead. At the PGA there were twenty-eight. Of those twenty-eight, six — Steve Elkington, Tiger Woods, and Davis Love (all two shots back of Singh), Mark O'Meara (three back), Hal Sutton (four back), and Paul Azinger (five back) — had won major championships. The rest were all trying to cross that great divide from professional golfer to major champion.

Steve Stricker left Sahalee on Friday night feeling good. He had gone to the range after his postround session with the media and redirected his focus from the mistake at 17 to what was to come on the weekend. Although he would have liked to have had the five-iron back, he wasn't unhappy to be one shot out of the lead as opposed to leading. "Less attention that way," he said. "Less questions about Nicki and the baby and what happened last year. All I really had to do was go through my round. That was no problem. And I was still in great position."

He and Walker went to dinner at an Outback Steak House near the hotel where Stricker was staying. They were finishing dessert when a very frightened-looking young woman came in the front door, looked nervously around the restaurant, and then made a beeline to the booth where they were sitting.

"I need to sit with you guys for a couple of minutes," she said.

Stricker and Walker looked at each other. "Are you in trouble?" Walker asked.

"No big deal," the woman said. "I just need to sit here for a little while, okay?"

"Okay with us," Stricker said. "But we aren't staying very long."

The woman was looking around the restaurant. Other than apparently being quite scared, Stricker and Walker had no sense that she had been drinking or was on drugs of any kind. "Do you want something to eat or drink?" Stricker asked.

"No, you're very kind. I have to go."

And with that, she stood up and walked out the door.

"I wonder if this means I can tell people I had a date tonight?" Walker asked.

They were left to wonder what kind of trouble she had been in. They paid their bill, then walked across the street to a Safeway to buy some soda for the refrigerator in Stricker's room. As they were walking out of the Safeway, they noticed a police car. Standing next to the police car, wearing handcuffs, was Walker's date.

"Whoo boy," Stricker said. "You almost had to spend the night in the police station explaining why you were with that woman."

"Me?" Walker asked. "What about you?"

"She was your date, wasn't she?"

He had a point.

Stricker went straight back to his hotel room after that, figuring he would leave Walker on his own to pursue his social life. He called Nicki, told her the story about the restaurant, went through the round with her in detail, and went to bed. He slept soundly, feeling better about his golf than he had in a long time.

Saturday morning was cloudy and cool, a marked change from the warm, almost sticky weather that had been in place the rest of the week. The golf course would play softer under such conditions, meaning that low scores might be more prevalent than they had been. Fred Couples, even after his predawn wake-up, provided early evidence of that by shooting 67, finishing his round just as the leaders were getting ready to tee off. Surprisingly, though, no one who was within shouting distance of the leaders was making any kind of early move.

Stricker was in the second-to-last group, paired with Scott Gump, a thirty-two-year-old journeyman who had been back and forth between the big tour and the Nike Tour throughout the '90s and somehow managed to smile each and every time someone asked him if he was related to Forrest Gump. Singh and Colin Montgomerie were behind Stricker and Gump, and Davis Love and Andrew Magee were right in front of them, with Tiger Woods and Brad Faxon one group ahead of them. For someone who hadn't finished in the top ten in a major prior to Olympic, it was heady stuff.

But it didn't seem to faze Stricker. He got off to a quick start with birdies at number two and number three and quickly settled into the kind of groove a player dreams about getting into late in a major. For five holes, he didn't miss a shot. At the sixth, he pushed his drive into a bunker and had to lay up short of the green. From there, he hit a gorgeous pitch-and-run shot to within three feet to save par. Then, at the eighth, he slammed a six-iron through the wind to 18 feet and made the birdie putt. He was three under for the day, six under for the tournament, and in the lead.

Most of the other leaders were going backward. Montgomerie, who had talked excitedly about the putting lesson he had taken from putting guru Dave Pelz after the British Open, suddenly lost the touch he had wielded on Friday and couldn't make a thing. He shot 77, consigning himself to another winter of questions about when he was going to break through and win a major. Magee shot 72 to slide backward, and Woods shot 70, running in place throughout the day. Love managed to finish strong to shoot 69, as did O'Meara.

That left Singh to try and keep pace with Stricker, who looked for a while as if he was going to open a big lead. After he turned in 32, he looked capable of going very low. But his hot putter didn't stay hot, although his ball striking never wavered. "It was the best I've hit the ball in two years," he said. "Other than the drive at six and the drive [into a bunker] at 16, I can't remember a shot that bothered me."

If Stricker's putter had matched the rest of his game, he might have shot in the low 60s. He missed from 15 feet at 10, from 12 feet at 11, from 18 feet at 12, from 15 feet at 14. He missed three greens all day — 6, 13, and 18 — and each time he got up and down for par. His only nonpar on the back nine was a gorgeous birdie at 16 after his tee shot had gone into the bunker. He hit his best shot of the day, a 169-yard seven-iron that skidded to a halt 10 feet to the right of the flag. He rolled in the putt, which got him to seven under for the championship. He then hit another five-iron at the 17th, but, unlike Friday's, this one ended up safely on the green and he two-putted for a routine par.

Walking off that green, he glanced up at the scoreboard for the first time in a while and was stunned to see that he and Singh were tied for the lead. Singh had made the turn even par for the day, but then birdied 12, 14, and 15. "I really thought I was ahead by a couple of shots," he said. "But then it occurred to me that the roars I had been hearing behind me were for Vijay. It took me a couple of seconds to regroup, but then I was okay. I was even more surprised to see that no one else was really that close to us."

No one was within four shots of them. Love, Elkington, and Billy Mayfair, who had shot 67, were at three under, and O'Meara and Woods were in a group at two under. That meant that one of them would have to go low or Stricker and Singh would both have to spit the bit if someone other than the two leaders was going to win.

Stricker finished his day with a wonderful up and down, pitching to eight feet after he had hit his second shot under a tree at 18 and making the putt for par. He was standing outside the scoring area talking to a couple of reporters when Singh walked by. "Great save at 18," Singh said, having witnessed it from the fairway. "I guess I'll see you tomorrow."

"It should be fun," Stricker said.

They both laughed. Each knew that playing in the last group of a major championship was many things, but fun wasn't one of them.

Stricker and Walker went back to the Outback that night — more out of superstition than anything else — but specifically requested a booth a good distance from the door. Stricker had talked to Nicki before dinner and she had told him that CBS was sending a crew to the house to talk to her the next morning. She felt good, but missed being out there. For Stricker, the evening was bittersweet. He had worked long and hard to get to this position, to play in the last twosome at a major championship.

But a lot of that work had been done with Nicki by his side and now she couldn't be there to share it. He and Walker joked about finding someone to run onto the green for the traditional wife's hug should he win. "Maybe we can bail my date out in time," Walker joked.

Stricker was tired and was confident he would sleep well. Being on the west coast was a bonus because it meant the last tee time was at noon, instead of three o'clock, the way it would be on the east coast. The less time he had to wait, the better.

As it turned out, he was right about sleeping. He was asleep almost before he hit the pillow, worn out by the long day of golf, the postmatch interviews, and the time he had spent on the range before leaving the course. Staying asleep was an entirely different issue. He was awake well before dawn, lying in bed thinking about the day to come. He was confident he could win. He had come a long, long way in just a couple of months, from qualifying at Woodmont for the Open to playing in the last group of the PGA. His game felt as good as it had felt in a long time, and even though he hadn't made any long putts on the back nine, he hadn't been close to a three putt or, for that matter, a bogey. And when he had to make key six-to-ten-foot putts, he had been rock solid.

A few miles away, Singh was just as restless. He too had traveled a long way — literally and figuratively — to get to this day. At thirty-five, Singh was an enigma to most people on tour, a quiet man who kept to himself most of the time, preferring to find a tucked-away corner of the range where he could pound balls until dark. From the day he had joined the tour full-time in 1993 he had replaced Tom Kite as the tour's number one range rat.

Getting to the tour had not been easy for him. Raised in Fiji, he had learned the game there, playing on golf courses growing up that had sand-based greens. He had played on the Australasian Tour early in his career but had been suspended from that tour after an incident in which he was accused of signing for an incorrect score at a tournament in Indonesia when he was in jeopardy of losing his exempt status on the tour. Singh has emphatically maintained his innocence whenever the incident has been brought up through the years, but the fact that it happened and that he is still asked about it years later has clearly been a factor in his often uneasy relationship with the media.

Singh had to go back to work as a club pro after the scorecard flap, spending two years in Malaysia. He came back and joined the European Tour after that, and grew into a solid player who could hit the ball as well as anyone but couldn't putt to save his life. That was still his reputation on tour: great hit, no putt. He had gone through so many putters and putting grips and putting stances that he had given up counting them years ago. In 1998 alone he had used a half-dozen putters and several grips. After the U.S. Open, his wife, Ardena, had suggested he go back to putting cross-handed and he had seemed to find comfort putting that way again.

He had been in position in majors before, especially at the PGA. In both 1993 and 1996 he had been in serious contention on the back nine on Sunday before his putter had done him in. He had won six times on tour, and other players would tell you the number would be closer to six-teen or twenty-six if he could putt. Singh knew all that. He also knew that there was only one player in the field within four strokes of him and that player (Stricker) had even less experience contending for a major ti-tle than he did. He had shot 66–67 the last two rounds and felt as com-fortable on the greens as he could ever remember.

It was well after two o'clock in the morning when Ardena Singh rolled over in bed and looked at her husband, who was staring at the ceiling.

"Are you sleeping?" she asked.

"Oh yeah," he answered. "I'm sound asleep. Can't you tell?"

As David Duval had said earlier in the week, someone was going to be handed the Wanamaker Trophy on Sunday afternoon. Singh and Stricker knew they might never have a better chance than this to kiss a major championship trophy.

"I would take it back to Wisconsin," Stricker said, grinning on Sat-urday night, "and fill it up with milk."

Stricker finally gave up on sleep at 7:30, got dressed, and went across the street to McDonald's for breakfast. He needed to get out of the hotel and get some fresh air. It was raining for the first time all week, the tem-perature comfortable, the wind light. Once again, the golf course would play wet. Stricker smiled at the notion that someone might go low on a day like this. Maybe if it were Thursday or Friday or even Saturday. But on Sunday at a major? Not likely.

While Stricker and Singh were fighting nerves, Mark O'Meara was excited when he woke up. He was five shots behind Stricker and Singh, but there were only three players between him and the leaders. He knew Stricker and Singh were fine players. But he also knew what kind of nerves could come into play the first time you were in serious contention to win a major. "I remembered how I felt the first couple of times I played late on Sunday at a major," he said. "It's an easy thing to think you're ready for but not that easy to actually deal with."

O'Meara was convinced that if he could get off to a good start and put some heat on the leaders, he would have a legitimate chance to win and make history. He had tried very hard all week to low-key the enormousness of such an achievement, but now he actually had a shot at it and he couldn't help but think about it — at least a little. "Ben Hogan and me," he said. "That would certainly be nice company to be keeping."

O'Meara was paired with Frank Lickliter, whose highest previous finish in a major championship was a tie for sixty-seventh, three groups from the end. That meant he would be playing about two holes in front of Stricker and Singh all day. They would probably hear his birdie roars; he would hear theirs.

The rain had stopped by the time the leaders began teeing off and the day was actually perfect for golf: cool and comfortable. If Sahalee could guarantee another week of the weather it produced, the PGA might consider selling Valhalla and moving all future championships to the Pacific Northwest.

Both Stricker and Singh could feel their stomachs tightening as they finished their preround routines. They had played together often in the past — including the previous Sunday — and got along fine. "Vijay doesn't say much and I don't say much," Stricker said. "So we're very happy to be paired with each other."

They both made pars at number one, Singh leaving his second shot short of the green before pitching to two feet. The second shot had been the product of a nervous swing, and Singh seemed to understand that. Walking off the second tee he had a little talk with Dave Renwick, his caddy, but his words seemed to be directed more at himself than at Renwick. "All I can do, Dave, is go out and try to play good golf," he said. "If I hit my shots and somebody beats me, I have no problem with that. There's no reason really for me to be worried or uptight."

Perhaps he should have given Stricker that same talk. Having not mishit a ball since the 17th hole on Friday, Stricker hit a wild snap hook off the tee at number two. It genuinely surprised him because he had no idea where it came from. He had been absolutely solid with his three-wood off the tee all week. But, as he had noted to himself earlier in the morning, this wasn't Thursday, Friday, or Saturday, and those cameras following his every step weren't there because he was about to become a dad in two weeks.

When he got to his ball, the news wasn't very good. It was buried in the trees and his only play was to slash it a few yards forward. He then chipped across the fairway into the right rough. He was now lying three and still had 175 yards to the hole — over water. Walker knew he had to get him to slow down and calm down. Singh, seeing Stricker's troubles, had passed on the idea of trying to clear the water with his second shot and had safely laid up just short of the water. Stricker had to get out of this hole with no worse than a bogey or his dream could die a quick and painful death.

"Hey, we're fine," Walker said to Stricker. "Let's just hit a solid shot to the middle of this green and go play the rest of the golf course. Long, long way to go."

Stricker knew he was right. He didn't need to pull out any miracle shots here and chance getting wet and taking a huge number. He hit a comfortable six-iron onto the green and almost made the par putt from 30 feet. He happily took his bogey and felt even better about it when Singh missed his 12-foot birdie putt. After all that, he had dropped only one shot. "I actually walked off the green feeling pretty good about it all," he said. "It could have been so much worse."

It got much better at the third. Stricker laced a six-iron to 18 feet and drained the birdie putt to get back even with Singh. He managed a smile walking off the green — it was as if the birdie had given him his sea legs. He looked even more solid on the fourth, draining a 12-footer for another birdie. Now he was rolling again, just as on Saturday. He was also leading at eight under. Singh had made four straight pars and trailed by one.

At the fifth hole, the players got their first look at a leader board. One name and one red number jumped right at them. The name was O'Meara and the red number was 5. Stricker and Singh had heard one huge roar early on but hadn't been sure who it was for. It could have been for Woods (who, as it turned out, made no move at all during the day) or it could have been O'Meara.

It was O'Meara. Knowing he had some serious ground to make up, O'Meara had gambled at number two, going for the green, and had cleared the water, the ball ending up 18 feet from the hole. He made the putt for eagle and all of a sudden thoughts of Augusta and Birkdale on Sunday came flooding back. Now he had a chance, a very real chance. When he birdied the fifth, he was at five under and alone in third place with lots and lots of holes left to play.

"I felt great at that point," he said later. "Very, very pumped. In all the years I've played golf I can't remember hearing a crowd like that just for me. I mean, they were really into it and I was enjoying every second of it."

Given a choice, most of the crowd would have opted for Fred Couples as the winner. That wasn't going to happen. Couples played well again on Sunday, shooting a 68 that enabled him to finish the tournament at even par in a tie for thirteenth place. It was a solid comeback, a nice way to end the week, but not what he had in mind coming in. "I had a ball the whole week," he said. "The way the crowds were it was like playing 72 straight 18th holes, walking on the green to an ovation every time. I was happy I played well on the weekend, but let's face it, the pressure was gone. I knew I couldn't win."

Option two for the crowd probably would have been Woods. He had started off superbly on Thursday, but never got anything going after that, with rounds of 72, 70, and 71. He had finally straightened out the putting problems that had plagued him earlier in the year, but now something had gone awry with his swing. Even without his driver he couldn't keep the ball consistently in the fairway and, as he put it, "I made a lot of putts, but most of them were for par."

Woods talked about how encouraged he was with three top-ten finishes in the '98 majors (eighth at the Masters, third at the British, now tenth at the PGA), and there was no doubting the progress he had made in terms of course management and maturity. There was also no doubting the fact that he was not going to go home and jump up and down about three top tens and zero wins. He would be twenty-three when the Masters rolled around in 1999, still just a kid in golf years, but considerably older and wiser than the twenty-one-year-old who had made it look so easy in 1997.

With Couples and Woods out of the picture, the fans were left to root for history, and O'Meara was the one with the chance to make it. They were hooting and hollering when he made the birdie at the fifth, figuring that Stricker and Singh were bound to hear him coming. But even for great players, golf remains the most fragile game. O'Meara hit his drive off line at the sixth and made bogey. Then he missed the green at seven, leading to another bogey, and then he missed a third straight green and bogeyed the eighth. Bogey-bogey-bogey. He had hit three slightly nervous shots — one at each hole — and each had cost him. No one knew better than O'Meara how narrow the margin was on Sunday at a major. Five shots back at the start, he couldn't afford three mistakes. All the work to get into contention on the first five holes went down the drain just that quickly. Standing on the ninth tee, O'Meara looked a little bit stunned.

"I was, a little bit," he said. "But that's golf. I made a couple bad swings, hit a couple bad shots. I didn't feel as if my mind wandered or I got too excited, I don't think I'm that way. But you never know. Something happened."

O'Meara had been places all year where he had never been before and had come through. He had closed at both the Masters and the British with amazing cool. He had stood over a 20-foot birdie putt to win a major, the kind of putt every golfer dreams about lining up, and rolled it in. He had made an almost as dramatic birdie on the 17th hole at Birkdale and been flawless in the playoff. But when you are stalking history — from *behind* — there is no margin for error. Everything has to go right, and one mistake — much less three — can sink you. Those three holes ended the dream for O'Meara.

Standing on the ninth tee, he knew what had happened. He was six shots back with 10 holes to play. If he had been chasing one player, there might have been a slim chance to come back. But he was chasing two, and it was highly unlikely that both would collapse and give him a chance. O'Meara gave himself a pep talk. The only thing to do was to try and hit every fairway and every green the rest of the way and finish as high as he could. There was no reason to give up, even if winning was now almost out of the question.

"If I couldn't win, I wanted to finish as high as I possibly could," he said. "I wanted to be able to look back and say I gave it everything I had for 72 holes, and if someone was better that was fine. I can live with that."

O'Meara was almost perfect the last 10 holes. He made eight pars and two birdies, to shoot 68. He had been remarkably consistent all week: 69–68–70–68. The one thing he hadn't done was throw in a really low round, which, in the end, was why he didn't win. He finished in a tie for fourth, the second highest finish anyone had ever produced in the PGA after winning two majors earlier in the same year. At forty-one, after having a "nice" career, O'Meara had produced a historic year.

Once O'Meara slipped, the tournament became, for all intents and purposes, match play between Singh and Stricker. Steve Elkington, the 1995 champion, made a late charge, but would have needed a miracle finish on 18 to have any chance. Instead, he bogeyed the hole, clinching third place.

Stricker's lead didn't last very long. After his back-to-back birdies at three and four, he made par at the fifth, but Singh hit a gorgeous six-iron to within six feet and made his first birdie of the day. Once again, they were tied. Stricker then bogeyed the sixth. Having pushed his drive to the right on Saturday, he overcompensated and pulled it left into the trees. He almost pulled off a miracle from there, punching a low four-wood through a tiny opening. He was 229 yards from the green, and he got the ball to within 10 yards. But his chip was mediocre, rolling eight feet past the cup, and he missed the putt. Singh led again, eight to seven, as the players liked to put it.

The next hole proved to be a major turning point. Stricker hit a superb nine-iron second shot to about seven feet, setting up what looked like an almost certain birdie. Singh pushed his second shot to the right of the green into some high grass. He looked the shot over for what felt like forever, then flopped a wedge 10 feet past the hole. His par putt was longer than Stricker's birdie putt. But Singh — the mediocre putter — made his. Stricker — the excellent putter — missed. Instead of Stricker retaking the lead, as seemed possible, even likely, Singh still had the lead.

"I never got a feel for that green," Stricker said later. "I missed a short putt there on Saturday too, and I was thinking about it on Sunday. There seemed to be a little ledge right around the hole and I never figured it out."

Stricker saved par at the eighth after missing the green, but on nine he came over a three-iron badly and the ball made a beeline for the water, way left of the green. It was the third time in four days Stricker had drowned a ball on a par-three, and it looked as if his chances to win might drown for good at that hole. But, after dropping in the fairway, he almost holed his wedge shot, the ball spinning to within a foot of the hole. That gave him a bogey when five had seemed inevitable and kept him in the game. He walked to the 10th tee trailing Singh by two: eight to six.

It was now Stricker's turn to give himself a talking-to. The walk from the ninth green to the tenth tee at Sahalee is a couple of hundred yards. Stricker was almost oblivious to the fans lined up along the ropes yelling encouragement at him. He was angry with himself. After the birdies at three and four there was no reason to play scared or nervous, but he felt he had. He had missed three of the next five greens and had let his best birdie chance (seven) slip away. And yet, two down with nine to play, he could still win.

Both players parred the 10th, bringing them to the par-five 11th. The 11th is Sahalee's signature hole because of two huge trees that pinch into the fairway about 75 yards short of the green. The trees form what look like a pair of football goalposts. To get to the green, a player has to squeeze a shot between the trees. Throughout the week, players who managed to make the shot had taken to throwing their arms into the air the way a football referee does to signal that a field goal is good.

The players had to wait on the tee because Davis Love and Billy Mayfair were still in the fairway waiting to play their second shots. Stricker killed the time chatting with Larry Startzel, the rules observer assigned to the last group. Startzel was a club pro from Stowe, Vermont, and he and Stricker, joined by Singh, chatted about the wonders of New England in the summer and fall. They sounded like three guys waiting out slow players on a summer Sunday. Which they were. Except there was a little more at stake than a $5 nassau.

Once Love and Mayfair started walking to the green, Stricker and

Singh both hit good drives, Singh on the left side of the fairway, Stricker on the right. Both decided to try for the field goal. Stricker pushed his three-wood off the right upright (tree) and the ball landed at the base of the tree, a good 80 yards from the green. Given that opening, Singh badly pushed his three-wood off the same upright. But his ball had come from a different angle — left to right — and it hit off the inside of the tree and ricocheted between the uprights onto the green.

Field goal good. Singh had a 20-foot eagle putt. It was the break of the day and of the week.

For a moment, Stricker — like everyone else — stared in disbelief. Singh's ball could have gone anywhere. At best, he should have been looking at a third shot similar to Stricker's. But he wasn't. He had a two-shot lead and an eagle putt. Walking to his ball, Stricker turned to Walker and said, "Earl, we gotta make birdie here."

So he did just that. Forced to play pitch-and-run under the tree, he ran the ball onto the green, eight feet to the right of the cup. Singh's putt for eagle slipped past the hole, and now Stricker could get off the hole without losing any ground if he could make his birdie putt. It went dead center. Singh's three-footer for birdie actually looked for a split second like it might die to the right of the hole, but it caught the corner and curled in. The margin was still two.

But Stricker now had a little momentum for the first time since the fourth hole. He had been staring at a three- or four-shot deficit after Singh's ricochet; now it was just two, and he knew Singh had to feel as if he had blown an opportunity. For the first time all day, Singh looked just a little shaky. The championship was down to six holes. Singh had the lead, but Stricker hadn't gone away.

Singh pulled his tee shot on the 12th hole into the left bunker. From there, he had no chance to reach the green and his third shot came up seven feet short of the hole. He missed the par putt for his first bogey of the day. Stricker also missed the green, but blasted from the left bunker to within a foot to save par. Now the margin was one again: eight to seven. Stricker was convinced that if he could get even with Singh, he would win the tournament. By his own admission, Singh was tight, un-derstandably so.

They both parred 13 and 14. At 15, the 417-yard uphill par-four,

Stricker split the middle with his tee shot. Singh took a long time on the tee deciding what club to hit. "I'm thinking two-iron," he said to Renwick.

Renwick is one of the most experienced caddies on tour. He worked for José María Olazabal when he won the Masters in 1994 and for Elkington when he won the PGA in 1995. He had been in the heat on the last day of a major more than his player had. So he didn't feel the least bit reticent about telling him exactly what he thought. He had already lectured him a hole earlier — after another hooked drive — telling him he needed to loosen up and play, that he was playing tight and nervous, and that he wasn't going to win the golf tournament playing that way.

Now, when Singh suggested two-iron, he shook his head emphatically. "You've hit driver on this hole every single day, even the practice rounds," he said. "Why change now? Do what you've done all week. Hit the driver and trust your swing."

Singh knew he was right. He took out the driver and hit his best tee shot of the day, bombing it a good 50 yards beyond where Stricker's three-wood shot had landed. That swing seemed to shake Singh loose from the tightness he had felt for several holes. Stricker was coming at him now and he was ready. After Stricker had planted a fabulous seven-iron shot 18 inches from the hole, Singh answered with a pitching wedge that stopped six feet from the cup. Knowing he had to make the putt to keep the lead, Singh curled it just inside the right corner of the cup. Stricker tapped in, and the lead was still one. They both missed birdie chances at 16, and they marched up the hill to the 17th tee with two holes to play and one shot separating them.

The hole location was a dangerous one: right front. Go for the flag and the water — front and right — came into play. Remembering Friday, Stricker selected a four-iron and tried to play for the middle of the green. But nerves got into his swing, and, as he had already done a couple of times earlier, he got over the ball and pulled it left, into the bunker. At least, he thought, it's dry.

Singh's turn. He stood on the tee taking a couple of deep breaths. His competitive senses told him he had a chance for the kill here. "Just put it on the middle of the green," Renwick said. "Right in the middle."

"I know what to do here," Singh said. Renwick was telling him what he already knew. But knowing it and doing it were two different things.

On what he later called his most nervous swing of the day, he hit a shot that was almost a carbon copy of Stricker's. It landed almost on top of his ball in the bunker.

They marched down the hill. With all but one twosome now finished, the crowds following them had become massive. Each heard cheers and shouts of encouragement as he walked to his ball. Each knew that he had to forget the water behind the pin and take a normal swing and try to knock the ball close.

Singh was first. Try as he might, he couldn't exorcise the water from his brain. His shot stopped 12 feet short. Now Stricker had the advantage. If he could get his ball close, the pressure on Singh to make his putt would be almost overwhelming. But Stricker couldn't do it. Just as Singh couldn't execute on the tee, he couldn't execute in the bunker. His shot also checked up short, bouncing perhaps a foot closer to the hole than Singh's.

That meant Singh putted first. It was, arguably, the most important putt in his checkered career as a putter. But he had made several clutch putts earlier in the day and was feeling more confident than he often felt on the greens on a Sunday afternoon. The putt went straight into the hole. Singh was so happy he almost smiled.

Stricker had to make his to have any realistic chance. He knew it and he took his time looking it over. But, as had been the case for much of the day, the ball just wouldn't drop. It slid two inches low. Stricker stared at it in disbelief. His stomach felt as if it had just had a hole gouged in it. After 71 holes of grinding, of believing he was going to win his first major, it would now take a miracle on the 72nd hole for him to win.

It had started to rain, and Stricker suddenly felt wet and cold. He forced himself to think positively as he walked to the 18th tee. "Birdie isn't impossible," he told himself. "And he could get nervous and make a bogey."

All the nerves were gone for Singh now. He blasted his drive around the corner into the fairway. Stricker hit a good tee shot but still had 241 yards to the hole. He and Walker debated on club selection. Walker wanted a two-iron to try and run the ball to the back of the green, where the pin was. Stricker was thinking four-wood. He finally decided Walker was right. He had to try and get the ball close, not just land it on the green and watch it stop 30 feet from the hole. But he was left again, probably overswinging, and the ball ended up in the left bunker. Singh, with almost no pressure remaining, hit a perfect four-iron 25 feet below the flag. The only thing left for him was to take a victory stroll up the 18th fairway.

Like everyone else on tour, Stricker was happy for Singh. He knew how far he had come from the controversy in Indonesia to the pro shop in Malaysia to the hours and hours on the range. Stricker was devastated that he hadn't played a little better, that he hadn't been able to fight through his nerves just a little more. But he was happy for Singh. He came out of the bunker to within five feet, and knowing he had to make the putt to avoid dropping into a second place tie with Elkington, he drained it. Singh, knowing he could three-putt and still win, lagged to four feet.

"Nice run at it, huh?" he said to Stricker.

Stricker couldn't help but laugh. "Yeah," he said, "real aggressive."

Singh didn't need to be aggressive. With a putt to spare, the four-footer might as well have been a four-incher. He knocked it in for a 68 and a four-day total of 271 — nine under par. Stricker was two shots back, Elkington three, O'Meara and Frank Lickliter five.

The rain had stopped as Singh and Stricker came up 18. There was no Davis Love rainbow, but when Singh's eight-year-old son Qass came out to greet him as he walked off the green, there were smiles everywhere.

Stricker looked at Singh, looked at Qass, thought about Nicki, and felt like crying. "Please," he said to reporters a few minutes later, "don't ask me questions about Nicki and the baby. It will make me cry."

He was standing just outside the pro shop, which had been used all week as the scoring area. Several yards away, the victory ceremony was taking place on the putting green. All the PGA suits were out there and, just as David Duval had predicted, the Wanamaker Trophy was indeed being given to someone. That someone was Vijay Singh, and, like everyone else who wins his first major championship, his reaction was disbelief.

"I really never thought this day would come," he said. "I can't really believe it's finally happened."

They never can.

Epilogue

Golf doesn't go away after the last major has been played. After the PGA, there are still eleven weeks left on the official PGA Tour calendar, weeks that are crucial to many players. A few are fighting for postseason awards: money title, player of the year, Vardon Trophy for lowest scoring average. A few more are jockeying to make the top thirty on the money list in order to qualify for the season-ending Tour Championship and — more important — a spot in the next year's Masters and U.S. Open.

"Making the Tour Championship is nice," said Dudley Hart, one of those trying to make the top thirty in the season's final weeks, "but making the Masters and the Open is *important*."

And many players are fighting for their professional lives, trying to make the top 125 on the money list to remain exempt for the next year or, if that is out of the question, trying to make at least the top 150 to retain partially exempt status.

But for the players who expect to compete and contend in the majors, the last day of the PGA is the last day of the golfing year that really and truly matters. "You play in the fall and you try to play well, but it isn't the same," Fred Couples said. "Once the PGA is over, you've spent your emotions. You can't get the same kind of rush you get when you're getting ready for the majors."

Couples had kept his promise to Thais to play a bare-bones schedule during the summer so he could spend more time with her and her two children. He had greatly enjoyed the time at home, adjusting to his new role as husband (to-be on September 26) and step-dad. "The only time I regretted it at all," he said, "was when I was on the golf course."

Try as he might to hit balls at home to stay sharp or even go out and play on occasion, there was absolutely no way to peak his game without playing any tournaments between the majors. After winning the Memorial, Couples played three times in the next eleven weeks: the U.S. Open, the British Open, and the PGA. After the PGA he played even less, if that was possible: the World Series of Golf, Las Vegas, the Tour Championship.

"From a golf standpoint there's no question that wasn't brilliant scheduling, and it showed in my results," Couples said. "If I had worked as hard during the summer as I worked the first five months of the year, who knows what kind of year I could have had.

"But you know what? I started the year out not even knowing if I could play. I had no idea where I was with my back or how I would be after everything that went on in '97. I won twice, I had a great Masters, and I had a great time being with Thais and the kids all summer."

Couples turned thirty-nine in October and believed that as long as he took care of his back and didn't push himself too hard, he could be a top player for another five years. The Masters had reminded him how much he enjoyed being in contention in the majors. He hoped he could put it all together at least one more time at one of them so he could again have the feeling he had at Augusta in 1992. He would no doubt be checking with Jim Nantz for omens.

Mark O'Meara's dream year ended with all the honors and accolades he could have hoped for. He was the PGA Tour Player of the Year even though there was talk in October that if David Duval, who won the money title and the Vardon Trophy, could finish the year off with a victory in the Tour Championship, he might sneak past him in the voting — which is done by the players.

In truth, there was no way for that to happen. Duval had a fabulous year — four victories, second in the Masters, and more than $2.5 million in prize money. But he didn't win two major titles. O'Meara did. "Look, David is a great player and he had a great year," Couples said. "But the fact is, if he had won eight times and Mark won two majors, Mark is the player of the year. The only players who might not understand that are guys who have never contended in a major. Once you've been in the hunt in a major and know what it feels like, you would never ever compare winning a bunch of regular tour events with winning a major."

Duval, who has certainly contended in majors, agreed. "In my heart of hearts, I know Mark wins," he said in October. "I'd just like to finish as strong as I can and make it interesting."

Nothing wrong with that. But the award was going to O'Meara. He added the World Match Play title to his résumé, beating Tiger Woods in a 36-hole final, in September just in case anyone thought he was going to fall off a cliff after his spring and summer performances.

The highlight of his year — among many — may have come on an October afternoon at home. Two friends from Ireland were visiting, returning the trip O'Meara had made with Woods in July before the British Open. On their second day in town, O'Meara decided to surprise them by bringing the Claret Jug with him to the clubhouse at Isleworth. He and the jug showed up in the men's grill along with two bottles of champagne. O'Meara hadn't gotten around to drinking champagne from the jug in the aftermath of his victory. Now he did.

"It was just great," he said. "To those guys, being from Ireland, seeing the Claret Jug up close was a thrill. To get to drink champagne out of it made it that much better. It was great for me too. It reminded me how lucky I'd been to go through the year and have the things happen to me that happened."

There were other benefits from his victories. Perhaps the best of all, as far as O'Meara was concerned, was seeing the way the British Open affected his nine-year-old son, Shaun. "Getting to stand on the green with the Claret Jug, seeing all those people around the 18th green, taking pictures, the whole thing really excited him," O'Meara said. "Ever since we got back from that trip he's looked at golf in a completely different way. He's really into it now, which is exciting for me. I never wanted to push him into it, but if he wants to play, I'm thrilled."

O'Meara did find himself in the middle of some controversy in the fall when Tiger Woods and his father decided they had seen enough of Hughes Norton's act and asked (demanded) that IMG assign another agent to handle the Woods account. Why this divorce came about was —

as you might expect — the subject of endless speculation on tour. Norton chose to place a chunk of the blame on O'Meara, who, he said, had influenced Woods to drop him. Norton went so far as to call O'Meara's father while O'Meara was out of the country to tell him what he thought about Mark poisoning his relationship with the Family Woods.

O'Meara is not the president of the Hughes Norton fan club. Like a lot of players, he sees Norton as a slick, bottom-line guy whose only loyalty is to himself and — perhaps — to IMG. There were rumors everywhere at the time of the split that O'Meara and Woods were going to leave IMG, take O'Meara's agent, Peter Malik, with them, and form their own company.

Someday Woods will leave IMG and form his own company. But at the moment, his long-term contracts with IMG make it almost impossible for him to leave without paying IMG a huge amount of money. O'Meara could have left, but starting out on his own at forty-one, even as the Masters and British Open champion, would have been a big gamble. Both stayed put.

The real reason for the split had more to do with Earl Woods and Hughes Norton than Tiger Woods and Mark O'Meara. When Tiger didn't perform in 1998 the way he had in 1997, someone had to be blamed. It certainly wasn't going to be Earl. Fathers never get fired (except in gymnastics). That left Norton as the most visible and important member of Team Tiger. Earl decided Tiger had been overscheduled, which was a little bit like Bill Clinton claiming it was his lawyer's fault that he was oversexed. Earl had pushed Tiger every bit as hard — if not harder — than IMG. He had wanted all the deals and all the overseas money and all the photo ops. Norton gladly went along because the more Earl cashed in, the more IMG cashed in on fees.

But when the train went off the tracks a little, Norton was an easy target. He had antagonized a lot of people, and a good deal of that antagonism had ricocheted in Tiger's direction. He did want as much control of the Tiger empire as he could possibly get. And, finally, Earl felt as if Norton had been in it strictly for the money, not for the money and the making of an icon. In a sense, that was unfair. Agents are paid to make money for clients, and Norton had done what he had been paid to do. But as had been the case in the past, his arrogance did him in. When he was holding all the cards, he not only made everyone else fold, he made them crawl across the floor to fold. Earl and Tiger Woods figured out that they could hold the cards without humiliating all their opponents. In the end, Earl held the one card that trumped Norton: Tiger.

David Duval didn't win the player of the year award, but he did walk away from 1998 feeling very good about where his golf game was. Not only had he won four tournaments, he had almost won the Masters, and had finished tenth at the U.S. Open and eleventh at the British Open. "Before this year I hadn't really contended in a major," he said. "Now someone had to make a twenty-foot putt at the Masters to keep me out of a playoff, I threw in a couple of 75s at the Open and finished tenth, and I was eleventh at the British. My only real disappointment was not handling my dislike for Sahalee better."

Duval turned twenty-seven in November, meaning he was still just a baby by PGA Tour standards. There was no doubt in the minds of those who followed golf that it was just a matter of time until he won his first major title. Duval, of course, was having none of it. "I think I have the game to win at the majors," he said. "Augusta taught me a lot. But until the day I win one, I'm going to wonder. I think that's human nature. Do I think my time will come? Yes. Do I hope it's real soon? You better believe it."

Justin Leonard's time had come at Troon in 1997. He had then started 1998 with an encouraging eighth place finish at the Masters. But the rest of the year hadn't been nearly as much fun. There had been the Kuchar controversy at Olympic, the disappointing British, and, finally, the missed cut at the PGA. Not the summer he had in mind.

"It wasn't exactly what I was hoping for at the start of the year," he said. "But in a way, it was almost bound to happen. I had been able to peak my game at the majors so well for two years that I almost started taking it for granted that I would play well in them. If I learned anything this summer, it's that it isn't that easy. All of a sudden, I noticed the ankle-high rough and the slick greens and the wind. That's what happens when your game isn't right where you want it to be at a major.

"But I think I learned from it, and I think I'll be a better player next year. It also helped me appreciate how great it is to play well in the majors. There's no feeling like that in golf. Now, because I didn't have that feeling this year, I really want to get it back next year."

By year's end, Leonard was finally able to laugh about Peter Kuchar. "What we're going to do next year is get World Championship Wrestling to put on a cage match," he said. "Me against Peter for the championship belt." He paused and laughed. "Of course I'll be the bad guy in the mask."

If he was looking for someone to referee the match, John Daly might be available. No one needed comic relief at year's end more than Daly. His summer started well at the U.S. Open with his opening 69 and went downhill from there. He missed the cut at the British Open and the PGA, producing embarrassing numbers at both (the 10 on the 18th at Birkdale and the 80 in the first round at Sahalee). He was clearly frustrated with his game at the PGA and appeared far less happy than he had been in the spring, when his golf was good and his family was first back with him.

Two weeks later at Vancouver came a real scare. Late in the first round of the tournament there, Daly got the shakes. Wearing a windbreaker in 80-degree temperature, he began shaking almost uncontrollably on the 15th green. One of his playing partners, David Frost, put his arm around him to try to comfort him, but Daly was so upset he began to cry. The scene was recorded by TV cameras and played back on every sportscast in America during the next few days. Daly finished his round that day and, unlike in the past, he came back and played the next day, even played fairly well.

But the rumors were everywhere that he was drinking again. He wasn't, but he was having serious trouble with his weight, with his emotions, with his frustrations, with his golf game. As hard as he had tried to put his life back together, he clearly wasn't out of the woods yet. He went back to California, back to the 5:30 A.M. meetings, and sought more help. He came back in October and played in the Dunhill Cup at St. Andrews and played well enough to win all his matches for the U.S. team.

Even so, life was still a struggle for Daly. As long as he was in Palm Springs and going to meetings and watching his diet, he was okay. But when he left that cocoon to venture into the world to play golf, life became difficult for him. By year's end, he and Paulette had split again and he had filed for divorce. What lay ahead for him in 1999 was anybody's guess.

The same could be said, in a very different sense, for Phil Mickelson. Financially, he had another great year in 1998, winning twice and finishing fifth on the money list with just under $2 million in earnings. But at the events he wanted most, he couldn't come up with his best golf. At Augusta he played well enough on Saturday to be in serious contention on Sunday. That appeared to be a step in the right direction. But at the other three majors, his Saturday doldrums cropped up again: the back nine got him at Olympic on Saturday, the entire golf course killed him at Birkdale on Saturday, and he couldn't buy a single putt on Saturday at Sahalee en route to shooting 78.

Mickelson has never been an excuse maker or a rationalizer. He wasn't happy with the way he had played in the four weeks that mattered most. He believed that a player good enough to win thirteen times on tour in seven years should be good enough to start winning majors. He knew he was still young — twenty-nine in June 1999 — but he also knew that he wouldn't be young forever. Like Duval, he didn't want people telling him his time would come. He wanted it to be his time.

Jim Furyk, who is one month older than Mickelson, felt much the same way. He wasn't as rich or as famous as Mickelson, and he hadn't won nearly as often on tour — his victory in October at Las Vegas was the third of his career — but he had been a lot closer to winning a major title than Mickelson. Furyk had a remarkable record in the majors. He had six top-five finishes in fourteen attempts (Mickelson had three in twenty starts as a pro) and had been in serious contention to win at both the Masters and the British in 1998.

That was all well and good, but in some ways Furyk was more frustrated than Mickelson, because he had been a putt or two away from breaking through and hadn't done it. "For some reason the Masters bothers me more than the British," he said. "Maybe it's because it's the Masters, and I always wondered if I had the game to play well there. I know I had more chances at the British, but the Masters is the one I think about more." He smiled. "Right now, I'd take any of the four. Just give me one of them and I'll be very happy."

That was exactly the way Steve Stricker felt. He had trouble sleeping for a week after getting home from the PGA. Once he left the golf course on Sunday evening, the reality of being so close without winning hit him hard. He so much wanted to get home and put Sahalee behind him that he spent much of the evening searching for a red-eye flight that would get him out of Seattle that night.

He didn't find one. But when he did get home the next day — "No brass band at the airport, just Nicki," he said, smiling — he had trouble putting the tournament behind him. Maybe if he had been playing that week, it might have been different. But he was home waiting for the baby to arrive and he had a lot of time to sit around and play the dreaded what-if game, which only made him feel worse. He had committed to play in the Wisconsin State Open the following week and he played — and won — but he still wasn't really over the PGA.

He was finally shaken from his doldrums on August 31 when Bobbie Maria Stricker arrived, healthy and happy, after thirteen hours of labor. Stricker didn't cry in the delivery room because, he said, "I was in such awe of the whole thing."

The timing of Bobbie Maria's arrival couldn't have been better. The tour came to Milwaukee that week, and Stricker was able to play and then go home every night. Seeing his friends, receiving congratulations on the baby, getting back to competing, helped greatly. What's more, he played well, finishing second to his friend Jeff Sluman. Then he went home to enjoy being a father.

"I was going to play a couple times in the fall before the Tour Championship, but when it came time to go I didn't want to do it," he said. "I was having so much fun with Nicki and the baby I just said the heck with it."

He had already made enough money to qualify for the Tour Championship, and he would go into 1999 with a place secured in all four of the majors, a far cry from where he had been at the start of 1998. He knew he still had to work on being more confident on the tee, especially late on Sundays. He wanted to win again, and he wanted to have another shot at a major. But he felt a lot better about his game and his life than he had a year earlier.

"Everything is so much better now than it was," he said. "I learned from my mistakes at the end of '96. I'm not going to play at all in November and December, just rest and get ready for next year. Nicki is thrilled to be a mom and I'm very comfortable with Earl [Walker] caddying for me. My swing isn't exactly where I want it, but it's a whole lot better now than it was at the end of '97. I've got my confidence back and, most important, I'm enjoying golf again. That's the best part of it all."

He smiled, thinking of his daughter. "Make that the second best part."

Brad Faxon felt a lot better at the end of 1998 than he had at the end of 1997, but it had little to do with golf.

Slowly but surely during '98 he had picked up the pieces of his life that had been shattered by his divorce. He and Bonnie were getting along well enough that they could work together to try and make the right decisions for their children. He had found a girlfriend he was comfortable with — Alison Tighe, a personal trainer who worked with Faxon, Tom Watson, and Justin Leonard — and, just as important, with whom his girls seemed comfortable. "Alison has two children," he said. "That alone gives her credibility with my kids. They like her. She likes them. Right now, it's a very good situation."

His golf had never really come around the way he had hoped during the year, but it had improved. He had finished eleventh at the British and thirteenth at the PGA and been one of that small group of seven players to make the cut in all four majors. His earnings had plummeted from more than $1.2 million in 1997 to $336,000 in 1998. But he knew there was a reason for that: a lot of the time the last thing on his mind when he was playing golf had been golf.

The only thing really bothering Faxon about his golf as the golf season came to a close was the Masters. Faxon hadn't yet qualified for the tournament he loved most in 1999. "It's killing me," he said one afternoon, standing around on the putting green at Williamsburg. "I've thought about the fact that if I had made one more putt at Augusta I would have made top twenty-four and that would have been it. Or if I had made top sixteen at the Open. Now I have to win a tournament the first three months next year to get in.

"That isn't all bad. I remember in '95 when Davis was in that situation it really focused him and he played well. Maybe that will happen to me." He smiled. "But I still hate it."

As it turned out, though, there was redemption for Brad Faxon. Late in November, at the end of a year full of changes (including redesigning several holes on the golf course and Hootie Johnson replacing Jack Stephens as club chairman), Augusta National announced a number of adjustments in its qualifying standards. One of those changes, which went into effect for 1999, added all players ranked in the world's top fifty at the end of the year to the list of qualifiers. Brad Faxon finished 1998 ranked fortieth in the world. He would play Augusta in 1999.

Dudley Hart had the same problem as Faxon at year's end. He had made progress in terms of the majors, playing in all but the Masters and making the cut in both the British Open and the PGA. But he hadn't finished high enough in any of them or high enough on the money list (fifty-third) to lock down a spot in any of them for 1999.

"I did better this year because I got to play in three of four," he said. "Obviously, I want to play in all four, and the next step is to be really competitive in them. I'm glad I made the cut at the last two I played, but next year I want to get to the point where my goal on Sunday isn't to play in two hours so I can catch a plane. I want to be there at the end, see what it's like, feel what it's like. I haven't done that yet."

Neither had Scott McCarron, although he had felt for one brief moment on the back nine at the Masters that he had an outside chance to win. He had ended up sixteenth — good enough to get him back to Augusta in 1999 — but that had really been the last piece of good news in the majors for 1998. He had made the cut at the U.S. Open but faded to a fortieth place finish, then didn't play in the British because he wasn't exempt and missed the cut at the PGA.

"I took a step back this year, and it really started when I lost my exemption to the British," he said. "I got upset and decided not to go qualify and that was a mistake. I want to be a top player — well, a top player plays in all four majors. I did that in '97 and I didn't do that in '98. I think that affected my confidence, and I was upset at myself for not going. If I didn't qualify, it would have been tough, but it still would have been an experience. And what if I had? I would have gone into the tournament with all sorts of confidence from playing well in qualifying. Instead, I'm home playing at Quad Cities. No knock on Quad Cities, but let's face it, Quad Cities isn't the British Open."

If attitude means anything, Scott McCarron will be back playing good golf for a long time to come — especially in the majors.

Jay Haas knows his time is far more limited than McCarron's. He turned forty-five in 1998 and began the new year knowing he was in the Masters again but unsure about the other three majors. Haas had a good year overall, making $510,000, to finish fifty-second on the money list. He almost won in Texas, which would have made a good year into a great one.

At least he knew as 1999 began that when spring came he would be back at Augusta, playing a practice round with his uncle Bob, enjoying the beauty of the golf course and the feeling that every player has when he walks inside the ropes at the Masters. "I'd like to be able to do that for the rest of my life," he said with a smile. "Of course I'm the only one who can make that happen."

The 1998 majors will be remembered for two things: Mark O'Meara's emergence as a star and lucky breaks. In fact, it may be remembered first and foremost as the Year of the Lucky Break.

Consider: Lee Janzen's ball falling out of the tree at Olympic; O'Meara's ball being found by the spectator and the fact that Reed McKenzie happened to be the observer with his group at Birkdale; Vijay Singh's bank shot off the trees at 11 at Sahalee. If you want, you can even throw in O'Meara's tee shot at number two on Sunday at Augusta, which went straight left and, instead of diving into the trees, kicked off a tree back toward the fairway, from where he was able to make a birdie.

Of course luck and breaks — good and bad — are a part of golf. It is just that when they happen in critical moments during a major championship, they become a part of golf history and golf lore. If a ball falls out of a tree at the Byron Nelson or the Bob Hope, it is a footnote. At Olympic it is remembered forever. Janzen's tree will go down with Sarazen's four-wood, Watson's wedge, and Palmer's 65 at Cherry Hills in the history books.

That's what makes the majors so special. Every year, history is made. Some moments — Tiger Woods at Augusta in '97, Nicklaus at Augusta in '86, Watson at Turnberry in '77, all the way back to Harry Vardon at Chicago Golf Club in 1900 — are more dramatic than others. But every major championship is a piece of history. A victory changes your place in golf's pantheon forever. If Mark O'Meara never wins again, he will go down in history as an important player, a two-time major champion. Before 1998, he was a guy who had made a lot of money.

"Now I catch myself wondering if I might have a shot to win all four of them once," he said late in the year. "I don't think many guys have done that, have they?"

Four: Sarazen, Hogan, Nicklaus, Player.

Thinking about those four names, O'Meara smiled. "You know, if I could do that, I think I'd have to stop saying I'm a nice player. I'd have to say then that I'm a great player."

He would, of course, be right.

If the U.S. Open, as Sandy Tatum once said, identifies the world's best player, it is fair then to say that the four majors together define history's great ones. That isn't to say that the other tournaments don't matter. They do, very much. They set up a pecking order for the game, from the stars to the Q-Schoolers, from the Nike Tour to the mini-tours. Winning any event on the PGA Tour is a major achievement. Just playing on the PGA Tour means you are a superb player.

But the majors separate the good from the great, the nice players from the ones who are remembered. Every year is different. In 1997, the majors were dominated by youth. Woods was twenty-one when he won the Masters; Ernie Els was twenty-seven when he won the U.S. Open; Justin Leonard had just turned twenty-five when he won the British Open. The old man in the group was PGA champion Davis Love, who was thirty-three. A year later, Lee Janzen, who is four months younger than Love, was the youngest player to win a major. O'Meara was forty-one, Singh, thirty-five. Nothing stays the same in major championship golf, which is one of its charms.

Years ago, just before his football team took the field to play a game that would decide the national championship, Vince Dooley, the longtime coach at the University of Georgia, walked into his team's locker room for a pregame pep talk. Instead of talking, though, he walked to a blackboard and wrote down three words:

Today is Forever.

Georgia won the game.

Four days a year, golfers go out to play for Forever. Those are the four Sundays at the major championships. They all know what is at stake. They all know that winning will change their lives and, in some cases, define their lives. They also know that losing can do those things too.

Greg Norman stood on the first tee at Augusta in 1996 with a six-shot lead. He holed out on 18 four hours and 78 shots later trailing Nick Faldo by five. His life hasn't been the same since. Mark O'Meara stood on that same first tee two years later as the King of the Bs. Four hours later, his birdie putt dropped into the left corner of the cup on 18 and his place in the champions locker room was reserved for life.

Those days, those moments, are what bring us back to the majors year after year. Norman's heartbreak; O'Meara's joy; Janzen's tears; Duval's kick in the stomach. The list goes on.

And, thankfully for all of us, will keep going on for years and years to come.

Afterword

In 1999, Tiger Woods came back. He pieced together one of the most remarkable years in the history of golf, winning his second major title (the PGA), winning eight PGA Tour events, and — including European Tour and unofficial tournaments — thirteen events in all. He became the first player since Johnny Miller in 1974 to win eight times on tour in a single year, and the first since Ben Hogan in 1953 to win four straight starts when he finished his tour season by winning the World Series of Golf, the Disney World Classic, the Tour Championship, and the American Express Championship. His earnings for those four weeks: $3,540,000, leading to total earnings of $6.5 million, doubling the record David Duval set in 1998.

But the most amazing thing about Woods's sensational year was this: It didn't even come close to being the story of 1999. Joyously and tragically, the story of the year in 1999 was William Payne Stewart. Twelve months after losing his four-shot lead on U.S. Open Sunday at the Olympic Club to Lee Janzen, Stewart made three glorious putts at 15, 17, and 18 on the final day at Pinehurst to snatch the championship from Phil Mickelson. It was a story of redemption — a golfer overcoming himself and his past to win a title few thought he could win at the age of forty-two.

And then, a little more than four months later, Stewart was gone, killed with five others in a bizarre plane crash in South Dakota. His sudden death, so soon after his extraordinary victory, not only stunned the golf world, it shocked millions who knew little or nothing about golf. Tiger Woods was the player of the year in 1999, but Payne Stewart was the story of the year.

To begin at the beginning, 1999 began with David Duval. He had won the money title in 1998, but Mark O'Meara had been voted player of the year for two reasons: the Masters and the British Open. O'Meara had won both, while Duval had come agonizingly close at the Masters and then hadn't seriously contended again in a major. Carrying the extra weight in his bag of the "BPNTHWAM" title, Duval began the new year as if he intended to lose the dreaded initials quickly.

By the time CBS began cuing up the schmaltzy Augusta-in-the-spring music, Duval had won four times. He lapped the field at the season-opening Tournament of Champions (a.k.a. the Mercedes Championships, in PGA Tour corporate lingo), winning by nine shots. Two weeks later, he made golf history by shooting the third 59 in the history of the tour and the first on a Sunday to come from seven shots down and win the Bob Hope Chrysler Classic. He took a breather after that before coming back to win in consecutive weeks leading up to the Masters, first at the Players Championship and then in Atlanta.

The victory at the Players was especially emotional for Duval. The Players is his hometown tournament, and he won on the same day that his dad won for the first time on the Senior Tour. It was the first time in history that a father and son had won tour events on the same day. Given the difficulties Bob and David had endured in the aftermath of Bob's divorce from Diane Duval, the twin victories and the pride each felt in the other meant a lot. The normally imperturbable Duval even got a little choked up during the awards ceremony in Ponte Vedra.

By the time Duval returned to Augusta, fifty-one weeks after O'Meara's putt on 18 had left him feeling kicked in the stomach, much had changed. To begin with, Duval was now officially the No. 1 ranked player in the world. It had taken a while for the silly rankings system to figure out that Duval had surpassed Woods — he had won eleven times in eighteen months, during which time Woods had won twice — but that finally happened, months after everyone in the game had come to the conclusion that Duval was the world's best golfer.

What's more, the 59 had given Duval a huge publicity boost. Now it was Duval that all the magazines wanted to profile; Duval who had to do a Tuesday press conference every time he played; Duval who all the TV programmers wanted to interview, regardless of what he had shot that day. Duval was bright enough to understand what was going on, and he handled most of it with a sense of humor. He knew he was the anti-Tiger. The biggest news connected to his 59, other than the number itself, had been his fist-pump as his six-foot eagle putt disappeared into the hole at 18. That made the career fist-pump score something like Tiger 5,864, Duval 1. Every time someone asked Duval why he didn't smile more often, he took it as a challenge to make sure not to smile more often.

Duval came into the Masters as the clear favorite, with Woods 1A and everyone else an afterthought. Golf seemed to have found its next great rivalry.

Woods heard all the Duval talk and was keenly aware of just how well Duval was playing. As different as the two men were, they got along just fine. Knowing how much he disliked the attention that came with stardom, Duval respected the way Woods had handled all the hype that had followed him for so many years. Woods liked the fact that Duval never big-timed anyone, that he seemed to stay on the same even keel no matter how many times he won.

Which is not to say that Woods was even the least bit happy to lose his No. 1 ranking to Duval or to hear and read constantly that Duval had surpassed him. He didn't necessarily disagree with what was being said, he just didn't like it. And so he began remaking himself. He had been on cruise control since his crushing Masters victory in '97, playing well enough for most mortals but nowhere near the level he had produced during his first ten months on tour, when he had won six times.

He was still good, very good, but those weren't words that were supposed to be used to describe Superman. He caught himself talking about how he had really done a great job grinding to shoot 71. Tiger Woods grinding? To shoot 71? What was going on here?

Woods knew he had to be more consistent off the tee. He had to get his short irons closer to the hole. He had to get himself back into the killer mindset that had made him so good, so fast. He had ended 1998 by firing Hughes Norton, his confrontational agent. He began 1999 by firing Mike ("Fluff") Cowan, his over-publicized caddy. In both cases, Woods believed that Norton and Cowan were a little too caught up in their own agendas and not involved enough in his. If that sounds egotistical, so be it. Agents and caddies serve at the pleasure of the player, and if the player isn't happy with them, they get fired. Whether they deserve to get fired doesn't matter. It is the player's call.

Woods brought on a more low-key agent (Mike Rosenberg of IMG) and a more low-key caddy (Steve Williams, who had worked previously for Raymond Floyd) and went back to work with his teacher, Butch Harmon, who was studiously staying in the background as much as possible. Gregarious and outgoing by nature, Harmon became Mr. All Business on the range when the boss was anywhere in sight. And he and the boss put in hours and hours reworking the golf swing so that it would become less wild, less apt to send golf balls in the wrong direction.

The makeover hadn't quite happened at the Masters. What's more, the golf course *had* been Tiger-proofed. The Lords of Augusta had made a point of not making any major changes after Tiger's blowaway 270 in '97 because they weren't going to publicly admit they were concerned about what Tiger had done to their masterpiece by changing it in the immediate aftermath of his performance. But a year later, after Tiger had tied for eighth and barely broken par for the week (two under), they could change the golf course and claim it had nothing to do with Tiger. Certainly, no one was going to accuse them of O'Meara-proofing the golf course.

The second tee was moved back to bring the hole's huge fairway bunker back into play. The green on the 11th hole was changed to bring Rae's Creek into play. The mounds on the right side of the 15th fairway were removed to prevent drives from kicking off them and down the fairway. And new trees were planted between the 15th and 17th holes to impede wayward drives and to force players to play more toward the once-famous Eisenhower Tree off the 17th tee.

Some thought the changes would play into the hands of long hitters like Woods and Duval because they made the course longer. But they also made the course tighter. The reaction to the changes among the players was mixed. Some liked the idea of toughening the old golf course. Others thought the members had gone too far, especially at 17, where the landing area for a driver had been narrowed to the approximate width of a bowling alley.

The members insisted that the changes were nothing more than part of the constant tweaking Augusta National was perennially put through. Others knew better. The memory of Woods hitting nine-irons into the back nine par-fives wasn't going to fade anytime soon, and clearly, the club members didn't want to see it repeated.

Woods had gone through considerable changes himself since his '97 tour de force. He wasn't as impatient with the media or autograph-seekers as he had been then, and he was much more comfortable in the locker room. He was more one of the guys now, very much a star, but less into the trappings of stardom. Even his father had taken a couple of steps back, in part because of health problems, in part because it was clearly time for Tiger to stop being the Wonder Kid and head out on his own to try to become Superman.

He wasn't quite ready at Augusta. The week belonged, not to Generation Next, but to two men almost no one thought would ever again be factors in a major. It was Friday afternoon when Greg Norman's name popped onto the scoreboards around the grounds, and the buzz could be heard all the way back to Atlanta. Three years had passed since Norman's infamous Sunday collapse had set up Nick Faldo's third Masters victory, and Norman had been nothing more than a blip in the majors since then. He had missed most of 1998 after neck surgery and, at forty-four, hardly seemed contender material.

Of course, the one person less likely to be a contender might have been José María Olazabal, the 1994 champion. On the day that Norman had blown the six-shot lead to Faldo, Olazabal had watched from his bed at home in Spain, barely able to walk to the bathroom. He had endured incredible pain in his foot for more than a year, only to learn from a German doctor that the pain was coming from a back problem that caused him to walk improperly. Olazabal had wondered if he would ever play golf again. Now, he was again contending in the Masters.

Others lurked all weekend. Duval actually closed to within one shot of the lead making the turn on Sunday, but splashed a ball into Rae's

Creek on the 11th hole and made double-bogey. Davis Love III, still trying to win the title he wanted almost as desperately as Norman, holed a miraculous chip shot at the 16th hole — backing the ball into the cup after intentionally popping it eight feet long and spinning it back — and got to within one shot of the lead.

But the day belonged to Norman and Olazabal. And their duel was decided, as it turned out, on the 13th green. Olazabal, leading by two shots, had laid up short of the water and pitched to about 25 feet. Norman had reached the green in two with a pair of gorgeous shots, and when he rolled in his 30-foot putt for eagle, the cheers were bouncing off the trees as if it were 1986 again and Nicklaus was chasing Norman down. This time, though, Norman was the darling.

Olazabal had seen this before. In 1994, he had been in the last group with the unheralded Tom Lehman and had felt (and heard) the crowd pulling for Lehman all afternoon. Now, they were pulling even harder for the very heralded but as yet un-green-jacketed Norman. "I actually enjoyed the cheering," he said later. "I knew they were for Greg and I understood. But all the cheering was very good for me."

Apparently. Coolly, Olazabal rolled in his birdie putt to maintain a one-shot lead. He couldn't help but smile. Neither could Norman, who pointed at him as if to say, "Good stuff, game on."

It wasn't good stuff, it was *great* stuff. But Norman couldn't quite keep up the pace. He pushed his drive at 14 and made bogey, and by the time they reached 18 — after a miraculous par by Olazabal at 17 — it was Love who Olazabal was holding off. Norman would finish third.

If there was ever any doubt about Olazabal being a true champion, it was doused for good on that Sunday at Augusta. He played fabulous golf to win, and then, walking toward the 18th green at a moment when he had every right to be thinking only of himself, he proved again that great golfers are often different from great athletes in other sports. As he reached the crest of the hill, he stopped and waited for Norman, who had dropped behind to leave the stage clear for the champion. Olazabal didn't want it that way. He insisted that he and Norman walk on the green together.

"I was very happy at that moment," Olazabal said. "But I knew it was a difficult moment for Greg."

Difficult and disappointing. But Norman was clearly thrilled to at least contend again. The nonwinner who was clearly crushed was Love. In 1995, when he had finished second to Ben Crenshaw, part of him had been happy for his close friend, especially in the wake of Harvey Penick's death the previous Sunday. Love had great respect for Olazabal, but he had thought this was going to be his Masters. After it was over, he kept talking about learning from the experience — but the look in his eyes made it clear he was sick and tired of learning.

Two months later at Pinehurst, it was Phil Mickelson's turn to learn. In all the Woods–Duval hype — which continued to build even after neither won the Masters — Mickelson had almost become a forgotten man. He was not yet thirty, had won fourteen times on tour, but still hadn't made a serious dent at a major. He knew there were whispers — and magazine covers — asking whether he had what it took to win a major title.

Few people expected him to be a serious factor when the U.S. Open finally came to Donald Ross's masterpiece, Pinehurst No. 2, after years of buildup and questions. After all, there was a decent chance that Mickelson would not even be around for the finish, since his wife, Amy, was home in Arizona about to give birth to their first child. Mickelson arrived at Pinehurst wearing a beeper, saying he would be on the first plane out of town the minute the beeper went off, no matter where or when it happened.

"Need to get that beeper number," John Daly joked on Thursday. "Because if he's leading Sunday and I'm second, I might like to set it off. I'd just tell him, 'Phil, you go on home and I'll take care of that child's education, don't you worry about it.'"

Half of Daly's prediction came true — Mickelson did lead on Sunday. Sadly, after being one shot out of the lead on Thursday, Daly was nowhere close to second. In fact, he was close to getting thrown off the golf course. Daly's year — and life — was sliding downhill quickly. He had split with Paulette again at the end of 1998, meaning he was seeing his children only on a limited basis. He seemed to put on weight just by looking at food and was beginning to look a little bit like a Thanksgiving Day Parade balloon. His golf was awful. He had finished his work at the Memorial two weeks earlier by *six*-putting the 18th green for a 10. "The saddest part of it," he said, "was that I was actually trying on the first four."

Daly wasn't drinking, but he openly admitted that he craved alcohol. "Imagine if someone said to you that you could never again eat your absolute favorite food in life," he said. "That's what not drinking is like for me."

After playing well on Thursday, he went rapidly backward the last three days, ending up last among the players who made the cut. But his worst moment came on Sunday, when, aggravated by Pinehurst's upside-down bowl-shaped greens, he hit a moving golf ball as it was rolling back to his feet after a poor chip. After being admonished by USGA officials and told he might be removed from the golf course if he did anything similar, he managed to finish the round without further incident. Then he blasted the USGA for the course setup — which had been praised to the skies by other players — and vowed not to play in the U.S. Open again.

He was long gone from the golf course when Woods, Mickelson, and Payne Stewart made the turn in a cool, steady rain on Sunday afternoon. One of the great fears about playing at Pinehurst had been the kind of heat that can bake North Carolina in mid-June. It hadn't happened. The weather had ranged from cool and rainy to warm and comfortable all week. Sunday was more like a British Open day than a U.S. Open day, and no one was complaining.

The only reason Stewart had received any serious pre-tournament attention had been his near-miss at Olympic a year earlier. Stewart had played well in 1999, winning the rain-shortened (surprise) AT&T Pebble Beach Pro-Am in February, and had come to Pinehurst feeling good about his game. But he was forty-two and he had missed his big chance to win a second Open a year earlier.

But Stewart wasn't the least bit haunted by Olympic. In fact, it had given him confidence that he still had the game and the mentality to win another major. "All I'm playing for now," he said, "is the chance to win another major. If I didn't think I could do it, I wouldn't be out here. I'd be home with my family."

And so, the least surprised person in the place, and perhaps the calmest, as the players came down the stretch was Stewart. He and

Mickelson, in the last group, jockeyed for the lead all day, with Woods and Vijay Singh trying to rally from behind. Woods almost caught them, but two missed short putts on the back nine did him in. Then Stewart staged one of the most remarkable finishes in Open history. At 15, facing a possible two-shot deficit, he rolled in a 25-foot par putt. What was most amazing about the putt was Stewart's reaction to it: nothing. He simply walked up, picked his ball out of the cup, and kept on going.

"I just had a feeling right then we were going to win," said his caddy, Mike Hicks. "Payne's always had to fight his tendency to get hyper when the pressure's really on. That day, he could not have been more calm. I didn't have to say a word to him."

Tied for the lead, Stewart and Mickelson both hit superb shots to within eight feet at the par-three 17th. Stewart made his birdie putt; Mickelson missed his. Stewart led by one. But at 18, after driving into the long, wet rough, he had to lay up. His wedge left him with a fifteen-foot par putt to win the tournament. No one in the ninety-nine-year history of the U.S. Open had ever made a final putt of that length to win. Stewart made history. The putt went in, his arms went up, and Hicks, both caddy and close friend, was in his arms.

A moment later, Stewart found Mickelson standing by the side of the green, took his head into his hands, and said, "Phil, you're going to be a dad. *That* is the greatest thing in the world."

Twenty-four hours later, Phil Mickelson found out that Stewart was right. If there had been a playoff, the beeper would have gone off on about the 10th tee.

The year was now half over and the two major champions were a forty-two-year-old many had considered finished and a thirty-four-year-old many had considered finished. Duval had contended for two days at Pinehurst before shooting 75–75 on the weekend. Woods had been right there almost to the finish before being undone by his putter. People couldn't help but be amused by the fact that he insisted the two four-footers he had missed had been "about eight feet."

"Yeah," someone had said on Sunday night at Pinehurst, "eight feet *total*."

Even though he finished third at Pinehurst, it was apparent that Woods was headed in the right direction. He had won in Europe in May against a good field and then a week later at the Memorial. In July, just before the British Open, he won at the Western Open for the second time in three years.

When the players arrived at Carnoustie for the Open Championship and began to play their practice rounds, the groaning began. It started loud and only got louder, reaching a crescendo when no one in the field could shoot better than six over par for 72 holes.

Carnoustie is one of Scotland's great old links golf courses. It had been part of the Open rota until 1975 — the year Tom Watson won his first major title there — when the lack of hotels and access roads into the town, combined with a sense that the golf course had not been well taken care of, brought about the R & A's decision to take it out of the rota. But the course had been sold to new owners who put millions of dollars into it, a brand-new luxury hotel had been built right behind the 18th green, and the roads had been improved — at least a little.

So, the Open was back at Carnoustie. But the R & A wanted to make sure the old golf course didn't get beaten up by the game's young stars and their new equipment. It narrowed the fairways to the point where players practically had to walk single file to avoid the rough and let the rough grow to U.S. Open length — or longer, considering the relatively tame stuff the players had faced at Pinehurst.

With the wind blowing on Thursday, no one broke par 70. Each day the scores went up, even when the weather became more benign. Duval got into trouble with the British tabloids for being critical of the setup, and most of the game's stars were nonfactors. By Sunday afternoon, the tournament clearly belonged to Jean Van De Velde.

Yes, *that* Jean Van De Velde.

Van De Velde was a European Tour journeyman who had won once on the Continent. He was a charming Frenchman with a self-deprecating sense of humor who kept getting himself into impossible positions and then getting out of them with an amazingly hot putter. By the time he reached the 18th tee on Sunday, he had survived every disaster possible and had a three-shot lead on Paul Lawrie, an unknown Scot who had shot a remarkable 67 to move up the leader board and position himself for a big check; and Justin Leonard, the '97 Open champion, who had doggedly pursued Van De Velde all day, only to see his last chance to win drown on 18 when, forced to play for the green from way back in the fairway, he had landed his three-wood shot in the burn that runs in front of the green. That led to a bogey and Van De Velde's three-shot lead.

"Sometimes," Curtis Strange said on TV, "you're just meant to win."

And sometimes you're not. Reckless as he had been throughout the tournament, Van De Velde played driver off the tee, when five iron would have been a perfectly reasonable shot. After all, three irons to the green and three putts would win the tournament. But, Van De Velde hit driver. And again got away with it, pushing the ball so far right that he cleared the burn that runs between 17 and 18 and landed on dry land near the 17th fairway. All that was left was a simple layup and a wedge to the green.

Van De Velde still wasn't laying up. He tried to play a two iron over the burn to the green. He pushed it right and watched the ball ricochet off the huge grandstand and back *across* the burn into deep rough. Now, Van De Velde had made things interesting, but he was still in control. He needed to get the ball on the green in two more shots and then two-putt to win. He could have pitched straight to his left to find the fairway and then pitched over the burn from there, but he tried to hack the ball out of the rough to the green. Instead, he knocked it right into the burn.

Van De Velde was making history. He actually considered trying to play his fourth shot from the burn — setting up the picture seen on magazine covers everywhere of him standing forlornly in the burn in bare feet looking at his ball. Realizing he couldn't possibly play the ball, he dropped, then hit his fifth shot into a green side bunker. From there, he actually made a remarkable up and down — holing an eight-footer for his seven.

That left him tied with the stunned Leonard and Lawrie, who had been waiting for the awards ceremony, since the runners-up are required to take part. Leonard never could get himself back into a competitive mindset; Van De Velde was a basket case; and Lawrie, who had finished more than two hours earlier, won the four-hole playoff, finishing with a flourish by birdieing the virtually unbirdieable 18th. The

Scots went wild over his victory, and sports had a new term for complete brain-lock under pressure: pulling a Van De Velde.

"Ah well, two hundred years from now no one will remember this," Van De Velde said bravely when it was over.

He was wrong. His 18th hole at Carnoustie will be remembered for ever.

As will Sergio Garcia's 16th at Medinah.

The last major of the year was played at Medinah Country Club, outside Chicago, on the longest golf course (more than 7,400 yards) in the history of major championships. By the time everyone reached Medinah, Woods and Duval were still the talk of the game, but not for reasons that made either one of them happy.

The trouble had started when IMG and ABC, looking for ways to cash in on the Duval–Woods hype, came up with the brilliant notion of an 18-hole big-bucks match play, a made-for-TV event between Woods and Duval. Since the two of them hadn't yet managed to come down the stretch at a major — or for that matter any tournament — fighting for a title, IMG and ABC decided to create an event where they would *have* to come down the stretch together. Various corporations jumped on board, guaranteeing $1.2 million to the winner; a mere $400,000 to the loser.

If such an event had been concocted for the Silly Season — November and December — no one would have minded very much. After all, Woods–Duval was just like all the Silly Season events: a money grab that proved nothing except that golf fans will watch almost anything if there are big names involved. But the so-called Shootout at Sherwood wasn't scheduled for the end of the year. It was scheduled for a Monday night in August, ten days before the start of the PGA. ABC scheduled it in prime time and promoted it as if it were an event that was slightly more important than a major.

To make things worse, just before the Silliness at Sherwood, Duval was quoted in a long Q-and-A in *Golf Digest* on the subject of the Ryder Cup. He really didn't understand, he said, why everyone made such a big deal out of it; after all, it was just an exhibition. What's more, he thought the players should be paid more than $5,000 in expenses, given that the PGA of America stood to walk off with $17 million for the week.

Duval wasn't wrong about the fact that the players — or charities they were involved with — should share in the Ryder Cup riches. But asking for more money on the eve of a one-day *exhibition* for which he was to be paid a minimum of $200,000 (he and Woods had pledged $200,000 each to charity) didn't sound good. And calling the Ryder Cup an exhibition when he had yet to play in it sounded foolish.

The made-for-TV match proved to be a major non-epic. Woods won and both players looked bored throughout. TV types bristled at media criticism of the event, and everyone moved on to Medinah, where Woods jumped right into trouble with Duval by agreeing with his notion of the Ryder Cup as an exhibition. "Of course it's an exhibition," he said. "I don't see anyone collecting a check for winning."

Ouch. Woods's old foot-in-mouth disease, seemingly in remission, had jumped back up. An event was an exhibition if no one collected a check? Did that mean that his three U.S. Amateur titles were exhibitions? Did it mean that Bob Jones had won a bunch of exhibitions when he won the Grand Slam in 1930?

Things really turned ugly in a Ryder Cup team meeting that week. Woods, Duval, Mickelson, and O'Meara argued ardently that the team should play for pay. Others, led by Love and Lehman, were just as ardently against it. "Let's be honest," Love said. "This isn't about you guys wanting to give money to charity. You can all do that today if you want to, we all can. It's about you guys getting paid."

Team captain Ben Crenshaw added even more fuel when he publicly ripped the Medinah Four at a press conference. At that moment, the U.S. Ryder Cup team had all the closeness and camaraderie of the 1968 Democratic Convention.

Against this backdrop they played the PGA and it evolved into a final-day duel between Woods and Sergio Garcia, the nineteen-year-old Spanish wunderkind, who had won the British Amateur a year earlier, then been low amateur at the Masters before turning pro and winning a European Tour event in his third start.

Garcia was a dream come true for golf. He had a lot of Woods in him, without the edge. His heroes as a kid had been Seve Ballesteros and Olazabal, and he had their imagination on the golf course, especially when in trouble. He clearly loved to play, loved the crowds and the attention, and wasn't the least bit bothered by being a celebrity. He was funny and charming, and he could really *play*.

The last day of the PGA ended up being a duel between Woods and Garcia. Playing one group in front of Woods, Garcia rolled in a long birdie putt at the par-three 13th, then shot a look back to the elevated tee where Woods stood watching as if to say, "Take that!" Woods later claimed he didn't see the look, but he certainly heard the birdie roar, and for one of the first times in his career — perhaps the first time — he flinched. He airmailed the green with his tee shot and took an ugly double bogey, allowing Garcia to get to within one shot of him. It was the first time in his life Woods had been challenged by someone younger than he was, and it was a bit unnerving.

Garcia hung in until the end, hitting the golf shot of the year on 16, a seven-iron off a tree root onto the green. Replays of the shot showed him actually closing his eyes at impact, waiting to feel the pain of hitting the root as he swung. As the ball flew toward the green, Garcia flew down the fairway after it, finally leaping into the air in a decent imitation of a hurdler in order to see where the ball had landed. It was wonderful theater.

In the end, Woods made a gutsy par putt at the 17th from ten feet to hang on and win, but the look on his face — exhaustion and relief — when he holed out on 18 made it apparent that the kid had given him all he wanted and a little bit more.

No doubt the IMG folks were all thinking: "Shootout at Sherwood II: Woods vs. Garcia."

Just what golf needs.

The U.S. did manage to win the Ryder Cup in September even after all the squabbling. The team came together on Saturday night, trailing 10–6, knowing that the world was ready to rip them all for being selfish, money-chasing louts if the no-name European team beat them on home ground. The Americans were bonded — finally — by the notion that everyone was ripping them.

They set up Johnny Miller, NBC's analyst, as the bad guy for actually pointing out that they weren't playing terribly well. Crenshaw brought in Texas governor George W. Bush to give the team a pep talk, and Bush read a poem to the players about the Alamo. Whether he or anyone else bothered to note that the Americans *lost* at the Alamo and everyone *died*, no one knows for sure.

The U.S. team played superbly on Sunday, rallying to win 14½ to 13½. The dramatic charge was sullied by the boorish behavior of the American fans, especially the way some of them treated Colin Montgomerie, and by the celebration staged by the players and their wives after Justin Leonard's putt on 17 that, as it turned out, clinched the Cup.

The celebration wasn't nearly as bad a moment as some — especially the European media — made it out to be. For one thing, it was completely spontaneous, an instinctive reaction to Leonard draining a miraculous, across-the-green 45-foot putt. Yes, it was wrong to make Olazabal, who still had a chance to keep Europe alive by making his own 30-footer, wait until everyone unpiled. But no one stepped in his line, and unlike some of the gamesmanship that goes on at the Ryder Cup — like the slow-playing tactics the Euros have perfected — it was unintentional.

Wrong, but unintentional. The crowd behavior, on the other hand, was inexcusable, and it was caused by the fact that the PGA of America, cashing in on every possible nickel, sold way too many tickets; sold way too much beer, and tolerated way too much misbehavior. It made for an ugly ending.

Which was rescued, to some degree, by Payne Stewart. Paired in the final match with Montgomerie, he came to the 18th green tied with the Scotsman. By then, Leonard had clinched the cup for the U.S., and the two men were playing strictly for pride. On the 18th green, Montgomerie had a twenty-foot putt to win the match. A two-putt would probably mean a halve. Before Montgomerie could putt, Stewart walked over, picked up his ball, and conceded the putt and the match to him.

"We had already won the Cup," Stewart said later. "I saw why he should have to make that putt. I didn't care if I won or not, my *team* had won. After what Colin had been put through all week, I thought giving him the putt was the right thing to do."

It was Stewart's final moment on golf's grand stage and perhaps, it can be argued, his best. On a day filled with rampant misbehavior and flagrant chauvinism, Stewart ended it with a gesture of uncommon grace.

And while his putt to win the Open and his reaction to making that putt will be the everlasting memory of Stewart for many, for some it will be that final act at the Ryder Cup.

Payne Stewart's exit from life in 1999 was a tragedy that will cast a shadow over the game of golf for a long time. But the legacy he created, especially in that final year, will last far longer.

Acknowledgments

Early in 1998 I was fortunate enough to be asked to rejoin my old newspaper, the *Washington Post*, to write a monthly column for its Sunday magazine. When I told my wife about my new assignment, she thought it sounded like a great idea.

"How many words per column?" she asked me.

"Nine hundred fifty," I answered.

Her eyebrows went up. "Nine hundred fifty words?" she repeated. "You can't get through your book acknowledgments in nine hundred fifty words."

How true.

But I do have an excuse. The books I write require the help of an amazing number of people. Most of them have to be very patient and very understanding. The least I can do — and I'm good at doing the least — is thank them for their efforts.

So, as briefly as I can, here goes:

The players who put up with me for an entire year: Fred Couples, David Duval, Mark O'Meara, Justin Leonard, Jay Haas, Dudley Hart, Scott McCarron, Jim Furyk, Steve Stricker, Phil Mickelson, John Daly, and Brad Faxon. Special thanks to Faxon, who never backed away from the project even though he was going through an awful time in his personal life. And to Nicki Stricker and Paulette Daly for their time and patience.

More players: Payne Stewart, Lee Janzen, Tom Watson, Tiger Woods, Larry Mize, Jeff Thorsen, Howard Twitty, Patrick Lee, Jay and Marnie Williamson, Kirk Junge, David Havens, Eric Meeks, Michael Campbell, and John Huston.

Old friends who happen to be players: Davis Love III, Jeff Sluman, Billy Andrade, Paul Goydos, Brian Henninger, Nick Price, Tom Kite, Bruce Fleisher, Mike Donald, Curtis Strange, and John Cook.

Caddies: Jim (Bones) McKay, James Earl Walker, Bob (TV guy) Riefke, Joe LaCava, Jerry Higginbotham, Mike Hicks, Bruce Edwards, Craig (Woody) Cimarolli, Ryan Scott (my stand-in), Steve DuPlantis, John (Cubbie) Burke, Dave Musgrove, Jeff Weber, Tony Navarro, Frank Williams, Brian Alexander, and Mitch Knox.

Golf big-wigs: David B. Fay, Thomas P. Meeks, Trey Holland, Ron Read, Tim Moraghan, Sir Michael Bonallack, Jim Awtrey, Will Nicholson, Joe Steranka, and Tim Finchem.

Golf P.R. types, each of whom deserves extra consideration for putting up with me on more occasions than anyone should. *PGA Tour:* Lee Patterson, John Morris, Dave Lancer, James Cramer, Joe Chemyez, Mark Mitchell (now a computer geek), and Denise Taylor. Special thanks as always to Wes Seeley. *USGA:* Craig Smith, Suzanne Colson, and Andrea Solamita, with a special nod to Andrea for dealing with the idiots posing as marshals on the range at Olympic Club. *At Augusta National:* the indefatigable Glenn Greenspan, who somehow answered all questions and responded to all requests without once saying, "Won't you *please* go away." *At the R & A:* Stuart McDougal. *At the PGA of America:* the world's grooviest guy, Julius Mason, Jamie Roggerio, and Bob Denney.

Rules Guys: Mark Russell, Ben Nelson, Jon (still the best) Brendle, Mike Shea, Slugger White, and Arvin Ginn. I cannot in a few words express my gratitude to this group for all they have done to help me during the past six years.

Curmudgeons: Frank Hannigan (he counts for at least two).

Friends and colleagues: Dave Kindred, Mike Purkey, Larry Dorman, Keith and Barbie Drum, Tom and Jill Mickle, Bob and Ann DeStefano, Terry Hanson, Tony Kornheiser, Jackson Diehl, Len Shapiro, Mark Maske, George Solomon, Carole (Princess) Kammel, Tom Denes, Kevin

Morrissey, Michael Fell, Jason Crist, Ed Brennan, Peter Gethers and Janice Donnaud, Tommy Bonk, Tom Ross, Jim Frank, George Peper, Art Spander, Hubert Mizell, John Hawkins, Geoff Russell, Ron Sirak, Jerry Tarde, Brian Hewitt, Jeff Rude, Dave Seanor, Steve Hershey, Melanie Hauser, Beth Sherry, Beth Shumway, and, of course, Nobert Doyle, the world's most underrated golfer.

Photogs: Fred Vuich, Sam Green, Phil Hoffman.

Agents: Only one, Esther Newberg. Never needed another. Or had a better friend.

Editors: Michael Pietsch. Makes me think all those terrible things I've said about editors through the years are untrue. At least partly untrue.

Agents and editors' assistants: Jack Horner, David Gibbs, Nora Krug.

Little, Brown P.R. honcho: Holly Wilkinson, who dresses so well it almost balances the way I dress. Almost.

Family: They all know. But just so they don't complain about not being mentioned by name: Mary, Danny, Brigid, Dad, Margaret, Bobby, David, Jennifer, Jim and Arlene Kacky, Stan, Annie, Gregg, Jimmy, and Brendan. (No wonder I need so many words.)

And finally, a word from my mother, who would have accosted me for not *starting* with my family: "The best thing in life is being with your family. The second best thing is having too many friends."

Mom also said the only place it was okay to curse was on the golf course.

She was a very wise woman.

Seven hundred and ninety-two words. My wife will be impressed.

Index